PRAISE IN ST. AUGUSTINE
READINGS AND REFLECTIONS

NIHIL OBSTAT:

John J. Gavigan, O.S.A.
Censor Deputatus

IMPRIMI POTEST:

Joseph A. Duffey, O.S.A.
Prior Provincialis

PRAISE IN ST. AUGUSTINE:
READINGS AND REFLECTIONS

By

JOHN M. QUINN, O.S.A.

THE CHRISTOPHER PUBLISHING HOUSE
NORWELL, MASSACHUSETTS
02061

COPYRIGHT ©1987
BY JOHN M. QUINN, O.S.A.
Library of Congress Catalog Card Number 85-70592
ISBN: 0-8158-0430-X

PRINTED IN THE UNITED STATES OF AMERICA

To my mother
and
to the memory
of my father
whose simple lives
of faith and love
first taught me
how to praise God

Preface

Augustinus Magister, or *Augustine the Teacher,* was the title felicitously selected for studies in 1954 commemorating the sixteen-hundredth anniversary of Augustine's birth.[1] The avowal implicit in this title is not an extravagance, for Augustine has scarcely an equal among the doctors of Catholic truth. It is hard to put one's finger on a tract of Christian thought that his brilliance has not illuminated and developed. To touch on only a few areas, his insight that relation constitutes each divine person has become part of the living nerve of the doctrine of the trinity; his explanation of the Church as an organism mystically one with Christ seems without peer in acuity and range of treatment; his penetrating critique of Pelagius and company earned him the title, *doctor gratiae,* teacher of grace. In the opinion of Fr. Hugh Pope, Augustine can aptly lay claim to another title, *doctor orationis,* teacher of prayer.[2] In a related step we may suggest that Augustine also deserves the designation *doctor laudis,* teacher of praise.

Augustine never authored a treatise systemically propounding the meaning and attributes of praise. But a scanning of his works, principally his commentaries on the psalms, lays bare the general lines of a well-constructed theory of praise. (As its title indicates, his *Confessions* devotes itself to praise of God, but the structure of praise is by and large assumed rather than explicitly exposited.) What the reader holds in his hands ventures a rough sketch, no more than an elementary examen, of some of Augustine's basic notions. Though it does not wholly neglect underpinnings of scholarship, the account that follows subordinates analytical considerations to existential or moral-personal themes. Analytical lineaments subserve spiritual reflections keyed to Augustine's expositions of certain psalms. In short, we are adopting the Augustininist style of nourishing the soul through the feeding of the mind.

In recent years the market for books of a religious character has reportedly expanded, with readers evincing a resurgence of interest in books on prayer especially. In addition to providing foundational conceptions for the worship that is praise, Augustine's view, insofar as praise is associated with prayer, may help furnish a framework and strategy within which contemporary inquirers into prayer can locate and organize their experiences and perceptions. The Christian message must always be adapted to the outlook and state of soul of a particular era. But such relevance can be genuine only if it has its wellsprings in earlier Christian sources. Relevance in the present requires rootage in the past. Clearly Augustine did not say the last word on praise, but, as inspection of his spiritual exegesis of the psalms assures, his relatively first word seems rich with insights and analyses shedding light in exemplary fashion on the nature of praise. Though close to sixteen hundred years old, the ideas of a thinker whom Bossuet called *doctor doctorum*, the teacher of teachers, are not outdated but seem significant for every age. Begotten of a mind gifted with genius and a heart steeped in holiness, they seem in a measure time-transcending, for they stream from St. John and St. Paul and, through these giants of prayer and praise, from the Spirit of Jesus.

This volume grew out of the main portion of a paper delivered at an institute on Augustinian spirituality and subsequently published as one of a collection of essays.[3] I wish to thank Augustinian Publications in Rome for kindly permitting me to make free use of this material.

It is a fraternal pleasure to express my gratitude to the Augustinian community of Villanova University for their day-by-day affirmation sustaining and encouraging me in this and other projects. My loving thanks go to my dear family, relatives, and friends, whose spiritual affection keeps quickening hope and rekindling enthusiasm. I want to thank the nuns of the Visitation Monastery in Philadelphia for their prayerful support and for the sympathy and patience with which they listened to sections of this little work while it was in the making.

Notes

Enarrationes in psalmos, translated from the Corpus christianorum, series latina, volumes 38-40, is referred to as EP. Other works, which unless otherwise indicated, are translated from the Migne edition, are cited according to familiar abbreviations. All translations from Augustine are the writer's.

Augustine's numbering of the psalms follows that of Old Latin translations of the Septuagint, whose enumeration, as does the later Latin rendering which we call the Vulgate, varies somewhat from that of the Hebrew text. Citations of the psalms in the notes below retain Augustine's Latin numbering, with the corresponding Hebrew numbers in parentheses. Parenthetical references to the psalms in the body of the text, nearly all of which are inserted in the selections from Augustine, also use the Latin enumeration, followed by the appropriate Hebrew numbers in brackets. While nonCatholic versions of the psalms since the Reformation opted for the Hebrew enumeration, roughly until Vatican II Catholic editions and translations of the psalms (such as Douay and Knox) remained faithful to the Latin numbering. In recent years Catholic editions and translations generally employ the numbering of the Hebrew text, some putting the numbers of the Latin text in the margin.

In the light of a literal Greek text Augustine produced an "original" translation of the psalter by emending three pre-Vulgate versions available to him at various times. Hence his rendering does not always coincide with early modern and recent English translations. See Dom D. de Bruyne, "Saint Augustin, reviseur de la Bible," in Miscellanea Agostiniana, 2 (Rome, 1931), especially pp. 544-78, which volume is fully cited in the introduction, p. xvi, n.5 below.

[1]See Pierre Courcelle, "Le 'maitre' Augustin," in Augustinus Magister, 2 (Paris: Études augustiniennes, 1954), pp. 9-11.
[2]Hugh Pope, O.P., The Teaching of St. Augustine on Prayer and the Contemplative Life (London: Burns, Oates and Washbourne, 1935), p. 1.
[3]John M. Quinn, O.S.A., "Praise in St. Augustine: Some Reflections" (Rome: Augustinian Publications, 1981), pp. 57-91.

Contents

Introduction

One initially curious-looking feature of human knowledge is the fact that we can know an object without being able to pin down its proper meaning. St. Augustine makes this point with apparent paradox when at the outset of his treatise on time he remarks: "What then is time? If no one asks me, I know. If I want to explain it to a questioner, I do not know."[1] Prior to analysis, Augustine is saying, we know time in a vaguely speculative and a clearly practical manner. It requires no training in philosophy to know that ten yards does not refer to the dimension to which ten hours is related. No one with any sense would for one moment consider using a yardstick to calculate the duration of a work period or a clock to measure the length of a room. But determining the exact meaning of time is quite another matter, a task ordinarily beyond the reach of most men. As with time, so with other common coins of knowledge: most of us surely know in a realistic, operative fashion what motion, place, space, and life are yet just as surely are hard put to supply adequate definitions.

A similar gap between practical awareness and sharp analysis roughly obtains with regard to objects of spiritual theology. The majority of Christians know what prayer is, for off and on over a number of years they have engaged in prayer. Yet many Christians do not know what prayer is in the analytical sense, and fall mute if asked for an exact, defensible definition beyond a formula or two retained from school days. Though the disparity between practical familiarity and analytical precision may be somewhat larger, the case of praise seems similar. Praise figures notably in Christian worship; over and over Christians recite or sing the "Glory to God in the highest" and the "Holy, Holy, Holy" and join in a rousing hymn like "Holy God, We Praise Thy Name." In fact, attempts to define praise might prove more awkward than ventures to specify prayer proper. Perhaps these more halting efforts to provide a definition of praise evidence in part a dimmer practical awareness of praise. Leaving to one side the one or two million reportedly influenced by charismatic renewal, a good number of Catholics apparently do not regularly praise God in their normal round of personal devotions. They petition the Lord for release from burdens and for miraculous interventions, beg forgiveness for sins, and pay him thanksgiving, all these acts rising up with a pleasing fragrance to the throne of God. Yet many do not explicitly praise him. A number of priests and religious daily praise God in the *Liturgy of the Hours* yet seem somewhat deficient in a sense of praise. After faithfully praying the divine office, not too many seem to give themselves over to praise as such in other devotional exercises. Cries for relief from anguish, yearnings for peace, prostrations of the soul sorrowing over sin that dominate certain psalms seem to stimulate more fervent intercession and contrition, but much less commonly do accents of praise in the psalms resound in repeated outbursts of praise in meditations and aspirations.

To recover or deepen the sense of praise we may ask God for more of the gift of praise, or make our own the exclamations of praise in the writings of the saints so as to imbibe some of their spirit, or concentrate on expressions of praise in the Mass or psalms that are pure praise. Any one of these avenues can prove no doubt profitable and, in individual cases, sufficient for growth in praise. It may benefit some, in addition, to quarry nuggets of theoretical and practical praise from Augustine's discourses on the psalms now entitled *Enarrationes in psalmos*, literally *Enarrations on the Psalms*, an enarration being a running commentary. This collection of commentaries, his longest work, is, I believe, the lengthiest single spiritual explication of the psalms ever authored by a major Christian thinker. Along with sifting other notions in the psalter, it articulates the main lines of a broad analysis of praise. The chapters that follow contain passages mostly selected from Augustine's interpretations of the psalms, from which can be distilled some chief motifs of praise. What we may name his theory of praise leads naturally to musings on the practical side that nourish heart as well as head.[2]

From every theoretical truth, some thinkers hold, it is possible to harvest practical results. But in some speculative domains the promise of practical yield is, for a good many truths, only a remote possibility. In theology, however, most truths bear a proximate practical import, and implicitly contain directives for resolution and action. Augustine's considerations of praise wear an especially pragmatic face since they occur in sermons, which are nothing but pieces of applied theology. On Augustine's showing, the ideas of praise he so lucidly lays bare are to be lived as well as learned, to be treasured in the heart as well as grasped by the mind. However sketchy, our account of his theory of praise serves then as a sort of introduction to a practice of praise. Thus after short exposés of leading notions that precede excerpts from his *Enarrations on the Psalms*, I make bold to offer some reflections or meditations geared to their respective themes and to complement these with passages oriented toward praise. It would be pretentious to esteem these spiritual pointers elements of a manual of praise. The follow-up remarks are only suggestions, seedling-stimuli that may help trigger a greater spirit of praise or simply spur the retrieval of intimate ways of praising the Father. While it is doubtful that anyone can produce a handbook of praise equivalent to a book detailing, say, how to play better golf, it does not seem unrealistic to offer a few thoughts that may occasion new personal lights in the spirit and stoke anew the fires of the heart, feeding mind and will with fresh fuel to dispose them the more to the downrush of the Spirit who originally came down, and still descends, albeit invisibly, under the sign of fire.

It is the Holy Spirit who teaches each soul how to pray, and this he does in tutorial fashion, i.e., one to one, his instruction jibing with the needs, possibilities, and limitations of this person here and now. To adapt a phrase from Augustine we will discuss later on, the Spirit cares for and teaches each individual as if each were all, as if each were the only one alive. Or if, in line with Augustine's doctrine of illumination, we focus on Christ, it is Jesus who is the one teacher, it is he who enlightens every man coming into the world, it is he, Truth itself, who communicates truth to each spirit, it is in his light that we see light, it is through his teaching that each of us prayerfully assimilates truths of the interior life as uniquely relevant to oneself.[3] So the musings that follow may be viewed as raw material that the movement of the Spirit helps us appropriate and fashion into fresh tissues of light and love in our spirits. These reflections function only as dispositive tools, instruments in the learning of and in prayer and praise. But lowly and ancillary though they be, they can play a role. In personal terms, we have a role to play. We cannot pray unless and except as the Holy Spirit prompts us, but it is no less true, however redundant it sounds, that we cannot pray unless we pray, i.e., try to pray. It is our privilege to cooperate with God in the shaping of the moral universe and the upbuilding of the mystical body of his Son, but we do not co-pray with God. The Spirit prays in us only in the sense that he moves us to pray, urging us not as inert lumps but as receptive yet active persons hospitable to his particular lights.[4] The loosely constructed meditations in these pages aim at no other than the rudimentary goal of opening readers to touches and illuminations of the Spirit.

Since Augustine was destined to be the teacher of Western religious thought, the finger of God, we may conjecture, directed not only his inward spiritual development but also helped cultivate the fruits of his analysis.[5] Though obviously his doctrinal achievements cannot be called inspired, he was led by the Spirit, we may think, to elaborate a theory of praise. While few of us may feel equipped to formulate a similar analysis, we can, and the Father wants us to, compose an interior set of enarrations or commentaries on the psalms and indeed, where possible, on the whole of the word of God. These expositions to be inscribed on the heart, and never to be published for human eyes, will be read and loved by the Spirit of the Father of Jesus. Supposing that we remain faithful to our call to become one with and like God and that we go on progressing in his love, our personal expositions of love-pervaded praise will be stored forever ineffaceably in the divine ''memory,'' never to be lost, everlastingly to remain as tiny sub-chapters of the divine history of the world, to be seen and enjoyed by all the blessed in the vision of the all-holy Face of God. Both the signature of the Spirit and our spirit will mark our "writings." Moreover, they will be part of us, and we one with them. When we know an object, our mind objectively becomes what it knows. When we pursue some good, our will subjectively becomes, loosely speaking, the good that nourishes us. We possess abstract truths, we are possessed by concrete goods. As we lovingly "write" our commentaries on praise, we become more Jesus-like, we become, like him, love, we become, like him, incarnate praise, a sacrifice of praise. A lofty ideal, yes, surely not wholly attainable by most in this life, still an ideal that Augustine sets before us, an ideal graven in gold in the psalms (and other parts of Scripture) by the Holy Spirit himself.

To couch this in language more characteristically Augustinian, an understanding of Jesus in his Spirit is available to every Christian believer, no matter how limited his analytical acumen. The words, "Unless you believe, you shall not understand" (Is 7.9; Septuagint), that Augustine doctrinally capitalized on[6] have been taken by scholars as a charter shaping all of Catholic theology. Faith is the root, and understanding the outflowering, of Christian awareness of revelation. Unquestionably a structured theology is meant to develop out of a living faith. But this pregnant line in Isaiah holds the key to Christian life as well as thought. For Augustine understanding springs from faith not only in the doctrinal mode but in the affective mode also. Peasants and largely unlettered factory hands whose analyical grip on faith hardly extends beyond a grade-school catechism can come to know Jesus Christ, can gain true understanding, can reach a measure of Christian wisdom, can become learned in what may be dubbed a theology of the heart not through analytical devices but through instruments of spiritual affectivity like prayer and praise. It is in the love-knowledge they achieve that eternal life consists, so that the knowledge in the next life is a continuation of the wisdom of the heart in this.[7] As we said one paragraph back, the "writings" of those learned in heart will last into eternity as part of the treasures of the wisdom of his children that the Father gathers up and retains forever in "memory."

The points for reflection consistently employ the first-person pronoun to underscore the close bond between God and the soul, the secrets of whose sharing in Christian wisdom will be fully revealed only in the everlasting light. It seems worth mentioning that Cardinal Newman favors this style in many of his prayers and meditations printed in *Meditations and Devotions*.[8] Not that my scribblings match in any wise the literary mastery and spiritual depth of a Newman. But his use of the personalistic "I" suggests that judicious recourse to it can express the seeking of the human for the divine heart without smacking of the egocentric.

First-person usage meshes with the long-maintained Christian view that in prayer we converse with God. In Augustine's words, "Your prayer is a conversation with God. When you read, God speaks to you; when you pray, you speak to God."[9] The soul enjoys an I-Thou relationship with the Father, the "I" of God evoking in reponse the "I" of the soul. The "I" in the reflections and sections on praise serves to make explicit each person's unique interchange with the Lord, the inimitable converse of friend with friend, lover with lover. According to Augustine, affective converse expands the heart: "The spiritually expanded heart is a heart indwelt by God with whom the soul interiorly converses."[10] Through the suasion of the Spirit the various meditations may help each reader to set in vibration like chords arising from his own experience and to initiate his own dialogue with God. In other words, the "I" in passages of reflection and praise is intended to shade into and be superseded by the "I" of the reader venturing his own musings, murmuring his own affections to the Father.

As he talks intimately with the Father, the reader may rediscover, through Augustine disclosing that mind which is in Christ Jesus, his own vocation of praise in union with the Lord who is head of his mystical body. He may find in Augustine's view of praise an existential or concrete, practical solution to one of the persistent problems of daily Christian living: how to see the hand of God in the simplest and most beggarly-looking of circumstances, how to discern the eternal at work in the here and now. Through further rethinking and re-praying, he may come once again to grips with suffering, not suffering in general but his own suffering, and that of his family and friends and those he prays for and ministers to, personal suffering that strikes without warning and harbors more anguish than expected. In filial interchange with the Father mediated through Augustine's account of praise the soul can learn afresh that, while we cannot eliminate suffering, we can transcend it by turning it into a sacrifice of praise. But crests usually outnumber the troughs of existence and, praying and praising with Augustine, the seeker after God may carry supernatural gladness to the point of jubilation. In some souls, though the pages that follow do not expressly deal with the point, the way of ordinary praise may become a launching pad to higher orbits of inward communion where absorption in him who is all beauty excites mystical paeans not of this world.

In line with the first-person approach the passages of meditation and praise are garbed more informally than the comments introducing each translated excerpt. Though the language is not austerely technical, the reflections and sections on praise should be read slowly, ever so slowly, to afford the Spirit more opportunity to impress the Jesus-suffused lights of Augustine on the spirit. Teachings of our faith, Augustine tells us, are to be stored in the memory, which functions as a kind of rumen; from time to time we can bring them to the surface and mentally chew them, retaste them with new delight.[11] Personal musings on St. Augustine's luminous presentation of old truths have to be similarly mulled over and ruminated to capture, according to one's personal leading, more of the spiritual nutrients with which the word of God is so rich.

In short, the analysis of praise is first but its use is foremost. May I then offer this summary suggestion to the reader: quickly peruse, if you will, the principal aspects of praise; then ponder in prayer, dwelling perhaps on part of one selection each day, Augustine's illumination of the praise that he perceives originating in the mind of God.

Finally, a word or two on the method of translation may be in order. Without forswearing all liberties, I have generally pursued a fairly literal rendering of Augustine's familiarly styled expositions of the psalms. While a more free, partially paraphrasing approach has its merits, a translation a bit more faithful to the text may claim the advantage of better catching the direct, plain tone, offhand remarks, colloquial asides, spontaneous observations, and repeated phrases and emphases in the sermons as actually delivered. Since the Italian pun about a translator being a traitor probably holds true at least in part, it seems next to impossible to reproduce in English all the fine shades and connotations of Augustine's Latin turns of phrase. Should, in spite of circumspection, a disputable interpretation occasionally make an unwelcome intrusion, it will not, I trust, obscure the main drift of a passage nor deflect the benign reader from the overriding intention of this volume, drawing the heart deeper and more sweetly into the heart of God.

Notes

[1]*Conf.*, ed. M. Skutella, in *Oeuvres de saint Augustin*, 13, 14 (Paris: Desclée de Brouwer, 1962), 11.14.17.

[2]Viewed strictly, theoretical knowledge aims at understanding an invariant order of things; in this sense physics, biology, and psychology are provinces of theoretical knowledge. Strictly speaking, practical knowing concerns human conduct or value-laden activity; in this wise ethics, sociology, and history occupy sectors of practical knowledge. Thus in this rigorous purview discussion of prayer and praise falls in the practical domain. However, academic usage sanctions extension of theory to cover any general analysis of a subject matter, enabling thinkers to speak broadly of ethical theory and sociological theory, and, in the technical-practical field, theory of art and theory of medicine. From this standpoint practical knowledge, broadly taken, signifies any particular application of general propositions. Our discussion of praise takes the theoretical and practical dimensions in the broad sense. Theory of praise focuses on analyzing the meaning and principal attributes of praise, while praise on the broadly practical side refers to concrete application of the general features of praise to the existential plane, i.e., to the individual human condition.

[3]*De mag.* 11. 38; PL 32, 1216.

[4]*De an. et eius orig.* 4.9.13; PL 44, 531. Ep. 194. 4. 17; PL 33, 880.

[5]In the first paragraph of *Ad salutem*, the encyclical marking in 1930 the fifteenth centenary of the death of Augustine, Pope Pius XI hailed Augustine as a star of the highest magnitude: "a greater, more powerful mind can scarcely be found anywhere in past eras." "Vast blessings" were garnered for the Church through "the wealth of divine gifts poured out" on Augustine. *Ad salutem*, reprinted in Antonio Casamassa, O.S.A., ed., *Miscellanea Agostiniana*, 2: *Studi Agostiniani* (Rome: Tipographia Poliglotta Vaticana, 1931), p. x.

[6]S. 139.1.1; PL 38, 770.

[7] De lib. arb. 2.2.6; PL 32, 1243.

[8] Meditations and Devotions of the Late Cardinal Newman, 3rd ed. (London: Longmans, Green, 1894).

[9] EP 85 (86).7; CC 39, 1182.

[10] EP 4.2; CC 38, 14.

[11] EP 46 (47).1; CC 38, 529. EP 103 (104) (S. 1). 19; CC 40, 1491.

Chapter I

The Meaning of Praise

Man is a seeking animal, ever searching for goods that will satisfy his needs, ever questing for values that will assuage yearnings of mind and heart. Whatever our particular likes or dislikes, we evince warm approval of things and persons that swell our fund of happiness. When we utter appreciation of anyone or anything, we praise him or it. We praise the generosity of a friend who unselflessly thrusts into our hands a large sum to tide us over financial distress; for a nuanced, acute paper we congratulate a scholar; a musical group that expertly uplifts and leads a congregation at Mass wins our praise for its gifts in the service of the altar. So closely linked to the true, the good, and the beautiful is the praiseworthy that the more we know of an object and the more sensitive we are to its value and order, the more we utter praise within or without. Undoubtedly when a thinker becomes crabbed and narrow in outlook, an increase of knowledge may dry up the springs of appreciation. But ordinarily the farther down a scientist digs into the intricacies of, say, the cell, the more striking he finds the phenomenon of life. The cell that was first pictured as a sort of mushy blot is now disclosed as a tiny city of dazzling architecture. At the root of praise also necessarily lies a spirit of wonder coupled with a child-like heart. No matter how learned, the scientist must at times stand back and simply look wonderingly upon the object that he is probing into. It is here that the common man joins the company of the scientist as contemplator, seer, wonderer, appreciator, praiser. Whatever our measure of knowledge, the order and beauty in an object stimulate our praise. However wide and deep our knowledge, what we do not know far exceeds what we do know; and the rounded scientist, though knowing more than the ordinary run of men, seems more explicitly conscious of the magnitude of human ignorance. When observing the sublime in nature — such as the roaring of the ocean deep, the apparently limitless span of the starry heavens, or the rich crimson of a setting sun — we realize that puny human ideas and words cannot capture this grandeur. Lost in wonder, we can only softly say, "How stunning! How breathtaking! How gorgeous!" An astronomer studying the staggering size of the universe, a cosmos of roughly ten billion galaxies each with an average of ten billion suns, is brought

up short by the labyrinthine ways of symmetry and laws beyond complete
human comprehension, and may quietly gasp, "This is overwhelming."
When a doctor who has delivered thousands of babies reverently reviews
the trillionfold processes at work in the making of a viable child, the latest
baby in his hands does not elicit a yawn but evokes a sense of awe that
prompts him to say almost incredulously to himself or a close colleague,
"Every birth is a miracle." The rhetoric may be more restrained but the
wonderment and the spirit of praise are in essentials the same: in the presence of the orderly and beautiful, partially understood but mostly beyond
human understanding, we at first ponder and analyze and describe, next
share our analyses and descriptions with others, then, coming to a halt,
because no longer able to articulate in detail, fall back at last on murmurs
of wonder, sighs of appreciation, outcries of praise.[1]

Praise of God as Unchangeable

Man, we may think, is by nature a praising animal. Processes in nature,
works of art, deeds of justice and love awaken his praise. As praise is natural
to man, so in a Christian context praise is supernatural to man. Because
of his orientation man is by nature a praising animal; because of revelation
man is by supernature a praising animal. In the light of faith man's voice
of praise rises from his religious orientation: he is directed toward God.
For a Christian all praise is ordered in some way to God. But the highest
praise is immediately centered on God alone. The same features of knowing
and not knowing, that, we saw, awaken mundane praise evoke praise of
God. We know him, and the more we know him, the more we realize the
depths beyond depths of incomprehensibility in the divine nature. We do
know him even here below, but our thought catches only glimpses, however
sure, however valuable, of his life and love. At a certain point we hit a
dead end, we can go no further. So vast is the Being that we encounter
that we can only, so to speak, stammer and stutter. Yet we need feel no
frustration, for stammering and stuttering can give way to praise, repeated
exaltation that intensifies knowing and loving of the Unutterable One.

Surely a Christian praises God because his mercy is all over his works,
especially those that are human beings recreated through grace. "O God,"
Augustine prays, "let the would-be praiser praise you not at all if he does
not ponder your mercies that I confess to you from my innermost self."[2]
The religious man voices praise of God because, never spurning the creature
who spurned him, he moved him to inner cleansing that renders him care-
free.[3] But the heart praises God for the second and higher reason that God
is God. Rudolf Otto's well-known description of God as *mysterium
tremendum et fascinans*,[4] an aweful yet all-alluring mystery, catches in
a phrase the Augustinist God who incites thoughts and words of praise.
He is utterly transcendent yet utterly attractive, the Wholly Other whose
charm causes us to delight in praising him.[5] As texts we will presently

examine argue, his sacred name signifies pure existence: he is the incomparable Is. Transcending past, present, and future, this eternal Is, the ever-faithful God of love, is incomprehensible in the sense that our thought only partially utters him and our language less than our thought.[6] When the soul trains its eyes steadily on Super-Being, it is overcome with awe and can only break forth in exclamations hailing the goodness of God, making its own the psalmist's cry with which Augustine begins his unparalleled prose-song of praise: "Great are you, O Lord, and highly to be praised."[7]

These few remarks yield a brief, elementary statement of the source and make-up of praise. Praise originates in the self-abasing reverence for the Creator by "a minute part"[8] of his creation and is elicited by wonder approaching amazement at the greatness of God. Praise, it seems, is the adoring proclamation of the perfections of God that excite admiration, whether seen as God or in God or whether seen as the font of salvation. Praise climbs to the outer boundaries of speaking about and to God, where, unable to go one analytical step further, we deliver ourselves over to dwelling upon God as God, extolling his attributes one by one, hearts set aglow by the unconsumable "I am who am" we homage.

We know, Augustine tells us, more of what God is not than of what he is.[9] As Maker and sustainer of all finite things God is in this world: without him nothing finite would exist. But God is not of this world: hence he is able to cause all things. Examine each and everything in the universe, Augustine bids us, and you will find that none of these, however grand in being, is God. Take the universe as a whole and think of its possessing a highest, integrating point: this greatest thing conceivable in this world falls short of the status of God. Thus God is outside the world not in a gross spatial sense but in the sense that he transcends all things created. As transcendent, God is ineffable, i.e., the full meaning of his nature eludes our grasp. As noted, it is easier for us to say what he is not than what he is. What is he not? He is not finite, not material, not bound by time and space, and so forth. What is he in his inner life? He is partially intelligible; in some respects, Augustine indicates, we know what he is. But ultimately he is incomprehensible; the finite human heart (here signifying mind) cannot completely understand an infinite being, though the soul in glory, the text from 1 Corinthians implies, will see him not darkly but in the light that is divine knowledge.

> "There is none like you among the gods, O Lord" (v. 8). A man can think of whatever other thing he wants to so long as it is not like him who made it. God apart, everything that is real has been made by God. Who can adequately think of the gulf lying between Maker and made? So the psalmist said, "There is none like you among the gods, O Lord." He did not, because he could not, say precisely how unlike the gods God is. I ask you in your charity to pay attention to me: God is ineffable. We more easily say what

God is not than what he is. Consider the sea; God is not that. Take all the beings inhabiting the earth, men and animals; God is none of these. Take all the things dwelling in the sea and flying through the air; God is none of these. Take whatever shines in the heavens, stars, sun, and moon; God is none of these. Take the heaven itself — God is not even that. Consider the angels, virtues, powers, archangels, thrones, seats, dominations; God is none of these. What then is he? I can say only what he is not. Do you want to know what he is? He is "what eye has not seen nor ear heard nor heart conceived" (1 Cor 2.9). Why do you want to form on your lips what your heart cannot conceive? "There is no one like you among the gods, O Lord, and there are no works like yours."[10]

A universe whose various sectors are constantly building up and breaking down has to be stamped with the seal of time. Each thing exists from moment to moment. Its past is gone, its future is up ahead, it exists in an ever-passing present. But God, wholly unmarked by time, has no past or future. He is timeless and, more, he is beyond all time. He is eternal, living in and perduring in a present that does not pass, a duration that unalterably abides. Indeed he is his eternity. The name of names that he lovingly gives to Moses bespeaks his changeless and eternal nature. "I am who am" is ever the same, eternally at rest yet never resting in his life of love, eternally ruling the universe and directing his people. Wave after wave of men may rise and fall but in the succession of generations the God who is "I am who am" remains the same, the absolutely stable being in a universe of flux, the peak of rest for the unrestingness of men, "the great Is" who is existence itself or fullness of being, the eternal present unaffected by ongoing time but sovereignly giving meaning to all of past, present, and future.

It is interesting to note that Augustine is not bothered by the opposition, which some of our contemporaries insist upon, between a God of reason and a personal God or a God for us. In his large-minded perspective the God who is rationally understood as unchangeable is one with the God who reveals his holy name, "I am who am," to Moses.

In time as we know it, every day comes, then ceases to exist; so it is with every hour, every month, every year. Not one of these time intervals lasts. Before anyone of them comes, it will exist; after it has come and gone, it no longer exists. But your years, O God, are eternal, your years are ever unchanged, your years will exist from generation to generation. . . . For the years of God are not one thing and God another, the years of God are the eternity of God. Eternity is the very substance of God that can suffer no change. In him there is no past that no longer is, there is no future that is yet to be. In him there is only is; in him there is no was or will be; because what was no longer exists and what will be is yet to be; but everything that is God is and cannot cease to be. God appropriately missioned his servant Moses with this word. Moses asked the name of the One sending him. He asked, he learned the name, the yearning of his good heart was not in vain. He was not curious in a presumptuous way; he asked this because he needed this knowledge for serving the Lord. "What," he says, "will I tell the children of Israel if they should say to me, 'Who sent you to us?' " (Ex 3.13). So as to show himself as Creator to creature, as God to man, as the Immortal to the mortal, as the Eternal to the temporal, the Lord answers: "I am who am" (Ex 3.14). If you were asked such a question, you might say, "I am," but we would ask further, "Who are you?" One person would say, "I am Gaius"; another, "I am Lucius"; still another, "I am Mark." But suppose you did not speak your name: would you say nothing else? So Moses was waiting for God to say more. This is why he put the question: "What is your name? What shall I respond to those asking who sent me?" The Lord answers, "I am." But who are you? He answers, "I am who am." Is this your name? Is this your entire name? Would existence itself be your name unless whatever is distinct from you is deemed not to truly exist in comparison with you? This is indeed your name. But express it once more, this time more clearly. "Go," he says, "and tell the children of Israel, 'He who is sends me to you!' I am who am. Tell them, 'He who is sends me to you.' " How great is Is, how great is Is![11]

God stays ever the same, invariable. Because he is Is, he is the Selfsame. This name capsulizes the unchanging nature of God, his absolutely immutable self-identity. God is himself and no other in the sense that he can in no way become other. God is simply that which he is, i.e., that which is in the fullest sense. He does not arise from what has been, he will not degenerate into or fuse with what will be. He is eternal, unendingly the same, everlastingly the one changeless self. The name "selfsame," derived from the psalms, takes on a clearer personal reference in the divine name that God reveals to Moses. "I am who am" emphatically betokens a God with personality, a God for us, a God who communes with and forms his own people, a God whose very name pledges rocklike fidelity to his convenanted chosen ones. We cannot fully grasp, Augustine cautions, the meaning of this name of God. Acutely aware as he is of how hard it is to think about an unencompassable God, Augustine is not claiming, as do some modern Catholics, that God is beyond concepts. For the human mind always directly or indirectly knows by concepts or ideas, and if we have no ideas of God, we simply cannot know him. Augustine is stressing not that God is unintelligible, but that we cannot know him adequately. We do know him as unchangingly existing, as eternal, as the Selfsame. But we cannot wholly understand, we cannot sufficiently conceive, just how God is unchanging. We know that God is eternal, always present without past or future, but we do not know this in the line of acquaintance, we have no experience of an eternal mode of existence. The time-conditioned setting in which we do know that God is eternal prevents us from adequately, concretely, knowing what it means to live immutably, to live as the Selfsame, to live and be an eternal life.

The ascent of the soul to the Selfsame is not sheerly intellectual. Besides sharpening our analytic power, we are to rid our spirit of "the darkness of the flesh" and to cauterize "the eye of the heart." We can never banish all mystery from the Selfsame, but the more charity and its cognates break the darksome fetters of pride and egoism, the more steadily and clearly do we see, still obscurely however, the Selfsame as fully real. In living the truth, in surrendering our spirit to doing good, we come to know the Selfsame as somehow luminous in his mysteriousness.

> Let the words that follow banish any doubt that we should read in a nonfleshly fashion the line, "Jerusalem which is built as a city; whose fellowship is in the selfsame" (v. 3). So now, brothers, anyone who lifts up the gaze of his mind, strips off the darkness of the flesh, and purifies the eye of the heart is able to see the selfsame. What is the selfsame? What can I call it but the selfsame? Brothers, understand, if you can, the selfsame. For however otherwise I express it, I do not express the selfsame. Nevertheless, let us try some approximate expressions and rough senses to lead our weak mind to ponder the selfsame. What is the selfsame? That which always exists in the same way, that which does not now exist in one way, now in another. The selfsame then is none other than that which is. What is that which is? It is this: that which is eternal. For that which always exists now in one way, then is another, does not exist because it does not last. It does not altogether lack existence but it does not exist in the highest sense. And that which none other than he who, when sending Moses, said to him: "I am who am" (Ex 3.14). That which is is none other than he who replied to Moses. In replying to the request of his servant, "Look, you are sending me; if the people ask me, 'Who sent you?' what should I say to them?" He refused to give a name other than "I am who am." Then he added: "Thus you will say to the children of Israel, 'He who is sent me to you.'" This is the Selfsame: I am who am. You cannot comprehend this, so much is there in it to understand, so much to apprehend.[12]

As we gaze upon the unchangeable Selfsame in his infinite beauty, we are moved to prostrate our spirit in adoration, offering him worship, reverence, holy fear, love. Bowed down before him in wonder and awe, we are moved to praise his manifold magnificence. So Augustine, captivated by the grandeur that is the Selfsame, cries out in exaltation of the Lord. Dwelling on the all-enveloping infinity of God, Augustine groups his attributes in apparently contrasting pairs — apparently because any opposition is relative rather than contradictory. Certain features complement each other: God is most merciful and most just. He is transcendent and immanent: most hidden and most present. His attributes he possesses eminently without lack or limitation: his love is passionless. Certain qualities we ascribe to him metaphorically: so he is said to be angry while actually remaining tranquil. Yet even as we list these attributes, we inwardly start at the multitude of perfections radiating from the one Selfsame and wince at how poor and limping our outpourings are. When all is said and done in worship, little, we find, is or can be said and done in praise of God. Even the most resounding of praise seems muffled, almost soundless, in the presence of the Selfsame who is all.

> What then is my God? What, I ask, but the Lord God? "For who is Lord other than the Lord? Or who is God other than God?" (Ps 17 [18].32). O God, you are the highest, the best, the mightiest, the all-powerful, the most merciful and most just, the most hidden and the most present, the most beautiful and the most strong, abiding and incomprehensible; unchangeable yet changing all things; never new, never old, innovating, initiating all things and leading the proud into decrepitude without their knowing it; ever active, ever at rest, gathering in and needing not a thing, upholding and fulfilling and protecting, creating and feeding and completing; seeking although you want nothing. You love and do not burn with passion, you are jealous and free of care, you repent but do not grieve, you become angry and stay tranquil. You change your works and do not change your plans. You find and regain what you have never lost; you are never in need and you rejoice over gain; you are never greedy and you demand interest. . . . And what have we said, my God, my life, my holy sweetness, or what can anyone say when he speaks of you? But woe betide those who speak no word about you since even those pouring out torrents of words are as if mute.[13]

Reflections

1. The cosmos is unimaginably huge, obscure in its outermost boundaries. The giant strides of modern science adventuring on to new frontiers leave large stretches of nature chartless. In some regions of inquiry each new answer provokes fresh problems, each new area of light ushers in newly noticed areas of darkness. And to go beyond the precision-lined precincts of philosophy and science, who can analytically formulate the meaning of any one person? Who can draw a diagram making sense out of the history of a single nation? Who can hope to weave together into a

pattern all the loose, scattered threads of all history? O Lord, we see only a part, perhaps only a speck, of this universe you have wrought in number and weight and measure. So much of its meaning eludes us, so much fades away into mystery. And what a mystery is each man! A being of question marks, a being perplexing to himself, a person who frequently surprises, perhaps disconcerts himself. If the world your love designed escapes our comprehension, how can you, Lord, be other than the mystery of mysteries, overtopping all our ideas? It is because you are God that human ideas grasp you only sketchily. No wonder man does not, in speaking of you, comprehend your Godness. For if the mind comprehends God it is not comprehending God.[14] Why are you incomprehensible, Lord? In one way because you are all-holy, utterly different from the whole universe, wholly other in your nature, infinitely beyond any possible creature. You are holy in your inner life, holy in your wisdom, holy in your love, holy in your creative action. You hold counsel only within yourself, needing no other thing, relying on no being without. Holy, hidden, secret, mysterious are you through and through, my Lord, my God. I can only cry out, "Holy, holy, holy are you, Mysterious One, incomprehensible God!" As I adore your mystery, light from your life floods into my spirit. As I hail your holiness, a glimmer of your sanctity caresses my spirit. As I lie prostrate, speechless in awe before you, your kindness raises me a little nearer to your majestic presence.

2. Everything in the world is streaked with change. The sun rises, the sun sets; spring follows winter, autumn follows summer. Earth, the planet man calls home, daily rotates at 1,000 m.p.h. and moves in orbit about the sun at 18,000 m.p.h. The Milky Way, our galaxy, is itself moving rapidly through space. Nature is in constant flux. In your being you, O Lord, are infinitely distanced from this world your hands have made. You are absolutely unchangeable; not the smallest shadow of variation falls across your life. You are always stable, abiding, totally immobile, ever the same. And what changes mark the story of man and each man! Physical variation is matched, perhaps outdone, by psychological variation. Youth passes quickly; then come cataracts, hardness of hearing, diabetes, ulcers, colitis, heart trouble, and the contemporary many-faced scourge, cancer. The human mind and heart are burdened with aches and pains and diseases of the spirit. Cheating destroys a career. Granitic selfishness spoils a marriage. Disappointments, obstacles, reverses, traps of enemies, treacheries of friends, vile slanders, bitter quarrels — all these data of psychic flux beset and bedevil and bemuse and bewilder the human spirit. In this life man cannot find a rock, a resting-place, a source of peace. All is process, all is change, that leaves the soul whirling rather than tranquil. Then the candle slowly sputters or is suddenly snuffed out: everyone dies. I am a changing individual in a universe never standing still, ever on the go. Without and within I know myself borne along by unceasing movement. Before me I see, possible at any moment, my death. I turn to you,

Father, everlastingly the same, absolutely deathless, and beg you to breathe into me more of your life, more of your steadfastness, more of the conviction that only in you can I experience the constancy I need for my peace. Only you are fixed in a world in flux, only you are a sure foundation on which to build a life that lasts and perdures. Come, changeless Lord, come, take hold of me, sweep me up in your strong arms, press me close to your heart, still my restlessness in the rest of your heart, in the Rest that is yourself.

3. You are eternal, your life is not spread out along a time-line: you live without beginning and without end, without succession of any sort: you exist totally, completely, all at once. You live only in a changeless present untouched by past or future yet a present that embraces all of the past, present, and future of the cosmic time that numbers my life. You simply are your eternity! You are the "I am"! You are the Is! O God, O timeless Lord, I bow down before you. Touch me once more with the light of your eternity. My life is parceled out in time; I grasp the things of nature only bit by bit. My life is a distension resembling that of the time-line itself; I tend to live fragmented, part sundered from part, scattered in my desires, hopes, purposes.[15] You are the great Is: touch me with the unity of your ever-enduring present, gather up the shattered pieces of my self, repair the broken parts of my being, knit together my tattered purposes into one act of love for you. You are the Burning Bush that is never consumed: plunge me into that never-changing fire, melt me in flames of your eternity and mold me anew, make me a fully new creation, one and stable and firm and harmonized in and through your eternity. Enfold me in the eternal fire of love that is yourself, eternalize me so far as possible in a time-bound world so that even as my eyes fail and my gait becomes feeble, even as I wilt under the remorseless gnawing of time, within I will be growing greener in your eternal vigor that sharpens the inner eye and makes the heart leap and bound forward. Through the wear and tear of time my body is slowly breaking down, becoming more and more dilapidated, and one day not too distant it will fall into ruins. Dearest Father, even as my temporal habitation slowly falls apart, pour your eternal power into my spirit, building day by day an interior mansion to outlast time and rise above the ravages of change.

Teach me to live in the eternal by living from moment to moment, by treasuring each drop of time that flows from you. Teach me to relate my present of time to your present of eternity. Let the light of your eternity shine more brightly on my soul, enabling me to see vividly that every instant of my life springs from and depends on your eternal instant. Thus my poor energies will be less dispersed as I stop morbidly rehashing defects of the past and anxiously vexing myself over uncertainties of the future. Let the fire of your eternity illuminate me: then will I rest in confidence in your rest that is eternal activity, then will I focus on the today that lives by your eternal today.

Praise

1. How magnificent you are, Lord! My vision is narrow, my phrasing maladroit, my contemplation of your greatness halting and spotty. Who can know and love you then without turning to simple praise? You will forgive these childlike utterances, since before your Super-Being I can only stare wide-eyed like a tot and go on repeating and repeating words of praise. Ineffable Father, I praise you for piercing my darkness with your eternity that pinpoints segment by segment the path of truth lying before me. Your eternity has ended my zigzag wanderings in the trackless wilderness of time. I praise you for the direction your eternal light has given to my hitherto shuffling and meandering. I praise you too for your eternal power upholding me at every step in a life so outwardly banal, so undistinguished, so like a worn string of dull beads. I praise you, Fountain of Mercy, for the steady inflow of strength bearing me up from moment to moment, from hour to hour. I praise you for stamping eternal meaning on a life-history so often punctuated by the meaningless.

2. Praise to you, everlasting reliable Lord, for making me a child of hope in a shifting drama of pain and tragedy — in a world of reverses and losses that sting and numb into hopelessness men living solely on their own resources. I praise you, Father: you are always there, always sustaining me, always assuring me of changeless power through the ups and downs of a chancy existence. Legions of totalitarian lying and murder fathered by Satan may enslave our land; I may be struck with blindness; I may agonize through long years of cancer; I may sink into senility; I may lose my sanity; yet I can never lose hope, I can never rage against the night, I can never collapse into depression, weeping and whining over the absurdity of human existence.

3. Praise be to you, Yahweh, for revealing yourself in the name proclaiming your everlasting self-integrity. Praised be the God who is "I am." All praise to you who are simply Is because in your self-identity I claim and maintain my self-identity. Because you are "I am who am," I can seek to know who I am, I can be sure that my "I am" will outlast the destruction wreaked by time. Praise be to you, Deathless One: in you I can aspire to be deathless. I praise you, Burning Bush: through you I can burn on and on, ever renewed in your eternal life. You are Fire, you are Love eternal. I praise you for thus revealing my own identity: I am intended to share in your eternal being, I am called to share in the endurance of the Burning Bush, I am meant to be fire, I am destined to be enduring love that infinitesimally, yes, yet truly mirrors never-ending love. All civilizations may crumble to dust, all the treasures of art and culture may be ground to powder, the galaxies may be broken to pieces, the universe may be torn apart from seam to seam — yet I will go on and on, perduring, unshatterable, impregnable in my self-integrity because I live by your everlasting life. I praise you, eternal love: you have made my life stronger than death,

you have fused my love with yours, so that I can be deathless love in your deathless love.

Praise of God as Merciful

God cannot be truly God, we saw, unless he is wholly other. An infinite divide yawns between himself and finite things. He is not just, figuratively speaking, countless light years apart from us: he is truly infinitely distant from his creation. He is God, the only God, the God needing only God. Before the universe existed, he dwelt serene in his beatitude, and after creation he remains infinitely tranquil, inwardly unperturbed by the incessant changes beneath him, inwardly unaffected by the successes and failures, delights and woes in the drama of his creatures. Some critics of the Christian religion have therefore found fault with this portrait of God. In their eyes an infinite God, absolutely unchangeable, resembles a despot icily aloof and callously heedless of struggles and sufferings in a universe of change. Such a charge, however, caricaturizes the Christian God. Leaving aside more subtle points, suffice it to say that a stonily uncaring God could not have created the world nor would he now be conserving and providing for it. A finite world emanating from an infinite, self-sufficient being can be accounted for only by his generosity. Sheerly out of his goodness, out of his desire to share himself, God freely and magnificently made the universe and instant by instant keeps it running. One beautiful line from the Old Testament concretely registers his tireless concern: "I have loved you with an everlasting love" (Jer 31.3). No frigidly sequestered potentate-deity could love creatures with a love one with his eternal being. God took one further, miraculous step to overcome the gap between infinite and finite that not we but he alone can bridge. In Jesus Christ the Word became flesh and pitched his tent among us. In him infinite and finite natures are really joined in one person. Unlike the prophets of old, Jesus spoke with the authority of God and worked miracles in his own name. But the power of this greatest of prophets mighty in word and work was the instrument of divine mercy. God is love, and Jesus is principally the human revelation of divine love. In relation to the ills of man God's love is mercy, and Jesus is the enfleshed mercy of God. Thus though God remains infinite, wholly other, he is present to us by his activity, especially in the salvific work of the incarnate love that is Jesus Christ. God is truly a God needing no other, but in Jesus he manifests himself in an unsurpassable manner as our God, a God for us, a God with us, a God among us.

It is to this question of the apparent remoteness of God that Augustine addresses himself in the two following texts, the first of which is a con-tinuation of a text we quoted above. A God who is "I am who am" seems infinitely far off and therefore infinitely inaccessible to the human heart. But God who in himself is Is, is for us the God of Abraham, Isaac, and Jacob, the God whose fullest epiphany in time is realized in the God-man, Jesus

Christ. In Jesus the Word of God summons men to be temporal and makes them eternal: in him the Word lifts time-constricted men up to the eternal dimension. In Jesus the Word became temporal so that man might become eternal. The Word became a servant subject to time and change so that we servants might become eternal and in some way changeless. He died that we might become deathless, he rose that we might live an everlasting life sharing in the unchangeable life of the God who simply is. In Jesus the God whose name is "I am who am" becomes a God living and dying and rising for us, and in and through him we become by participation as deathless and eternal as "I am who am."

How great is Is! How great is Is! In comparison with the grandeur of this Is, what is man, whatever he may be? Who can understand this existence? Who can pant after it? Who can presume the power to attain it? Do not despair, man, though your name is frailty. "I am," he says, "the God of Abraham and the God of Isaac and the God of Jacob" (Ex 3.15). In effect, he says, "You have heard what I am in myself, now listen to what I am for you." So this eternity has called us, and the Word has sprung forth from eternity. Eternity already existed, as did the Word, but time was not yet in existence. Why was time not yet in existence? Because time also was made. How was time made? "All things were made by him, and without him nothing was made" (Jn 1.3). O Word before time, through you all time was made, O Word born in time, although you are eternal life, you summon beings to be temporal and make them eternal! This is the generation of generations. For one generation goes and another generation comes (Eccl 1.4). And you see that the generations of men on earth are like leaves on a tree or at least like those on the olive or laurel or any other tree perennially garbed in green. So the earth bears the whole of mankind like leaves; it is full of men, while those who die are succeeded by the newly born. So it is that such a tree is always dressed in its green garment; but look underneath: notice how many dried-up leaves you tread on.[16]

"You indeed are the same and your years do not fail" (v. 28). But in comparison with those years what are we to do with our tattered years? And what are these rags of years? However, we should not give way to despair. Already in his majesty and sublime wisdom he had said, "I am who am," and, nevertheless, to console us he added, "I am the God of Abraham and the God of Isaac and the God of Jacob" (Ex 3.15). And we are the seed of Abraham, and, abject as we are, dust and ashes though we are, we hope in him. We are servants but for us our Lord took the form of a servant (Phil 2.7), for us mortals the Immortal One willed to die, for us he showed the example of the resurrection.

Let us then hope that we will reach those changeless years in which the revolution of the sun does not determine days but in which that which is remains what it is because it alone truly is.[17]

Because in his concrete, historical condition man is sunk in sin, he could not ascend to the heights of divine life. But God could and did descend to man. Jesus, divine and human, reunites fallen man with the all-pure God. If Jesus had been only God and his bodily appearance had been just that — appearance — and no more, a mere external vesture of flesh, God would have been as far out of reach as ever. If he had been only man, his life and sacrificial death could not have won divine redemption and reopened the gates of paradise. As the one mediator Jesus enables us to feed on the bread of angels, not in the sense of the full vision of God, which the angels enjoy, but in the measure that Jesus nourishes us with the fruits of divine life. The spiritual meaning of sweet bread does not derive from the narrow import of the term reserved for foods like cake and candy. Bread that is sweet strengthens, refreshes, satisfies, delights the hungry frame. Analogously we taste the sweet bread of God when in and through Jesus we experience the love, truth, wisdom, and power of the Father. Strength restored by and heart relishing the sweetness of the Lord, we praise his name for feeding us with his power and glory.

To what length can we not go in speaking of his goodness? What heart can conceive and encompass how good the Lord is? But let us return into ourselves and let us receive him within ourselves and let us praise the Maker in his works, for we are unable to contemplate him in himself. We will be able to contemplate him later, when our heart will be so purified by faith that we will at last rejoice in the truth. Now because we cannot see him, let us view his works so that we may not go on without praising him. Therefore I said, "Praise the Lord because he is good; sing psalms to his name because he is sweet" (v. 3). Perhaps he might be good yet not sweet if he did not give you the power to taste him. So generously did he show himself to men that he even sent them bread from heaven (Jn 6.32, 51). He gave his own Son, equal to himself, a Son who is what he himself is, to become man and to die for men so that because of what you are you can taste what you are not. It was a great privilege for you to taste the sweetness of God; for he was far off and unapproachably lofty, while you were utterly abased and prostrate at the bottom of the abyss. A mediator was sent to overcome this enormous gulf. As a man you were unable to attain God, so God became man. As a man who was unable to attain God, you could relate to a fellow man; thus as a man you could approach God through man; and the man Christ Jesus became the mediator between God and man (1 Tim 2.5). But if he had been only man, you would never have attained God because you would have been relying on what you are. If he had been only God, you would never have attained God because you could not have grasped what you are not. God became man so that, by following man, which you are able to do, you might attain God, which you were not able to do. He is the mediator; hence he became sweet. What is sweeter than the bread of angels? How can the Lord not be sweet when man ate the bread of angels (Ps 82.25). Man does not live on one bread and an angel on another. This bread is the truth, it is the wisdom, it is the power of God. But you cannot enjoy it as the angels do. How do they enjoy it? They possess it in the way he exists: "In the beginning was the Word, and the Word was with God, and the Word was God" (Jn 1.1), through whom all things were made. But how do you attain it? You attain it insofar as the Word was made flesh and dwelt among us. So that man might eat the bread of angels the Creator of angels became man. "Sing psalms to his name because he is sweet." If you have tasted this bread, sing psalms. If you have tasted how sweet the Lord is, sing psalms. If you have relished what you tasted, praise him. Suppose an individual delights in a meal cooked and served by his host: wouldn't you think him a sorry ingrate if he failed to thank him by praising the delicious food? If we do not pass over in silence feasts like these, shall we be silent about him who gave us all things? "Sing psalms to his name because he is sweet."[18]

Reconciliation with God requires the cleansing of the human heart. It is Jesus who heals us, binds up our wounds, anoints us with the oil of gladness of his Spirit. No infirmity is so debilitating, no disease so advanced, no disfigurement so ugly that it cannot be healed by the gently probing power of his divine heart. However skilled, a physician, Augustine notes, may inflict remedy-related suffering to no avail; the patient may die within days. No human doctor can absolutely guarantee a healing. It is happily otherwise with Jesus, the divine physician. As the Maker of the human body and soul he penetrates with utmost precision to the innermost workings and malfunctionings of the human spirit so that he can cure all our spiritual ills. We need not shrink from him in fright or dismay — he *will* heal us as quickly and painlessly as possible. But we must yield ourselves to his care, must surrender ourselves into his hands with total confidence. Too we must want to be healed, and a valid index of that desire is our willingness to keep his commandments, the loving directives of his heart that assure spiritual health. Indeed Jesus is our health as well as our healer. When we are cleansed in his blood shed to pay the price of our redemption, when we grow in the fruits of the outpouring of his blood, we are made healthy by him who is health itself, the incarnate love of the Father.

"He heals all your ills, he redeems your life from corruption" (vv. 3-4). . . . Illness you have, but he heals all your ills. All your ills will be healed: do not be afraid. "They are great," you say; but the physician is greater. For an all-powerful physician no illness is incurable. Simply yield yourself to his healing. Do not push aside his hands; he knows what he is doing. Do not rejoice only when he gives you relief but bear with it when he applies the knife to you. Bear with the pain of the remedy by keeping in mind the healing it will bring. Look, my brothers, at how much men put up with in their bodily ailments. Yet they may die in a few days anyway, and even these few days are not guaranteed as certain. Indeed many men, after enduring great suffering under the physician's knife, either die while under treatment or, after recovering, are shortly stricken by and die from another disease. If they had expected such an early death, would they have chosen to expose themselves to such enormous sufferings? You at least do not suffer with the outcome in doubt; he who promised you healing cannot fall into error. At times a physician makes a mistake and promises a patient that he will become well. And why does he make a mistake? Because he is not treating a body he made. God made your body, God made your soul. He knows how to recreate what he created, he knows how to remake what he made. All you have to do is give yourself into the hands of this physician, for he does not love those who spurn his healing hands. . . . So as your soul blesses him, bear with his hands that bring healing, and do not forget the health he has restored to you. . . . He made you so as never to be ill on the condition that you truly desire to keep his commandments. Will he not then heal you? . . . He fully heals every ill person but he will not heal anyone unwilling to be healed. . . . Here then is what I am telling you: . . . if your condition convinces you that you are ill, think first of all about your health. Christ is your health; think then about Christ. Take up the cup of his salvation: "He heals all your ills." If you truly desire health, you will obtain it. . . . Don't have one bit of anxiety. . . . He has negotiated a business deal, he has paid the price, he has poured out his blood. Indeed the only Son of God, I am telling you, has poured out his blood. Indeed the only Son of God has poured out his own blood for us. O my soul, raise your spiritual self-image: at what a great price you have been purchased! "He redeems your life from corruption" (v. 4). He showed by the example of his resurrection what he promised as your reward. "He died for our sins and rose for our justification" (Rom 4.25). Let the members hope for what they see manifested in their head. He has lifted up the head into

heaven: will he not also heal his members? So "he redeems your
life from corruption."[19]

Jesus did not walk the earth like some Greek god in pseudo-human
flesh caparisoned with pomp and the panoply of power. Rather, according
to a theme that Augustine returns to again and again, Christ lived among
men as the humble healer, the utterly self-effacing physician of souls.
Simplicity and the poverty of the anawim characterized his early years as
a village carpenter. During his public mission he was constantly on the
go, established in no fixed abode or headquarters, frequently sleeping under
open skies, living from hand to mouth, relying on followers and benefactors
for provisions. He came not to be served but to serve (Mk 10.45): his
unexampled gifts were devoted to the healing of as many as possible, among
whom were the sweaty, the coarse, the fickle, the many times thankless
individuals, in the multitudes that pressed around him. In his suffering
and death his lowliness blazed with the greatest brilliance. On the cross
he drank the cup of humility to the full.[20] As Augustine underscores in
the following text, Jesus exhibited humble patience also in struggling to
teach the crowds infiltrated and partly infested by fractious enemies. He
was abused, insulted, slandered, insolently upbraided, ridiculed, sneered
at, but in his humility he loved his enemies, prayed for his persecutors,
turned the other cheek to his attackers, and anointed them with the
compassion of the Father. His humility was the surgeon's lance that cut
away and healed the rotting tumor of pride in men.[21] The surgical knife
seems hard but the touch of Jesus is soft and delicate. The embrace of his
self-forgetful love pierces our hearts, drains away our pride, and infuses
into us his own lowliness. Only the radical humility of the Jesus who is
love can cleanse us of the age-old, radical disease that is pride.

> Just as the seducer of Adam said of himself, "I will set my throne
> toward the north" (Is 14.13), so too he persuaded Adam in these
> words, "Taste and you will be as gods" (Gen 3.5). It is then
> through pride that we have fallen, a fall culminating in this present
> mortal condition. And because pride had wounded us, humility
> healed us. God came as a humble man so as to heal man of his
> gaping wound of pride. He came, for "the Word was made flesh
> and dwelt among us" (Jn 1.14). He was seized by the Jews, who
> heaped insults on him. During the reading of the Gospel you heard
> what they said and to whom they said: "You have a devil" (Jn
> 8.48). And he did not respond, "Rather, you have a devil because
> you are sunk in your sins, and the devil possesses your hearts."
> He did not say this, though, had he said it, he would have spoken
> the truth. But this was not the time for such a response. Other-
> wise he might have seemed concerned not with preaching the truth
> but with repaying insult with insult. He ignored what he heard
> as if he had not heard it. For he was a physician who had come

to heal a delirious man. A physician does not bother about what he hears from a delirious patient but is interested only in restoring him to health. He remains unconcerned even if struck by such a patient: he is opening new wounds to heal an old fever. So also to a man delirious in his sickness the Lord came, ready to brush aside whatever he might hear and suffer. By such forbearance he taught men humility so that, by learning this lesson, men might be healed of pride. Here the psalmist prays to be freed from this pride: "Let not the foot of the proud touch me, and let not the hand of the sinner move me" (v. 12).[22]

Reflections

1. Today a confrere in his sixties died suddenly of a heart attack. A month ago a relative in her prime succumbed to galloping leukemia. Weeks before, a young man of college age sustained fatal brain damage in a freakish automobile accident during a heavy rainstorm. Old, middle-aged, young — all of us can die easily and quickly from one of a thousand causes. Mysterious though the beginning and ending of a single human life may be, there is no mystery in the brute fact of death. Every man is marked for death, each of us carries his own death warrant in an organism programmed to decompose. Death is the plainest, most poignant sign of our temporality: we are mortal, we are beings of time. In Augustine's graphic figure men are so many leaves on the evergreen tree of nature, whose base is always carpeted with dead leaves. How trivial mortal life, my life, seems! A few years, some piddling accomplishments, then the irremediable coldness of death, then the endless oblivion of the tomb. Another leaf falls, and all that remains of one life dries up, disintegrates, and sinks into the earth whence it came. How petty and inconsequential seems the brief episode that is my life. Measured against the long stretches of geological time, my life is only a bit, an infinitesimal fragment, of the course of nature, its few feeble gestures toward ideals apparently an exercise in futility because eventually buried under layers of succeeding epochs. But, sweet Father, you are not just God but God for us. You sent your Son into the world to make our wasteland of time abloom with the eternal. When your Word became flesh, you inserted eternal meaning into ever-vanishing slivers of time. Through your eternal Word you have made me a being of time in order to make me over into a being of eternity. My vocation to the eternal will not cause my life to last any longer than the ordinary. Shortly, perhaps very shortly, I will close my eyes in death and be laid in the grave. But now my evanescent existence glows with new significance. Because the Word of eternity took on the flesh of Jesus in time, my fleshly span is lighted with some of the radiance of the eternal. Though absolutely immortal, Jesus, you took on a mortal nature. So, though headed for death, I can share in your deathlessness. Jesus, in rising from the dead, you raised

my hope for ending my days not in the blankness of death but in union with you in your eternal day. I am an earth animal, fettered to time, swept along in the flux, but because of your Father's eternal love expressed in your journey through time, I can hope, after a swift voyaging through time, to be lifted to an eternal home of deathless tranquility.

2. It would be blinking unpleasant facts to blame time or the flux it measures for my woeful human condition. Time is only the natural setting for my decisions. It is I who am guilty; I am responsible for my failures. I am a sinner, one who never seems to learn the lesson of the deformity of sin. I fall again and again, and rise only to return to former lapses. I am covered with wounds and scars, yet in my partial blindness I seem to go on living for the day, the dupe of immediate impulses, never widening my horizons to live fully in your never-failing light, Jesus, my eternal lover. Heal all of my wounds, loving physician of my soul, in particular, the darkness of my mind, my slackness of faith. Time flows on without respite, yet at each instant without respite you shine your light into my soul, and very frequently I neglect to heed your presence. At every moment you try to speak a word of guidance or comfort but the ears of my soul, dulled by the din of preoccupations, hardly catch a syllable. Heal my spiritual eyes and ears, make them sensitive to every least ray or note of your presence. Make my faith whole, free of all doubt and wobbling: then I will truly believe that you, my Jesus, my all-giving healer, are always in the center of my being, always ready to cure all that is crippled and tumorous in my spirit.

Heal me especially of my lack of trust. While insisting that I want to be transformed by your Spirit, secretly, in the recesses of my soul, I shrink from such radical change. I am like a patient who wants to be cured without undergoing the necessary major surgery, I am afraid of the suffering and pain that spiritual growth entails. I say yes to your entreaties but within my yes is concealed a no. I want all of you, but I do not want all of you because I fear, and at times am terrified by, the possible anguish and distress this "all" may demand. Calm the disquiet of my heart, kind physician, and empty me of all vain anxieties. Once more show me your wounds and bid me enter with my wounds. Your heart will tranquilize my heart, persuading me that any pain permitted by your perfectly skilled hands will always be a sweet pain, a pain infused with your consolation, a pain tempered by your gentleness. Now I do notice your presence, ever-tender healer, now once more I do hear you pleading, "Come to me." So again I say yes to your invitation. I yield myself to your medicines of the spirit, knowing that the more I give myself in trust, the more I will be healed; the more I yield myself as a child, the more assured I am that my spirit will be made more virile.

3. Lord Jesus, you healed not with éclat and histrionic flourish, not with ostentation, not with a spectacle of staggering power. You came as a humble healer, laden with weariness and hunger and affliction from heat

and cold. Your life is a book teaching us humility; you urged your apostles and urge us still: "Learn of me for I am meek and humble of heart" (Mt 11.29), you lived and died as the humble servant of the Father, you were obedient even to the point of saying yes to death on the cross. You called us not to imitate your divine strength but your human weakness. You do not ask us to learn of you to create the cosmos or to raise the dead to life or to give sight to the blind or to restore hearing to the deaf or to still the raging sea. Your request is simple and feasible: learn my humility of heart.[23] Lord Jesus, you are our medicine, our source of healing,[24] you are our life and healing. You are my healing, your humility is my healing. I totter under burdens, especially my sins, and the chief of these is my pride. Speak to me again with all your charm, lure me by your sweetness, draw me by a fresh anointing to learn of your humility so as to be disburdened of my pride.[25]

I know the abstract meaning of humility, Lord, but I have a long way to go in mastering its concrete, existential sense, in living humbly. If I become humble, I can know myself not as less than what I am but just as I am: a fragile vessel, a man appointed to die, a creature dependent on you for my slightest breath and smallest thought.[26] I can realize that you are Being, Existence, Super-Existence while by comparison I am nonbeing. I can live as your obedient servant, accepting all from your hands as tokens of your love, rejoicing in the awesome fact that I totally rely on you, that I can do nothing supernatural without you. This is the lesson I must impress on every fiber of my being: I am weakness, you are strength; I am sinfulness, you are infinite purity; to you do I owe all that I am and hope to be.[27]

Jesus, you said a number of times, "He who humbles himself will be exalted" (Mt 23.12). You supremely exemplified this key truth in your own life and death. You are exalted: every knee bends before you, every voice hails you as Lord of lords because you chose the most shameful of deaths, crucifixion as a despicable criminal (Phil 2.5-11). When I see myself as little and lowly, I can share in your exaltation. When I recognize my weakness, I become open to your strength; when I confess myself a sinner, I dispose myself to be cleansed and rise to your divine life. I can aspire to touching the peak of your sublimity by drinking of your cup of humility.[28] Take me into your heart so that, cleaving to you within, I can livingly grasp your humility and know you, incarnate humility, and, resting there, reach for the heights of eternity. I bow to the exigencies of living in time as I interiorly deliver myself over to the turmoil and torment of an existence subject to matter and human perversity. Here below I can be in some way lifted out of narrow confines of time into the breadth of the divinely timeless. No matter how often I falter in my resolve, I can, by acquiescing in my call to live in time, enter in some measure into my vocation to live in the eternal, to share, ever-attractive Jesus, in your eternity, in your peace not of this world, in your rest immune to the fluctuations and blows of time; to share in your everlasting knowledge of the Father that you lovingly choose to reveal to me (Mt. 11:27), knowledge, however faint and shadowy, of him whose sacred name is "I am who am."

Praise

1. Dust we are and unto dust do we return. Vessels of clay are we, frail, unstable, feeble, insignificant-looking. Flowers of the field are we, destined to blossom briefly, then to vanish like smoke. Praise be to you, all-loving Father: you have transfigured this dust, you have lit up this earthen vessel with divine life, you have made us for time so as to remake us for eternity. Praise and glory to you for your wisdom in sending your Son to live among us to deify the dust, to dwell as God in this tent of clay, to hallow each moment that was, fleetingly is, and will be with the presence of your "I am who am.' I praise you for this gift of gifts, Jesus. Since you have not refused me this greatest of gifts (Rom 8.32), dower me your lesser gifts, especially the gift of understanding and the gift of praise.

How obtuse of spirit I am, how like a witless child unaware of the countless blessings showered on him by his parents. Illumine my mind, Father, so that I can perceive, yes, spiritually see, that Jesus is the eternal in time. Grant me also the gift of tireless praise for your Son whom I boldly name my Jesus. Let me never cease praising you for Jesus! Let me never cease praising you in Jesus! Glory to you, eternal Father! Praise to you, Jesus, eternity in the flesh! Praise to you, Holy Spirit, everlasting fire who makes me burn with the desire to praise Jesus! Praise to you, mercy three-in-one! You are mercy that can never end, you are mercy pouring yourself out at this very moment, you are mercy that eternalizes human time in Jesus, you are mercy that is always there, always the same, yesterday, today, and forever. Praise to you, Father, for being eternal mercy. Praise to you, Jesus, for making time alive with the eternal in you. Praise to you, Holy Spirit, for leading me as a son of God: you inspirit me to walk the way that is Jesus, you breathe the eternal that is Jesus into my spirit, you spur me to praise, indeed within and through me you praise the boundless mercy of the Father in Jesus.

2. Praise to you, Jesus, for being Jesus. As Jesus you are savior, healer, my savior, my healer. Praise to your holy name: Jesus, Jesus, Jesus! May I never stop repeating this holiest, this sweetest, this most precious, this most healing of names. Live, Jesus, live! Live in me as Lord, as master, as king, but first of all as loving healer. I praise you for tirelessly pursuing me, for lovingly battering down my resistance with your overpowering charm. Praise to you for all of my life, even for my infidelities, betrayals, greed, anger, sloth, coldness to others, self-centeredness, deceit, Janus-faced behavior, hypocrisy, bitterness — all my sins and frailties and twisted desires, all that tells of my muleheadedness, all that springs from my seeking of self in defiance of your love. I praise you for my misery because my repulsiveness attracted your mercy. I praise you for my ugliness because

this drew the beauty of your redeeming touch to my spirit. Come now, Jesus, come with your scalpel: cut deeply and strongly and widely, remove every tumor and abscess, burn away every diseased tissue, cleanse me of all my darkness to make room for your light. I praise you, doctor of doctors, for sowing in me the yearning to be healed, I praise you for not sparing the circumstances, inner and outer, aimed at lopping off my malignancies, I praise you for being so gentle, so caring, as you cut to heal, as you destroy to build, as you inflict pain to insure more of the pleasure of your peace. Glory to you, Jesus, stronger than steel but mildest of healers! Praise to you, Jesus: you hurt when you heal but even as you hurt, the sedative of your peace and the balm of your joy flow into my soul.

3. All honor and praise and worship to you, Jesus! You are Lord, you are king of glory, all-glorious in your humility. Praise to you for your absolute self-surrender to the Father. I praise you: for us who are nothing, you nothing-ed yourself. I praise you for being despised and spat upon and whipped like a dog, for handing yourself over to the horror of the cross. Praise to you, king of glory, in your abominable death. Praise to you, king of power, king of love, for manifesting your power in being powerless, your love in being hated. I praise you for your unspeakable lowliness: most despised of men, you invited men to grind you to powder, to make you a zero in their eyes, to strip you of all human dignity, to nail you to a tree of hate you transmuted into a tree of love.

I praise you, king of glory, for showing me the way to true glory: the glory of self-surrender, the glory of utter abjection. Glory to you, Jesus, for showing me your holy face — the face of rejection and triumph, the face so hated that has loved so much, the face so beaten and mangled yet so handsome and glorious in its humility. I praise you, all-disfigured and all-lowly one: and as I praise you, let your Spirit imprint more of your face on the face of my soul. I praise you, king of glory: let each moment of praise teach me how to share in the glory of self-annihilation. Praise to you, Jesus, most mighty in your mercy, most exalted in your humility. As my heart in its praises embraces you, plunge me into the depths of your humble heart to believe and understand the way to the glory and power of a little one. I praise you, king of humble glory. Make me delight in the humility I praise, show me how to taste as inwardly sweet the outwardly bitter draught of humility. I praise you, lowliest of kings: let my praise, always simple, many times insufficient, now and then feckless, become the praise of your heart; let me know your glory, let my heart by its praising become like the humble heart I praise.

Praise in Relation to Modes of Prayer

Today it is not uncommon to hear references to the prayer of praise with the implication that praise is a mode of prayer. This way of speaking, however, was not employed by Augustine. In his usage prayer is never

general, always specific in import. He did not see prayer as a genus sub-
suming various specific modes or divisions of prayer. In his vocabulary
prayer ordinarily meant, as the Latin nouns *oratio* and *precatio* indicate,
what we designate the prayer of petition, which is, by the way, the usual
sense of its New Testament equivalents.[29] Just as the Lord's prayer prefaces
its petitions with praise of our Father in heaven,[30] so, we are told, praise
should precede all invocation and propitiation. God "hearkens to the seeker
whom he recognizes as a praiser: he recognizes as a praiser the lover whom
he attests."[31] In the life to come when all our needs will be everlastingly
satisfied, prayer that is petition will necessarily disappear while praise will
eternally chant its alleluia.[32]

Plainly Augustine's language draws a sharp line between praise and
prayer, but it does not do violence to his thought to roughly relate praise
to what are currently taken to be the four modes of prayer: adoration,
contrition, thanksgiving, and supplication, or acts, as one mnemonic device
has it.[33] We shall vary this order slightly, beginning with thanksgiving,
then moving on to petition and sorrow for sin. Because we have dealt with
it earlier as a springboard for praise, we shall pass over an explicit treatment
of adoration. A fine line divides praise and thanksgiving. We praise God
simply because he is God — unexcellable in all his attributes. We praise
him for being God, infinite and merciful, all love, all beauty, all sweetness.
But we thank God for his benefits to us. We praise and thank the God who
is a God for us, but in praise we underline God while in thanksgiving we
lay more emphasis on the "for us." Clearly distinct, these two modes of
prayer resemble blood brothers or fraternal twins, so closely related that
in the first selection below Augustine intermingles the two.

All too often the thanksgiving of some Christians, Augustine points
out with melancholy, seems cramped as the horizons of their too earthbound faith. Some Christians chant and shout the praise of God when he
showers material benefits upon them. But let them suffer financial reverses
along with personal woes, marital headaches, pain of body and spirit, and
they whine over the apparent injustice of God, perhaps screaming curses
at the God whom a few days before they were heartily blessing. Such bizarre
vacillation branches off from a shortsightedness that fails to see temporal
evils as a discipline reluctantly permitted by a loving Father to help shape
souls for everlasting treasures in heaven. Measured on the scale of faith
and love against "the eternal weight of glory," troubles that gall us in time
count for comparatively nothing. Temporal afflictions are brief and unsub-
stantial, eternal joys in God endless and super-satisfying.

"He will praise you when you do good to him" (v. 19). Pay
attention to this line, nourish your soul on it, absorb it into your
hearts.... Brothers, how numerous are the Christians who
thank God when their hands gain more money. For this type
of Christian the verse, "He will praise you when you do good
to me," takes on a one-sided meaning. Such a Christian will

utter praise in the words, "You are truly my God." Or he will say, "Because he freed me from prison, I will praise him." He makes a profit, so he praises him. He is left an inheritance, so he praises him. But he suffers a loss, so he blasphemes him. What kind of a son are you if you become displeased with your father when he corrects you? Would he correct you if you did not displease him? Or would he bother to correct you if in his displeasure with you he hated you? Then thank your corrector so that you may receive an inheritance from the God who corrects you. When you are corrected, you are taught a lesson. But he corrects you a great deal because he has a great inheritance prepared for you. Weigh the correction against what you are to receive, and you will find it amounts to nothing. As the apostle Paul tells us, "For this light and momentary affliction is achieving for us an eternal weight of glory beyond all measure" (2 Cor 4.17-18).[34]

People of the eschaton or the end of time, with eyes lifted up toward the world to come, Christians are people of hope. In his love our Father has planned every inch of our lives. All our gifts and limitations, all that occurs in line or at cross-purposes with our desires, all that happens for weal or woe, all our good fortune and mishaps — all are touches, direct or indirect, of love from the Father who is all love. The Christian response to continuous love is continuous giving of thanks. We thank him always, when he consoles and when he chastises, when he gives prosperity and permits adversity. True Christians are "everywhere thankful and nowhere thankless" because the joys and sorrows that are intermixed in every human life are only passing phenomena, instruments to ready souls for happiness that will not pass. In this present life we try to always thank the Father, for he lays his loving hand, whether soft or hard in pressure, upon our hearts, impelling us to believe the promises of the risen Jesus and to fasten our hope on the life that is simply an eternal present.

We are Christians only in view of the future life. No one should hope for the good things of this present life, no one should promise himself happiness in the world simply for the reason that he is a Christian. Rather, he should use the happiness of the present life as he can, how he can, when he can, as much as he can. When such happiness befalls him, he should give thanks to the God who consoles. When deprived of it, he should give thanks to the God who is just. He should be everywhere thankful and nowhere thankless. He should be thankful to a Father who consoles and caresses him, he should be thankful to a Father who corrects and chastises and imposes discipline, for God's love is ever the same, whether he caresses or threatens. He should say what you heard read in the psalm: "It is good to praise the Lord and to sing psalms to your name, O most high God" (v. 2).[35]

Because we are so weak, so mired in difficulties, so troubled, so perplexed, so unsure, so conscious of pressing needs, needs spiritual, psychological, physical, and economic, petition is probably the most common mode of prayer — "O God, help me" is the core of the greater number of our prayers. Lying in between the lines of the words of supplication is the note of praise: God will answer our prayer because he is God, he is all-powerful. The praise that should explicitly precede petition is implicitly present in our very asking.

The good things we seek in the prayer of petition are principally faith, hope, and charity or virtues having an affinity to them. Perhaps Augustine is here intimating that whatever we pray for and whatever the external outcome of our prayer, we are always compensated with an increase of the faith, hope, and charity that quickens praise. With a bit of wrenching and forcing of similar texts in Luke and Matthew he interprets the fish of the parable as faith, the egg as hope, and the bread as charity. Their look-a-like opposites, the serpent, scorpion, and stone, stand for respectively disbelief, lack of hope, and hardness of heart. In contrast to the foot-dragging householder annoyed because his deep sleep has been broken, the Father is eager in his generosity to enrich our hearts with his choicest good things, stronger faith, hope, and love in him through the Spirit of Jesus. Indeed the Father does not sleep because he need not. In fact, as Augustine wittily perceives, it is we, the petitioners, who are nodding or slumbering, and it is the Father who stirs us from sleep, the inertia of the flesh, to ask, seek, and knock for the goods that make us people of love and praise.

> According to another parable, a certain man, whose friend had come from a journey and sought three loaves, which perhaps symbolized the very trinity of one substance, did not have anything to serve him. Though he and his servants had gone to bed, the petitioner was so extremely insistent and annoying that he got up and gave him as many loaves as he wanted; and he was concerned not so much with exercising charity as with getting rid of vexation. The point of the story is this: if a man roused from sleep feels, however reluctantly, bound to give to a petitioner, how much more kindly will he give who has no need of sleep and who rouses us out of our sleep to ask of him.

> This is why he continued: "Ask and you will receive; seek and you will find; knock and it will be opened to you. Everyone who asks receives; whoever seeks finds; and it is opened to anyone who knocks. Which father among you, if his son asks for bread, will hand him a stone? Or if he asks for a fish, will hand him a serpent? Or if he asks for an egg, will hand him a scorpion? So if you who are evil are ready to give good things to your children, how much more will your heavenly Father give good things to those who ask him." (Mt 7.7-11; Lk 11.9-12). In line

then with the three virtues the Apostle commends, we may take the fish to mean faith either because of the water of baptism or because it remains intact amid the turbulent waves of this world. In contrast to faith is that serpent whose poisonous deceit persuaded men not to believe God. The egg represents hope because the life of the chick does not yet exist but is yet to come, Not yet seen, it is hoped for, for "hope that is seen is not hope" (Rom 8.24). In contrast to hope is the scorpion because a person hoping for eternal life forgets what lies in back and stretches out to what lies in front; for it is dangerous to look back; so we are warned not to touch the back part of the scorpion, where is lodged its poisonous and sharp sting. The bread represents charity. Just as "the greatest of these is charity" (I Cor 13.13), so bread is the most highly valued of foods. In contrast to charity is the stone because hard hearts spurn charity. These three foods may more felicitously symbolize other spiritual objects, but this key idea remains: he who is ready to give good things to his children urges us to ask and seek and knock.[36]

Many times Augustine depicts each of us in our seeking as a beggar. Before God we have and are nothing of ourselves. Each of us is an absolute mendicant, dependent on the Lord not just for a substantial alms but for everything; for food, clothing, the air we breathe, the very body that is fed and clothed, the very soul that begs for sustenance. What we implicitly beg for in every prayer is God himself, the life of our life. The bread we beg for is the living bread that is Jesus who enables us to live, as he does, by the life of the Father.

> When we pray, all of us are beggars of God: we stand before the gate of the great Father of the household. Indeed we also lie prostrate on the ground, groaning in our supplication, longing to receive something; and this something is God himself. What does a beggar ask from you? Bread. And what do you ask from God but the Christ who says, "I am the living bread that has come down from heaven" (Jn 6.31).[37]

The posture of begging implicitly bespeaks praise of God, for in his shabbiness and indigence man has to recognize and totally rely on the munificence of an infinitely rich God. It is the poor in spirit who, in casting themselves down before God, in beseeching his generosity, in effect, praise his name. By contrast, those who are swollen with pride seek themselves, praise themselves, worship themselves, and win as recompense for their self-adoration the most meager and miserable of rewards — themselves. Spiritual beggars, however, raise their eyes in praise to God, who banishes their poverty by filling their hands and hearts with himself.

> "The poor and needy will praise your name" (v. 21). You see that the poor and needy belong to God. "Poor" refers to the

poor in spirit "because the kingdom of heaven is theirs" (Mt 5.3). Who are the poor in spirit? They are the humble who tremble before the words of God, who confess their sins, who put no trust in their own merits or in their own righteousness. Who are the poor in spirit? Those who praise God when they do something good and blame themselves when they do something evil. "On whom will my Spirit rest," says the prophet, "if not on the humble, peaceful man who trembles at my word (Is 66.2). So now understand this, no longer is he attached to the earth, no longer does he pursue the earthly promises of the Old Testament. He has become your beggar, your poor man. He thirsts for your rivers, for his own have dried up. Since he became so different, don't let his hope be cheated. He has sought you at night with hands upraised in your presence: don't let him be fooled. "Do not let the humble be turned away in confusion: the poor and needy will praise your name" (v. 21). Those who confess their sins will praise your name, those who yearn for your eternal promises will praise your name. But not those who are bloated with temporal goods, not those who are haughty and puffed up into pride by their own righteousness; not one of these. But who then will praise your name? "The poor and needy will praise your name."[38]

According to the sound and realistic account of Augustine, the universal call to poverty is a call to poverty of spirit. Were it not, large segments of the human community would be barred from the happiness promised in the first beatitude. Were it not, the moral rule proposed by Jesus would be unlivable. For men and women with families cannot simply strip themselves of all material possessions — they are bound to earn and use these to raise their families. Thus whatever the economic condition or social status, all are called to poverty of heart, to lowliness of spirit, to self-abasement before the God who is infinitely rich. Augustine's perceptive comments on what we call the story of Dives and Lazarus supply Scriptural foundation for the distinction between poverty of spirit as essential and material poverty as accidental. It is noteworthy that the abode of glory to which Lazarus is lofted is described as the bosom of Abraham. This symbolic phrase substantiates the truth that Lazarus was raised to a realm of joy and peace not because he was destitute but because he was humble. Wealthy by the standards of his day, Abraham was nonetheless poor in spirit. Aware that he owed all to God, he was ready to forfeit all his wealth, even his most prized possession, Isaac, in obedience to the will of the Lord. If material poverty were a necessary condition and criterion for gaining paradise, Abraham's riches would have barred him from happiness in the life beyond. In fact, Lazarus is depicted as entering the bosom of Abraham, i.e., as sharing in the felicity of the just whose Old Testament father is

Abraham. What the Abraham of history and the Lazarus of parable hold in common is not a similar economic status but a kin poverty of spirit. Only men poor and needy in spirit or empty of self can be filled with God. The unfortunates who coldly scorn God or the more common run of men who drop him as a traveler disposes of useless baggage are empty in another, more terrible sense. In abandoning God, they become filled with self, i.e., enslaved to pride, spiritually barren and desolate, patches of desert that resist even the seeds of divine life.

But do not, brothers, take my statement that God does not incline his ear to the rich to mean that God does not hear those who have gold and silver and servants and estates. If they happen to be born to such a class or if they enjoy such status in human society, let them only recall what the Apostle says: "Charge the rich of this world not to be imbued with pride" (1 Tim 6.17). Those not imbued with pride are the poor before God, and he inclines his ear to the poor and needy and penniless. For they know that their hope does not lie in gold and silver nor in any goods that they seem to have in abundance for a time. It is enough that their riches do not wreck their lives. It is enough that they do not harm them, for riches can bring them no benefits at all. Clearly a work of mercy brings benefits to both rich and poor. The rich can desire and do it, while the poor can do no more than desire it. So when a man scorns in himself the springs of a bloated pride, he is a poor man of God. God inclines his ear to him for he knows how sorrowful is his heart. Undoubtedly, brothers, the poor man who lay covered with ulcers in front of the rich man's door was borne by angels to Abraham's bosom (Lk 16.20).... But is it true that the poor man was borne by the angels solely because he was poor? Is it true that the rich man was thrown into torments solely because he had riches? Not at all. Let us understand this well: it is humility that was honored in that poor man, it is pride that was condemned in that rich man. I am going to prove to you in a few words that not riches but pride in that rich man caused his punishment. Undoubtedly the poor man was carried into Abraham's bosom, but of this very Abraham Scripture says that he possessed a great deal of gold and silver and was rich on earth (Gen 13.2). If every rich man is dragged off to torment, how could Abraham have preceded the poor man in felicity so as to receive him into his bosom? But in the midst of his riches Abraham was poor, humble, respectful of, and obedient to all the commands of God. So completely did he consider his riches nothing that on the order of God he was going to sacrifice his son for whom he was saving all his wealth (Gen 22.10). Whether or not you possess anything in this world, learn then to be needy and poor. For you can find a beggar bursting with pride and a rich person confessing his sins. God resists the proud (Jas 4.6), whether dressed in silk or rags; he gives grace to the humble, whether or not they possess this world's goods. God looks at the interior: it is there that he weighs, there that he measures. You do not see the balance of God; on those scales he places your thoughts. Notice that the psalmist gives the reason why he deserves to be heard, that is, his title to being heard, in his avowal, "For I am poor and needy." Be careful, make sure you are poor and needy. If you are not, you will not be heard. If there is around you or in you anything that may foster presumption, get rid of it. Make God the whole of your presumption. Be in need of him so that he can fill you with himself. For, all that you possess without him will only serve to enlarge the emptiness within you.[39]

Confession of sins also implies the confession that is praise. The sinner crying out for forgiveness from the Lord is, in effect, lauding divine mercy. Underlying the hope in the publican's begging for mercy was faith in a good and merciful God. As his lips spoke his plea for healing, his heart was praising the mercy of God.

When anyone confesses his sins, he ought to confess them along with praise of God. Confession of sins is devout only if it is free of despair and implores the mercy of God. Thus it harbors praise of God whether in words that hail him as good and merciful, whether in unspoken acts of affection that evidence belief in his goodness and mercy. In this sense are we to understand the only words of the publican recorded, "Lord, be merciful to me, a sinner" (Lk 18.13). Although he did not say, "Because you are good and merciful" or words of that sort, he would not have uttered his prayer for mercy if he had not believed that God is good and merciful; because he prayed with a hope that could not exist without faith. Where there is no confession of sins, there can then be true and devout praise of God, a praise repeatedly named confession in Scripture. But there can be no devout and fruitful confession of sins where there is no praise of God, whether in the heart alone or whether as well in words falling from the lips.[40]

Misery is the name of man, mercy is the name of God. Interwoven in the confession of misery is the confession or praise of mercy. Because divine mercy always responds to human misery, the greater the sinner, the more powerful the mercy and therefore the stronger our tribute to God's generosity. The more crushing the onus lifted, the more ringing the praise of the divine healer. The more contrite the confession lamenting sins, the more the confession that is praise sings the glory of God.

What is the meaning of "Let us come before his face in confession" (v. 2)? It means this: since he is to come, let us do this first before he comes; by confession let us condemn what we have done so that he will find in us not sins to condemn but merits to crown. But does the confession of your sins not concern the praise of God? Yes, it does truly, in the fullest sense, concern the praise of God. Why does it concern the praise of God in the fullest sense? Because the more desperate the case, the more praiseworthy the physician. So confess your sins then as readily as you sank into despair at the sight of your sins. The greater the abundance of the sins of the penitent, the greater the praise of the pardoner of the sins. So let us not think that, by taking confession to mean confession of sins, we have departed from the sense of praise in this psalm. Confession of sins also concerns the praise of God because, in recognizing our sins, we extol the glory of God. "Let us come before his face in confession."[41]

Reflections

Thanksgiving. 1. How stingy we are with gratitude, how nonchalantly and rapidly we forget the blessings showered upon us. Frequently we neglect to repay by heartfelt thanks all that parents, relatives, friends have spent of themselves for us, and at times it is only as we mourn over the cold body of a dear one in the coffin that we are pierced to the heart for our ingratitude: so many times we took his or her kindness for granted, tendering at best a perfunctory thank-you. And how much more grievous is our thanklessness toward you, Lord, for all of our life, natural and supernatural, continually forth-streaming from the fount of your limitless life.

Teach me, Father; to thank you for the ordinary natural gifts, which I have blandly accepted save where I must face their diminution or loss. There flashes across my mind an image of a resourceful, self-reliant blind student picking his way around the Villanova University campus with a long metal stick. How fortunate I am to be able to see the spacious fields, the roses, the trees, the cloudless blue sky, the sunset, the beaming faces of friends through two tiny organs so exquisitely shaped out of their millions of parts. How fortunate that the rest of my senses — hearing, taste, smell, and touch — are able to capture the beauties of your creation and to rejoice in the voices and handshakes of my fellow men. I have never been esteemed physically attractive, but thank you for giving me a normal appearance — no warped features, no blotches, no limbs gnarled by disease. Thank you too for endowing me with at least normal intelligence so that my mind could gradually expand through schooling. Thank you also for letting me grow up in a land of unrivaled political freedom, a freedom that gleams the brighter against the backdrop of Communist tyranny that forces over 1.5 billion people to submit to its grinding heel. Thank you especially, all-bountiful Giver, for the most basic gift of all — life itself. How laced with enigma my life has been! And among the most obscure of its facets is the banal-looking fact that I have survived these many years. So many risks I took as a youth, any one of which could have been a final encounter with death, yet your hand kept me cupped in your care. At ten I was hit by a truck and suffered a fractured skull. Perhaps a slightly different angle of contact, a more direct impact of my head on the street, and I would have died on the spot. Yet for some reasons still unclear to me I was spared — thank you for the ongoing burning of a flame so close to being snuffed out.

2. I must learn to thank you, Father, when you visit me with reproof. Disciple implies discipline, and I can become wholly your follower only through testing and chastisement. Since I can be one with your heart only through walking the rock-strewn road of suffering, instruct me, Lord, by the light of the Spirit of Jesus to understand that you let afflictions befall me to curb ego, to make me savor humiliation that exalts the soul, to drill in once more the lesson of my littleness. Thank you for this stern but gentle schooling in love, for you bruise only to beautify, you hurt only to help, you wound only to heal, you cut only to cure, you break only to build up, you make me die to self only to live more fully for you.

3. I will come to see your sweet touch in punishment, the more I praise and thank you for the boundless riches of the supernatural that you have heaped on me from the day of my birth. How many born on the same day as I grew up in darkness, far from the fullness of the truth. Alas, perhaps a good number are still groping in the night. Never for one day have I been without access to your light and life: thank you for this gift of your inner life through Jesus and his Church. Stirring and gripping are the tales of those befuddled, wandering souls who under the impulse of your Spirit, crawled their way out of the wasteland into our holy faith. Thank you, Father, for those miraculous conversions, but I prefer the direct road to your light you prepared for me through my beloved parents. No initial slumbering in illusions of the Zeitgeist, no careening from one cheap nostrum to another, no empty complacency in a cold universe from which the warmth and light of the sun of justice have been evacuated, no agonizing search for the truth. Your grace will, I trust, magnetize individuals trapped in errors and delusions, drawing them to your heart. Without being condescending, I am simply thanking you for choosing me from the beginning, for implanting me in the only ground that comes anywhere close to resembling a paradise on earth, your holy Catholic Church.

Quicken me most of all, Lord, with a spirit of thanksgiving imitating in some way the style of gratitude remarkable in a spiritual woman with whom I was once privileged to be acquainted. Exceedingly generous herself, she would deprecate the value of what she selflessly gave in time and energy. Yet the smallest benefit, the slightest good bestowed, would excite her to wave after wave of thanksgiving — warm, repeated, zestful, childlike, entirely innocent of show or effusiveness. Her gratitude was a spiritual gift, a quasi-charism of wholly delighting in any favor and responding with quiet exuberance. This is of course the gratitude that welled up endlessly, Lord, in the souls of your saints, a spirit that springs from the Spirit that filled Jesus as he constantly gazed on your Face, Father, with ever-fresh expectation and ever-renewed gratitude. Come, pour more of the Spirit of Jesus into me, bringing me your love and power in the red and white roses in the garden, the image of your steadfastness in the worn countenance of a Christian great-grandmother bowed down by self-sacrificing labor over the years, the sign of your presence in any service done me. Teach me to say, "Thank you, Father," now, then again and again and again, then without ceasing, until my gratitude in time rises to an everlasting thanksgiving.

Petition. 1. Purify my heart, Lord, cleanse my sight anew. Make me never-failingly desire the highest and most precious goods of the Spirit of Jesus. Dim-sighted and selfish, I have often avidly hankered after and kept pounding on the door for lovely-looking goods for body and spirit that, however enriching for others, would have turned me away from you. In your Fatherly care you said, "No, I will not give you this stone; it will only leave your soul dessicated. I will not give you this serpent and scorpion, for their bite and sting will poison you." Light, more light, Father, so that, whatever I pray for in particular, I will be praying for more of the fish, the egg, and the bread, for more faith, hope, and love in regard to Jesus. Let my every petition have locked within it an entreaty for more of Jesus, let my every prayer make me decrease and him increase.

As self decreases, let me learn that my loftiest role is to be the lowliest, to be a beggar. So sluggish is the imagination of my faith that I find it hard to see that all I have flows ultimately from your hands. Your wisdom and power weave together combinations and interconnections of persons and things to accomplish your work of love. You did not directly manufacture the clothes I wear, you did not sow the potatoes and carrots I eat, you did not directly produce the pen and paper that communicate these slight thoughts. But over the many agencies and multiple channels of making and distribution presides your all-providing sovereignty. So it is as if you yourself immediately, without itermediary or instrument, clothed me, fed me, supplied me with materials and tools for writing. All that conspires to sustain and uplift me comes as a personal token of your love. Open wide my eyes to see that you are all giving all, show me how to beg from you my morsel from moment to moment. As I go in and go out, as I sit down at table and then leave, as I go to bed and get up, teach me how to have my palms outstretched as a mendicant, as one utterly destitute of ultimate self-support, with not a scrap of provisions I can call sheerly my own. Following thanksgiving after communion one morning, while admiring the sweep of a college chapel, I reflected that, even were I to live a million years, I would not be able to construct just by myself the chapel with its striking stained-glass windows, its massive walls, its intricately carved sections of marble. In that minute of meditation I realized anew my dreadful limitations. Now, carry me one stage farther to realize that without your sustaining touch I can do nothing of myself. Without your undergirding I cannot take a single step, I cannot speak a solitary syllable, I cannot write one word. Father, I am a beggar, totally dispossessed, bereft of anything I can claim as my own.

2. Father, make me love to be a beggar, however degrading it seems at first blush. A beggar has to brace himself to meet the shock of rude stares and chilling looks of curiosity, and, when aided, the offhand, patronizing attitude of almsgivers. How it rubs one's face in the dust to stand hour after hour, the target of the capricious unkindnesses of the passing crowd. Even in a less status-conscious era a beggar's lot seems repulsive, acceptable only as a last resort preferable to starvation. But it takes only a few minutes' meditation on you who are infinite love to see that the lot of a spiritual beggar need not repel. Because your generosity is not crabbed or stinted, because you are absolutely faithful to your covenant of love, you do not distribute your alms grudgingly and fitfully. Indeed you want to thrust into my hands and heart as much of the inner wealth of your life I can compass. Nothing in my life is unimportant to you. The food and sleep I need, my intellectual interests, the success of projects and pursuits, however trivial or exiguous to human eyes — all these you are profoundly concerned about. Every particle of my being, every smallest incident call forth your concern, for each of these involves some bit of goodness, which refracts your infinite goodness. Captivate me with yourself: you are love, and all you bestow manifests love. Make me love to beg for what is really more and more of your love, make my begging a continual act of love seeking you, my love.

3. Because of your call of love, Lord, those not materially poor can sincerely aim at achieving the happiness promised in the first beatitude. So sky-high have the quantity of goods and quality of life shot upward in the last few centuries that many in the West now live like kings in comparison to their ancient and medieval kin who scrimped and scraped just to survive in scarcity economies. Though many of us live middle-class, we can strive to be poor in spirit after the model of Abraham. Affluent according to the indicators of his culture, he was a poor man in the life of the spirit. Rich in the wordly sense, he was dispossessed of self, stripped of vanity, humble, ready to give all in return for all. Indeed against every instinct of nature, against the powerful pull of fatherly affection, in obedience to you, Father, he prepared to sacrifice his own son for whom he and Sarah had waited so long. The knife had to be driven into the miraculous child of their old age, Isaac had to be immolated simply because God required it. A stupendous sacrifice; yet unhesitatingly Abraham said yes: he loved you, Father, more than his own son. Nothing, not even his own son, was to come between him and you, his God, not even Isaac could cause him to break his covenant with you. Faithful to his commitment, totally submissive, seeking your way alone, Abraham was truly poor in spirit. Thus poverty of spirit is not incongruous with a bank account or social status. It is for all, for rich as well as poor, for middle-class dwellers

in suburbia as well as Latin American peasants. But like others ensconced in a middle-class lifestyle, if I am to imitate Abraham, I must be prepared to sacrifice my Isaac or a string of Isaacs, all that counts most to me within and without. I must hold nothing back. Build into me the spiritual sinews of an Abraham so that I can be devoid of all that smacks of self. More, configure me more to Jesus, the supreme exemplar of all the beatitudes. He was most blessed because he was the poorest in spirit, exempt from the least taint of self-seeking, wholly centered on you, Father, eaten up with a zeal for your glory alone, so permeated with the sacrificial spirit that as the new Isaac he let himself be killed as a sacrificial lamb.

Shortly before Christmas, 1979, a middle-aged nun suddenly suffered a nervous breakdown. Feeling inner anguish as she was plunged into the depths, she prayed at first that God would take her home to himself. Then slowly light filtered in, assuring her that Jesus was asking her, "Can you drink the cup that I drink?" Around six months later, after gradually pulling herself out of her illness, she came to see that she had in part undergone the battle of the desert temptations and had in part agonized in Gethsemane. In this more purifying stage of her inward journey she had been compelled to let go of her purse containing the riches of Mass and divine office, the staff of work and friends, and the sandals of her former outer self — the shell was simply removed. At the time of her writing she had been enclosed in, and was still experiencing, a kind of dark night of the spirit, a way not her own, a path saying no to all her normal desires, a vise gently squeezing natural inclinations to death. For the first time in her life she had found herself totally powerless, totally alone, totally receiving and submissive to God's will in place of inspecting and discerning it. By her suffering this chosen soul learned and is learning the obedience (Heb 5.8) concretely one with poverty of spirit. Thank you, Father, for this living instruction in poverty of spirit. May it bulwark my soul to walk with a similar childlike acceptance whatever stony uphill path through whatever stormy night your veiled wisdom may choose to lead me. For perhaps such a road of imposed self-forgetting and self-annihilation lies before me to help rid me of my conceit and pseudo-independence. How smug I am in the thought that I am managing my own life, how cocksure in the conviction that I am running the show. Teach me that in myself I am a zero. Cast out my false emptiness, my shallow and worldly ways, my self-centeredness, my greed for the half-thoughtless, fickle respect of men. You can, and want to, do what is impossible for man. Though I seem hopelessly frozen in mediocrity, your love can melt my hardness, your fire can set me more aglow. Wrap me round in your inscrutable wisdom and love that enlighten by darkening and fill up by emptying. Make me blessed with the poverty of spirit of Jesus and his imitators under the Old and New Law.

Confession. 1. Let me murmur with the publican, "Lord, be merciful to me, a sinner." Whether I plead for forgiveness in or outside the sacrament of penance, I believe, Father, that you heal me through the Spirit of Jesus.

The firmer my faith, the more fruitful is the inflow of your restoring grace. Whether or not I advert to it, every act of contrition that calls down your mercy is implicitly praise of you, O God of wonders, sublime in your power but sublimest of all in your mercy. The more explicitly I believe this, the more melodious the praise I lift into your presence. Take me by the hand and tell me again that I am a child of your mercy: in constantly leaning on your mercy, I can constantly praise you. "Depart from me, Lord, for I am a sinful man" (Lk 5.8), said Peter in a moment of illuminating sorrow. Now since Jesus in the bravest and humblest of acts sacrificed himself to purchase our spiritual freedom, I can say, "Come to me, Lord, for I am a sinful man." Without straining for effect, without melodramatic posturing, I confess that I am a sinner. From my earliest years I resisted your grace, chased after passing pleasures, caved in to lower appetites, luxuriated in selfishness. But you forgave and forgave and forgave, so that I can vault from swamps up to skyey mountaintops, and even with the story of my past wretchedness before me can sing the praises of your wondrous name. Whether seen in retrospect or prospect, your healing is always there to be welcomed and praised. At every moment I can seek pardon in the words of St. Bernard, "Jesus, be to me a Jesus," i.e., "Savior, be to me a savior," and so at every moment I can celebrate your name, Father, with the most exalted of names, "the name before which all in heaven, on earth, and under the earth bow the knee" (Phil 2.11): Jesus. How swift and smooth the course to the benediction of your mercy. I need only cry out or whisper, "Jesus," to be laved in your peace and proclaim your praise.

2. Except for the barest outlines my future looks fuzzy, but I know for certain that there will never be a day without spot or blemish. Yet out of this initially dismaying prospect blossoms fresh hope because, Father, your mercy overtops the highest of the mountains of our sins. Given the smallest crack in the armor of my pride, you are able to break down my defenses and easily pardon the seemingly unpardonable. No matter how wicked or rotten I become, so long as I am ready to fall prey to your ever-redeeming love, I can be shriven and in the very pleading for pardon chant your praise. The greatest of my miseries only releases your greater mercies. Toppled by sin yet prostrate in repentance, I am raised up to praise you through and for your mercy.

3. Never stop then feeding me, Father, with the food I seek through Jesus: the fish symbolizing faith that sees beyond all darkness and doubt that the meaning of my life is your mercy; the egg standing for hope anchored in your timeless, unfailing power; the bread representing the love that covers a multitude of sins (1 Pt 4.8), love that gathers up all the detritus and rubbish of my life and transforms them into inner strengths shining with some of the beauty of Jesus.

Praise

1. How great you are, O Lord, how great you are! The most complex movements of the farthermost galaxies fall under your sway, coming and going inexorably in obedience to your command. You are infinite, beyond all human measure, appointing all things within your frame of order, yet mysteriously, against all human expectations, you fasten your limitless attention and affection on fallen humanity and, yes, on each one of us. We praise your wisdom: you lower yourself to raise us up to you. Father, we praise you because your pedagogy is so effective: prompt and prod me to lower myself so that I can be raised up by you. How generous are your ways, O Lord! Ordinarily, to reach a high point on, say, the outside of a building, we have to resort to ladders and machinery. To reach you the reverse is the case. Needing no contrivances, I have only to lower myself to be lifted up by you who have come down to me. I praise you for this enchanting way of humility that brings me, lowly in my sins, into communion with you, the Most High.

I praise you, Father, because you are God, because you are goodness pouring itself out on me unwearyingly, ever patiently, in spite of my rebuffing you. I thank you for being a God for me, my dearest benefactor, a God who acts as both father and mother; a Father in that you call, command, and govern me; a mother in that you caress, feed, nurse, and take care of me.[42] As gratitude falls from my lips, let my heart ring with your praise. Because it is your holy will born of your love, I desire to feast my eyes for all eternity on the inexhaustible loveliness of your Face. But should the impossible occur, were I to be strictly annihilated, I would want my praise to linger on in your "memory," indissolubly wedded to the heavenly chorus of angels and saints. Let no thanksgiving escape my lips that is not in the company of praise. I thank you, I adore you, all-holy God, I greet, I salute you as savior and lover. And I praise you, I praise you for simply being God. Come, instill more of the Spirit of Jesus into me so that I can praise you with all Godliness possible, so that I can praise you with some of your self, so that my praise may arise from the abysses of your own love.

2. Had you so willed, you could have gifted us with all we need right at the beginning of our lives. But mysteriously, i.e., lovingly — for your mystery is your love, and all you are and all you do is love — you have ordained that we ask for what your hands dispense to fill and fulfill us. Praise to you, Father, for your plan: every desire I express to you conveys praise. Purify my desires so that my praise may ascend as a holy perfume before your Face. Every gift you originally bless us with, every good we seek from you, is a treasure. Let my seeking become only a seeking to praise you, let the gift of praise be the richest treasure you apportion to me amid all the other gifts of prayer and all the other affluence of the spirit you surround me with. Thus whatever my quest or request, I will at all times

consciously praise you as my Treasure of treasures. And as I praise you, I will enter more into Jesus, and he more into me. So I can truly say in his Spirit, "Yet I am not really alone because the Father is with me" (Jn 16.32). I am never alone, never without you, Father, never without Jesus, and his heart will be my companion in praise uniting me with you and your Spirit. Soon my asking in his name will be praising in his name, and not one, not the most petty-seeming, of my prayers can go unanswered. As I ask and praise, I will become more and more a being of praise, my life imaging more and more the Jesus through and with whom I praise, my actions burning the more with the fire of the Spirit in whom I praise. As I ask and praise, I will receive everything because you, the source of all, will sweetly conquer more and more of my spirit. All-providing Father, I praise you for opening all the doors of infinite life any time I lightly knock on the door. How exquisitely you clothe the lilies of the field, how more splendidly you garb me in the rays of your inner sunshine whenever I pray for the smallest of favors. Hasten the day when I will become a child of praise, a child holy like Jesus, wide-eyed, liberated from self-adulation, guileless and trustful, with arms uplifted to receive your bounty and embrace, with heart that is content only to praise you, that asks only to praise you, that praises so as to be more purified for asking. Praise to you for turning my lackluster prayers into golden hymns of praise. Praise to you, glorious God, for breathing the Spirit of Jesus into this dust to convert it into a temple of praise, a temple grand in its littleness because it wears the face of a child.

3. In Philadelphia a plastic surgeon with remarkable gifts of brain and hand has rebuilt numerous horribly disfigured faces, enabling the restored individuals to lead lives free of social taunt and aversion. One young child's bulging brains gave her the appearance of a monster, but, after Dr. Linton Whitaker, with the help of a colleague, pushed back the brain and adjusted cranial and facial bones, her reshaped countenance looked, as it was, strikingly normal.[43] What admiration we feel for so dedicated a doctor. Yet how faint seems my praise, sweet surgeon of my soul, when I try to proclaim your mercy. How hideous-looking my spiritual face has been. How often, after being restored to inner beauty, I have once more marred and scarred the face of my soul — yet unquestioningly, most patient of physicians, again and again you have recast my crooked features in the image of Jesus. Father, how lovely are your merciful heart and healing hands! I praise you for your mercy: no tribute soars higher yet it brings you closest and presses me to your bosom. Praise be to you for making your power perfectly manifest in my infirmity (2 Cor. 12.9). Let my power of praise be as great as my weakness: then my misery can truly celebrate your mercy, then my old unsightliness can hymn your beauty that you share with me, then my tormented spirit refashioned into praise can sing its admiration of your healing touch. Come, Father, send, so to speak, your "other selves," Jesus and your Spirit, into me so that I can praise you fully

and fittingly. Come, Jesus, enter my heart, let your mercy praise the mercy of your Father, let the munificence of your Sacred Heart praise the generosity of your Father. Come, Holy Spirit, rekindle my spirit with the fire of your love, let your love praise the healing love of the Father, let your holiness praise his holiness that aims at making me whole and holy. You are Gift: be my gift of praise to the Father.

Notes

[1] In *Praise: A Way of Life* (Ann Arbor: Word of Life, 1976). Fr. Paul Hinnebusch, O.P., gives an incisive, vibrantly devotional account of praise. See also C.S. Lewis's perceptive chapter, "A Word About Praising," in his *Reflections on the Psalms* (New York: Harcourt, Brace and World. Harvest Books, 1958), pp. 90-98.

[2] *Conf.* 6. 7. 12.

[3] EP 30(31). 20; CC 38, 614.

[4] Rudolf Otto, *The Idea of the Holy*, 2nd ed., tr. John W. Harvey (New York: Oxford University Press, 1950), pp. 12-40.

[5] *Conf.* 1. 1. 1.

[6] *De Trin.* 5. 12; PL 42, 911.

[7] Ps. 47 (48).1; 95 (96).4; 144 (145).3. *Conf.* 1. 1. 1.

[8] *Conf.* 1. 1. 1.

[9] *De ord.* 2. 16. 44 and 2. 18. 47; PL 32, 1015 and 1017.

[10] EP 85 (86).12; CC 39, 1186.

[11] EP 101 (102) (S. 2). 10; CC 40, 1445.

[12] EP 121 (122).5; CC 40, 1805.

[13] *Conf.* 1. 4. 4.

[14] S. 117. 5; Pl 38, 663.

[15] *Conf.* 11. 29. 39.

[16] EP 101 (102) (S. 2). 10; CC 40, 1445-46.

[17] EP 101 (102) (S. 2). 18; CC 40, 1449. See Étienne Gilson's masterly reading of the text and its earlier parts (see nn. 11 and 16 above) along with cognate texts in *Philosophie et incarnation selon saint Augustin* (Montreal: Institut d'Études Médiévales, 1947), especially pp. 34-55.

[18] EP 134 (135).5; CC 40, 1940-41.

[19] EP 102 (103).5-6; CC 40, 1454-57.

[20] *Serm. Guelf.* 32.5; MA 566-67.

[21] EP 18 (19) (S. 2). 15; CC 38, 112.

[22] EP 35 (36). 17; CC 38, 334-35.

[23] S. 69, 1. 2; PL 38, 441. EP 90 (91). 1; CC 39, 1254-55. *Serm. Wilmart* 11. 11; MA 702-03.

[24] S. 142.7. 7; PL 38, 782-83.

[25] S. 142. 6. 6; Pl 38, 781-82.

[26] S. 137. 4. 4; PL 38, 756.

[27] S. 161.4; PL 38, 875.

[28] S. 96. 3. 3; PL 38, 586.

[29] All the holy desire that is prayer is epitomized in seeking God and his love for us and a burning love for him, the imperishable fount of all goods in time and eternity. See EP 85 (86). 8; CC 39, 1183. For a deft synthesis of texts on prayer see Thomas A. Hand, O.S.A., *St. Augustine on Prayer* (Westminster, Md.: Newman, 1963).

[30] *De serm. Dom. in monte* 2. 4. 15; PL 34, 1275.

³¹EP 104 (105). 1; CC 40, 1535. Too we are to exteriorize praise not only in good deeds but in never-flagging prayer that is meant to be continual conversation with God. EP 85 (86). 7; CC 39, 1181-82.

³²EP 85 (86) 11; CC 39, 1185. The precise lines of the distinction and nexus between praise and prayer seem to require further textual exploration. Neither of two fairly recent pieces, the "Introduction" of A.-M. Besnard, O.P., to Saint Augustin: prier Dieu, les Psaumes; ed. A.-M. Besnard, O.P., and translations by Jacques Perret (Paris: Cerf, 1964), pp. 9-52, and the "La teologia della lode secondo S. Agostino" of Cipriano Vagaggini, O.S.B., in La preghiera nella bibbia e nella tradizione pastristica e monastica by Cipriano Vagaggini, Gregorio Penco, et al. (Rome: Edizione Paoline, 1964), pp. 399-467, seems to wrestle with the problem. May I mention also that both these commendable essays, while corroborating some of our conclusions, came into my hands only after I had finished nearly all of the main draft.

³³In addition, praise is distinguishable from and relatable to glory and jubilation. In the adapted classical sense glory is "established renown accompanied by praise" (Tract. in Joh. 105. 3; PL 35, 1095) or it is "clear knowledge attended by praise" (C. Max. 2. 13. 2; PL 42, 770). Jubilation, to be discussed in Chapter V, is praise that overpasses the limits of stock utterance. While glory is not an ingredient of praise, praise is an essential or at least a sine-qua-non component of glory. Jubilation of course falls within the category of praise.

³⁴EP 48 (49). 9; CC 38, 372-73.

³⁵EP 91 (92). 1; CC 39, 1279.

³⁶Ep. 130. 8. 15; PL 33, 500.

³⁷S. 83.2. 2; PL 38, 515.

³⁸EP 73 (74). 24; CC 39, 1020-21.

³⁰EP 85 (86). 3; CC 39, 1178-79.

⁴⁰EP 105 (106). 2; CC 40, 1554.

⁴¹EP 94 (95). 4; CC 39, 1333-34.

⁴²EP 26 (27) (S. 2). 18; CC 38, 164.

⁴³Marshall Ledger, "A Sense of Beauty," The Pennsylvania Gazette (April, 1980), pp. 23–29. May I mention here that in recounting incidents in the text above and below, many of which are drawn from personal knowledge, I have here and there altered minor details to safeguard the anonymity of individuals whose lives are touched on.

Chapter II

The Supremacy of Praise

It may come as a surprise to some that Augustine rates praise as the supreme work of man.[1] He goes much further than singling out praise as a superb work of the spirit. Praise is lifted up to the pinnacle, it is rated the summit of religious activity, second to none. The sovereignty accorded praise is puzzling as well, for other passages seem to appoint an equivalent first office to charity, thanksgiving, and inner healing. The work of God to which Jesus summons us is faith, not simply doctrinal faith, but faith working through love toward full spiritual stature.[2] This encompasses the whole of the law and prophets, involves all physical philosophy, all ethics, the whole foundation of logic, and is central in the shaping of the other virtues, each of which is an order of love.[3] Jesus, the impeccable exemplar of this supreme law, in commanding us to love one another as he loves us, i.e., to love God in one another, puts his finger on charity as the unique emblem and bridal song of his disciples.[4] Moreover, Augustine here and there deputes preeminence to thanksgiving. "The whole worship of God mainly lies in the fact that the soul is not ungrateful to God."[5] Still another text seems to give first rank to healing: "Brothers, all our works in this life consist in healing the eye of the heart through which we see God."[6] All hearkening to the word of Scripture, all partaking of the sacraments, all taming of the flesh, all acts of virtue, all works of mercy are geared to this one end, the achievement of total metanoia, a purification enabling the inner eye to receive the light that is eternal wisdom.

Praise Relatively Supreme

It would seem foolhardy to trace these seemingly paradoxical strains to rhetorical flourishes that Augustine indulged in to suit homiletic needs. Not varied pastoral occasions but diverse but related uses of the same term iron out apparently irreconcilable claims. Absolutely speaking, it seems incontestable that the law of love imposes the supreme obligation because it calls for unconditional self-surrender. "He who made all of you requires all of you."[7] In giving all of his heart, a person becomes a new man aflame with love that he expresses in the new song to the Lord. In short, praise

is the supreme work of man insofar as it flows from and enunciates the
supreme law of love. Thus praise as the outpouring of love in song is relatively supreme. Indeed only praise stemming from love is true praise, for
we sing the new song when we live a life of love. In action that squares
with the will of God who is all love, love and praise concretely blend. The
new man, a being of love, is a living praise. The new man is the new song
that is a hymn of praise. As new, the new man singing his love is praise
itself. Hence as one fruit of charity, as concretely fused with love, praise
may be called the supreme work of redeemed man.[8] Absolutely, charity
remains the supreme attainment of the graced heart. Relatively, as the
utterance of charity, as the concrete equivalent of divine-human love, praise
may be legitimately said to be the highest work of the human spirit. A
secondary relativity, this with its foundation in praise, makes thanksgiving
describable as the principal act of worship. As already remarked, in praise
we sing homage to God because he is all goodness, but in thanksgiving
we pay recompense of heart for his goodness to us.[9] Thanksgiving, as based
on praise, may then be considered to be the greatest act of worship. Finally,
preeminence accorded healing also seems relative. Healing of the eye of
the heart may be given the highest priority because it is associated with
the charity joining hearts to the heart of God. Healing is the necessary precondition of intimacy and union with God: we must drastically prune self-
seeking to love him with our whole heart. From another angle, if we
telescope such healing into confession of sins, confession harbors praise
of God. As we saw earlier, the publican within all of us begging for healing
implicitly praises God as merciful. We can praise God without confessing
sins but we cannot confess sins without praising God.[10] The more advanced
the cancer of sin, the more vibrant the praise of the divine healer.[11] Thus
charity stands as the primary law of man, but, since love in action is living
praise, praise becomes man's supreme work. Since all gratitude rests upon
praise, thanksgiving also may be called by extension the finest of human
works. Insofar as healing is a precondition to loving union, insofar as confession of sins includes praise of divine mercy, we may, in addition, analogously maintain that all our works consist in the healing of the inner man.
    Praise is the highest accomplishment of the human spirit because it
is addressed to the heart of the Lord of heaven and earth, all-beautiful in
himself, all-alluring to the eye of the human heart. What God, simply by
being God, gives us is the spiritual pleasure of resting our gaze upon his
beauty. What we are to give in return for this joy is praise of his beauty.
This praise, because it is the exaltation of supreme beauty, is the supreme
work of man. We are free not to praise God but we are not free not to praise
some object we practically reverence as highest. If our works do not praise
God, they will probably be aimed at praising ourselves. The alternative
to love and praise of God is love and praise of self. The individual deluded
into self-love and self-praise does not truly exalt himself but degrades his
spirit as he dissipates the gifts of God in pursuit of illicit pleasures. The

cult of "the imperial self"[12] enchains the spirit in callous and gross vices. But the mercy of God that is meant to elicit praise tracks down the prodigal son and draws him back into his arms. The divine beauty that evokes true praise seeks out the sinner to heal the uncomeliness that issues from false praise. The touch of divine pity raises the dead soul to life, and, purified of his old blemishes, the returned son is wrapped in the arms of the Father and begins again to sing the beauty of his Face.

Some have understood the words of the psalmist, "My heart over-flowed with a goodly theme" (v. 1), as the verse of a hymn. (From the heart of anyone singing a hymn to God overflows a goodly theme, while from the heart of someone blaspheming God over-flows an evil theme.) He intended the adjoining sub-verse, "I speak my works to the king," to mean: the supreme work of man is nothing other than praising God. It is proper to him to please you by his beauty; it is proper to you to praise him in thanks-giving. If your works are not praise of God, you will begin to fall in love with yourself, joining the company of those of whom the Apostle says, "There will be men in love with themselves" (2 Tim 3.2). Be displeased with yourself, and let him who made you be pleasing to you, inasmuch as you are displeased with what you yourself have made in yourself. Let your work then be the praise of God, let your heart overflow with a goodly theme. Speak then your works to the king because the king has made you so that you might speak these works, and he gave you what you offer to him. Give him back what is his: do not take your share of the father's wealth and run off to a faraway country and squander every cent in the company of prostitutes and end up feeding pigs. Remember that line from the Gospel, but also keep in mind that we are told: "He was dead and has come back to life; he was lost and has been found" (Lk 15.32).[13]

The greatest of works draws down upon us the greatest gifts of God. In offering God praise, in performing this greatest of actions, we grow more and more in Godly estate. As with prayer proper, so with praise: hymning his attributes does not alter him but us. The unchangeable God who is "I am who am" does not break forth in a spiritual smile when we praise him nor does he slump into distress and gloom when we curse him. Man, not God, becomes better or worse through praise or dispraise of his name. In praising the Lord, we commune with him and participate in some measure in his perfections. When we come into his presence singing his praises, we sun ourselves and wax more holy in the light of his goodness and holiness. When we praise his mercy, we receive more mercy and become more merciful, and when we praise his wisdom, we advance in wisdom. In short, praise of a particular attribute of God wins for the praiser a share in that attribute. The fruit of praise is not more for God from us but more of God for us. We are his servants, dependent in every way on his bounty and mercy. For all is gift. Every bit of goodness, every smallest blessing, streams from his love. So we are bound by cords of justice and love to praise him. But there is more — we are his sons, enjoying all the intimacies of members of the family of God: so this more of love demands more praise burning with more intense affection.

> The exhortation this psalm makes should be very sweet to us, and we should rejoice in its sweetness. For it says: "Praise the name of the Lord" (v. 1). And it immediately adds the reason why it is just to praise the Lord: "Praise the Lord, you who are his servants" (v. 1). What work is more just? What more fitting? What more delightful?...The psalm exhorts us, the prophet exhorts us, the Spirit of God exhorts us, finally, the Lord himself exhorts us to praise the Lord. Not he but we grow stronger through our praise. Your praise does not make God better nor does your dispraise make him worse. But in praising him who is good, you will become better, and, in dispraising him, you will become worse; he, however, stays just as he is — good....But because it benefits us to praise the Lord, he orders us not out of arrogance but out of mercy to praise him. Let us then listen to what he says: "Praise the name of the Lord." As his servants you do nothing unseemly in praising the Lord. And if you were to remain forever no more than his servants, you would be bound to praise the Lord. How much more should you, his servants, praise the Lord so as to deserve to live as his sons as well?[14]

Praise's Song of Love a Foretaste of Eternity

Our praise as servants and as sons of God readies us for a life of unending praise. This life is a school in which we are to channel our energies into becoming able and expert in the one major area of concentration which is praise. Our short earthly career is to be principally devoted to mastering praise in preparation for an eternity of unbroken, undistracted praise. The skill in praise we achieve here below will determine the level of praise to which God's mercy lifts us hereafter. The slothful individual who rejects or neglects praise will be, in turn, praiseless in eternity. As the praiser on earth continues his vocation of praise in heaven, so the man mute with respect to praise in this life will continue dumb in the life to come, his lips sealed, his soul shut off from God forever. Though praise on earth and heaven are essentially continuous, the wholly divine atmosphere in heaven makes them discontinuous in mode. Praise in eternity is far superior in quality. Praise in time is successive, multiple, pluralized; temporal praise is actually praises. Praise in eternity is one, stable, simple act focused on the one God who is the Selfsame. In Augustine's language, in passing from earth to heaven, we go from praises to praise.

Our meditation in this present life should be focused on praise of God because praising God will be everlasting rejoicing in our life to come. And no one not now practiced in praise can be prepared for the life to come.[15]

So begin to praise God now if you are going to praise him for all eternity. The person who refuses to praise him in this passing world will remain mute when there comes the world without end.... So praise and bless the Lord your God day after day so that when this succession of days comes to an end and there comes the one day without end, you will go from praises to praise as from strengths to strength (Ps 83 [84].8).[16]

In heaven praise will be always intertwined with love.

What will we be doing in heaven? Praising God, praising him in our love, loving him in our praise.[17]

In our earthly journey praise and love are similarly interconnected. Praise bespeaks love, and love excites praise. The rejoicing praiser is a lover, and the lover praises his beloved. When we celebrate the beauty of God, love flames higher in our hearts. As our love burns brighter, we intermingle sweet murmurs of praise with whispers of affection.

A person singing praise not only praises but praises with gladness. A person singing praise not only praises but also loves whomever he is singing about. The song of the praiser celebrates the person he praises, the song of the praiser pours out the affection of a lover on the person he praises.[18]

Living through and in Christ, the Christian is the new man and sings the new song of redemption, the anthem of the new kingdom and its new covenant. The song is or bespeaks the new commandment of love in union with and in imitation of Jesus. We sing the new song when we live with the love of Jesus, when we love with the love that unites Father, Son, and Holy Spirit. Our new song takes its melodic line from and is chanted in unison with the eternal song of love and praise in the choirs of heaven whose Beloved is ever ancient, ever new.

The building of the temple after captivity was noted in the words of another psalm: "Sing a new song to the Lord: sing to the Lord, all the earth" (Ps 95[96].1). What the psalmist spoke of as a new song the Lord spoke of as a new commandment. For what does a new song contain but new love? Singing is the outpouring of a lover. The voice of this singer is the ardor of holy love.[19]

We are urged to sing to the Lord the new song. The new man knows the new song. A song is a thing of delight and, looked at more closely, it is a thing of love. So anyone who knows how to live the new life knows how to sing the new song. It is the new song that reminds us of what the new life is. For to the one kingdom belong all three, the new man, the new song, the new covenant. So the new man will both sing the new song and belong to the new covenant.[20]

The new song is sung by the whole people of God, children of praise who dwell in every nation under the sun. The partial darkness of separated Christians, like the Donatists of Augustine's day, keeps them from singing the new song. Singing the new song liberates fully spiritual Christians of worries and disquiet and, inwardly secure, they march forward confidently to the celestial promised land. Wayfaring Christians are like travelers journeying on foot at night who sing to forget their fears and bolster their spirits. Perhaps the growls of wild beasts or the tramping of feet in nearby fields send tremors racing through them. More frightening at other intervals is the silence that stirs foreboding about the rapacious beasts or men it might conceal. At any moment robbers may leap from behind a clump of bushes to waylay them. Christians sing in union with Jesus, they are wholly secure, wholly care-free, internally invulnerable to attacks of predators. Robbers can victimize not those who walk the way of Jesus but only those unfortunates who drift from the path of Christian truth and love. Their song guarantees the people of God security of spirit because it is a twofold confession — a confession of sins pleading for the mercy of God and a confession that is praise of the God who is all mercy. The divine mercy that the new song sings acts for the new people of God as a cloud by day and a pillar of fire by night.

"May all peoples praise you" (v. 4). Walk on the way with all nations, walk on the way with all peoples, O children of peace, sons of the one and only Catholic faith, walk on the way, singing as you walk. This is what wayfarers do to relieve their fatigue. Sing on this way, I beg you, by the Way himself. Sing a new song, don't sing old sons. Sing songs expressing love of your heavenly homeland. . . . The way is new, the wayfarer is new, the song is new. Listen to the Apostle exhorting you to sing the new song: "If then any man is in Christ, he is a new creation, the old things have disappeared; now everything has become new" (2 Cor 5.17). Sing the new song on the way that you have known "on the earth." "On the earth" in what sense? In this sense: "among all nations." This is why the new song does not belong to a part of the earth. A person who sings in only part of the earth sings an old song. No matter what he sings, he sings an old song, and the old man does the singing, a man severed from the whole people of God, a carnal man. Certainly insofar as he is carnal, he is an old man; insofar as spiritual, he is a new man. . . . As a spiritual person, then sing the new song on the way, sure you are secure. This is how wayfarers sing, and quite often they sing at night. They hear dreadful sounds round about them; or rather, not sounds but silences, and the deeper the silence, the more dreadful. These wayfarers, however, go on singing, even those afraid of robbers. How much more secure you are when you sing in Christ! Along this way no robbers lurk, and only by abandoning this way do you fall into the hands of robbers. So I say again, sing the new song on the way, sure you are secure. "May the peoples praise you, O God." They have found your way: may they praise you. The singing itself is a confession, a confession of your sins, a confession of the power of God. Confess your sins, confess the grace of God. Blame yourself and glorify him, reproach yourself and praise him."[21]

Divine Likeness Through Inner Cleansing

The heart must be cleansed, the inner eye of the spiritual self healed if we are to live the love that animates the praise which is the highest work of man. As mentioned earlier, it is exceedingly difficult to grasp the exceeding great. Indeed what we know about nature seems far outbalanced by what we do not know. Further, though each of us is intimately acquainted with himself, it is hard to crisply define the self, or, in Augustine's vivid phrasing, to "comprehend the me within me." If we cannot lay hold of what is about and within us, how can we understand what is above us? The impulse and the light to know what is above come from above through the revealing word of Jesus. But in order to see God we must drive out the darkness of sin, denude the self of all that rebels against the Father. Our wickedness extinguished, we can escape from the region of unlikeness, the sphere of sin-drenched humanity, to enter the region of likeness, the sphere of the interior man no longer defaced by sin, the region in which man is like God because recreated in his image. Thus remade, we love with the very love of the Father who distributes sunshine and rain evenhandedly to both good and evil men. When we love in the image and by the power of the Father, we experience God, we taste him, we see him, we overleap the abyss that divides the finite from the infinite. God is not spatially but affectively near to or far away from the human heart. It is by likeness or unlikeness, by love or its lack, that we draw near to or distance ourselves from God. A person imprisoned in the region of unlikeness resembles a blind man who is physically present to the green of trees, the blue of the skies, light shimmering on the water, yet sensorily not present to them: his blindness unhappily blocks all visual access to light and color. Similarly a wicked man is present to yet absent from God. He is physically present in the sense that God is everywhere at work in the things his divine power causes, but he is affectively absent, spiritually separated, from God. His sin that makes him unlike God puts God out of reach. A miserable condition, a sadly paradoxical moral situation, Augustine remarks: a sinner, because immured in darkness by his blindness, is far away from the divine light with its love that is ever near because it is everywhere.

> Just as these bodies about us are seen by the eyes, so God is perceived only by the mind, recognized and seen by the heart. And where is the heart that is the source of seeing him? The Lord says, "Blessed are the clean of heart for they shall see God" (Mt 5.8). I listen, I believe, I understand so far as I can that God is seen through the heart and that he cannot be perceived save by a clean heart. But I listen to another verse from Scripture: "Who will boast that he has a chaste heart or who will boast that he is cleansed of sin?" (Prv 20.9). So far as I am capable, I have then taken a look at the whole of creation, I have observed the corporeal make-up of things in heaven and on earth, I have observed in myself the spiritual constituent in virtue of which my members utter sounds, move my tongue, pronounce words, and use various powers. And when do I comprehend the me within me? How then can I comprehend what is above me? Nevertheless, the vision of God is promised to the heart of man, and man is required to strive for a cleansing of the heart: this is what Scripture tells us. Obtain the means to see what you love before you come to see it. . . . To draw near to God and to receive his light you have to be dissatisfied with your darkness. Condemn what you are so as to deserve to be what you are not. You are wicked, you ought to be just. You will never lay hold of justice as long as you are complacent in your wickedness. Grind it to powder in your heart; cleanse your heart. Drive it out of your heart, there where he whom you desire to see desires to dwell. Thus the human soul, so far as it is able, draws near to God: this is the interior man, recreated in the image of God because he was created in the image of God. Man had become distant from God insofar as he had gone off into a region of unlikeness. It is not in terms of spatial distance that you draw near to or withdraw from God. When you become unlike him, you withdraw from him. When you become like him, you draw very near to him. See how the Lord desires us to draw near to him. First he makes us like him so that then we may draw near to him. He tells us, "Be like your heavenly Father who makes the sun rise on the good and the evil and sends rain on the just and unjust" (Mt 5.45). Learn to love your enemy if you want to stay clear of your enemy. Now insofar as charity grows in you, shaping you and restoring you after the likeness of God, it extends to your enemies as well. So you come to be like him who makes the sun rise not on the good alone but on both good and evil, and sends

rain not on the just alone but on both just and unjust. As you draw near to his likeness, so do you progress in charity, and so do you begin to experience God. And whom do you experience? The God who comes to you or the God to whom you return? For he has never left you. God withdraws from you only when you withdraw from God. All things are present to the blind as well as to those with sight. Suppose a blind man and a person able to see are standing in the same place; both are surrounded by the identical features of the things there. Yet one is present to things, the other absent from them. Two men are standing in the one place but one is present, the other absent, not because the things themselves draw near to one and withdraw from the other but because their eyesight is different. A person is called blind because in him there is snuffed out the light of eyesight that is in sympathy with the light garbing all things. So he is present but in vain to things he does not see. More precisely, he is indeed said to be absent rather than present. For a person is rightly said to be absent from a place of which he has no sensory perception; for to be sensorily apart from a place is to be absent. It is in this wise too that God is present everywhere and wholly everywhere. "His wisdom reaches from end to end mightily and orders all things sweetly" (Wis 8.1). What is true of God the Father is true also of his Word and his Wisdom, Light from Light, God from God. What then do you desire to see? What you want to see is not far from you. Indeed the Apostle says that God is not located far from each one of us. "For in him we live and move and have our being" (Acts 17.27). What an immense misery it is then to be far away from him who is everywhere![22]

The likeness of God is imprinted on those communities that live in his peace because joined by his love. The forgiving love at the core of every Christian community comes not from man but from God. In the world apart from and against God, forgiveness is usually regarded as capitulation in the face of greater prowess or at best as part of a tactic of waiting for a more opportune retaliation. Worldly men, unable to abide enemies, count the days for a chance to strike back at those who have wounded them. Sadly the lips of some Christians piously blessing the Lord routinely curse their enemies, even, it may happen, while engaged in prayer itself. Only by an anointing poured down by the Holy Spirit can we drive out the darkness of cursing from our hearts. Lifted up in faith, already breathing in some respect the atmosphere of heaven, overshadowed by the love the Spirit brings from the Father, our hearts bathe our enemies in divine compassion and forgiveness. In the world men feel penned in by enemies, with no recourse other than cursing and counterattacking their besiegers. If we hearken to the loving imperative, "Lift up your hearts," we break loose from the iron ring of attackers by dwelling by faith and love in a heavenly haven of peace where we live immune to all assault.

"Because there the Lord has ordered a blessing" (v. 3). Where did he order it? He ordered it in the midst of brothers who dwell united. There he has prescribed a blessing, there those who dwell in concord bless the Lord. For in discord you do not bless the Lord. It is idle to say that your voice resounds with the blessings of the Lord if they do not resound in your heart. You bless with your mouth and curse in your heart. "They bless with their mouths and curse in their hearts" (Ps 61 [62]. 5). Are these words our very own? They point the finger at certain individuals. When you are praying, you bless the Lord; and while going on with your prayer, you also curse your enemy. Is that what you heard from the lips of the Lord himself: "Love your enemies" (Mt 5.41)? If, however, you act on his word and love your enemy, you will also pray for him: "there the Lord has ordered his blessing," there you will possess "life for all ages," that is, life for all eternity. For many men enamored of this life curse their enemies; and for what object but this world, for what but the advantage of this world? Where does your enemy have you so beleaguered that you feel compelled to curse him? Are you beleaguered on earth? Then fly from the earth and dwell in heaven. "How," you will say, "can I dwell in heaven since I am a man clothed in flesh, engrossed in the flesh?" Go first in heart to the place where your body will arrive later. Do not listen with deaf ears to the words, "Lift up your hearts." Keep your heart lifted up and in heaven no one will beleaguer you.[23]

Reflections

1. Once more, dear Lord, I feel unresponsive to the sublime truths of your kingdom. I am called to exercise as my supreme work the praise of your name, called to praise you, as Jesus does, singing his song in your heart, celebrating you in all the workings of your power and the nearly unbelievable sensitivity of boundless love. A magnificent vocation this; praise is a priceless gift, so entrancing, so magnetically attractive. But much of my praise seems near-lifeless and dry as dust, a vapid and near-spiritless utterance of my laggard spirit. All too often few of the splendid qualities associated with praise sprout in my soul. This greatest of works does not set my spirit tingling but leaves me cold and unmoved.

My cry is that of the apostles to Jesus: "Lord, increase [my] faith" (Lk 17.5). Teach me to put aside merely natural gauges of growth in praise. Your saints, we may surmise, were not always intoxicated with delight in reading your holy word and chanting the psalms of your Spirit, and at times may have found recitation of the so-called opus Dei or the work of God (that some have wittily and all too realistically labeled onus diei, the burden of the day) a taxing obligation, an unappealing requirement to be got through as quickly and painlessly as possible without offense to reverence. Yet they persevered in faith, stoutly believing that they were truly praising you in heart in spite of the absence of sensible consolation. Drill into me over again this pivotal truth of my life as your son: I live by faith, not by sight, by your word, not by sensory indicators. Though the heavens seem closed, dropping down no refreshing dew, though a suffocating indifference stifles devotional warmth, impel me, Father, to go on speaking and singing your praises. Teach me to measure union with you in praise not by human appearance but by pure faith, faith bereft of all secondary supports and marginal sensory features, faith that bears me up to bask in peace and joy not of this world, fruits discernible only by signs not of this world.

In spite of cruelty in war and licentiousness perhaps at times not much less marked than those in other periods in Christendom, the people of the Middle Ages lived by a transcendent faith evidenced in their worship of you, Lord. Knowing nothing of modern affluence, often just barely scratching out a subsistence from day to day, these little ones did not grumble about the expense of constructing huge cathedrals that even to this day thrill and elevate hearts. The age of faith created many of the finest works of worship, massive edifices of praise. Father, encourage me to aspire to be, in some modest sense, a living cathedral, or, pehaps better, a living chapel on a minor scale. Let it be my glory to give you glory, let my arms be uplifted in this highest of works, like two towering spires glistening in the sun, reaching up to touch the sky. Teach me how to put aside the gewgaws of this passing world, show me how to give myself first and foremost to this topmost of works, my whole being a sacred edifice of silence ever ready to soar upward in celebration of your name.

What cleverness you use, Father, in winning us to a life of praise! When we forget you, we heap praise on ourselves and throw up gaudy towers to enshrine our power and glory. But shortly, in a year, a decade, a century these proud structures are smashed or wither away, and men quickly turn away from the rubble to stare with mouths agape at some new wonder thrusting itself upward yet doomed like its forebears to come tumbling down. But when we prostrate ourselves before you, then, rising, raise our voices and hearts in praise, you gain nothing but we gain all. As we dispraise self and praise you, you fill us with your light and power, and begin to build each praiser as a humble tower meant to climb to the very summit of existence. Make me a living tower of praise, lowly and abased, so that I can be raised up in your might to praise you with all the energy of a son of God. I am again struck by St. Paul's words wrung from his own experience: "When I am weak, then I am strong" (2 Cor 12.10). Let all exterior taste for praise turn to ashes in my mouth, let acts of praise be drained of vigor, let sessions of praise, however canonized by your Church, become entirely dull, boring, irritating, let me be despoiled of all zeal for praise: then will my praise thunder upward, divested of self so as to make way for more of the voice of Jesus praising in me, then will my chapel of praise rise stone upon indestructible stone, resplendent with all the strength of your love.

2. Lord, the temple of the spirit fashioned in us by your Spirit is intended to sprout and last for all eternity, a treasure that neither rust nor moth can consume. This treasure beyond the stars will endure because it will be a cathedral of love, invincible love, love mightier than death. In the life to come, Father, we will praise you in love and love you in praise. So here below our praise is shot through with love. Thank you for making love the quiet essence of our praise. Now I can pray with more hope and I need not be depressed when my praise seems flaccid, when outwardly I hit false notes, when I cannot match the gusto of your enthusiastic disciples. Now I see the kernel of praise: it is love, love, love! I need only love, love intensely, love with a supernatural passion, to praise you in some authentic way. In all my praising I am singing the new song that celebrates the new commandment. So in living by the new commandment, in striving to be on fire with love, in obeying, however ploddingly, your command-ments epitomized in the one commandment of love, I am praising you, however off-key my singing, however wooden-sounding my phrases, however platitudinous my expressions, however saccharine-seeming my affection.

I am supported by the chant of love that my brothers and sisters all over the world unceasingly sing. As people of the new covenant of love we sing the love inbreathed by the Spirit who is love. Old or young, educated or uneducated, well or sick, outgoing or reticent, each of us sings differently, each walks a different path in different circumstances with a unique destiny. But through all the variation and diversity runs the one common theme of love. However individually scattered the paths, all are walking the way of Jesus that is love. How cheering to know that, wherever I go, wherever anyone travels, north, south, east, or west, the song of love is being sung in the melodious language of the Spirit open to all without boundaries or restrictions, available to slave and free, Jew and Greek, male and female. Because it is the love of Jesus, it is new, and, because it is new, it is as universal, in a way, as you, our Lord and God, are. This is the song that the tongues of angels peal, the song of heaven, the song divine, the song of Jesus himself.

As wayfarers we sing as we walk, especially at night when we are most exposed to beasts — in our day human beasts ready to claw and tear with the cunning of crafty brains. So the song of love drives away our fears, covering us with its protective mantle. More often, Lord, I find darkness lying in the ordinariness of my life. It seems so banal, distinctive only in its lack of distinctiveness. It is here, Lord, that, like so many other believers, I must learn to discover love and, in loving, praise your name. I have yet to completely unriddle the simple-looking question: who am I? Thank you,

Lord, for illumining my spirit with the general and many particularized answers to this question revealed in the doctrines of your Church and afforded by the Spirit of Jesus in prayer. But withal, in spite of the light of revelation and many intimate lights I still grope forward, unsure of myself, unable to tie together all the loose ends of my existence.

And your Church, O Lord — how roiled and riven with dissension it is, how wounded by disobedience and individualism disguised as personal leading of the Spirit. So much in your Church seems opaque, impenetrable even to faith seeking understanding. It is torn by so much division, so much bitterness, so much unbridled egoism in members formerly unified in and loyal to holy doctrine and disciplined practice. Yet however exteriorly sleazy her garb, the Bride of Christ, I believe, remains interiorly clothed in raiment of gold.

Teach me, Father, to sing more enthusiastically the song of love. It is love that shines in the dusk; it is through a heart of love that I will be able to comprehend in some manner the concrete meaning of my existence and the meaning of the dissension that at present agonizes your Church. Soak me in the mystery of your love and I will come to know, vaguely but serenely, obscurely yet peacefully, the mystery of my own life and the mystery of your suffering Church, Give me the voice of the Spirit of Jesus to sing his song of love: then I will truly know the inner beauty, the very meaning, of my life and your Church.

3. Once more I sorrowfully perceive that it is I who am blocking awareness of myself. Only by confessing more thoroughly can I confess more vibrantly, for my sins muffle the sounds of praise. Cleansing the inner eye, I can love and praise as an interior man. How tenacious the grip with which original sin seizes the soul of every man. *Facile descensus Averni,* how easy it is to fall into the pit. Because the bent to evil is so marked in every man, sin soon contaminates the social environment. After Mount St. Helens erupted in Washington state in May, 1980, thick volcanic ash almost as heavy as cement covered homes, sidewalks, streets, and cars in nearby towns and cities. To their dismay residents found that as soon as they hosed the ash off sidewalks, cars driving by stirred up fresh dust that blanketed the pavements anew. The ash of sin coats the souls of nearly all, and, almost as soon as the ash is scrubbed away, another layer settles on many souls. A partially lame comparison perhaps, for sin lives and reigns universally, in deserts, along the seashore, on the plains, in mountainous regions, holding sway wherever human beings set foot.

It is this evil within that beclouds and distorts knowledge of self. How much knowledge contemporary man has amassed about the body and mind yet is hardly closer than the ancients to achieving in full measure the meaning of the Socratic dictum, "Know yourself." Contemporary man continues to make scientific advances in genetics and physiology and to garner data disclosing much about the senses, emotions, drives, and the measurable side of intellectual performance. But none of the biological analyses or psychological facts can fully come to grips with the existential, moral question: who am I? For self-knowledge in the line of the heart comes from the light of God. So the thrust of Augustine's question remains as forceful today as it was nearly sixteen hundred years ago: how can I grasp "the me within me"? How can I existentially know myself, i.e., live fully and consistently by the ideals I cherish? How can I release all the potential good within me? Simply how can I become a good man? First I have to recognize that I am tainted with the evil that pervades the universe of man. Come, Father, let me know myself: I am a sinner. Let me see myself as a prodigal son, drifting in a region of unlikeness, where darkness rules as lord and master. Come, take me into your light and let me discover myself in you. Restore the interior man, remold the evil-stained self in the image of your self, shaping another son of God. Cut the cords that bind me to my exterior self, worldly illusions, seductions of the flesh, subtle lies of the Evil One. Becoming like you, I can make your ways my ways, I can love with your love, I can reach out with compassion as wide as the world, I can forgive according to the French saying, "To understand all is to pardon all." I can look on fellow men and women with your eyes and be moved with pity rather than anger toward or contempt for their apparent mediocrity and meanness. I can come to see with an understanding heart that many faults arise in part from a person's genes and individual history. Then with your mercy within I will be able to forgive enemies, individuals who for whatever motive are embittered toward me or vexed by my defects.

Through your spirit of mercy poured into my spirit I will be protected from my enemies, an elusive phrase in Augustine that probably means that, in taking care of my enemies, I will take care of them, i.e., in loving them, I will lose them as enemies. Armored in love and wielding the sword of love, I can only love and only know love — spears and arrows of enemies break and fall harmlessly to the ground against a soul shielded by love. Further, in loving my enemies, I will put on more of the mind of Jesus and so, Father, I will more intimately experience you, taste your sweetness, hear your honeyed voice whispering my name, breathe in the fragrance of your tenderness, relax in your embrace, and see you within my heart and, gradually, within the hearts of others. I am your child, I yearn to be wholly like you: give me your heart of forgiveness. I am still partially blind: you are present everywhere yet often I overlook your presence. It is your love that makes the lover perceive your love, it is your love I need to enable me to "annihilate" my enemies with love, to "exterminate" them with mercy, to conquer them with compassion, to subdue them with solace, to vanquish misunderstanding and hatred with understanding and forgiveness. I am your child: make your kingdom of mercy come in me, and through me let your love reign wherever I go. Make me your apostle of love, your missionary of mercy, so that, as I am bathed in your infinite love, others may be soothed by my mercy and love (really yours working through me), however paltry the portion, however fragile the vessel.

Thank you, Father, for coupling the two imperatives, "Love your enemies," and "Lift up your hearts," for the first cannot be practiced without the power promised in the second. Enemies, it cannot be denied, straiten and besiege the soul with cutting words, cold stares, insulting attitudes, and disparaging comments behind one's back. It takes the utmost restraint not to lash back in kind, not to go on the offensive, not to repay nasty remarks with equally mean replies, not to combat persistent knifing in the back with a counter-campaign of backbiting. But as your son chosen to live as another Jesus, I must return love for hate and exchange a blessing for a curse. I can do these impossibilities only through Jesus, who has bridged the chasm between earth and heaven. Following this Way, I can mount to heaven itself. Dwelling in heaven through his heart, united through him to you and your Holy Spirit, I can live in the atmosphere of your love and peace. With your heavenly love I can love my enemies. Fused with your unity, I can seek to be one in heart and mind with my brothers who for whatever reason exhibit disdain and aversion for me. Blessed with your peace, I can bless and extend peace to those who put themselves at odds with me. True, I am still burdened by demands of, subject to fluctuations of, the flesh. But inwardly, according to the interior man, I have been raised up with Jesus and dwell in heavenly places. Without the duality that entails being in two incompatible places at once, without the polarity that causes unhealable tension, my heart already resides in heaven: all the love and tranquillity from on high are mine not by sight, not by endless and full possession, but by faith.

What a life you call me to, Father! By faith and adoption I am to live the life Jesus lived by intuition and natural sonship, a life wedding heaven to earth and earth to heaven. Lifting up my heart, I feed on the love and peace of the holy three. Living in the body on earth, I feed my enemies with the love and peace of heaven you share with me. At home in heaven, I can use the power of its open and spacious fields to batter down barriers with which enemies compass me. In the risen life of Jesus I can continually ascend and descend the ladder of Jacob.

Praise

1. Thank you, all-wise Father, for making me a being of praise, a being of nature whose highest work is beyond any work of nature. I praise you for breathing a living soul into the dust that is the foundation of my body. For raising me above other beings of nature, I praise you; for patterning my inner self on your own likeness, I praise you. Wonderful are you for touching me with your finger of creative power that sent life pulsating through my frame. More wonderful are you for gracing my inward eye with light from him who is Light from Light and causing it to be turned upward to your Face, hidden but even now beautiful, its faint contours eliciting my admiration and awe. I praise you for this gift, this supreme vocation,

of praise. I praise you for weaving each of my trillions of cells perfectly into place so that my first cry might be a cry of praise to you or, if not one of praise, at least its infantlike anticipation. You released normal growth processes during those long years up to maturation, readying me for normal-voiced praise. But mine has been a normal praise too often subnormal, praise coarsened by the dusty lower self, speckled with distractions, rushed through in the heat of less-than-heavenly pressures. Praise be to you, Father, for the "blindness" of your love that benignly neglects the crudities of my offering and smiles on my clumsy efforts.

Father, make me a child again! Then I will praise you as Adam did at the dawn of the world, worshipping you in the innocent accents of wide-souled wonder. Then I will praise you as your first children in the Spirit did on the birthday of your Church and shortly thereafter: what uninhibited joy sang out in their spirits, joy inflowing from the Spirit of Jesus! Fill me with unquenchable gladness in you, Father, and I will never stop praising you. Let success turn sour; yet I will praise you. Let pestilence more virulent than the Black Death sweep across our continent; yet I will praise you. Let calamities beyond description torture contemporary man; still I will praise you. Let demons be unleashed to lay waste the earth and turn it into a living hell; even then I will praise you. With the heart of a child newborn in the Spirit, nothing can separate me from this love that is in Christ Jesus — nothing, because all the forces of nature in disarray, all the battalions of malignancy marshalled by the prince of darkness and death are as nothing before the might of your mercy; so I go on praising you. Let others jeer at this vision of mercy and my vocation of praise as vaporings of a revivified Don Quixote, the weird outpourings of an arch-fantasizer, the crazy reveries of a dreamer; still I will praise you. However shoddy my praise, I will not stop believing that I have been chosen to perform this loftiest of activities. If I resort to words vacant of practical meaning, I praise you for putting them in my mouth, for I trust that what you move me to clothe in word will be somehow embodied in fact. Nothing but lack of confidence can discourage, deter, or detain me from chanting your praise and glory.

2. Father, let me now continue my praise through interior and near-voiceless murmurs and sighs, all of love. Jesus sweetens the yoke of praise and lightens its burden by companioning it with love. Let me now celebrate your beauteous Face with the love that is implicit praise. It is love that makes my voice true and my singing on key, it is linkage with love that makes my praise of you my supreme work. All things in heaven and on earth well up from your bosom, all love springs from your primal love. Out of you unendingly courses love because you are love (1 Jn 4.16). Lead me to close the door and in the inner room that is the heart of Jesus generate love anew in me that I may praise you with the love of a son.

You are love: so you have me seclude myself in a spiritual hermitage of love. You are love: when I praisefully love you in secret, you reward me in secret with the finest of rewards — more of yourself, more of the love that is your very substance, more of the wages of life that is love, the greatest treasure, and in one respect perhaps the only treasure in heaven or on earth. Praise to you for calling me to the divine mansion of love. There I sing the new song of love-filled freedom gained by the sacrificial love of Jesus. There I sing the new song of the glory that is your mercy. There I sing as a new man risen out of the old self entombed in the passions. There I sing as a being living in but marvellously dwelling apart from the world, caught up into a new, unimaginable dimension. There I sing the song of the new covenant whose binding force is love. In Jesus I am covenanted with you, united to your whole self and its relationships, covenanted with the holy three, a kin spirit by adoptive love with you and the Son and the Spirit. I am new! I am a Godly man as Jesus was and is the God-man! I am divine love in the finite as Jesus is infinite love in finite flesh. Thus in a small way I am a being of love, I am love incarnate. I am love: your love is what makes me new, love is my new song, love is at the center of my new covenant in Jesus. I am love: let every loving word or sigh I emit help compose a symphony of praise to love that has made me love.

3. I praise you, Father, for making me a part of the new people formed by your love. I am never alone: I praise you for always being with me as you were always with Jesus. I am never alone: I praise you for giving me hundreds of millions of brothers and sisters all over the earth. What a super-city of love is your Church on earth! How mildly yet invincibly, secretly yet efficaciously, her mighty currents of love circulate through her members! I praise you for the desire and power to write this sentence, some of the sustenance for which was perhaps won for me by Legion of Mary members·working clandestinely in Shanghai in the midst of a hideous totalitarian state. I praise you for fidelity up to this hour, due in part to the supporting arms of contemplative nuns who lose themselves in the heart of your Son in prayer and penance offered to secure holiness in priests. I praise you for all the nutrients of love channeled to me through this polity of love. And what holy ones you are cultivating in your garden of love, thousands and thousands, some perhaps to be canonized in the centuries ahead but, whether to be raised to the altars or not, they are at this moment generating stations of your life and love. I praise you for linking my heart to their hearts in the heart of Jesus: even without my knowing it, I am right now growing by the appeal of their example and the force of their character. In my physical body cell is interwoven with cell to drive off invading microbes, to heal wounds, to fight off fatigue, to rid the body of poisons, and to perform a million-and-one activities ordinary in their appearance but extraordinary, by criteria of human making, in the conveyance and coordination of processes. How much more wondrously does your mystical body function! Every least good work, every grace received, every progress in virtue, every new exercise of a gift, every touch of love, every consolation, every whiff of the fragrance of divine beauty that any one soul

profits from are shared in by all the members of the body of Jesus. I thank and praise you for so many brothers and sisters so varied in their gifts and strengths. Who but you can tell what outstanding saints you are shaping in your Church at this hour? Each of your saints is unique, but in every age you plant and bring to fruition new saints resembling at least in some respects the sequoias and redwoods of the past. In this sense then I praise you for privileging me to share in some measure in the wisdom and zeal, at its maximum in a St. Augustine, now partially ornamenting one of your living saints; in the love of evangelical truth of a living imitator of St. Dominic; in the spirit of poverty of a soul now walking the path of St. Francis of Assisi; in the mystical illumination of a soul anointed with prayer like that of St. Teresa of Avila; in the gentleness of one mirroring St. Francis de Sales; and in the plainness and childlikeness of a tiny one modeled after St. Bernadette. Praise be to you, Father; some portion of all of these graces are mine because I belong to this universal community of love. How lovingly deft you are in designing this body. Spiritually it realizes the naturally unrealizable utopian dream: here it is all for one and one for all, here perfect unity in diversity and the most minute diversity for unity. As I praise you for the wealth raining upon me from the saintly, teach me to descry and love those who are, like myself, less than saintly. What succor and affirmation from so-called mediocre brethren firm my tottering resolves! Praise be to you for all the dynamism that streams into my spirit as an elect member of this society of divine love; an army of the Spirit of Jesus that in spite of all defeats and disasters and apparent decrepitude miraculously leaps up higher in every generation, its forces waxing ever more vigorous as they resistlessly roll back the massed legions of the Dark One. Yours is the kingdom, the power, and the glory: the kingdom of love, the power of your mercy, the glory of your unceasing triumph of infinite love over finite hate.

4. I praise you, dearest Father, for draining hate and other poisons out of my spirit, for touching me with your mercy. Christianity has been vividly described as the religion of the second chance. But perhaps it is more: it is the religion of an infinite number of chances. You are always there, ready to excuse as soon as I sincerely accuse myself. How swift is your mercy, how quick your healing. "Betwixt the stirrup and the ground he mercy sought and mercy found." Incalculable miracles of your mercy you work in the last instant of life to sweep sordid sinners into your arms. But at this moment you are yearning to cleanse the eye of my heart: at any moment I can plead for your bath of forgiveness. I praise you; teach me how to confess my sins now so as to praise you more. Plunge me into the abysses of your mercy: then I can praise you with something of the pellucid eye of your holy ones. I praise you for so loving me that I am able to love my enemies. Supersaturate me with this love: then I will praise you as I should. Consume me in the fire of your love: then I will be able to pour coals of fire on my enemies, coals lit by your love, coals in whose bright

burning I will sing all the more lustily your praises. Press your yoke of love on my shoulders. Then my love will respond to your love. Then my love will speak praise of your love. Then healing rather than hurting others, I will experience your family of love. Then heart lifted up to you, my spirit will praise you in heavenly tones even while my body is riveted to the earth.

I praise you for the wonder of littleness producing great fruits that shine in Jesus's kingdom on earth. Father, what power you exercise in championing your Church. In Jesus, the Lamb of God, you still send its members forth as lambs among wolves. A flock of lambs surviving amid and indeed overcoming packs of wolves! I praise you for this fold of the helpless and weaponless before the teeth and fangs of the wicked. All glory to you for this kingdom of weak children: all glory indeed because a flock of lambs of itself cannot for a minute stand against the lying and violence of those pledged to serve this city of evil. I praise you for this unity and robustness of hearts coming down from above. It is the sharing in your love for Son and Spirit and their love for you that binds together members of this mystical polity. Praise to you for this community of the divine that mirrors your fully divine community. Resting in your love, energized by your mercy, refreshed by your life, I can live a life of love, I can do the humanly impossible, I can forgive enemies seventy times seven times, I can forgive with every beat of my heart. Praise to you for your mercy that can make me a being of mercy worthy to praise you.

Notes

¹EP 44 (45).9; CC 38, 500-01.

²Tract, in Joh. 25. 12; PL 35, 1602. S. 144. 2. 2; PL 38, 788.

³Ep. 137. 5. 17; PL 33, 524. De civ. Dei 15. 22; PL 41, 467.

⁴De mor. Eccl. Cath. 1. 18. 13; PL 32, 1316. Tract. in Joh. 65. 2-3; PL 35, 1809. Fr. Robert Russell, O.S.A., in "The Nature and Foundations of Augustinian Spirituality," the first of three excellent articles in the Second Annual Course on Augustinian Spirituality (Rome: Augustinian Publications, 1976), pp. 19-23, sheds light on the central role of love.

⁵De spir. et litt. 11; PL 44, 211.

⁶S. 88. 5. 5; PL 38, 542.

⁷S. 34. 4. 7 and 5. 8; PL 38, 212.

⁸EP 72 (73).1; CC 39, 986. S. 236. 1. 1; PL 38, 1472.

⁹"Louange," Dictionnaire de spiritualité, 9 (Paris: Beauchesne, 1935-   ), 1022. Augustine's handling of praise and thanksgiving generally reflects this Biblical distinction.

¹⁰EP 105 (106).2; CC 40, 1554. A. Solignac, "Introduction aux Confessions" (in the edition cited on p. xvi, n. 1 of the introduction), pp. 9-15, discriminates the senses of confessio, basing his view in part (p. 9, n. 1) on the research of Joseph Ratzinger, "Originalität und Ueberlieferung in Augustins Begriff der confessio," Revue des études augustiniennes, 3 (1957), pp. 375-92 (but he parts company with Ratzinger on the signification of sacrifice: p. 15, n. 2).

¹¹EP 94 (95). 4; CC 39, 1333.

¹²James Hitchcock, "The Imperial Self," The New Covenant (July, 1980), pp. 4-6.

¹³EP 44 (45). 9; CC 38, 500-01.

¹⁴EP 134 (135). 1; CC 40, 1937-38.

¹⁵EP 148. 1; CC 40, 2165.

¹⁶EP 144 (145). 2-3; CC 40, 2089.

¹⁷EP 147. 3; CC 40, 2141.

¹⁸EP 72 (73). 1; CC 39, 986.

¹⁹S. 336.1; PL 38, 1472.

²⁰S. 34. 1. 1; PL 38, 210.

²¹EP 66 (67). 6; CC 39, 863.

²²EP 99 (100). 5; CC 39, 1395-96. (For further references to the region of unlikeness see Conf. 7. 10. 16 and S. 7. 7; PL 38, 66.) The twelfth sentence from the end of this selection describes a blind man as an individual devoid of the light of eyesight, because, in accord with the Platonic tradition, Augustine maintained that the physiological state of a sense organ is congruous with its proper medium: the eyes contain light in sympathy with the physical light conveying brightness and color. See De mus. 6. 5. 10; PL 32, 1169 and De Gen. ad litt. 4. 34. 54; PL 34, 319-20.

²³EP 132 (133). 13; CC 40, 1934-35.

Chapter III

The Cosmic and Divine Role of Praise

Man praises God because he radically tends toward God. If the sovereign work of man is praise of God, man is made to praise God. God actualizes this drive to praise by making praise a thing of joy. "You spur man to delight in praising you because you have made us for yourself and our hearts are restless till they rest in you."[1] Man is oriented toward God as his lasting home of rest, and this orientation is the reason why God incites man to praise him. In short, man is made to praise God because man is made for God. It is impossible in this order for man open to God not to praise God. No more than he can cast aside his nature or erase his basic orientation can he not praise God. Praise intensifies this radical directedness, inducing the wandering heart to let the Father gather it more tenderly to his breast. His clasp damps fitful oscillations through a sustaining serenity. Indeed praise and rest become locked in a virtuous circle: praise overcomes restlessness, and interior rest fosters more fruitful praise.

Praise of God by God

The God who lovingly designs and directs man to praise him instructs his rational image how to praise him. Because of our halting reason and the partial darkness of the most luminous faith we feel inadequate in our efforts to praise God. The sense of our inadequacy would have become sharper and more painful if we had had to depend on utterances of our own making to celebrate his holy name. A finite mind and heart cannot devise formulas of praise appropriate to an infinite being. Whether we opted for simple expressions or strained for excessively rhetorical modes of praise, we would never be able to shake free of the nagging fear that our patterns of praise were inapt, inconsonant with the majesty of the all-holy one. But God spares us this uncertainty by revealing the proper way to praise him. In Scripture God praises God, and, in praying the word of God in faith, we learn to praise him. A man praising himself is ordinarily a dupe of vanity or pride, but God praising himself is not indulging in arrogant self-advertising but dispensing mercy. As indicated before, God reaps nothing from our praise, and the praise of himself to which he gently goads us boosts us to heights divine, where we come to partake of the lovely attributes we praise. In his Spirit we praise him with formulations of praise that he has fashioned for himself and thereby in his Spirit the face of our spirit is irradiated with the love and the kin lovable attributes of his Face.

> We have desired to praise the Lord with you. Since he has deigned to grant us this blessing, the praise we utter should be offered with due order and we should avoid offending by some showy extravagance him whom we praise. So it is better for us to look for the path of praise in God's Scripture, making sure that we do not wander to the right or left from this way. For I dare to say to you in your charity: to insure that God be aptly praised by man God praised himself; and because God deigned to praise himself, man discovered how to praise him. For we cannot say to God what has been said to man, "Let not your own mouth praise you" (Prv 27.2). It is arrogance for man to praise himself, it is mercy for God to praise himself. It benefits us to love a person we praise; when we love someone who is good, we become better. So because he knows that our loving him benefits us, in praising himself, he makes himself lovable; and he makes himself lovable just for our benefit. So he urges our hearts to praise him, and he has filled his servants with his own Spirit that they might praise him. And since it is his Spirit in his servants that praises him, what else is he doing but praising himself?[2]

So we find praise newly interlinked with love. In praising himself, God gives a glimpse of his lovely Face so that, in growing in praise, we assimilate the divine good and grow in love. Just as the praise we offer God first emanates from God, so the love we give God originates in God. We cannot help loving, but we do decide what or whom to love. Yet we choose to love God only because he has first chosen to love us. The disproportion between an earthbound man and a transcendent God nullifies any possibility of our taking the initiative in love. How, Augustine asks, can death-oriented man first love the deathless God, how can a sin-ridden creature presume to first love the all-pure one? He asks also, perhaps more subtly, how can things to be made first love their Maker? Things to be made, i.e., beings not yet created, surely cannot love their Maker before they come into existence. Creatures are first made out of divine love, then they are gifted with at least a radical capacity for loving God. Our love springs from the creative love of the Father, the redemptive love of the Son, the sanctifying love of the Holy Spirit. Because we are loved by God, we love God. Indeed we can go on loving God only by the steady influx of his love. Augustine exhorts us in a striking phrase, *Amemus Deum de Deo*: "Let us love God by God."[3] Hearts lit by the Holy Spirit, we can truly love the all-holy one. As we meditate on the love poured forth in our hearts by the Holy Spirit, we may come to experience some of the "sober inebriation"

John knew as he rested upon the bosom of Jesus and captured a faint glimmering of the awesome truth he was later inspired to write: "God is love."

There is no one who does not love, but we do inquire about what a person loves. We are then instructed not to forego love but to choose what we love. But what do we choose unless we are first chosen? Because we do not love unless we are first loved. Listen to John the apostle. This is the apostle who rested upon the heart of the Lord, and in that banquet drank in heavenly secrets (Jn 13.23). Because he thus drank and became blessedly inebriated, he proclaimed the words, "In the beginning was the Word" (Jn 1.1). What a towering lowliness, what a sober inebriation! So this grand preacher, drawing upon other mysteries that he drank from the Lord's breast, proclaims this also: "We love because he first loved us" (1 Jn 4.10). He did man a great honor by speaking the words, "We love," precisely in reference to God. Who are expressing this love? Whom are they loving? Men love God, the mortal the Immortal, sinners the absolutely Sinless, the fragile the Unshatterable, things to be made their Maker. We love: and what is the source of our love? "Because he first loved us." Search for the source of man's love for God, and you will never discover any other than this: God first loved him. He gave himself as the person we are to love, he gave the source of our love. Listen to the apostle Paul telling us more plainly what he gave as the source of our love: "The love of God is poured forth in our hearts." What is the source? Are we ourselves perhaps the source? Not at all. Then what is the source? We received love "through the Holy Spirit who is given to us" (Rom 5.5). Buoyed up then by such solid confidence, let us love God by God. Indeed because the Holy Spirit is God, let us love God by God. But what more can I say? Let us love God by God. This is absolutely true because, as I just said, "The love of God is poured forth in our hearts through the Holy Spirit who is given to us." From this it undoubtedly follows that since the Holy Spirit is God, we cannot love God except through the Holy Spirit: let us love God by God. A further consequence follows. Listen to what John himself more plainly tells us: "God is love, and he who abides in love abides in God and God in him" (1 Jn 4.16). It is not enough to say: love comes from God. Who among us would be bold enough to say what has just been said, "God is love"? John said this because he knew what he held in his heart.[4]

Since love and praise are two sides of the same coin, we may be permitted to complement his telling phrase, "Let us love God by God," with a similar one summing up his reflections on the source of praise: *Laudemus*

Deum de Deo: let us praise God by God (though Augustine never expressly employs these exact words). Praise is supreme because it initially flows from the heart of God. A compost of "dust and ashes," we can aspire, without the slightest hint of arrogance, to this topmost of works only because his Spirit inspires us. One with the heart of God, our hearts praise him with his own praise.

At times even the stoutest of praising hearts may feel downcast or listless and, partly chilled by the prevailing secular winds of doctrines of our day, may pose questions about the value of praise that verge on religious doubt. Are my exercises in praise divinely worthwhile? Are my cries piercing the cast-iron vaults of heaven? Augustine brushes such difficulties aside with the reminder that the very fact that Scripture is the written word of God lends extra weight to its genuine character. God formalizes and certifies his promises by putting them in writing. Appealing to the ordinary man's business sense, Augustine depicts Scripture as a financial statement containing a list of promised items, most of which God has already paid for. He has sacrificed his Son, sent his Spirit, and infused fresh strength into his Church through martyrs' blood. A God scrupulously faithful in paying these debts can be trusted to reward our praise by filling us with the loveliness and sweetness of his own ineffable life.

> ' The Lord is faithful in all his words and holy in all his works''
> (v. 13)....For what has he promised that he has not
> given?...He has promised certain things and has not yet given
> them. But let us believe him because of what he has already
> given....We would believe him if he only spoke his word. He
> did not want us to believe his spoken word alone but he wanted
> us to have his Scripture to hold onto. It is as if you were to
> say to a person to whom you had promised something: "You
> do not believe me; look, I am putting it in writing for you."
> Indeed because one generation goes and another comes and
> because these generations hurry past, with earlier generations
> of mortals yielding place to their successors, it was necessary
> for God's Scripture to perdure and for a sort of document in
> God's handwriting to remain, which all those passing by on
> this earth might read and thereby cleave to the path of his
> promise. And how numerous are the things he has paid for in
> line with this document! How can men raise doubts about
> believing his word about the resurrection of the dead and future
> life, the only promises that remain to be fulfilled, when
> unbelievers themselves are bound to be chagrined if he calls them
> to account? Think of God saying to you, "You hold my
> document in your hands. In it I have promised judgment, the
> separation of the good from the evil, an everlasting kingdom
> for those faithful to my word, and do you still refuse to believe?
> Read there in my document all that I have promised and take

into account my written words. By tallying what I have already paid, you can believe without a doubt that I will pay all that I owe. In this document you have my only-begotten Son promised, whom I did not spare but handed over for all of you (Rom 8.32). Count that among the items already paid. Read this document: there I promised that I would give through my Son the pledge of the Holy Spirit. Count that as paid. I promised there the blood and the crowns of the most glorious martyrs. Count that as paid. Let the mass, the large group of holy martyrs, remind you that I have paid this debt.''...And what else has to be paid? Do you not yet believe him even after he has paid all these debts? What else has to be paid? See, you have examined his account; look at the huge debts that he has paid. Does he become faithless because a few bits remain to be paid? Certainly not. Why? This is why: ''The Lord is faithful in all his words and holy in all his works.''[5]

Reflections

1. From the moment of my birth, indeed from the moment of my conception, Father, you pointed me toward you. Though only a being of nature controlled by laws of matter, I have been made for you who infinitely surpass nature. Though my life is a flickering candle soon to gutter out, I am made for an unending life in you. Now and then it seems almost laughable to claim this, for, like other animals, I have to assuage my physical needs, else I quickly die. As seems the case with most men, few of my waking thoughts center on you. I am caught up in a round of mainly human activities, many having hardly the barest link to your life. A being made for God yet a being that seems to spend most of his day coolly detached from God! A being made for God yet one that actually expends most of his energies on the purely human! But you cause me to delight to praise you: the way of praise is the way to you, for in praise I know, now concretely, that I am made for you. In praise my helter-skelter mind pauses for a breath, stops running in circles, drops its fretting and fussing, and rejoices in resting in you. Let the rationalist say, ''No, you can't be God-oriented. Don't be silly, you are programmed for manlike goods alone. Forget this deluded desire for a God moderns have outgrown.'' Let a secularized world insist, ''God may be up there but he doesn't count down here. Whether he exists or not, we are running this human world with human resources for human goals. Get rid of this fantasy about being made for God.'' All the misleading arguments, all the involuted dialectical traceries come to nothing when I am launched into praise of you, Father. In praise I know you, however hard to articulate, as the end of all my longings, as my highest good, as the beloved I long to embrace, as the companion whose hand I want to hold and not let go of forever. In the irrefutable power and exultation of praise all the spiderwebby subtleties

of misguided rationalism pass like mists dissolved in the rising sun. When I praise you, I know why I exist: I am made for you, I am made to praise you.

Thomas Carlyle once said, "If I could give only one sermon, it would be brief and to the point. I would simply say, 'My dear brethren, you all know what you ought to do. Well, then go out and do it!' " His mother, sitting nearby, observed, "Aye, Tammas, but don't ye think ye should tell 'em how." Man schooled in the what and why of praise still has to learn how to praise God. It seems impossible for the human mind and heart to form expressions of praise worthy of the All-High. I could be endowed with the analytic sweep and power of Plato and Aristotle combined, I could enjoy a creative imagination equal to that of a Dante and Shakespeare rolled into one, I could master every strategy of thought and writing — yet I would fall far short of hitting upon phrases that could truly praise you, Father. How pale and gauche my or anyone's humanly coined praise sounds over against the boundless, super-brilliant Reality! Left to myself, disconsolately and near-despairingly I would have simply tossed praise aside — an exercise falling pitiably below the mark. Thank you, Father, for your words of perfect praise mirroring your wisdom, echoing your love for us. Choosing not to speak in scientific terminology, you bared your heart and mind to the hearts and minds of myself and other little ones in unsophisticated formulations that in our reverence we may have otherwise spurned as childish and disrespectful. Thank you for teaching us the elusive how, how to praise your splendor in an unadorned style that ordinary mortals like myself are at home with. Thank you for your self-praise, for stooping down in compassion to put on my lips and in my heart what the French call *le mot juste*, the right word, of praise, or, literally, the just word, the word that is due you, that fits you perfectly, that is just right for you, properly attuned to you who are both awe-inspiring and alluring. Each word of praise going straight to your heart carries me straight toward you, and, in fixing me deeper in you and you deeper in me, breathes new peace into my spirit. In praising you, I rest in you, my Peace, my Serenity, my Tranquility without end, the bottomless, limitless sea in which I am absorbed without sinking, the ocean of Peace that washes away all perplexity and anxiety.

2. But this is also an ocean of love, the self-giving and union that make the heart at peace in itself and with brothers and sisters. I praise you, Father, because you are supremely lovable. Again, I stand before the mystery of love. Even on the natural level love is hard to catch and catalogue. Why do John and Jane fall in love with each other? Multiply reasons as we can, the reciprocal pull and fusion of their personalities defies final analysis. How much more enigmatic is my love for you and your love for me. I bear the seeds of death within my body. Sometimes I walk the planet as if I were never to die, but in a few years my body will return to the earth and disintegrate into dust over the millenia. You are deathless, suffering no alteration, no decay: you are fullness of life. My love fires up and blows hot, then becomes cold as stone. Yours always burns with maximum

intensity — steadfast, ultra-dependable, transccending all the to-and-fro of the human heart, absolutely immutable, unwaveringly faithful. Yet it is your love for me that seems more inscrutable. Out of your freedom one with your goodness you chose to make me out of nothing. Why did you create me? Why did not you leave me unmade? Why did you not let me remain as one of the billions and billions of beings no more than possible? Why? Why? Perhaps I shall never know the answer. Or rather, I do know the answer, one wrapped in layer after layer of mystery, which I may never fully comprehend. The answer is your love; the mystery is your love, Father. You are love, love, love — nothing but love. Because you are love, I was chosen. Because you are love, I can love you. Because you say "I love you," I can say, "I love you." Because you show your loveliness within, I can cry out, "I praise you, Father." Because you are love, I lovingly praise you and in that love-praising desire to be like you: I want to become love, all love, nothing but love, so far as possible for a creature at home in time and space. I want to be all love: then I will become all praise.

If some of the pseudo-sages of this generation read or hear of aspirations like these, they may mock and hoot at me. Pietistic nonsense, half-crazy enthusiasm, dream-world fatuities perhaps betraying an incipient senility — these and other aspersions might be hurled by men of this age who, shackled with backs to the light, waste their lives in the contemplation and pursuit of shadows in a cavern darker and more dreadful than that sketched in Plato's allegory of the cave. The heavier and more cutting the chains, the louder the cries of its prisoners vaunting their freedom; the more obscure the shadows and the fuzzier the sight, the more the slaves of darkness boast of their light and truth. Poor fools, dupes of the Enlightenment, pour out your mercy on them, Lord. They scoff at your magnificence because they do not know love. They have never been enfolded in your love, or, if they have tasted it, they have, for some reason or another, turned their backs on you. In repudiating you who are love, they forged around their spirits irons of night and unlove. Mercy; anoint them with your mercy, Father. Free them with your love. Burn away their slavery with your love. Strike dead their old selves and recreate them by your love. Lead them out of their cave into the super-daylight of your love. Give them, as you have given me, a hunger and thirst for your love, drawing them to eat and drink of your love. Then knowing peace, they will begin to know the secret meaning of themselves, each coming to see that he is purposed to become love. Then each will realize, as I realize, however feebly, that his vocation is to love in praise and praise in love. O beautiful one, dear, dear, Father, how wonderful you are! You are love! Make me, along with others trying to be your friends, all love. Make each of your enemies all love. Consumed in this mystery that is love, I will understand the more: I will become love, I will become like you in all things because love is the reason why all things, God and angel and man, are. Love is the infinite reason beyond all finite reasons. Your final explanation is love.

Make me love then I will know my sufficient reason, then I will know why I am: as love I will understand myself in your love.

3. How faithful you are, Father, in your covenant of truth and love! You could have restricted yourself to oral communication, perhaps by successive waves of prophets. Choosing to bind yourself to us in writing, you cast your message in words to endure till the end of time, a testament to be interpreted by your Spirit illumining your Church. You have given us an unimpeachable warranty of the truth of your words and, in particular, have generously stamped your seal of approval on the passages of praise. Each line bears your affidavit, every expression of praise has been selected from all eternity by your Spirit of truth and love. How gracious of you to teach us infallible means of praising you! I cannot puzzle out all of Scripture — dark sayings and allusions dot its pages. But you spell out for us the words of praise, and in love-impregnated praise we can sing, at least in general, all the latent senses of words vibrant with the melodies of the eternal.

Thank you, Father, for your personalized messages. You address my individual condition in your words from the Spirit of Jesus. Of course I am not lapsing into a theory of private interpretation, a view that would leave your Holy Spirit contradicting himself and make any religious unity in doctrine unthinkable. Surely you interpret your word through the Spirit dwelling in your Church. Still, within that framework your word is morally, spiritually directed toward me. In your holy word you speak to me, you guide me to select forms of praise in tune with my peculiar self (peculiar in more ways than one!). Show me, Father, how to make my very own the words of praise and glory you have fashioned for my spirit. Inscribe your word within me by your light and love: then will I respond to your written word without. Let your Spirit within peel off veils overlaying the Word in your word. Feeding on the Word in your word, I will sing your love more joyously and, if possible, spiritually burst out of my cage of flesh and wing my way upward into your presence where, fascinated by the beauty of your eyes, I will celebrate your mercy with the Spirit-voice Jesus shares with me.

The words we read and speak through your Spirit we read and speak in time. But you are eternal, and the Word uttered in your temporal words is eternal, and the Spirit through whom I speak them is eternal. You everlastingly utter your one Word in your one Spirit, a Word of truth and love. Do you also utter an everlasting Word of praise in your Spirit? Yes, Father, it seems that you do, indeed that you must, for all three of you, in loving one another with an infinite love, must praise one another's beauty in infinitely marvelous song. As I praise you with your words in time, lead my spirit to praise you as do your Word and Spirit in eternity. Word of God, make my word of praise like yours, a word begotten, as so to speak, of the Father, a word that praises him by imaging his perfection within. Holy Spirit, the very Love of the Father and Son, make all my praise live by the flame of your love. Your praise of Father and Son is all love, and your love is all praise. Inspirit me anew, enliven my praise and love with eternal breath, ensoul my love with your eternal praise.

Praise

1. I praise you, Father, for putting in my heart and on my lips your words of praise. I praise you for making all praise, not just the praying of the liturgical hours, an *opus Dei*, a work of God, a work whose language you have fashioned. O God, how I yearn to praise you with all my heart, with all my soul, and with all my strength. How I desire to praise you with the sweetest music, with the most sublime of melodies, with the superlative singing of your saints! I praise you for sowing this desire in me, however slight its fruit. Glory to you for causing me to delight in praising you: let praise make my heart divinely one-track, uncompromisingly aimed only at your love. I praise you for adapting your words of praise not to the wise and clever but to the lowly and simple, to mere tots (Mt 11.25). I praise you, Father, for designing unornamented garments for your praise. What a generous God you are! Matchless in wisdom, you form words of praise that the simplest can use. O how accommodating you are, how considerate! For the performance of this supreme work you require words that look far from supreme. I praise you, I worship you in song for clothing your Word in weak flesh, for clothing accents divine in plain garb.

2. Homely though its dress be, your word is all love. I praise you, Father, for binding yourself in a covenant of love, for making your Scripture a story of love, telling me I am loved. Loved! Infinitely loved! Who can fathom the riddle of your choice of me? Before the foundation of the world, in an eternal decree shrouded in profoundest mystery, you decided to create this universe, and in that choice I was chosen. Why do beings of nature tend toward you and love you? Because you chose to love them. Why do I love you? Because you chose to love me. I praise you: you loved me at birth as I flew forth from the maternal nest, you never hesitated to love me as I fumbled and stumbled, you never stopped striving to entice me back as I rebelled against you. Ever-loving one, you ever elect to forgive me and rekindle my love amid myriads of shortcomings. I praise you for the sometimes seeming darkness of love, a darkness like light, a darkness not comprehended but comprehending all, a light-giving darkness.

How beautiful are the sun and the green earth and the millions of plants and animals! How lovely is every part of my body, how marvelous the least of the gifts you have bestowed on my ordinary mind! But the beauty of this world must pass; every gift and talent will lose all earthly use in the loss of my life. I praise you for the transiency of things of this world because there remains only the fruit of your choice, only love. Empty my spirit of every illusion: let only love and the sense of being loved by you stay. Then will I be love responding to your love, then will I be praise doubling the praise that circulates among you, Father, your Son, and Spirit.

3. Praise to you, all-merciful one, for adapting your constancy to my inconstancy, for casting eyes of pity on my fickle ways. How my moods shift like the wind, how rapidly I plummet from exaltation to gloom. How easily I am perturbed by some slick argument pretending to desupernaturalize your word or reduce the fullness of truth to the prettiest of myths. I praise you: you have built up and continue to reinvigorate a holy Church including many unholy men, you have raised up saints who defy the wisdom of the wordly wise. How faithful you are in your words: miracle after miracle testifies to their truth. How holy you are in your works: your saints lovingly proclaim your holiness. Make their praise of your unbroken fidelity fortify my fidelity, make my praise of your infinitely various holiness convert me into the saint you want me to be. Glorious God, you do all: trace the fidelity and holiness of Jesus in living characters on my spirit. Then will I praise you always as a living affidavit of your fidelity and mercy, irrepressibly proclaiming: how good you are, how lovely you are, Father! Let my whole being sing its song of praise! O incredible love that chose to make me love you! O faithful love! O love that never stops diffusing itself until all you have chosen diffuse themselves in your love.

Glory to you, Father. Every line of your covenant carries your autograph: love. I praise you for the one style threaded into all the diverse styles of Biblical writers: love; for the one theme: love; for the one message: love. I praise you for your love manifested in your fidelity to your promises. Father, you are love! Come, write your autograph on my heart, burn into my spirit your theme, stamp on my soul your message; then will my heart praise you with the theme and message of your word: love.

Praise of All Creation

Not only man but all creation is made to praise God or, more precisely, all material creation is so ordained through man: "Let all your works confess to you, Lord" (Ps 144.10). Rocks, trees, fish, birds, and cattle are evidently devoid of the voice that betokens intelligence. Yet like the three young men blessing God unharmed in the flames, we can regard senseless stones and dumb animals as praising God. The universe that stretches from visibles to invisibles is a perfectly ordered, stupendously beautiful system, a chain of beings proportionally and unbrokenly linked one to the other from least to greatest. This whole ensemble praises God through the insight of the human spirit: "In pondering this and noting its beauty, you praise God in it."[6] Observing the fecundity, the mysterious potencies, the marvellously coordinated strata of species upon species, the mind poses questions to these natures: whence their striking power and bewitching beauty? Their answer is voiced in confession articulated in the praise man accords God. The universe acclaims in one voice woven out of the innumerable voices of heaven, earth, fleas, gnats, worms, each bewilderingly intricate creature, prodigious or trivial in appearance, contributing its modicum to one combined chant: "You, O Lord, have made me, not I myself."

"Let all your works confess to you, Lord, and let all your holy ones bless you" (v. 10). "Let all your works confess to you." How can this be? Is not the earth his work? Are not the trees his work? Are not the cattle, fish, birds his works? Clearly all these are his works. And how will these confess to him? I see indeed that his works confess to him in the angels, for the angels are his works. Men too are his works, and, when men confess to him, his works confess to him. But do trees and stones have a voice for confession? Certainly they do: let all his works confess to him. What are you saying? Do earth and trees as well confess to him? Yes, all his works do. If all praise him, why do not all confess to him? Now confession refers not only to sins but also to praise. . . . There is . . . a confession pertaining to praise. Accordingly, how are we to take the words, "Let all your works confess to you, Lord"? This means: let all your works praise you. But this raises a question concerning praise similar to that concerning confession. For if earth, trees, and all things lacking sensation cannot therefore confess to him because they lack a voice for confession; so too they will be unable to praise him because they lack a voice for pouring forth praise. Nevertheless, did not the three young men enumerate these things in their canticle while they walked unscathed in the flames, in the midst of which they were not only spared from burning but even praised God? They tell all things in heaven and on earth, "Bless the Lord, sing hymns to him, and extol him forever" (Dan 3.19). Look how they sing their hymn. Do not imagine that a mute stone or dumb animal possesses reason that enables it to understand God. Many holding such a view strayed far from the truth. God has ordered all things and made all things. To certain beings such as angels he gave sense and understanding and immortality; to others such as men he gave sense and understanding with mortality; to others such as cattle he gave bodily sense but neither understanding nor immortality; to still others such as herbs, trees, and stones he gave neither sense nor understanding nor immortality. Nevertheless, these beings are not devoid of qualities proper to their type, and God ordered his creation by successive degrees from earth to heaven, visibles to invisibles, from mortals to immortals. This system of creation, this perfectly ordered beauty ascending from the lowest to highest and descending from highest to lowest, forms an unbroken chain forged out of diverse links: this is the ensemble that praises God. In what sense does this ensemble praise God? In this sense: in pondering this and noting its beauty, you praise God in it. The beauty of the earth is a sort of voice of the mute earth. You observe and see its beauty, you see its fecundity, you see its potencies, you see how it receives seed, how it often produces fruits that were not sown. You see its workings, and, in considering it, you, as it were, question it; and your inquiry itself is a way of questioning it. When your inquiry stirs you to admiration, and when you deeply ponder the universe, and when you discover in it great potency, grand beauty, and surpassing power; since in and of itself it cannot possess this power, it immediately strikes your mind that it cannot exist by itself but only by the Creator. What you have discovered in it is the voice of its confession: in recognizing this, you praise the Creator. When you reflect on the beauty of the whole universe, does not this beauty itself answer you with one voice: "I did not make myself, God made me"?[7]

God gives us the beauty of this world so that we may be lured to enjoy the beauty of his Face. Originally, before sin polluted the human heart and planet, the beauty of the universe could not seduce man and alienate him from God. Every rose, every stone, every clod, every mote dancing in the sun pointed the hearts of the first man and woman upward to worship and exult in and praise the beauty of the Maker of this incredibly beautiful heaven and earth. Today, whenever we are liberated from sin, the beauty of the universe, looked at broadly or in detail, makes us gasp at and adore the beauty of God. Whether we peer through an electron microscope to examine finely wrought fibers of a cell meshing with one another, or observe some of the farther stars through a giant telescope, we always encounter more order and, with it, more beauty, more intricately interlaced patterns that awe the mind and stir the heart. The beauty before us is a beauty no man made: it is beauty bespeaking the beauty of God. The most magnificent of human architecture cannot parallel the beauty of the simplest-looking contrivance of nature. How much more matchless has to be the beauty of the God who crafted works of nature with infinitely skilled artistry.

"His confession is on earth and in heaven" (v. 14). What is the meaning of this line, "His confession is on earth and in heaven"? Is God doing the confessing? No, here confession means the action that all things engage in when they confess to him and cry out to him. The beauty of all things is in a certain sense their voice with which they confess to God. The heaven cries out to God, "You made me, I did not make myself." How do these things cry out to God? When you ponder them and recognize their beauty, they cry out in your pondering, they cry out with your voice. "His confession is on earth and in heaven." Contemplate the heaven: it is beautiful. Contemplate the earth: it is beautiful. Both together are very beautiful. He made them, he directs them according to his decree, he marks out their periods of time, he renews their movements, indeed he renews them through himself. So all these things praise him, whether they are at rest or in motion, on earth below or in heaven above, in old age or in renewed youth. When you see these things and you rejoice, you are borne up to their Maker and behold his invisible attributes understood through the things that have been made (Rom 1.20), "His confession is on earth and in heaven." In other words, it is as representative of the things on earth and in heaven that you confess him. And because he made all things and because there is nothing better than he, everything he made is beneath him and everything that pleases you in these creatures is inferior to him. Do not let the things he made please you so much that you draw away from their Maker. But if you love the things he made, much more should you love their Maker. If the things he made are beautiful, how much more beautiful is their Maker. "His confession is on earth and in heaven."[8]

Reflections

What a paradox contemporary man is: so advanced in technology, so backward in religious sense; so adept in exploiting nature in engineering, medicine, and other applied sciences, so maladroit in grasping the ultimate meaning of nature. Thank you, Lord, for blessing Christians with a religious heritage that recognizes and celebrates the unbreakable bond between nature and you. Secular humanists of course would ridicule the suggestion that the things of nature praise God — mythology rooted in the pathetic fallacy, simple-Simon metaphor trying to pass muster as a statement of fact. Let them smile condescendingly and shake their heads, Lord. This universe is yours. Every bit, every particle, of nature was made by you and therefore for you. Every atom, every amoeba, every blade of grass, every bee reaches out to you as the grand overall end of all its lesser ends. How consummately organized, super-delicately designed are the tiniest of your creatures. The electron microscope that magnifies cells 200 times over even more sharply helps magnify your name. This German shepherd, this mockingbird, this lily, the sun and the moon and the planets tend toward you, and their beauty hails your generous heart. But they tell of your power and sing of your beauty without knowing it. It is in man, the highest being of nature whose highest work is praise, that they praise you. Though only one among billions, I can praise you in this beech tree, in this rose, in that swallow, in the scorching sun and in the cooling rain, in the exquisitely formed snowflake. Is this primitive poetry crudely masquerading as science? No, it is authentic religious thought born of and developed by such childlike wonder as adorns St. Francis of Assisi's "Canticle of the

Sun'': all nature is a vast family of types and individuals that takes on conscious aspiration and a voice in the heart and senses of man.

Just by being a Christian, I am a priest in the common or nonministerial sense, deputed to share in the worship Jesus continually offers you, Father. In union with Jesus I offer to you my body as a living sacrifice (Rom 12.1): I am consecrated to you. As a *pontifex*, literally a bridge-builder, as a priest of creation, I bridge the gap between nature and you, offering you along with my body every subhuman body in the universe. Unless I praise you, squirrels and bluebirds and butterflies and azaleas and oxygen molecules will not praise you. I am their priest, I stand before the altar of nature and raise up to you all their unconscious yearnings after you, all their masterful design, all their wordless exaltation of your love. Bathe me once more, Father, in your light and love, wash away all of my darkness. Then I will begin to see anew the beauty of creation, then I will start afresh to praise you in the name of the whole universe. All about me lies beauty longing to pay its worship and gratitude. As I kneel before you in adoration, all creation kneels with me. As I prostrate myself, the whole of the nonhuman universe bows down before you. As I rise and lift up my arms to you, all of infra-human nature raises its arms in praise of your name. As a man and as a Christian, I have been chosen to be a priest of praise: in my song all creation sings its song of praise, in my heart the whole universe celebrates the wonders of your love, on my lips all of nature chants its praise and thanksgiving. But how often my interior singing is flat, my dedication ragged. I hope it is not naive to think that, were a rose able to speak, it might say: ''I exist for a number of reasons but the root reason for my existence is simply this: I am meant to praise God; my beauty praises his beauty.'' Make me just as simple and direct: let me know my role, love it, exult in it, want to do nothing other than live out my priesthood of praise. What a calling is mine: I am a priest of creation!

2. All creatures proclaim their dependence on you, Father. ''Look beyond us,'' they seem to say. ''Not we ourselves but he made us. Look above, look to the summit of being, look outside the world, above all creation, and you will find the super-generous Artisan who shaped us down to the least particle. Look beyond our beauty, and at the source beyond us you will reach Beauty. We are all beautiful because he is the All-Beautiful One.'' Unless I find more than their beauty in your creatures, I will come to see less of their beauty. Unless I admire you in them, I will not properly esteem all the splendors of your creation. As a rational animal I refuse to trample on my reason in the service of a warped view of faith. Reason can know in a broad sense that and what you are. You are not exalted but demeaned when undisciplined zealots spit upon reason, your gift to man. Shackling reason does not liberate but imprisons the soul in a false faith. But while my reason can attain you, Lord God, it can hardly call you Father. While reason can sketch your attributes, your inner life remains somewhat

vague and abstract. It is faith that makes me a member of your household, and in its familiarity I long for more of your embraces. As I need to know you in order to know myself, so I need to know your beauty in order to appreciate to the fullest the beauty of the world about me. You first lead me up the steps of created beauty to reach your uncreated loveliness, but, to complete the circle, in order to properly value created beauty I must grow in communion with your beauty. Only by looking beyond this world can I prize the beauty about me, only by caressing your countenance, only by being touched by your cherishing care, only by speaking intimately to you and being charmed by your affection, can I praise you as a priest of creation, fully alive to all the overpowering beauty of you and your universe. Flood my soul with your light bearing new love so that in me the beauty of the world can praise you; so that, praising, I can know your beauty the more; so that, knowing your beauty the more, I can praise you the more through a voice made more beautiful in its song by a more sensitive prizing of a universe mind-boggling in the infinitesimal subatomic particle as in the most enormous and most glittering of the galazies.

3. Because I am a priest of creation, then nature itself is truly sacred, a colossal temple erected ultimately to worship and praise you, the divine Workman. Some of the ancients verged on this truth in only a fumbling and distorted fashion, imagining that nature was full of gods, paying homage to a god of the fields, a god of the woods, a god of the sky and stars, and so on. Yet, Father, in their gross primitive intuitions perhaps these children of philosophy and theology came closer to the truth than the darkened, however acute, minds of our day who ruthlessly tear out every trace of the divine from nature. The universe is full not of gods but of things signifying God, full of signs of you, Father. In this sacramental universe each thing is a visible sign pointing to your presence. The commonest blade of grass, an ordinary drop of rain, the rock by the road, each conveys your presence, wears your smile, speaks of your excelling care, proclaims your beauty. Each of these sacraments is also a sort of sacrifice telling me: "I belong not to myself but to him, I came from him — so my every action goes back to him. In making me, he gave me a share in himself and in return I give myself to him." In giving itself to you, each thing surrenders, sacrifices itself to you. All of the elements and stars and trees and horses articulate their sacramental dependence and sacrificial self-giving in my mind and heart. In my praise they cry out, "Father, we are yours, wholly yours. You made us to show forth your glory. So we say yes to you, Father, we consecrate ourselves to you, we pledge our whole being, we yield all of ourselves to you." In me the whole universe sings its collective affirmation of your beauty, Father. On my lips the chant of the universe rises to a crescendo. "Yes, yes, yes," its voices continually sing, "Amen, amen, amen, you alone are great and glorious, Father, you are the everlasting yes that makes our praise a yes, you are the eternal holy one who sanctifies our being as sacrament and sacrifice."

Praise

1. How heavy my heart feels as I try to live as a priest of creation. I am trapped in longstanding faults, buckling under the weight of my irresolute behavior. Again, Father, I stand before you in trust, relying on your understanding heart to render right and fitting my imperfect praise. I praise your goodness for making this endlessly dappled world that never fails to surprise and delight the purified and discerning eye of faith. I praise you for making me a microcosm of the universe, summing up in myself all the levels of nature. Like coal and sandstone, I am anchored to the earth by gravitation; along with tulips and oaks I feed and grow; in communion with terriers and horses I touch and hear and see and roam about. I praise you for weaving my body out of things of nature and their patterns. I am composed of carbon, hydrogen, oxygen, and nitrogen; and without iron in my blood cells I would suffocate; minus lithium and other elements in my brain I would become mentally unbalanced. As a priest of creation I praise you because nature is epitomized in my human nature. Come, all you elements, praise the Lord in me and with me. Come, grass and maples and orange trees, praise with me by praising through me. Come, humming-birds and gerbils and cats, praise with me by praising through me. I praise you, Lord of all, for making me a lord of nature, for giving me the best possible work in the cosmos. It would be sheer joy to climb to the peak of Mount Everest and there proclaim your glory, carrying in my uplifted hands all the exaltation of the whole of nature. How I would love to dive to the bottom of the ocean and there sing your praises, hailing your name in the name of all the denizens of the deep. I praise you for uniting your heart to my heart: I need not move one inch from where I sit or stand or kneel, I need only lift up my whole being to you in spirit as a priest of creation, laying at your feet the innumberable bounties of this, for me, most gorgeous of worlds.

I praise you, Father, for the superb "ecology" of the cosmos, so tightly knit in its harmony that some of the ancients misconceived it as an organism to which they appointed a world-soul. Thank you for this wondrous organization underpinning the economy of praise you ask of nature. I praise you for its near-flawless law and order, so reliable in its silent workings, so smooth in its noiseless running.

2. Highest praise to you, Father, for enabling me to gaze upon this beauty so as to behold your beauty. What a joy to realize that at the controls of this stupendous world-order is not a grim impersonal force, not a blind malevolent will, not a power-drunk Caesar, but a being who is all love. I praise you for being a God of love! Behind the world's beauty is your beauty; within, causing this beauty, is your sweet Face, always wreathed in a smile. O Beauty so charming, so winning, so enchanting! O Beauty so immeasurable yet so childlike that all my fears and shame and feeling of worthlessness melt away in the fiery cataracts of your love and

tenderness! O Beauty that never stops radiating its allure though my inward visage is partly blemished! O Beauty that calls me to contemplation even though my devotion wavers and wobbles and I wallow in distraction. Take me once more into your bosom and, forgetting all else, let me rest there to silently cry out all the praise of the universe, let my wordless waiting hymn the praise of all things for their burdenless dependence on you, let my stillness embracing cosmic synergy and unison utter how unutterable is your loveliness. Lackluster as I am, I will go on praising you in the name of all of nature because you are all pity, infinite compassion, that transmutes my offering into a divine gift: so does the universe in and through me offer you praise that electrifies even the hearts of angels.

3. "Time flies," goes the stock but pregnant adage. Time moves on steadily, inexorably, the cosmic clock skipping not a beat and thus signalizing the unstopping movement of the whole universe, a symphony ever striking new chords in its celebration of your name, Father. I praise you for attracting me to praise: now teach me to praise constantly or, at least, no matter how sporadic my inward singing, no matter how far down into the pits I may slide, galvanize me to fresh efforts. You will, I believe, hear my plea, you will make me an ever-fervent priest of praise. I will praise you even when I falter and fritter away special times of praise, I will praise you even when I want to throw up my hands, when living as a priest of your creation seems a piece of fanaticism. I will praise you, absolutely sure that you will miraculously transform my fickleness into fidelity, you will change this desert patch into an orchard singing your glory, you will heal my palsied gait and make me leap and dance constantly before your throne, every movement a gesture of praise, every word and action a signal for the cosmic orchestra, every breath an incontrovertible sign that I have become in defiance of all odds a priest of your praise. All praise to you, Father! Glory to you! Let uninterrupted glory be yours, continuous laudation on earth that echoes the unbroken chant of angels and saints above, a chant itself echoing the infinite round of fire and praise among the holy three.

Joint Praise in Head and Members

All things comprise a splendid chorus channeling through man the new canticle that hymns the super-beauty of the Creator who has restored all in Christ. The new vocation of man is then to see and praise God as Jesus did; to see behind natural agencies the personal love and power of the Father; to praise the loveliness of his Face revealed in the trillionfold face of creation. The highest pitch of this supreme work is uttered by the Word made flesh. Because of his dual nature we not only praise him as Logos, the Word uttered by the Father, but as priest he praises for us and as our head he praises in us. Our sometimes languid efforts gain muscle in the conviction that because two in one flesh and therefore two in one voice, we chant our praise in him and he his praise in us. Hence not only in man redeemed but also in Man the Redeemer all creation sings its song of praise. The new man who sings the new song is the whole Christ of co-praising head and members. So in and through our head our praise is robed in fully divine raiment. As we contemplate the beauty of things, they cease looking mute and praise the Father in us. As we contemplate the beauty of our head, our praises cease looking sleazy and resound with all the power of his voice. The chorus of things in unison with man now harmonizes with the nobler chorus that is the praising body of Jesus. Perhaps better, now there is only one chorus of man and infra-man directed by Jesus, one in head and members, one in divine melody and lyric, whose towering leitmotif of the variously modulated song is simple: alleluia! praise his holy name! Thus as a member of Jesus each man fulfills his vocation by praising through Christ, with Christ, in Christ. Praising as another Christ, praising as a being of praise, divinized through his Spirit, he truly praises God by God. By becoming God through God, he praises God with the very voice of the human God who is Jesus.

The chorus of Christ encircles the globe and covers all the points of the zodiac. A singer out of tune or tempo gratingly jars a choral group. In a like vein heresy drives a sharp wedge between individuals in the Church. Yet the Church goes on singing its new song and in spite of doctrinal disharmony of dissidents maintains its essential harmony.

' Let them praise his name in chorus" (v. 3). . . . A chorus is an organized group of singers. If we sing in chorus, let us sing in harmony. A member of a chorus who sings out of harmony grates the ear and upsets the chorus. If the discordant voice of one singer disturbs the harmony of the others, heresy causes far greater discord in the harmony of those praising God. The whole world is already the chorus of Christ. From east to west the chorus of Christ sings in harmony. Let us see whether the chorus enjoys this great breadth. Another psalm tells us, "From the rising of the sun to its setting praise the name of the Lord" (Ps 112 [113].3). "Let them praise his name in chorus."[9]

Through the mystery whose revelation never failed to leave St. Paul awestruck (Eph 3.8) Christians enjoying the fullness of truth and life form one mystical body with Christ. His prayer is our prayer, our prayer his. His praise is ours, ours his. Insofar as Jesus as the Word is one with the Father, we do not pray with but to him. God of God, he is also man among men, who opened himself to experience all in the human condition except sin (2 Cor 5.21). He perspired and ached as he worked, felt hungry and thirsty, ate and drank, sagged in weariness to the point of exhaustion, and was overcome by sleep. Jesus prayed constantly, favorite verses and pet phrases from the psalms resounding in his memory and falling easily from his lips especially when closeted with his Father. Indeed the psalms were singularly the prayer of Christ. They were truly his, for, according to Augustine's spiritual interpretation, it is Christ who is the dominant figure and voice in the psalms. Where the head is, there are the members: so Christians too speak in the psalms. In line with the personalistic accent of Augustine, each of us should not be reluctant to claim, "Because Christ is speaking, I am speaking in each and every psalm." We are wholly identified with the Jesus who so identified himself with us that, as he sweated drops of blood in Gethsemane, his Church was already mystically shedding the blood of her martyrs.

God could not have bestowed a greater gift on men than this: he made his Word through whom he created all things their head and joined them to him as his members. He gave this gift so that he might be Son of God and son of man, one God with the Father, one man with men. So when we speak to God in prayer, we do not separate the Son from him, and, when the body of the Son prays, it does not separate the head from itself. The one savior of the body, the Lord Jesus Christ, prays for us, prays in us, and is prayed to by us. As our priest he prays for us; as our head he prays in us; as our God he is prayed to by us. Let us then recognize our words in him and his words in us. When anything is said of the Lord Jesus Christ, above all in prophecy, which expresses a lowliness unbecoming to God, let us not hesitate to attribute this to him who did not hesitate to become one with us. Indeed the whole of creation is subject to him because through him the whole of creation was made. So when we gaze upon his sublime and divine nature; when we hear the words, "In the beginning was the Word and the Word was with God, and the Word was God. This was in the beginning with God. All things were made by him, and without him nothing was made" (Jn 1.1-3); when we gaze upon the divinity of the Son of God that far outstrips and exceeds all the sublime features of creatures, we also hear in some passages in Scripture the same Christ groaning, praying, and praising. So we hesitate to attribute these words to him because our mind shrinks from descending from the contemplation of his divinity to his lowliness. It is afraid, so to speak, of doing him an injustice by recognizing in a man the words of one to whom it was addressing its words of prayer offered to God above. Our mind often wavers and tries to alter the thrust of Scripture, but nowhere in Scripture do we come upon anything other than that we should have recourse to him and never stray from him. Our mind should then rouse itself from slumber and become wide-awake in faith. Thus it would see that the Jesus whom it was contemplating a short while ago in the form of God "took the form of a servant and was made in the likeness of man; and, appearing in the form of man, he humbled himself and became obedient unto death" (Phil 2.7-8). While hanging on the cross, he chose to make the words of the psalm his own when he said, "My God, my God, why have you forsaken me?" (Ps 21 [22].2). Thus in the form of God he is prayed to, in the form of a servant he prays; in the first respect he is Creator, in the second, creature. For while remaining unchanged, he assumed a created nature subject to change and made us with himself one man, head and body. So we pray to him, through him, and in him. We speak with him and he speaks with us; we speak in him and he speaks in us the prayer of this psalm that is entitled "A Prayer of David." In the line of the flesh our Lord is a son of David. He existed not only before David but also before Abraham, from whom David stemmed; but before Adam as well, from whom all men descended; but, in addition, before heaven and earth in and on which every creature dwells. No one then, when he hears the words of this title, should say, "Christ is not speaking" or "I am not speaking." Rather, recognizing that he himself is in the body of Christ, he should use both expressions, "Christ is speaking" and "I am speaking." Say nothing without him: he says nothing without you. Didn't we have evidence of this in the Gospel? There it is surely written: "In the beginning was the Word, and the Word was with God, and the Word was God: through him all things were made" (Jn 1.1). There we surely find also: "Jesus was sorrowful" (Mt 26.38), "Jesus was fatigued" (Jn 4.6), "Jesus slept" (Mt 8.24), "Jesus was hungry" (Mt 4.2), Jesus was "thirsty" (Jn 19.28), Jesus prayed and "spent the whole night in prayer" (Lk 6.12). Jesus, we are told, spent the night praying and never stopped praying; and drops of blood ran down from his body (Lk 22.44). The fact that drops of blood coursed from his body while he was praying clearly showed that his body that is the Church was already flowing with the blood of martyrs.[10]

Augustine sounds the same chord in another passage touching on these now familiar ways of throwing light on the mystical oneness of Jesus with those who live by his Spirit. Jesus is as intimate to the Church as bridegroom to bride; he and she are interpenetrated as beloved and lover. Thus Christ may be called bride as well as bridegroom: they are two in one flesh, the twoness being mystically absorbed into the oneness of supernatural bonding. Too Jesus and his Church are so related as head and body that the members are truly Christ. Again, he is the vine, we the branches: the sap of his love sets our hearts on fire with his love as we pray. Without him we can do nothing; with him we can do everything. Without him we cannot breathe a single prayer; with him we sing the super-powerful song of his body that surges up continually to delight the ear of the Father. Without him we are the blind being led by the blind, stumbling about, falling, crawling aimlessly in the wasteland that is the world which has alienated itself from God. With him we are friends and lovers of our Father, gladdening him as he gladdens us by his embraces and kisses. Our common bond with the lowliness of his humanity enables his heart to bear us up to the heights of his divinity. Because he is one with us in human nature, we can become with him mystically two in one flesh. Because he is one with the Father in divine nature, we can become with him two in one Godly life beyond all flesh.

Here then Christ speaks in the voice of the prophet; it is, I dare say, Christ who is speaking. In this psalm he will say certain things that may seem unbecoming to Christ, to the majesty of our head, and above all to that Word that in the beginning was with God. Perhaps certain other expressions will seem inapplicable to him who lived in the form of a servant, a form that he took from a virgin. Nevertheless, it is Christ who is speaking because Christ lives in the members of Christ. In order that you may realize that the one Christ is both his head and body, he himself tells us when speaking about marriage: "They will be two in one flesh. Therefore they are no longer two but one flesh" (Mt 19.5, 6). But was he perhaps saying this about any and every marriage? Listen to the apostle Paul: "And they will be two in one flesh: this is a great mystery — I mean in reference to Christ and the Church" (Eph 5.31). Thus from the two, from head and body, from bridegroom and bride, there is formed, as it were, one person. Indeed Isaiah the prophet also hails the wonderful and surpassing oneness of this person. For Christ prophesying through him also tells us: "As with a bridegroom he has put on my head a crown, and as with a bride he has adorned me with jewelry" (Is 61.10). At one and the same time he called himself bridegroom and bride. Why did he call himself both bridegroom and bride unless because they will be two in one flesh? If they are two in one flesh, why not two in one voice? Let Christ speak then because the Church speaks in Christ and Christ speaks in the Church, the body in the head and the head in the body. Listen to the Apostle expressing this point more clearly still: "For as the body is one and has many members, and all the members of the body, though many, are one body; so it is with Christ" (1 Cor 12.12). In speaking of the members of Christ, that is, of the faithful, he does not say, "So it is with the members of Christ"; rather, this whole entity that he is speaking of he calls Christ. For as the body is one and has many members, and all the members of the body, though many, are one body, so is Christ many members but one body. Thus we are all united with Christ our head, and without our head we are worth nothing. Why? This is why: with our head we are the vine; without our head (God spare us from this) we are branches cut off from the vine, destined not for the work of the vinedresser but for the fire alone. So he himself tells us in the Gospel: "I am the vine, you are the branches, my Father is the vinedresser;" and "Without me you can do nothing" (Jn 15.5). O Lord, if without you we can do nothing, in you we can do everything. For whatever work he does through us seems to be our own work. He can do much, indeed everything, without us; we can do nothing without him.[11]

Wherever members of the body gather, Christ prays and praises in them and they in him. Each assembly, especially that in a church, represents in microcosm the whole Church. Jesus prays and praises as one man, as the whole Christ, throughout the whole of the world, from east to west, from north to south. The song of the new creation in the new man is the song of the universe: its melody of light knows no boundaries in this world. Intermingled with the song of praise, however, are sighs, groans, and sobs of members still laboring. The Latin word for labor signifies all that is associated with work: perspiration, burning and stinging in the hands, and stabs of pain in the shoulders, back, and legs. But it also connotes suffering: the wounds from without and within, the agony of a fatal disease like cancer, the awful weight of mental illness on sufferer and relatives, and the impact of multiple sorrows striking an ordinary home like an avalanche, which turn ordinary family life into a nightmare. So the one man cries out for help, succor, a soothing benediction for body and spirit from the Lord. As head Jesus suffers with and cries out in his members. There are no limits to suffering, no limits to the cry that goes up all over the world, yet too there are no limits to the strength and solace Jesus pours into his members. Joined to him, Christians form one man, and their human work, become one with that of God, gains in and through him inward divine rest.

"I have called the voice of this psalm our own not in the sense that it is limited to those now present. Rather, it is our own in the sense that it belongs to all of us throughout the whole world, who live at any point from east to west. In order that you may realize that it is truly our voice, here he speaks, as it were, as one man. He is not, however, one man in the usual sense, but he is speaking as one man in the sense of the oneness of the Church. For in Christ we are all one man because the head of this one man is in heaven and its members still labor on earth. Now see what he says about them because of their labor.

"Hear, O God, my plea, listen to my prayer" (v. 2). Who is speaking these words? He is in a sense one man. See if he is one man: "From the ends of the earth I have cried to you while my heart was in anguish" (v. 3). In one sense then he is not one man but in another sense he is one man because there is only one Christ, whose members all of us are. For which is the one man that cries from the ends of the earth? This alone cries from the ends of the earth: that inheritance about which it was said to the Son himself, "Ask of me and I will give you the nations for your inheritance and the ends of the earth for your possession" (Ps 2.8). This then is the possession of Christ, this is the body of Christ, this is the one Church of Christ, this is the oneness that we form: this cries from the ends of the earth. But what is it crying? It is crying what I have just said above: "Hear, O God, my plea, listen to my prayer. From the ends of the earth I have cried to you." In other words, this desire to be heard is the cry I raised to you. It is a cry "from the ends of the earth," that is, it is everywhere.[12]

Reflections:

1. Because I am a man, I can clothe in words and bedeck in song all the voiceless aspiration and celebration of mindless creation. Because I am a redeemed man, I can clothe all my words in the power of the Word made flesh and bedeck my songs in the exhaustless praise unceasingly rising from the heart and lips of your Son Jesus, Father. Now I am slowly coming to perceive a little less obtusely why the Gospels assign such power to the prayer of a single Christian blessedly chosen to be a member of the body of Jesus. My prayer is not just mine: it is the prayer of Jesus himself. Through his Spirit he prays in me so that every slightest ejaculation, every half-distracted pleading for the needs of men, becomes a spiritual weapon of incalculable force and delicious fruit. It is Jesus, the almighty one in our flesh, it is Jesus, sweetness incarnate, who ensouls my prayer with his force and gentleness. No prayer of a Christian goes unanswered because true prayer, however slack-looking, is the prayer of Jesus, infinitely inviting, irresistibly attractive to you, Father. When I pray, it is the ever-same Jesus praying within me, with all infinite resources of his Godly self; the Jesus who prayed for forty days in the desert under the impelling of his Spirit; the Jesus who spent nights rapt in prayer and praise of you; the Jesus who prayed prior to the crucial selection of his twelve apostles; the Jesus who wept and prayed at Lazarus's grave before breathing fresh life into that rotting corpse. Within my prayer is latent the power that stilled the wind and the waves, within my praise is the ecstatic chant of Jesus super-affectionately looking into your eyes. O what a gift in my prayer and praise is this! I pray and praise with all the inimitable consecration of Jesus to you, Father. Always with you, Jesus as my head, brother, and my lover is always with me as he promised, "I will be with you always even to the end of the world" (Mt 28.20). Jesus is principally with me through his continuous prayer, which raises up my mind and heart till my personal world comes to an end. Till the last beat of my heart on earth Jesus will be praying with, in, and through me, each prayer as vital to the life of my spirit as each heartbeat is to the life of my body.

Reflections:

1. Because I am a man, I can clothe in words and bedeck in song all the voiceless aspiration and celebration of mindless creation. Because I am a redeemed man, I can clothe all my words in the power of the Word made flesh and bedeck my songs in the exhaustless praise unceasingly rising from the heart and lips of your Son Jesus, Father. Now I am slowly coming to perceive a little less obtusely why the Gospels assign such power to the prayer of a single Christian blessedly chosen to be a member of the body of Jesus. My prayer is not just mine: it is the prayer of Jesus himself. Through his Spirit he prays in me so that every slightest ejaculation, every half-distracted pleading for the needs of men, becomes a spiritual weapon of incalculable force and delicious fruit. It is Jesus, the almighty one in our flesh, it is Jesus, sweetness incarnate, who ensouls my prayer with his force and gentleness. No prayer of a Christian goes unanswered because true prayer, however slack-looking, is the prayer of Jesus, infinitely inviting, irresistibly attractive to you, Father. When I pray, it is the ever-same Jesus praying within me, with all infinite resources of his Godly self; the Jesus who prayed for forty days in the desert under the impelling of his Spirit; the Jesus who spent nights rapt in prayer and praise of you; the Jesus who prayed prior to the crucial selection of his twelve apostles; the Jesus who wept and prayed at Lazarus's grave before breathing fresh life into that rotting corpse. Within my prayer is latent the power that stilled the wind and the waves, within my praise is the ecstatic chant of Jesus super-affectionately looking into your eyes. O what a gift in my prayer and praise is this! I pray and praise with all the inimitable consecration of Jesus to you, Father. Always with you, Jesus as my head, brother, and my lover is always with me as he promised, "I will be with you always even to the end of the world" (Mt 28.20). Jesus is principally with me through his continuous prayer, which raises up my mind and heart till my personal world comes to an end. Till the last beat of my heart on earth Jesus will be praying with, in, and through me, each prayer as vital to the life of my spirit as each heartbeat is to the life of my body.

As Son of God Jesus is a being of power. As son of man Jesus is a being of weakness. His dual nature is the mystery of might enfleshed in frailty. Jesus exposed himself to all the privations and stresses of a first-century Palestinian living in a scarcity economy. He felt pangs of hunger, was parched by thirst, bowed down by fatigue, jostled and pressured by crowds, and, worse, bullwhipped by the hate-filled taunts of enemies. Then he agonized almost beyond belief in a crucifixion still a stumbling block to the Jews and a stupidity to the pagans. It is Jesus as son of man who also prays in me as I grope, now and then trembling, on the way to my final consummation. I cannot properly put my comparatively luxurious existence beside the utterly mortified life of Jesus. Yet even my bed of ease has its thorns, so that Jesus can pray and praise in me as I wince from the stings and stabs of circumstances. When I feel pressured, bogged down by an over-load, or driven near the breaking point, the weak Jesus infuses into me his fortifying prayer and praise. My little can become much when leavened by his spirit of littleness. When I am downcast because my small store of energy is running down, the prayer of Jesus within lifts my heart, and in the cheerfulness of his holy face I can praise you for my want of drive, for the chagrin of always being short-winded, for the discomfort of being unable to participate in the multiple activities and enthusiasms of others. Yes, power is made perfect in weakness (2 Cor 12.9) because it is Jesus who is incarnate weakness. Because he became weak, I can become inwardly powerful. Join my heart more closely to his, making his weakness my own as he has already made my weakness his own. The weakness of Jesus changed frightened men, women, and children into martyrs eager to be devoured by wild beasts or hacked to pieces by people of hate. This same weakness can transmute my fear into courage, my self-seeking into self-giving, my petty-souledness into great-souledness: I can do all things in him who became weakness incarnate (Phil 4.13).

2. As I pray, it is Jesus within who whispers his love to you, Father, and at one stroke whispers his bridal love to my spirit. Jesus is spiritually married to his Church, he the bridegroom, his Church the bride. As is true of every member of this holiest of communities, I am wedded to Jesus in the spirit: we are spiritually two in one flesh, we are two in one spirit or even in one Spirit. How this closest of unions ennobles and enriches my prayer and praise! Every prayer, every act of praise, is a joint act of love, one word uttered by two hearts, an outpouring of two lives fused into one. Father of all mercies and all delights, only you in your tender wisdom could have designed a bond in which individuals are no longer male or female but all identically spiritualized, a relationship in which each soul is espoused to Jesus, in which every prayer, every bit of praise, goes up as a common gift of marital union, a supernatural marriage in which Jesus penetrates his bride so as to beget the fruit that is love. In this one act of prayer-love I come to know him in the intimate Biblical sense of knowing, and in that knowing I come also to know you as Jesus knows you, because you and your Son and your Spirit mystically interpenetrate one another's divine personality in one act of divine nuptial love. No prayer in Jesus goes unheeded: each prayer is stamped with his nuptial love. The prayer of the two in one Spirit pierces to the deepest recesses of your divine life. No doors are barred, no special chambers sealed, no innermost sanctuary remains closed to a heart one with the nuptial heart of Jesus whereby he knows by loving and loves by knowing the most profound abysses of your infinite self.

The light Jesus radiates is love. Though many members, we are all made one with him and one another in the unifying force that is love. We live by the life of the divine vine that is ultimately love. Without Jesus I can do nothing: apart from his heart that is all love all my works are sounding brass and tinkling cymbal. Without his love I have no supernatural love, but with his love, in the merger of my heart with his, I can do everything. Not everything sheerly thinkable — I cannot write plays similar to Shakespeare's, I cannot produce a summa of theology rivaling that of a medieval master, but I can do everything desired of me, I can do works of love, I can become holy, fully a son of God, shining with all the measureless love with which Jesus wants to enfold me and set me aflame. If, by yielding myself to the ongoing miracle of divine love, I did become a saint, my prayer and praise could open up further treasures from on high and help rain down unimaginable riches on emaciated souls starving for the Spirit of Jesus. With Jesus, in Jesus, as Jesus I can do all things. I can be love. In union with the gentlest of hearts I can aim at, and perhaps come close to, achieving a heart that is nothing but love. Father, in being love and doing love, I can do everything, for love from Jesus sums up the whole law and the prophets, love in Jesus energizes every spiritual work, love with Jesus rides over every obstacle and resistlessly moves to accomplish your will. Let your fire melt the arctic tissues in my heart, let my soul be gripped by this omnipotence of prayer and praise: his prayer and praise and mine fuse in the one heart and voice of bridegroom and bride; prayer and praise form one act of love called forth by and imaging the one act of love everlastingly enlivening and constituting the three-in-one and one-in-three self-giving that is your innermost life.

3. Occasionally while strolling through a university library, I am dismayed at how scanty my knowledge is. Unless I become exempt from the need of sleep, unless I am granted an earthly near-immortality, I can never master millions of facts and analyses. Even if I did exhaust all the intellectual veins in a large library, I would remain tied down to a small slice of space and a sliver of historical time. Living in the northern hemisphere, I cannot simultaneously reside in the southern hemisphere. But in the body of Christ I can dwell all over the world, north and south, east and west. My prayer and praise, no longer particularized, take on a world-girdling quality. In Jesus my prayer and praise reach to the ends of the earth; at every moment I can lend my voice to universal cries of supplication and global chants of praise. So far as we truly know, our tiny planet orbiting about a middle-sized star is the only abode of intelligent life in the universe. However, the mind of man, because spiritual, is greater than all the billions of galaxies scattered to the outer boundaries of the cosmos. Slim knowledge of these island universes assures us that a similar order and beauty mark their least particles, these too exclaiming ''Not we but he made us,'' their beauty mutely proclaiming your beauty, Father. Their praise too is given voice and melody in mine united to the singing of brothers and sisters mystically espoused to Jesus. Blaise Pascal, a religious thinker and scientist of genius, poignantly said, ''The eternal silence of the infinite spaces frightens me.''[13] But in union with the one man the immense stretches of the cosmos that excite dread in minds

through the humanly limitless spaces of nature. Here is a gigantic chorus acclaiming you through me (in some modest sense). Here is a cosmic choir of beauty praising you through the one new man forming one body in head and members, blended as bridegroom and bride in one spirit. Here is the song of numberless species drowning out the horrible noise of the legions of evil. Their voice is like the sound of many waters, all the waters of nature, all the beings of the cosmos, joined in a thunderously roaring yet sweetest song, sound as charming as the sigh of a lover, more triumphant than the crescendo of all the finest orchestras in history playing in unison. For the voice is that of the gentle Jesus who is *pantocrator*, ruler of all things, proclaiming the praise that reduces to almost nothing all the snarling dispraise of those who transmogrify themselves into pure hate because you are pure love.

Praise

1. I praise you for your plan that makes us people of praise, a plan imitating in some way your oneness with your Son and your Spirit: one nature in three persons. So it is in the whole Christ: one Jesus in many members; all are in Jesus, all are Jesus. Father, Son, and Holy Spirit, each of you loves and praises the other persons distinctively yet your loving and praising are a co-loving and co-praising. So it is in the whole Christ: each of us distinctively loves and praises you, Father, yet each of us co-loves and co-praises with Jesus. I praise you for laving me as a baby in the holy waters of baptism. At that instant of purification and illumination I became your child capable of worshiping with Jesus, capable of lending my voice to his in praise, open to letting his voice praise in me. Dearest Father, let me always remain a child in heart, simple in faith, trusting .absolutely in your care, testifying in love to the belief that it is *all true!* I praise you for allowing me to waver about my role as a co-praiser with Jesus. Though I have been feckless, out of my staggering about and lurching you have drawn fresh sturdiness, a ramrod posture of faith. Praise be to you for making golden all the dross of my halting praise. I praise you: at every moment Jesus is praising in and through me, in every second of consciousness I can praise you with Jesus. How precious now is my least word of praise in union with Jesus! A sort of gabbler at times clinging to things divine only by the thinnest thread, now I can reach up in an instant to your throne, laud your wonders before your very Face, sing your perfections with praise beyond compare. The healing touch of Jesus that made the blind see, the deaf hear, the dumb speak, the crippled walk, and the diseased sound makes my languid praise vibrant, sets my cold heart on fire with the extolling of your name. How can I thank and praise you for this gift of praise of Jesus, indeed for the gift of praise that is Jesus? How can my praise image your gift? In one way only: in return for Jesus I give you Jesus. He is your praise: let him be my praise of you. I offer you the

praise that is Jesus: with the everything that is Jesus, your perfect image, I praise you.

2. I praise you, Father, for making my praise one with the sweet yoke of love. Your wisdom weds Jesus, the bridegroom, and my soul, the bride, in an act of love that is praise. In connecting praise with love, you enable me to leap over the divide separating praiser and praised. My act of loving praise and praiseful love in union with Jesus reflects the incomparable praiseful love and loving praise that eternally and reciprocally streams among the holy three: Father, Son, and Spirit, each of you is one act of love, one act of praise without end.

I cannot praise you with the tongues of men and angels, I am not endowed with prophecy that reads secrets of divine knowledge, I cannot claim faith that moves mountains, I am not moved to strip myself of everything to feed the poor, I quail at the thought of handing my body over to be burned. Bereft of these gifts and generous desires, I can still praise you in the highest possible way, I can praise you with the agape-love of Jesus. Without Jesus every gift is worth exactly nothing (1 Cor 13.1-3). With him and with his love-infused praise alone, apart from the gifts called charisms, I have everything. Praise be to you, Father, for Jesus-praise and Jesus-love: this is the loving praise that covers a multitude of sins in my cumbrous, vacant-minded stabs at prayer, that wins forgiveness for my eyes glazed before your presence in the numberless wonders of your creation. What a treasure is this praise in and with Jesus! Prophecy will cease, those speaking in tongues will fall silent, supplication and contrition will cede place to fulfillment and sinlessness, but praise, like charity, will never come to a stop (1 Cor 13.13). I praise you for emboldening me to praise and praise again though my praise is ungainly and faltering, like the initial phrases of a person abashedly trying to speak a foreign language. Confused and vacillating as it is, at times childish in its lalling, my praise becomes, when one with Jesus's praise, childlike. Stiff and unfluent though it may be, my praise harbors a little finger of light that will not go out, destined to blaze one day into a globe of unquenchable fire, to be fused with all the praises of the saints and angels in a super-sun of light and love continuously glorifying you, Father, along with your Son and Spirit, in the eternal day that is yourself.

3. So enamored of life and mind have been some ancient and modern thinkers that they claimed that all nature is alive and capable of perception and aspiration. Unfortunately for this view, stones give no evidence of knowledge and desire in the usual sense. I praise you, Father, for your plan that bids man surmount the wall that isolates speechless nature from himself. I praise you for having Jesus choose to reveal you to my soul (Mt 11.25-27). In you I can know myself and in you I can also know myself in relation to nature and, in a sense, nature in me. Out of yourself emanate all creatures, united in a gigantic ensemble, each bound to turn back to you because it has come forth from you. All the energies of creation below

man are offered to you, their hands upraised in an unbroken chain of praise sung through mind and heart like mine. In the voice of sun and moon and stars I praise you. With the voice of all the fish and flora in the seas I praise you. In the name of fire and rain, winds, mountains and hills, reptiles and birds and cattle I praise you. In unison with all my brothers and sisters in the flesh, prestigious and lowly, old folk and mere striplings, I praise your beautiful name. Glory, glory, glory to you, agelessly and limitlessly loving Father! May all creation ever without end sing in matchless melody the magnificence of your dear name!

I praise you, Father, for the love-praise bridging the gulf between my heart and the rest of nature. Perhaps virtually all of this megalo-cosmos lies beyond my ken, yet now some light shines through its mists because of the love and praise your heart planted in mine. In some very vague manner my questions about nature have been answered by love, my ache of alienation healed by a sympathy with creation through your priceless love. Praise to you: my hunger for a total analysis of the nexus between myself and nature has been assuaged by the praise that makes me a fellow chorister with all of the material world. Now I glimpse the deeper meaning of nature: alive and ringing with praise, my praise, it is divinely alive with the praise of Jesus, it is a super-grand cathedral whose adorers and praisers give themselves to you, Father, in the self-giving of Jesus. Praise to you for making all of nature one in man and one in the God-man in one cosmos-exciting cry: Amen! Alleluia! I praise you for the world-choir in which hydrogen and oxygen, grasses and trees of the forest, roosters and rabbits, horses and dogs sing in harmony: Amen! Alleluia! I praise you for making me a part of man, the steward and keeper of the garden that is the world, who carries the chant to a spiritual pitch: Amen! Alleluia! Above all I praise you for Jesus, the man of men, the God of God, who makes all the singing supremely and divinely one in his heart. Jesus is the incarnate Amen and Alleluia, he is complete praise, perfectly intimate with you, Father, perfectly praising your name in himself. Once again, Father, I praise you for giving me the golden key to the meaning of nature and myself in Jesus. In praise and love I vault to the apex and center that all of nature in the new creation quests for — Jesus, divine being of praise and love. I praise you; in that wonderment and praise I can know all things; along with all my cosmic kin I need only lovingly praise you in one vast choir, I need only sing with Jesus to become, like him, an incarnate amen and alleluia.

The Jesus-Heart, a Sacrifice of Praise

Borne up to realms divine, Augustine felt joys not of this world. "The delights of our spirit are the divine songs in which even weeping is not without joy."[14] Supersensuous pleasures these — joys of spiritual taste and touch and embrace captivating and enchanting the soul past description. The words of God, however, ravish only the heart that gives itself to him in response to his self-giving. "God is with us so that we may be with him."[15] The self becomes totally his here in order that it may not be here. Wholly absorbed in his lightsome word, the self is raised from the here of earth to the not-here of heavenly affections. Only those who have actually experienced these interior delectations can best grasp what Augustine is driving at: "How can anyone who has not tasted it within himself understand this good of the heart when described by someone else?"[16] If never so blessed, we can at least point out the path leading to it: a glad sacrifice of praise, one not of rams or bulls but of the heart singing the name of God. We offer voluntary sacrifice when we praise God gratis and disinterestedly, simply and solely for his own sake. Indeed it is foolish to beg for the whole earth from the Maker of heaven and earth who wants to enrich us with all of himself. Rather, if we are supernaturally astute, we praise God simply because he is all-holy and goodness unlimited, sheerly because he is God. Out of his own experience Augustine could say without the smallest tincture of extravagance: "My psalter is my joy."[17] But it was a joy born of psalming "in the presence of the angels,"[18] i.e., with celestial lights, a joy open only to those who self-obliviously offer themselves through Jesus as a total sacrifice of praise.

In praising God, we are lifted out of ourselves. The earthly word we sing carries us up to the Word praising in the bosom of the Father. "All the way to heaven is heaven," said St. Catherine of Siena, "because Jesus who is with us said, 'I am the way.'" Outwardly on earth, inwardly we soar to the heights of heaven in union with Jesus: our "life is hidden with Christ in God" (Col 3.5). We belong to God in Jesus, and, when we praise the Father in the Son through the Spirit we become piercingly aware that we are his and he is ours. By his power God dwells in us on earth, and by our praise of faith and love we dwell in him in heaven.

> The delights of our spirit are the divine songs in which even weeping is not without joy. For the man of faith journeying as an exile in this world no memory is more gladdening than that of his home city from which he started his journey; but the remembrance of his city is not without sorrow and sighing. Still the sure hope of returning home consoles and buoys us up when we grow downcast during our journey. Let the words of God ravish your heart and let your God to whom you belong claim his own possession, that is, your mind, so as to keep heart and mind from being diverted to something other than himself. To each of you I say: be wholly here so as to be not here. In other words, be wholly in the word of God, which resounds on earth, so that you may be raised up by it and thus no longer be on earth. Hence God indeed is with us so that we may be also with him. He descended to us to be with us, he causes us to ascend to him to be with him. During his earthly sojourn he did not disdain to share our exile's journey, for he who made all things is nowhere an exile.[19]

Grasped by the word of God, we can grasp him more closely, more lovingly, within the secret chambers of our heart. We are no longer exiles, or, perhaps better put, outwardly exiles, we still plod forward as pilgrims on the way back to our homeland, but inwardly we no longer feel like exiles because within we taste the presence of him who nowhere can be an exile in the universe made. We experience this union when we gladly offer a sacrifice of praise to the Lord. Elatedly, voluntarily, unstintingly we offer all of self as a sacrificial offering to him who has given all of self to us and in his Son has sacrificed all for us. In so praising God, we desire nothing but God; nothing that he has made, not even all possible riches of the earth heaped up before us; nothing but the Maker of heaven and earth; nothing but the God of love who enriches us with his love; nothing but the God who makes our heart sing and dance with his own joy. The Christian message of self-donation is the most exhilarating in the whole world yet all too often it seems frustrating to those trudging along paths far below the peak of perfect self-sacrifice. Wholly disinterested love, absolute self-giving, seems beyond attainment — a conclusion sadly extracted from personal experience even by some committed to a strict monastic pursuit of God. Perhaps it is only extraordinary saints, canonized and canonizable, who are able to denude themselves as far as possible of all egoism in this life. Probably the great majority of those seeking God seem called to be ordinary saints, individuals of commendable virtue yet besmudged with selfishness. But the call to ordinary sanctity is still a lofty vocation to self-giving whose source is the infinite self-giving of the holy three. Whatever the measure of the self-annihilation attained, it can come only from "the riches of the wisdom and knowledge of God" (Rom 11.33). However incomprehensible his ways and counsels in concrete particulars, his wisdom unfailingly prescribes mercy, his knowledge constantly appoints compassion to lift us out of ruts and encourage us to rise higher and higher. Because he is all goodness, his only desire is to diffuse his goodness as widely and deeply as our hearts will allow it room. As we endeavor to praise him just because he is good, he blesses us with more of his goodness, portions to us more of his selflessness that frees us from subjection to lesser things, and touches us with the divine equivalent of a simplicity that un-compromisingly concentrates our hearts and lives on him alone.

"I will voluntarily offer you sacrifice" (v. 8). How can anyone who has not tasted it understand this good of the heart when described by another? What does this mean: "I will voluntarily offer you sacrifice"? Nevertheless, I will try to describe it. If you are able to understand it, do so as much as you can. If you are unable, believe it and pray that you become able to understand it. Should we indeed skip over this verse without venturing an interpretation? I say to you in your charity: my love for this verse strongly draws me to say something about it, and I thank God that you are listening attentively. If I noticed that listening discomfited you, I would reluctantly pass over this verse in silence, and yet, inasmuch as the Lord deigned to grant me words, in my heart I would not pass over it in silence. So let my tongue utter the ideas my heart has conceived, let my voice express the thoughts stored in my mind. Let us say, so far as we can, what the words, "I will voluntarily offer you sacrifice," mean. What shall I take sacrifice to mean here? Or what shall I worthily offer to the Lord for his mercy? Shall I look for victims from a flock of sheep, shall I pick out a ram, shall I try to spot some bull in the herds, shall I bring incense, the real article from the land of the Sabeans? What shall I do? What shall I offer except what God specifies: "A sacrifice of praise shall honor me" (Ps 49 [50].23). Then why is the word "voluntarily" used? This is why: I love gratis, without self-interest, the object I praise. I praise God and I rejoice in that very praise. I rejoice in praising the God whose praise never makes me blush out of chagrin. For he is not praised as a charioteer or hunter or any sort of actor is hailed by a devotee of theatrical frivolities. Their praisers appeal to others to join them in praising and urge them to cheer along with them: and though they all have cheered, often they all have to blush when their hero goes down in defeat. It is not so with our God. Praise him freely, love him with a heart of charity, love and praise him gratis. What does "gratis" mean? We praise him gratis when we praise him for his own sake, not for the sake of something else. For if you praise God so that he may give you something other than himself, you are no longer loving God gratis. You would blush with shame if your wife loved you simply because you were rich and, if you were reduced to poverty, would start thinking about adultery. Since then you want to be loved gratis by your spouse, are you going to love God for any reason other than God? What recompense are you counting on from God, greedy man that you are? He holds in store for you not the earth but himself who made heaven and earth. "I will voluntarily offer you sacrifice." Don't do it out of necessity. For if you praise God for any reason other than himself, you are praising him out of necessity. If you already had in your possession what you love, with this attitude you would not praise God at all. Notice what I am saying. Suppose you praise God in order to get a large sum of money. If you were to obtain a large sum of money from another source, not from God, you wouldn't bother praising God, would you? Then if you praise God to get money, you are not voluntarily offering sacrifice to God, you are offering sacrifice out of necessity because you love not God but something else, whatever it may be. So we are told, "I will voluntarily offer you sacrifice." Despise all things, fix your eyes on him alone. These things he has given you are good because their Giver is good. For unquestionably he does give, he gives these temporal goods to some for their weal, to others for their woe, according to the height and depth of his judgments. Before the abyss of these judgments the Apostle trembled in awe when he said: "O the depth of the riches of the wisdom and knowledge of God! How inscrutable are his judgments and how unsearchable his ways! For who will penetrate his ways and who will comprehend his counsels?" (Rom 11.33-34). He knows when to give and to whom to give, when to take away and from whom to take away. Ask in the present for what will benefit you in the future, ask for what will benefit you for eternity. But love him gratis because in what comes from his hands you will find nothing that he gives is better than himself, or, if you do find something better, then ask for that. "I will voluntarily offer you sacrifice." Why is it offered voluntarily? This is why: it is offered gratis. What does "gratis" mean? It means this: "And I will praise your name, Lord, because it is good (v.8)." I praise it for no other reason than this: it is good. Does the psalmist say, "I will praise your name, Lord, because you give me fruitful lands, because you give me gold and silver, because you give me enormous wealth, a large sum of money, a very lofty status"? Not at all. But what does he say? He says, "Because it is good." I find nothing better than your name. So "I will praise your name, Lord, because it is good."[20]

The soul that utterly gives itself to God, holding nothing back, wanting only him, sacrificing the whole world if need be for him, sacrificing its most prized possessions, its bodily life if so constrained for the sake of the beloved — such a soul is touched, enfolded by, then filled with the joy of the Lord to whom it abandons itself. The love it gives him is his own divine love first infused by his Spirit, then offered to him in return. So the joy that transverberates it is also not of this world. It is a divine joy, a joy of the Spirit of Jesus, concealed from the eyes of those wrapped up in themselves or seduced by the pleasures of this world. Such joy sets the faces of the souls of martyrs aglow, makes their spirits luminous and glad in dark, filthy dungeons, starts their hearts dancing as they are led to execution. When we sing the praises of God with all of our heart, then we participate in some measure in this out-of-this-world joy. Our divine singing, our praising in the heart, is a divine joy: we hymn the Lord in the presence of his angels always standing before the holy three to sing their praises.

"And I will sing psalms to you in the presence of men, my joy

arising from higher goods in the presence of the angels'' (v. 3).
It is not in the presence of men but in the presence of the angels
that I sing psalms. My psalter, my psalm-singing, is my joy.
But my joy arising from lower goods occurs in the presence of
the angels. For the wicked man knows nothing of the joy of the
man of virtue. "There is no joy for the wicked, says the Lord"
(Is 48.22, 57.21). The wicked man rejoices in his tavern, the
martyr in his chains. In what ways did Crispina rejoice, the
holy woman whose feast we are celebrating today? She rejoiced
when she was arrested, when she was haled before the judge,
when she was thrown into prison, when in chains she was
brought out of jail, when she was lifted up on the scaffold, when
she was given a hearing, when she was sentenced to death. In
all these circumstances she rejoiced; yet these miserable people
deemed miserable a woman who was then rejoicing in the
presence of the angels.[21]

Reflections

1. In the late 1970's newspapers and magazines detailed the tragedy
of the boat people, refugees who fled the brutalizing and sickening oppression of Communism in Vietnam, Laos, and Cambodia. These wretched
people had to tear up their roots, abandon their homelands, each of which
had been turned into a kind of prison camp, a slave state run by Marxist
masters with the smoothly lying tongues and hard eyes and murderous
hands of polished gangsters.[22] Wherever they settled, their spirits still ache
with loneliness. Akin to the boat people were the D.P.'s, the displaced
persons, driven from their homes by the devastation of war and fear of
Soviet rule during and after World War II. The alienation the boat people
and the D.P.'s experienced so keenly was felt to a lesser degree by millions
of Germans, Irish, Italians, and Poles and, more recently, by Cubans, Puerto
Ricans, and Mexicans who came, at times in waves, to the United States,
most in search of a higher standard of living during the nineteenth and
twentieth centuries. However prosperous an immigrant, he cannot help
casting a fond eye overseas to the old country that bore and nursed him,
whose memories are woven in all the fibers of his heart. The abstract term
"social mobility" that rolls so facilely from the tongue betokens separation,
sorrow, a hole in the heart. How orphaned, how disoriented an exile feels.
Yet the sense of loss paining an alien is only a slight sign of the alienation
paining every human heart, in which you, Lord, implant a longing for a
far-off country, a supernatural home. I am a wanderer, a displaced person
on this earth. Father, though you created me an earth animal, you have
called me to my true home in heaven. So within me is this panting for
my abode in your kingdom. I do long for you, I desire to dwell in the courts
of your love forever. Often the longing is faint, the desire flickering and
short-lived. Set me free with your love, let me be nothing but love; then

my desire will be an élan, an upward thrust, ever reaching out to you, undistracted by passing fuss and bustle. How near that lofty new dimension at times seems yet how far off sinful ways put it. Touch me anew with the Spirit of Jesus: then will I burn with the intensest of desires for union with you as I journey onward. Bring me to taste again and again, unforgettably, your delights in psalms and other prayers to thread my weeping with joy. Because a wanderer, I have to know worry and depression and a sense of failure and inner defeat, but, while in exile, I can live by your love in my true home, your precious bosom. As my yearning daily increases, pleasure in the prospect of seeing you will daily grow apace. Time is short — like every human being, I am living on borrowed time. Come, Father, teach me through Jesus the secret of feeling the joy of home while being in exile, the key to rejoicing in your rest while making my pilgrimage here below.

2. Father, through the Spirit of Jesus you send forth your word continuously. Just as rain and snow fall from the sky to fertilize the earth and to furnish bread, your word flows from your infinite wisdom to take root in and grow to harvest in the human heart (Is 55.10-11). Make my heart soft and open, ready to let your word sink its roots deep, deep, seizing my heart with its light and power, becoming so one with it that its wisdom will be inscribed in my questings and struggles, my sufferings and frustrations. Captured and transfixed by your word, I will focus on your kingdom, seeking divine things first, untouched by the lure of lesser things. A narrow approach? Indeed, but broad in its consequences. Purified by your holy word, I can embrace all other things, seen as stemming from and hanging upon you. Living by faith affords room for "all other things besides" (Mt 6.33). Father, make me wholly here so as not to be here. Saturate me with your word. Seeing, as your word tells it, the universe oriented by your love, I will take on wings and be lifted to a heavenly realm. A few years ago as a woman who works in a downtown office building was about to enter one section of the building, another woman held the door for her and favored her with a warm, winning smile. A casual encounter, but her heart was joyed and energized by that fugitive smile. Father, you spoke to her in that transitory smile, an echo of your word of love sent her spirit briefly bounding upward. In every passing event you are smiling at me, indirectly speaking your word to me, reminding me that my heaven is in the making right now on earth. Your infinite love has planned each occurrence to reveal your heavenly smile so as to evoke in my heart a smile reflecting your joy.

On November 29, 1980, two days after Thanksgiving Day, Dorothy Day died. Fittingly her life reached its end as the 1980 liturgical year came to an end; fittingly, many of her friends believed, she entered immediately into glory: her Advent would be itself a celebration of an unending Christmas. If some of her concrete socio-political opinions were not altogether convincing, these slight shadows were swallowed up in the bliss of her simple, austere, resolute devotion to and service of the poor. Cardinal

Spellman once called her "another Francis of Assisi who walked the streets of New York."[23] The love and compassion that moved Jesus when he saw the crowds close to fainting from physical and spiritual hunger stirred her heart at the sight of bums, social rejects, the wreckage of New York City. Father, a self-sacrificing woman of such spiritual steel must have been blessed by familiarity with your heavenly life. When she fed the poor and handed out clothes to down-and-outers in the slum called the Bowery, she saw your Son Jesus in their wasted faces and watery eyes and disheveled, smelly apparel, and in and through him was lifted up to move about in a region not of this world. Lacking the mettle for such a heroic vocation, I must discover Jesus in less exacting circumstances. Awaken me to Jesus speaking your uplifting word in the most routine of events. As I stroll to the library, let me discern the face of your beloved Son. In the bite of the wintry air let me thank him for the legs that bear me forward. As I sit at community table swapping trivia with the brethren, let me hear the voice of Jesus. Give me the self-discipline to hang on the words of others as if listening to the Master himself. From time to time I meet a retired priest, the hardening of whose arteries has clouded his mind. Encourage me to offer him more than perfunctory cordial remarks: let my heart go out to his heart as to the very heart of Jesus, and so through Jesus will my heart truly leap from earth to heaven. In your will every encounter is to be a door opening into your courts, every happening a gateway to heaven here and now, every incident a partial unveiling of your secret presence.

In recent years I have been privileged to be the beneficiary of one whose special charism seems to be a gift of penning long, informative, unpretentiously spiritual letters, every one of which excites the heart to fresh love of you, Father, and affords a glimpse into a soul residing in a heavenly dimension. Shake me once more out of my laziness, train my inward eye to count every event a part-letter indirectly conveying your word, tenderly yet forcibly bidding me to go up higher, perhaps to the first seats at the banquet table. Faith, give me more faith in Jesus and I will be able to read your billets-doux, your love letters, inviting me to your embrace.

3. Jesus, your name is Emmanuel, God-with-us, so that our name may be we-with-God. In your descent among us you fulfilled your desire to be where we are so that through your ascension we may be where you are. Out of love for the Father you chose to walk the earth as an exile with us. Treading the path of a pilgrim, you knew, in the depths of your human nature in a way inscrutable to us, some of the sense of alienation of the traveler seeking the lasting city, a feeling that touched bottom in the dereliction that wrung from you the cry from the cross, "My God, my God, why have you forsaken me?" (Mt 27.46). Yet as Maker of all you were present to all and stranger to none. In any case, you were never alone. At every instant you were in perfect communion with your Father, you and he locked in the most rapturous of embraces. At no moment were the lips of your soul not pressed to his and in that continuous ecstasy binding him

and you in the Holy Spirit you heard every one of his words of love, so that you could do nothing on your own, love's sweet urging impelling you to speak only as he told you. You were immersed in his word, living by it alone. Come, Jesus, clasp me in your arms, take me up to the Father through the power of your ascension. Then communing with you, I will commune with him. Through you I will press my lips to his and in that kiss begin to hear his word with all my heart. In that embrace I will be consumed by the desire to do always only what pleases him (Jn 8.28-29).

On a high mountain, usually said to be Mount Tabor, to your inner circle, Peter, James, and John, you showed yourself as a living sun. Swept up in your ecstasy, they knew the shekinah, the very glory of God. The vision, however, aburptly ended, the cloud evaporated, and, putting aisde as a sheer wish the impetuous idea of setting up tents on the mountain, they had made their way to Jerusalem, on the outskirts of which they would silently witness you prostrate in agony in the garden of olives. Jesus, do not reckon me presumptuous or spiritually greedy if I make an apparently bold request: I would like to see your glory. Of course not by sight, not in an ecstasy, overshadowed by a cloud. Let me know your glory by faith, even by the simplest faith naked of all images, barren of all consolations. Manifest yourself to me, not shining like the sun, not arrayed in dazzling white but in faith alone. Long years afterward Peter, James, and John must have reenacted that scene again and again in memory. Reveal your transfigured self to me so that I can never forget that you are my brother, my companion, my dearest friend, my precious lover. Once a relative sent me a small plaque on which were painted the words, "Someone loves you," to spark courage on days when the temperature within the soul dips to an arctic low. Show yourself, Jesus: then I will be bolstered by the knowledge that "Someone loves me" — Someone who takes me into his arms and lets my heart nestle in his. Your unyielding love is enough to overshadow and wrap me in the brightest of your glory accessible even now by faith. Then I can burst out with the enthusiasm of Peter, "Lord, it is good for us to be here!" (Lk 9.33). How good it is to view your glory at the top of an invisible mountain, how blessed to hear the words of the Father, "This is my beloved Son on whom my favor rests. Listen to him" (Mt 17.5). As I become absorbed in you spiritually transfigured, I can listen to you with the utmost attention, with the firmest desire to obey and follow you. I hear you speak those heart-rending words portending horror yet awful in the unsurpassable love they promise, "The Son of Man must first suffer much, be rejected by the elders, chief priests, and scribes, [and] be put to death" (Lk 9.22). I must make my way to Jerusalem, I must suffer so as to enter fully into glory. A dismaying prospect: can I still honestly say, "Lord, it is good for us to be here"? With you at my side I can say yes, Lord, it is good: good because, within, you are bearing the cross with me; good because the glory of the not-here of your ascended presence becomes one with the suffering of the here on earth; good because you infuse the goodness of the Father into my cowardly spirit; good because the cross will gradually transfigure me into your image. O my Jesus, how good it is to hear your words about the cross of death that gives life, how good it is to be transformed into the very likeness of your inward life.

Praise

After you created all things in the beginning, Father, you surveyed your handiwork and found that it was good, indeed very good (Gen 1.31). How could a universe making its exodus from your infinite goodness be other than good? I praise you for being good — absolutely you alone are good (Lk 18.19). Beings distinct from you are somewhat good because their goodness rises from and leads back to your goodness. Glory to you, Father, for always seeking to have us partake of your goodness, to feel the overflow of your joy. Even as I journey as a stranger in a twilight world begloomed by sins and follies, you will not deny your own nature. You have to be and do good for me. In my exile you put into my heart divine songs of love that delight my spirit, that weave the silver lining of joy into clouds that weep. I praise you too for filling my cup of joy to the brim, even after my sins have made the world a bleaker place. How can I cease glorifying your name! O good Lord, who are purest goodness, I praise you; you simply will not stop being good to me no matter how often I have played the vagabond or with molelike blindness clung to prideful ways.

A lover writes to his absent beloved, "I miss you" — a reserved way of saying, "I need you, all of you, I cannot live without you; come to me or let me go to you." I praise you, Father, for letting me feel empty at your absence so that I can murmur, "Father, I miss you." How lovely you are, dearest one, God of my heart! How I hunger for your presence, how I want to have your arms wrapped around me! Glory to you for the mystery of your love for me; in seeking me, you are saying, in effect, "I miss you."

I praise you, Father, not for alienation — how could I ever be wholly happy apart from you — but for loneliness whetting awareness of my need for you, stirring afresh my love for you. To the irreligious ear this may sound nonsensical, but you are all-good, good beyond any stretch of imagination. I wander far from home but every step of my pilgrimage can be a closer link to you in all your inwardness. What delights of weeping are mine, how precious is the void within me! I praise you because the tears turn my face upward. Glory to you for telling me in my separation from you, "I possess you now in your not possessing me fully." How irresistible your goodness, how unflagging your pursuit of me! Let my spirit magnify your name for the "folly" of your insatiable love for me. Let praise, praise a million, a billion, a trillion times over, rise up in your presence attesting that I want to love you with boundless love, that I do not want to be outdone by your love, that I can never stop thanking you for you.

2. I praise you, Father of lights, for not permitting me to be gulled

into faith-denying darkness. Today many academicians are struggling to discover new methods of emancipating themselves from our sensate culture that entombs the soul in worldly success. However earnest, their endeavors to transcend self are stultified by spirit-destroying techniques they experiment with. I beg you, send forth extraordinary streams of your merciful light to loose these misled seekers from the novel death-traps into which their spirits have been tricked. I praise you for grounding me in your sober, enchanting truth. I can never stop thanking you for throttling any temptation of my sometimes overcurious spirit to search for expansion of mind in peyote or LSD; or to locate the meaning of the universe in absorption in Universal Mind; or to look for satori in trafficking with demon-gods; or to expect redemption in the art of sorcery. For always keeping your hand on me and sparing me from delusive devices of pseudo-mysticism, I praise you. Bound in your word, I am free. Because you possess me as your own, I possess my own spirit. Glory to you for satisfying me with this in-your-Spirit union, so sparing me from a ruinous hunt for out-of-the-body experiences.

Borrowing the words of Jesus (Mt 11.25), I praise you, Father, for concealing your truth from the wise of this world and revealing it to little ones. Though the body of Christ requires acute and subtle teachers, I need not be brilliant to learn the inner meaning of our holy faith, I need only say yes to your invitation to covenant love that burns away layer after layer of my pride, and I will be taken wholly out of my lower self to abide in you. I need not scale mountains or traverse deserts, nor be initiated into secret lore and cultist language, nor dabble in mind-blowing techniques, nor sit under renowned gurus. All praise to you; no one can be so wholly beyond the earthly as you, yet I mount from the here of this world to the not-here of your divine world through unenchanting duties. Your Word taking on flesh makes every place a haunt of the divine, every happening a shrine of your special presence. In Jesus I can transcend, without voiding, my self, and rise to live in the center of your life. In his life that was love through and through I come to understand your word: it is truth working in love, love lit up by truth. Irradiated by your love, I can be a messenger and minister of your word: at any moment, raised up to your presence, I can be used to speak the truth in love so as to raise others from the here of earth to the not-here of your bosom.

3. In a life parceled out in minutes, hours, and days my strivings must come to terms with time — all things take time and patience. For minds capable of conceiving things timeless, time can come to look like a cavern pitch-black save for tiny pulses of lights. Yet I praise you, Father, for making me a subject of the kingdom of time, a yoke hallowed by your Son's subjection to time. I praise you for sowing in my heart a desire to be constantly enclosed in your presence; but also for not bringing this desire to fruition. I cannot help repeating this: how I yearn to be overshadowed by the cloud of your glory. But you enable me to see that such transfiguring

awareness is a gift bestowed as you will out of your infinite generosity. Your way is sufficient for me: without a heart vibrant with joy I know by faith that, while time-bound, I am being transformed from glory into glory (2 Cor 3.18) as you put your arms around me as surely as Joseph put his around the boy Jesus in Nazareth.

Praise to you, Father, for the transports you accorded a number of your saints. However, these were rare super-banquets, exceptions to the daily bread of the spirit with which you nourish your own. Practically all your saints traveled the beaten path most of their lives. Praise to you for working a transfiguration cloaked by the commonplace. How wonderful you are in your saints! How extra-marvelous you are in saints like Joseph, so close to and intimate with Jesus, yet largely lost to us in the silence about nearly every detail of his life. Praise to you for making Joseph holy as you are holy, for making him your image on earth. Because you channeled your affection for Jesus through Joseph, he could, as you did, say, "This is my son — how I love him!" Praise to you for the light of providence in Joseph unerringly directing the holy child in their home at Nazareth.[24] What tender wisdom in one man! Yet he trod the path of the ordinary, leaving behind no pregnant phrases, no memorable gems of wisdom. I praise you for Joseph, among the greatest of the great, outwardly nondescript, inwardly splendid through your transfiguring power flowing through Jesus. To praise you more lustily, give me more of the spirit of Joseph with which to watch and wait upon your love that works its mightiest miracles within, secluded from the vacant stares of men who judge by appearance alone.

Reflections

1. Sacrifice — this word conjures up hardship, toil, struggle, perhaps pain and suffering and, at the extreme, death. But sacrifice also evokes respect, admiration, reverence, perhaps awe in the presence of the heroic. As Augustine says, we have to personally experience sacrifice before we can properly understand it. It is a "good of the heart," a pearl of great price, whose weight bears us upward to your throne, Father. What sacrifice do you ask me to offer? Not simply material things, valuable though these may have been in the low-grade economy of the ancient world, such as a lamb, ram, bird, or costly imported incense. Of course you do relish material gifts, you are pleased, touchingly so, when men offer you the fruit of the sweat of their brows. The imposing cathedrals built in the age of faith still proclaim the sweetness of the sacrifice of material things. Men whose names are known only to you invested their raw materials, their tools, their labor in churches that still cry out to those with ears to hear, "God is alive! God is Lord!" As *Dominus*, Lord, you alone can claim strict dominion over all the goods of the universe. But you are more pleased with a sacrifice of praise; the offering of my heart is more gratifying in your eyes than the wealth of the whole world. A chapel of the spirit in the most destitute of

men is more majestic than all the cathedrals around the world. All the king-
doms of the world in all their glory, all the great cities of man, all the
libraries of famous universities — all these are so much chaff in comparison with the inner splendor of a single human spirit. Once again I sacrifice
my entire being to you, I return to you all of myself, soul and body, every
least spiritual quality and every cell. See, all, all that I am and have, is
yours: take it, kind Lord, letting it rise as a fragrant evening sacrifice.

Father, anoint this offering of my spirit with the unction of your Spirit.
So often I write with faith but little fervor, so often without meticulous
regard for the existential import of words. Occasionally I have leveled strictures on mere word-mongers, venting disapproval of gentlemen of the
media who lash out at prejudice yet not too cleverly trot out their prejudices
against your Church, journalists who, while bemoaning the lack of moral
fiber in political leaders, do not scruple to wallow in various forms of self-
indulgence. It is so easy to score points while standing on the sidelines,
to toss off ringing slogans and eschew their practical implications. At times
I have dipped into verbalizing, uttering forceful phrases that go untrans-
lated into vigorous action. Rest your soothing hands upon my brow: then
will I not only speak but do the truth, then will I commit myself without
reserve to you, then will I offer you the sacrifice of myself.

Yet, Father, even when action fleshes out my bare rhetoric, I feel
unworthy to offer you sacrifice. After being newly set on fire, I lapse back
into lukewarmness. After being activated by your energy, I once again
hobble along in sloth. I am a sinful man, Lord. How tarnished is the offering
that is myself, how blotched with egoism. But in Jesus your Son, my closest
confidant, my dearest lover, I can make bold to approach you. The offering
of the Lamb of God, the most innocent and helpless of victims, purifies
my guilt-ridden and weakness-laden offering. As my offering goes up to
you, let your eyes fall on Jesus alone. You cannot say no to the all-pleasing
yes that is Jesus, you can say nothing but yes to my sacrifice become one
with his.

Such an offering invests death as well as life with point and value.
Apart from you, Father, death empties the greatest of secular lives of
meaning that no memorial-service grandiloquence can supply. Apart from
you death not only trivializes a single life but renders the whole of human
history senseless. But in union with Jesus I can surmount the dread of death
and the meaninglessness it inflicts. In recent years a lifelong Catholic
agonized as the cancer that had invaded his bones caused arms and legs
to break like matchsticks. Still his passage was one of peace and joy because
every day he faced death with the sober thought, "This may be the last
day of my life." Fr. Solanus Casay, a saintly Capuchin who died on July
31, 1957, evidenced perhaps a more moving mastery of death. Nearly
drained of strength as his life ebbed away in a Detroit hospital, he suddenly
sat bolt upright and exuberantly announced: "I give my soul to Jesus

Christ." Then, slumping backwards, he departed moments later.[25] His remarkable testimony culminated a life of self-oblation, daily iterated to you, Father, through Jesus. Father, teach me to live in the prospect of death, day by day uttering in word and action Fr. Solanus's sacrifice of praise. In the sacrifice of Jesus each of the fleeting bits of my life can take on eternal moment all-destroying death can be enlisted to minister to life lifted up in sacrifice.

2. Earthly loyalties and enthusiams frequently wind up disappointed. As Augustine observes, the athlete we feverishly try to root to victory often goes down in defeat. Father, cynosure of our existence, we never become crestfallen if we seek to love you for your own sake, not for a flush of fleeting glee when our favorite flashes first across the finish line. Yet how can we love you gratis, with absolutely no self-regard? In a dispute that raged some centuries ago certain theologians argued that a total elimination of self-interest seems impossible. This is not the place to reopen that controversy. Let it suffice to trust in your mercy to empower us to love you just because you are you, our Father. According to Augustine, some individuals, only feigning to love you, love out of avarice or vaulting ambition that recruits you to promote their wordly success. Such virtue is really vice, such love of God is really love of a god, idolatry of a manipulable otherworld monarch to be cajoled and wheedled by mechanical ritual into boosting income. I hope it is not blindness to think that you have delivered me from love of self masked as love of you. Yet freedom from irreligious religion still leaves me far from perfect detachment. Though I daily reconsecrate myself, I still cling to things of earth and lower impulses. How can I ever totally surrender to you alone? The witness of others fuels my desire to be the bond-servant of your heart. After the death of a young, holy Sister of St. Joseph whom I was privileged to know, one friend in her Chestnut Hill teaching community summed up her sanctity in three words: "She gave herself." How did she give herself unconditionally? Certainly by humility; no doubt she served him in the children she taught. Her daily prayer for humility was probably brief, to the point, simple, joyful, perhaps similar to the familiar aspiration that one spiritual woman keeps on her office desk for frequent recall: "Jesus, meek and humble of heart, make my heart like unto thine." Perhaps too she directly or indirectly prayed for the truth, the truth about herself, the truth about her Sisters and associates, some of whose actions she may have found at times disconcerting. Bring me into the truth, clothe me more in Jesus who is the truth. My inner self is in part malodorous. But do not hesitate, lay bare my vicious tendencies so that I can know myself as you know me, so that I can cry out more repeatedly for your healing that peels away hidden attachments. Cleansed of sordid ties, I will be able to love you the more for yourself. With some of the self-lessness remarkable in genuine human love the lover gladly does things ordinarily distasteful or unappealing simply for the sake of his beloved: "My darling," he says, "I am doing this for you." As Dostovieski said,

"To love someone is to see him as God intended him." Let me love you as my beloved, let me see you as you are intended to be known; then will I be able to pray, "Dearest Father, I love you and therefore I will do my best at this disagreeable job. I will spend my time and self doing just what you want. I love you, Father, or at least I am trying to love you — that is everything."

Father, give me the faith of Mary that flowered out in perfect love. O those beautiful words of hers, to be treasured and pondered in Marylike fashion again and again: "I am the servant of the Lord. Let it be done to me according to your word" (Lk 1.38). What a yes that was! What stupendous consequences were its issue! Mary said yes, and a new, the final, the greatest chapter in human history began. At that moment of the overshadowing of your Spirit your Son cast his lot with the human race. With her infused gifts of wisdom and knowledge Mary understood what a humanly insupportable burden was falling upon her shoulders, what terrifying trials lay ahead. All that was human in her may have recoiled at the prospect of being the mother of the Son of the Most High. Even if her reluctance had been magnified a million times over, Mary would have uttered her all-submissive yes. However powerful the tug of lower drives, the humble slave-girl of the Lord wanted you, God alone, only your will in any and all circumstances. Your will is love and power and beauty, and, no matter how staggering the office, your love and power and beauty were at her disposal or, more, were to be built into her very being. So pure was her faith that it glowed almost with the light of intuition in seeing that the all of your mercy supplied for her nothingness. You have formed me as your child to say a yes like that of Mary, not epoch-making, not world-transforming, but decisive and destiny-shaping for myself and perhaps for a few others. Overshadow my spirit with your Spirit, sheer off from my inner self all that is twisted and rotting. The words of Gabriel resound in my soul: "Nothing is impossible with God" (Lk 1.37). You can make my sterile soul big with self-sacrifice, you can turn wintry wastes in my spirit into land flowing with milk and honey.

3. Father, it is only by faith radiating love that I can come near to faintly discerning your wisdom in the distribution of goods. In Augustine's words, you know "when to give and to whom to give; when to take away and from whom to take away." Every life is shaped out of contingencies eluding strict scientific analysis, nonessentials somehow contributing to the core of personal existence. Your creative wisdom gathers up all the loose strings and bits, the odds and ends of each life, and weaves them into a tapestry. Some chance encounters seem quite significant. In 1591 at the age of twenty-four, while returning from law studies in Padua, Francis de Sales was denied space on a boat that had been hired by a well-to-do lady. Shortly thereafter the ship sank, with all on board lost.[26] Had Francis died that day, he would never have become a bishop, never co-founded the Visitation order, never penned his superb spiritual literature. Yet what of

those on board—why was it appointed that they be buried in a watery grave on that trip? Unsearchable mystery here. Indeed some mystery envelops the death of every individual. Apart from the millions hideously murdered by abortion, so many lissome youths die before maturity. Other individuals are cut down in their prime. Some pass away slowly, others drop dead in a moment. Humanly speaking, certain deaths seem without rhyme or reason. A mother in her late thirties succumbs to cancer while a woman in her nineties drags out a painful, near-senile existence in a nursing home. Goods of nature and wealth also seem unevenly apportioned. One youngster is born blind, another deaf, another lame with cerebral palsy, still another without arms. Marked differences occur along the spectrum of intelligence. Some are bright, the majority mediocre, some dull, a small number mentally handicapped and uneducable. Too what huge gaps obtain in economic opportunity. Hundreds of millions around the world live near or below the poverty line, scraping out a bare subsistence, with the doors barred even to elementary education. Many of the rock-bottom poor never visit a single doctor their whole lives long and lack ready access to modern medicine. Who can measure your mind, Father, who can fully fathom your plan? I can only adore you, stand reverently before your wisdom, endeavor to respond with love to your love. I can dimly catch snatches of the configuration of your plan only by growing in the height and depth and length and breadth of your love. Yes, it is by the love with which your Spirit anoints me that my heart can perceive what my mind cannot, in Pascal's phrase, "reasons that reason knows nothing of,"[27] reasons hidden in your all-loving bosom, Father.

In effect, Jesus urges me, "Ask for anything at all and I will give it to you." Through him, Father, send your Spirit of truth into me, enticing me to want only the truth, wooing my will to be wholly one with yours. Purge me of earthly desires, for it is only as I approach you with empty hands that I can be blessed with a heart full of grace.

Thus I will come to truly praise your name as you want it praised: because it is good. In becoming more detached, I will praise you more, and, in praising you more, I will become more detached. Though estranged from you in body and seeing through a glass darkly, I will feel less and less the alien. Throughout my checkered life you have been calling me, leading me to taste various goods and then to hunger again. Each savoring you intended as a sharing in your goodness that, as I was satiated, made me more hungry for you. What I have been panting for all these years is the goodness that is you: so I praise you, Father, simply and solely because you are good. Let my praise make me good with all your attributes, good particularly with your kindness and compassion, good with your very Godness. Made Godlike through this praise, I will voluntarily offer you sacrifice, the very goodness you have portioned to me through the Spirit of Jesus.

Praise

1. I praise you, Father, for accepting my sacrifice. Dwelling within your infinite life, diffusing infinite love within your own being, serene, incomprehensible bliss within, you need nothing, however invaluable, outside yourself. Were I to multiply the billions of galaxies a quadrillion times and the millions of species a quintillion times, this increase of external glory would add not one iota to your inner glory. Yet you generously choose to have my sacrifice glorify your name.

Praise to you for the gifts you lavish upon me: these I give back to you with glad heart. At the risk of tedium let me return to one theme. I praise you, dearest of Fathers, for simply bringing me into existence. From time to time there flashes across my mind the realization: I exist, I am alive! What a gift it is simply to live the life of a normal human being, enjoying the spectacle of life, eating, drinking, sleeping, thriving in mind and heart, sharing with friends. I praise you: how blessed I am to know you in Jesus! It is these gifts, natural and supernatural, that rouse, yes, thrill me to new inward melodies of praise. All-generous one, what return can I make, what recompense can I offer, except the prodigious gifts you have showered upon me? Glory to you, limitless goodness who require no exterior glory.

Praise to you for spurring me to make a voluntary sacrifice of praise. Not only do all gifts spring from your creative heart but the very spirit of sacrifice imitates your infinite generosity. Praise to you, Father: you give all of yourself, the all that is yourself, to your Son. Praise to you, Word of God: in return you eternally give yourself to the Father. Praise to you, Holy Spirit: you are the personalized love of Father and Son in their reciprocal self-giving. Praise to you, holy three: at the center of your infinite life lies the spirit of supreme self-giving that feeds my spirit of self-giving. Praise to you, holy trinity: you cannot sacrifice yourselves in our finite sense, for you are changeless, deathless, ever-faithful, ever-reliable in your love. Yet your triune self-giving that constitutes you as God is the divine super-equivalent of all genuine human sacrifice. Glory to you, Father, Son, and Holy Spirit: as God you are infinitely self-giving and, as infinitely self-giving, you are God. Praise to you, holy three: you could not be the three persons of the one true God if you did not eternally pour yourselves into one another. O God, how glorious you are! You are the all that is all self-giving. Gladly, with all the infinite power of your love, you give and give and give, without end, without limit, without restraint. Praise to you, holy three, for revealing yourself as total self-giving, as infinite self-donation.

But how can I measure measureless self-giving? Blessed be your holy name, Father, for, sensitive to the narrow range of a human mind, you chose to give as your greatest gift your Son incarnated as Jesus Christ. How can I ever stop praising you for disclosing yourself in Jesus. I bless you for making Jesus the way, the enfleshed image of your infinite generosity: he tells us, "He who sees me sees the Father" (Jn 14.9). You have always been one with Jesus, and he with you, and it was your work that he did on earth. Glory to you, Father, for that work of endlessly patient divine pity, a work of infinite self-giving transmitted through finite flesh. In Jesus I can haltingly, to a small degree, understand the boundless self-giving of you, your Son, and your Spirit that makes you God.

Now let me praise you, Jesus, since you are wholly one with the Father. I praise you for your passion and death on the cross: how voluntarily, how fully you gave yourself in this supreme sacrifice of praise. Glory to you: out of love you endured in those hours of horror all the punishment necessary — and much more — to expiate all the sins of self-worshipping man from the sin of Adam and Eve down to the last sin before the lightning-like arrival of the Day of the Lord. You gave all: there was no pain or suffering of body and soul to which you did not submit in order to satisfy for the unspeakable enormity of sin. Praise to you, sweet Lamb, beautiful image of the self-donation of the Father. You emptied yourself, becoming a worm and no man (Ps 22.6), shredded of every inch of dignity by your devilish killers. I praise you for showing me your thorn-crowned and bleeding heart as the symbol and reflection of the totally self-giving heart of your Father.

Praise to you, Jesus, for exhorting me to ask the Father anything at all in your name, with the guarantee that he will grant the request (Jn 14.12-14). Father, let my very praise of you count as an implicit petition entreating for the spirit of sacrifice of Jesus. As Jesus promised, you will work even greater miracles (Jn 14.12). Work this miracle in me, implant in me the very heart of Jesus, then I will offer you a sacrifice of praise voluntarily with a Jesus-heart, with all the unction and power of his imcomparable soul, so that in virtue of him who out of love became nothing I who am nothing can become all. Praise to you: I trust you, I believe that in some way you will insert in me the crucified heart of Jesus that alone can fully sing you a sacrifice of praise, that alone is perfectly nothing-ed, that alone is maximally childlike, your super-vessel of praise.

2. Are these desires bootless fancies, pseudo-devout follies? From the human standpoint they may look like castles in the air, almost comical fantasies. But I praise you, Father, for speaking with and in Jesus who tells me, "What is impossible with men is possible with God" (Lk 18.27). You can strip me of self and implant a Jesus-heart within. My past blunders, all my rock-ribbed selfishness counsel scepticism about a radical renovation. But I can do the impossible; rather, not I but you working by the power of the Spirit of Jesus can do the impossible in me.

Let me partake of your patience with me so that gradually, without adolescent haste, I can grow toward unconditional surrender. Glory to you, Father: give me courage to face myself, to drive out unhesitatingly one by one illusions clouding my vision and inflaming my passions. Let me love the truth about myself in you, throwing off all that is self-deceiving. In your truth show me the whole truth about myself, truth that, however searing, liberates me for total oblation.

Glory to you, Father, for the power of your word, "more piercing than any two-edged sword" that penetrates to my soul and spirit and lays open before your eyes all that I am (Heb 4.12-13). Let me praise you more ardently as you drive the sharpest and most burning of swords into my innermost parts, cutting away all that savors of evil and decay, cauterizing my wounds, washing my spirit clean in the white heat of your light. Glory to you for this piercing thrust that makes me docile to your truth. How brutalizing exposure to the truth can be in a purely secular setting. Here I am, the soul is forced to say: I am nothing but a phony, a whited sepulchre, bloated with corruption. Praise to you for mildly revealing the truth about myself in love. Your kindness calms my fears and extrudes merely human shame as I see myself in your judgment of mercy softening the glare of truth. O Father, how can I praise you enough for your love, in which I no longer turn the blind eye to the man within, in which I praise you for letting me know myself as you know me.

Father, I beg you, let my praise of your gentle might win an additional request: give me also a Mary-heart. As soon as Gabriel affirmed your miracle-working power in the words, "Nothing is impossible with God" (Lk 1.37), Mary said her irrevocable yes to your invitation to become the mother of your Son. Along with Mary I magnify your name and exult in you, my saving strength, who empowered her to utter that absolutely decisive yes. Endow me with her iron determination, her meek but unswerving resoluteness, then with her faith I will know that there is nothing you cannot, nothing you will not, do for a soul thirsting for your truth and love alone. All praise to you, most faithful in all your promises. Once I am gifted with her heart, every act will be a yes, a sacrifice of praise. With her heart I can transfer my mountains of pride and vanity into the sea, I can live confidently in your liberating word, I can, in some small measure, carry and bring forth Jesus to breathe new life into dead souls and to help your kingdom wrest one more slice of territory from minions of the prince of darkness.

3. All-just one, I offer you a sacrifice of praise for the order in nature and history out of which, in a manner imperceptible to human eyes, you are harvesting a cornucopia. The enormous differences among men you are knitting into a pattern you promise to unveil in all its beauty at the end of time. I praise you, Father, for your mercy in between the faith-testing lines of human history. Even a human mind capable of scientifically mastering all the laws of nature would be hopelessly baffled by the enigmas of history. Praise to you for this mystery of history since the greater the mystery, the greater the guarantee of your mercy.

Praise to you for your unfailing mercy to the hearts of men whose pride and injustice poison and corrode the human city. Ever-patient Father, your justice scoops up in its net those who abjure your dominion. Through your almost-paradoxical kindness the more bitter the revolt against your plan of love, the more abundant are the outpourings of your mercy. O what love, O what mercy is yours, Father! However repulsive the treachery, however acrid the scorning of your word, you ever reply with more mercy. How can I ever offer you praise commensurate with mercy that seems to always turn the other cheek. When a rebel shakes a fist of hate in your face, you answer with a smile, extend a hand of friendship that with the least acquiescence turns into a hug. Praise to you for the meekness with which the Spirit of Jesus graced the spirit of St. Francis de Sales, who, after being mockingly slandered, greeted his tormentor with a gracious smile.[28] Every day millions and millions of morally blind, arrogant men mock you and spit in your face, and daily you answer with the most engaging of smiles aimed at melting and withering the steel walls of their pride.

Blessed Father of lights, send down your light more intensely so that I can live the word of Jesus, "Seek first the kingdom of righteousness and all these things will be added unto you as well" (Mt 6.33). Praise to you for your generosity: even as I renounce everything for your kingdom of truth and love, you promise to give back everything I require and more as well. O Father, I praise you for being my Father: you simply cannot stop showering good things upon your child. Come, gather me up into your arms once more, clasp me with your infinite love. Then nestled in your bosom, I praise you: you are all, my all, wholly mine. Resting in you, abandoning all for you, I glorify your name, and in that abandonment I receive all of you, then, in addition, everything else I could possibly need. As I offer you a voluntary sacrifice of praise, I begin to perceive a little more clearly how canny is your kindness, how ingenious are the wiles of your love, how blessedly sly is your zeal to love me. You hoodwink me, so to speak, into detaching myself from everything so that you can whelm me with wave after wave of your exquisite affection.

Glorious God, how good you are! Praise to you, Father, for your inexhaustible goodness! I praise and praise and praise you, dearest one: you are goodness living only to spread your goodness as far and wide and deep as possible. I praise you for the epiphany of your goodness in every part of my life. I dare say that, if I were the only thing alive (an impossible hypothesis but you know what I am driving at), I would truly know you as God because you have been so unfailingly good to me. So let my song of praise be: Bless the Lord, all you works of my being. Bless the Lord, body so wonderfully made. Bless the Lord, soul so noble in its powers. Bless the Lord, story of my life so crammed with mercies. Bless the Lord, all the goodness of my being: praise him, exalt him forever! O God, how good you are in the least and frailest of your human creation. Let every impulse of my being praise you, let every breath rise up as a glad sacrifice of praise, whose goodness (really your gift) may come close in some way to hailing and, so to say, duplicating your goodness to me.

Reflections

1. Father, you have made me for joy, your joy. Unhappily ours is a nation that pursues joy day and night yet remains ridden with anxiety, reportedly consuming close to forty tons of aspirin a day. "Enjoy! Enjoy!" the ads on TV, in magazines, and in newspapers shout. "You owe it to yourself to take care of number one. Live it up — enjoy!" So the mad race for joy goes on and on, and, as a kind of law of diminishing returns casts its pall over the hectic chase, the more feverish the pace and the more ravenous the appetite, the more meager the delight and the more disappointing the satisfaction. Your displeasure at the idolatry of sensory pleasure in no way implies that you countenance a life-hating Manichean or Puritan attitude. For you join delight to eating and one of the most potent of pleasures to nuptial union. You are a God of joy who rejoices in wreathing my day with joys, the joys of being in good health, successfully solving a problem, conversing with friends, reading the *Confessions* of St. Augustine, finishing a small piece of manual labor.

Gratifying as these are, they are only human, excelled by the supernatural joy you distribute. Though I struggle in the foothills, it is a joy to sit or kneel in your presence, to feel your hand stroking the face of my soul to allay fears and anxieties. My stammering efforts toward intimate colloquy are scarcely periods of unbroken bliss, but every inch I crawl forward in prayer garners an ounce of loving exchange whose joy exceeds pounds of sheerly human elation. And how glad you make my heart, Father, when I encounter Jesus in the sacraments, especially in the Eucharist. What inexpressible joy that new manna contains! What spiritual cheer courses through my soul resonating feebly but really to the loving cadence of silent words spoken by his heart. The sacrament of penance also imparts your joy. Of course its dominant fruit is the peace that you sent Jesus to bestow, the peace that Jesus sent his apostles to communicate to all (Jn 20.20-23). When sacramental confession tears down the barriers sin has erected, accompanying this peace is a joy akin to the pleasure I feel after a bath has washed away dirt and grime. Other avenues of forgiveness yield a like joy. At the end of the day when I ask Mary to place her hands upon my bruised and stained spirit, the healing light she channels from your Spirit anoints me with peace and joy.

The joy you share with me, Father, is in danger of drying up unless I share it with others. Preparing a sermon is not a work of the Lord that the ordinary priest approaches with uninhibited gusto. If an individual is not a natural-born writer, a blank page does not instantly elicit a spate of sparkling original ideas. When finished, my homily does not usually incite temptations to pride. Set beside a sermon by a Bossuet, Lacordaire, or Fulton Sheen, my prose looks limp and unmoving. Yet you can use my mediocre endeavor to feed hearts famished for even a morsel of your word, and warm them in your joy. Any initial dissatisfaction of a clerical Father pales in comparison with the hard knocks to which many fathers year in and year out bravely resign themselves in order to rear their families. The boss may be a minor-league Hitler, the physical load taxing, and psychological defeats plentiful, yet these men hang on, and in sticking, albeit reluctantly, to their jobs, show a spirit of service to company and clients that increases joy among men.

Father, how good you are! Not only those who are served but those who serve receive joy. In your giving I receive; in my giving I receive; in trying to serve, I am given joy. For several years I have been hearing nuns' confessions at a nearby convent, and, because the pace is relaxed, administering the sacrament consumes around two hours. Not once have I completed confessions without experiencing an upwelling of your joy. How prodigally you bless everyone who, though imperfectly, does his job and does honor to your name.

So much are we your people dependent on your joy, Father, that without the affection with which others favor us we could hardly survive. According to the research of Dr. David Bresler, a psychologist formerly attached to the UCLA Pain Control Unit, a young child needs four hugs a day for survival, eight to maintain psychological health, and twelve to insure steady growth.[29] Dr. Bresler's findings suggest that adults also require affection for survival and growth. When I speak a word of praise to another, when I pat a friend on the back, when I do a community member a favor, when I offer a smile or word of comfort to an individual swamped by gloom or grief, I am giving each a hug of the soul. Father, without the spiritual hugs my friends bestow on me I might start to decline and fall apart emotionally. No more than I can do without food and drink can I last without these exchanges of love. You clothe the lilies of the field and feed the wandering birds of the air (Mt 6.26-29), and so you have to clothe me in your love and daily feed me with squeezes of your affection from friends and acquaintances. As I am indirectly embraced by your love, let me embrace you in spiritually embracing my brothers and sisters, and embrace them as I embrace you. You made the universe a macro-circle of love and my life a micro-circle of love, circles that are also circles of joy. Ring me round the more in your love and joy so that I may widen my circle to draw others into the joy of falling into your everlasting arms.

2. Your saints, Father, break forth in exultation beyond human analysis and power. As Augustine recalls, a martyr like St. Crispina rejoiced in all the dehumanizing stages leading to decapitation, a cruel death tasting more delicious to her than a gourmet feast to worldlings. How can chains and torture machines issue in delectation of the spirit? How can suffering that stunts the person gladden the soul? Only, it seems, in and through the Spirit of Jesus. In the passion of Jesus you furnish us with the key that practically solves the mystery of suffering. But in your plan not only does suffering pave the way to triumphant joy but the very suffering can harbor joy. Toward the baptism of the cross Jesus looked with joyful anticipation,

and in the holocaust itself, as a victim wholly on fire, he felt divine joy (Lk 12.50, 49). Jesus endured the shame and agony of the cross for the sake of the joy to be won (Heb 12.2), but since his act of the highest love glorified you and him, Jesus experienced the deepest of joys while suspended on the cross. The joyful victory over death at Easter is foreshadowed by the joyful victory over sin on Calvary as Jesus gladly finishes his work and commends his spirit to you, Father. You graciously willed that followers of Jesus could claim this humanly indecipherable combination of suffering and joy. In the earliest days of the apostolic age the apostles, when scourged at the order of the Jewish leaders, left the Sanhedrin in high joy (Acts 4.41). Perhaps the memory of this scene was still vivid at the time Peter counseled fellow Christians to rejoice when they were privileged to share in the sufferings of Christ (1 Pt 4.13). Paul rejoiced that his life was being poured out like a libation, a sacrificial offering to build up the faith of his flock (Phil 2.17-18). Writing from a dark Roman prison that denied him nearly every creature comfort, Paul was overbrimming with joy and burst out with an exhortation to continual joy: "Rejoice in the Lord always! Again I say, rejoice!" (Phil 4.4). Surely Paul's was the supernatural joy Jesus brought down with him from you and your Spirit. Paul had been hated, hunted, hounded by his own flesh and blood, scourged and beaten by rods, stoned, shipwrecked, exposed to danger from mobs and robbers, slandered and betrayed by fellow Christians, and, in becoming all things to all men, had suffered nearly all things from all sorts of men (2 Cor 11.23-24). Yet his travails filled him with a near-incredible joy that the most alluring goods of this world cannot cause.

How were Paul and your other early heroes, Father, able to exult in unbearable suffering, pain, and dishonor and to welcome death? One great line of the Apostle provides the answer: "I can do all things in him who strengthens me" (Phil 4.13). Though Paul's tolerance for pain was probably not substantially higher than that of most others, though he groaned in body and spirit, he rejoiced in suffering because the strength of your Son, who became Lord by suffering and death, was infused into him. As did Jesus on the cross, he anguished in pain yet joyed not only in spite of but because of his suffering. But could even the human Jesus feel both sensibly sad and glad? Where were the signs of joy in the holy face contorted by agony? Father, you are not a God of the absurd. Surely Jesus, and Paul later on, did not experience sensible joy in suffering. The joy born of suffering in divine love is spiritual, at work in the deepest recesses of the soul. More recently this was confirmed during St. Therese's final months; when tuberculosis was chewing up her body and fierce, demoniacally instigated temptations mocked her faith as delusion assaulted her soul. She experienced peace but no sensible joy; her unflinching perseverance in love amid wracking pain and frightful darkness could yield not sensible delight but spiritual joy.[30] Thus as your saints testify, the highest joy has to be a Jesus-joy. He is your beloved Son with whom you were most pleased at the moment of his death in love: your pleasure in him became his joy in his suffering. You are similarly pleased with those who suffer in Jesus, and your pleasure with them and the joy of Jesus himself become their joy, a balm of the spirit arising from the bitterest of sufferings.

St. Teresa of Avila prayed, "Lord, let me either suffer or die," and her fellow Carmelite, St. Mary Magdalen de Pazzi, entreated you, "Lord let me suffer and not die," desiring to be laved in a baptism of the cross and to taste the inexpressible joy of unendurable pain. I cannot imagine myself carrying crosses with the indomitable fortitude of your holy ones. I am spineless, scared by enormous, prolonged suffering. But take me by the hand, dear Father, and teach me how to accept the pinstabs of ordinary life. When upbraided, let me smile inwardly, content to be humiliated like Jesus. When crushed by reverses, let me experience some of the quiet delight your saints savored as they trudged through the valley of shadows.

Thus will I learn to praise and live in the presence of the angels, partaking of their "heavenly delectations." In recent years certain theologians have undercut the role of angels, some rashly reducing them to symbols of your attributes and operations. Father, you have clearly spoken in the word delivered to your Church and affirmed in her Scripture and liturgy: these prodigious spirits do exist, ministering to your Church and all men in every part of the globe. Skepticism about pure spirits marks one more cave-in before the pseudo-scientific pretensions of contemporary naturalists bent on constricting and even nullifying spiritual horizons. Father, liberate our minds from false liberalism that immures man in a strictly material universe. Saluting the angels as our compatriots, I can pray in their presence, I can endeavor to fix, as always do they, mind and heart wholly on you, I can praise you, and in suffering pray with spiritual joy. Mother St. Cecile of Rome, a twentieth-century Canadian mystic, prayed that angels would take her place in adoration before the Blessed Sacrament when duties or illness kept her away from the chapel.[31] So praying in the presence of the angels perhaps means also: when prevented from express praying, I can pray with them in the sense that they pray for and with me as they adore you in the Spirit through Jesus. Direct your angels to minister to me as they did to Jesus so that in their continuous adoration of you I will not forget to breathe his holy name moment by moment in the worship ascending from sometimes colorless routine.

Father, I sing psalms also in the presence of one mightier than the mightiest of angels: Mary, queen of angels and men, perfect adorer, perfect praiser, perfect lover, mother of sorrows, mother of joy. In a homily on the Assumption St. Thomas of Villanova waxes eloquent on "those delightful dialogues, those intimate conversations and hidden colloquies," she was privileged to have with her Son "when, lying on [her] lap, he disclosed heavenly secrets . . . and [she] in turn bestowed gentle kisses on him as fee for his teaching." Then he gently questions Mary: "I beg you, blessed Virgin, tell us why you have cheated us of such riches? . . . Why did you not commit these sweet conversations to writing for our instruction and consolation?''[32] A shrewd query, perhaps impossible of solution on this side. Your love decreed that Mary not commit to writing her intimacies with Jesus. It is not presumptuous, I hope, to venture one possible part-answer. Perhaps our immaculate mother did not write down these richest of secrets because she preferred to communicate them in some way personally to her children over the centuries. Father, it is by the wisdom of your Spirit distributed through Mary that I grasp the meaning of life through the meaning of your word. Through Mary my mother, I tap the veins and dig out the gold of Scripture that Mary pondered in her heart; rather, her heart pours these treasures into mine. As I pray psalms in the presence of the holy virgin, she opens up the center of the Scriptures: these always speak directly or indirectly of Jesus and, like St. Paul, your sacred writers know only Jesus crucified who is your power and wisdom. Brilliant with the light of your Spirit, Mary points out the way that is Jesus: "Do whatever he tells you (Jn 2.5), do whatever you see him do. Bring your dust-ridden water before him and he will transform it into wine, lay all your sufferings, even the slightest, at his feet and he will change them into joys gleaming within. As you drink of his precious blood, your way of the cross will be changed into a triumphant march of love and joy. Go to Jesus: he is the Lord of life that is suffering; he is Lord of joy." Father, draw me to kneel before Mary, seat of wisdom, who brings me to kneel before your crucified Son, and perhaps I will take steps to imitate St. Augustine, whose psalter was his joy. Through Mary let me learn to find my most ravishing joy in praising your name, to light upon spiritual delectation in the rebuffs and coldness of day-by-day life. Then in the flattest or most miserable of circumstances I will praise you in the presence of the angels through Mary bearing in her arms Jesus, our sacrifice of praise, whose death brings life, whose defeat wins victory.

Praise

1. Praise to you, Father, for your love surrounding me in what to the eye of an outsider was nothing but one more unprepossessing lower-middle-class dwelling. I praise you a thousand times over for unbreakable bonds of friendship you forged in my soul with my brothers and sisters. I could, perhaps I should, praise you a million times over for the love and strength with which my father and mother fed me every day — gifts that I can never repay in this life. Since the mother is the heart and the backbone of the home, let me focus my gratitude mainly on my mother. Like most of us, my mother is probably not a saint, but, like most Christian mothers, she lived a life of uncelebrated self-sacrifice day in and day out. I praise you for her often-taken-for-granted self-giving: how she devoted herself, with all the religious resonances of that word, consecrated herself to my brothers and sisters and myself. However rhetorically forced it may sound,

I believe that, had it been necessary, my mother would have laid down her life for me. Father, how faithful her unassuming selflessness was to all my needs! Perhaps never again on this earth will another human being grace me with such tenderness and power. I praise you for her discipline: hers was "tough love" fibered with justice and the need for responsibility. How nauseating this world would be had it no Maker; how barren my life might have been had I grown up in a home devoid of a heart like my mother's. I praise you for the unsung self-consummation of Christian mothers, for the care with which they carry offspring in the maternal nest, for grit during labor pains and the final pang of birth, for patience in coping with minor upsets, for fortitude in facing tragedies. All praise to you for the stamina of a mother who bolsters her husband still in his prime as a job-related cancer gnaws him into a living skeleton; for the bravery of a mother whose college-age son is swiftly struck down by a brain tumor; for the resignation of a mother whose youngest son is killed instantly in a motorcycle accident.

"Because God could not be everywhere, he made mothers." While not likely to impress a theologian with its precision, this pointed expression does vividly drive home that a mother's expansive love reproduces your boundless love, Father, that the love a mother gives springs from your motherly heart. According to an old Chinese saying, "God is the great motherly father and the great fatherly mother." Praise to you for showing your motherly side: "As a mother comforts her son, so shall I comfort you" (Is 66.13); and for drawing me into your bosom, where I "may suck fully of the milk of [your] comfort" and be "fondled in [your] lap" (Is 66.11-12; adapted). All glory to you for caressing and nursing me with your motherly love. Clasp me close, cuddle my spirit in your arms, then through Jesus I will become inwardly a lamb but outwardly a lion breathing the fire of your Spirit.

I praise you, Father, for instilling in men as well as women the spirit of self-immolation that is at the root of the most beautiful flower called motherhood. I praise your love: you can build in me a Mary-heart that sees in others the Jesus that Mary loved and served. With this Mary-love I can reach out to "hug" my brothers and sisters with unobtrusively kind words and deeds. Praise to you, Father: in this Marylike service of Jesus I can experience in a manner ultimately inexplicable the warming wind of your Spirit, your delightsome fondling, the more intimate throbs of the heart of Jesus you reserve for all who, however fumblingly, try to exhibit your motherly heart to the hearts of your sons and daughters.

2. Praise to you, Father, for the wonders of the universe, so various, so complex, so astonishing in the flight of the littlest gnat as in the wheeling of the greatest galaxy. More praise to you for the touch of Jesus that healed paralytics, cleansed lepers, opened the eyes of the blind, and raised three individuals from the dead. Glory to you for the unnumbered miracles of grace Jesus wrought. How many hearts of stone he changed into hearts of

flesh, how many broken hearts he made whole, how many dead in the spirit he raised to supernatural life. Praise to you for the healing Jesus still ministers to minds hurting from wounds of the past. Even greater praise, if possible, to you for the miracle of joy concomitant with suffering itself. Some of your saints averred that they would gladly spend eternity in hell if only you were there — a piously paradoxical way of saying that your presence would turn hell into heaven. Glory to you for your presence in suffering that makes joy present. Father, you are joy, you are joy unalloyed! All praise to you: following Paul, I will rejoice through your joy in every instant of worry, in the simplest case of spilt milk, assured that, should hard blows fall, I am being readied for joy yet more intense.

But isn't it true, Father, that at an earlier stage, when we stagger under trials, the best we can do is to alternate between sorrow and joy? After the sudden death of her beloved husband in a freak hunting accident Jane Frances de Chantal was engulfed by grief. Ordinarily her sorrow did not admit the slightest glimmer of consolation, yet on certain occasions she apparently experienced joy over his death, a comfort stemming from the indelible conviction that "God does all in his mercy."[33] Later, as Jane's inner face grew more beautiful, she no doubt felt joy in the secret suffering she described as a martyrdom of love. Praise to you for the lived wisdom of your saints. Let my smallest gestures of praise help mold in me a heart able, in spite of hankering after pseudo-consolations, to renew holy resolves hour by hour, able, in the bleakest hour amid a sinking feeling of near-despair that urges me to give up, to muster courage to offer myself once more. I praise you also for dividing our time-line into days. Now and then the long stretches of the future look pregnant with dread possibilities of unheard-of sufferings. Glory to you; I can partake of the glory of the cross of Jesus by taking up the cross in the confusion, uncertainty, rudeness, and occasionally overt hostility that dot my day. According to one pithy saying, these are not coincidences but God-incidents: you reluctantly permit contrary events in order to press to my lips your goblet of joy and let me sip the wine that in its fullness inebriates the blessed in heaven with an ecstasy divine. I praise you for putting my defiant neck under the sweet obedience of Jesus, which makes your Face shine upon me and in which I taste galling suffering savory with hidden rejoicing.

I especially praise you, Father, for the joy of Mary our mother. How she rejoiced as she first intoned the *Magnificat* after the spiritually discerning proclamation of Elizabeth! Yet how she sang in secret her unsurpassed song of joy in her seven sorrows, indeed in all her sorrows. Praise to you for inundating her soul with your enrapturing joy while she shed tears during the excruciating passion of her beloved Jesus. Every time we pray, "Holy Mary, Mother of God, pray for us now," we mystically invoke those tears. If I should feel the sting of insult or the stabbing pains of some illness, let tears from her immaculate heart moisten my heart to bring forth blossoms of joy. In that blossoming I can sing in a minor key some of the *Magnificat*, hail the mighty things you are doing within my spirit, exult in you, my savior, and hymn the holiness of your name that is almost compelled to make the toughest of trials mild by the joy you breathe into me. Truly, all-tender Father, you are nothing but joy! You mingle your joy with any grief I must undergo, you make my tears glisten with gladness under a rainbow that augurs even greater joy.

3. Thank you, gracious Lord, for letting us know the angels as prayer-partners, models, and guardians. I praise you for a mind that intuitively penetrates to the make-up of things, charts the movements of the stars, compasses in one general idea all the furniture of earth and heaven, and probes the broad whence and whither and what and why of my life. Over against the power of angelic intellect the output of a super-genius resembles the scrawling of a kindergarten child. Because their actions are unfettered by material conditions, St. Thomas Aquinas calls angels relatively infinite.[34] How their living that is sheer thinking and willing glorifies you, Father! I praise you for designating these stupendous spirits our associates in prayer and co-workers in the redeeming of all times. In their presence my praise becomes a trifle less distracted, a mite more fervent.

Praise to you, Father, for their burning concentration on your holy will, for never wavering in their total adoration of your Face. Praise to you for their swift, faultless ministrations to human needs in every corner of the world. Let my praise in the presence of these lofty spirits make me in some slender way angelic — angelic in undeviating devotion to your will, angelic in fulfilling whatever ministries you appoint.

An angel ministered to Jesus agonizing in the garden. I praise you: an angel ministers to me not only in suffering but in the agenda of the day, working, eating, exercising, straightening out my room. Praise to you for these luminous guardians who illumine my soul, relight faith when it is burning low, steer me away from pockets of malignity, nudge me toward the science of the saints. Father, lead me to pray more to these minds and hearts ablaze with light and love. Since it is no accident that my confirmation name is Michael, I ought to be particularly attached to these gigantic spirits so as to absorb lessons of humility and service. Praise to you: in some titanic struggle prior to the creation of the physical universe the yes of these brightest of spirits drove down to the nethermost depths the legions who snarled their irrevocable no into your Face. Make the praise I chant in the presence of the angels a hymn whose single chorus iterates the theme of their song: yes, I love you, Father, I want only to love, obey, serve you in whatever work you command.

Father, I praise you also for union with Mary, mother of the Church, mother of the communion of the saints, and mother of the city of God, concerned, as she stands before your throne in purest love, only to serve you in her children spread throughout the world. Thank you for this mother of mothers, on earth a perfect living psalter, in heaven an everlasting living *Magnificat*. As I praise you in her presence, garb me in her love, her lowliness, her meekness, all fused with her spirit of praise that is joy of uttermost abandon. Praise to you for Mary's continuous rejoicing: through her motherly counsel I will try to seize the holy joy in the most humdrum of circumstances with some of the gusto of a starving man devouring a filet mignon at a banquet table. Years ago I became a friend of a saintly nun who surrendered herself to you with utmost trust and joy. The source of her joy? She never let a day go by without praying for joy. Father, I praise you: impel me to pray every day for your incomparable joy; then will I praise you more gladly in the presence of Mary and the angels.

Praise Sung in Faithful Living

Because the vocalizing of praise is so exhausting, praise cannot be exhausted in the chanting of psalms. Toward the end of a long sermon Augustine compassionately and humorously remarks, "How can any tongue have the stamina to keep on praising God all day long? If I have fatigued you just in stretching out this sermon, how can you have the endurance to praise God all day long?"[35] To resolve the problem of continual praise he recommends, "Whatever you do, do well, and you are praising God."[36] A second, more profound reason underlies this proposal for unbroken praise. Both voice and action flow from within, from the heart that is the inner voice which the divine ear primarily heeds. Virtuous conduct serves not only as a psaltery accompanying psalm-singing but goes on after chanting has stopped. "After singing with your voice, you become silent for awhile. Sing with your life in such a way that you are never silent."[37] We praise God by never forsaking honesty in business, by eating and drinking moderately, by going to bed and rising with untroubled conscience. Unhappily a man sunk in sin is a living disharmony so that his praise insults rather than pleases God. The cacophony of his behavior drowns out the music of his lips. So praise is meant to encompass analogously the whole of human living. "Sing with your voices, sing with your hearts, sing with your lips, sing with your actions."[38] His life suffused with praise, each Christian is to be praise incarnate. As already mentioned, the new song that is the new man is primarily a song of love in the sense that we surrender to the Father our super-precious possession — ourself — in accord with the word from the lips of Wisdom: "Son, give me your heart" (Prv 23.26). Refusing to shrink back in fear, paying the price of oblation of heart, the new man is free to live the life of praise, a mountaintop of spiritual exaltation that finds its epiphany in the outwardly homeliest and most commonplace of circumstances: in eating bread and drinking coffee, we sing the new song of love. The divine poetry of charity in praise shines through all the prose of daily living.

One problem that troubles certain devout souls is the difficulty of praising God with one's whole heart and mind and strength. The spirit may seem to be willing but the flesh is weak. While the soul dreams of indefatigable piety, the body's stamina runs down, then, like a guttering candle, goes out. Brother ass falls to the ground exhausted, bringing sudden halt to the soul's aspiration to go on and on praising. The stringent limitations that imperious demands of the body impose on the soul apparently rule out unceasing praise as impossible. Certainly no one can offer strict praise to God without respite all day long. But we can continually praise God in a broad sense: any word or work spoken or done well that is offered to the Father through Jesus is praise in action. Less strictly but still truly, we can praise God all day long by uniting our hearts to his in love and obedience and service.

> O Jesus, our head, you who are one with your members, what will you say now? "Let those who desire my justice exult and be glad" (v. 27): here Jesus speaking through the psalmist is referring to those who cleave to his body. "And let those who desire the peace of the servant of God always say: Let the name of the Lord be glorified" (v. 28). "Then my tongue shall make known your justice and your praise all day long" (v. 28). How can any tongue have the stamina to keep on praising God all day long? If I have fatigued you just in stretching out this sermon, how can you have the endurance to praise God all day long? I will suggest a remedy enabling you, if you so desire, to praise God all day long. Whatever you do, do well, and you are praising God. When you sing a hymn, you are praising God. But what good is it to move your tongue if your heart does not praise him as well? Suppose you stop singing the hymn and you leave to eat a meal. Do not get drunk, and you will be praising God. Suppose you leave to go to bed. Do not get up and do an evil deed, and you will be praising God. Suppose you are engaged in business. Engage in no wrong dealing, and you will be praising God. Suppose you are tilling your field. Do not provoke a quarrel, and you will be praising God. Your upright actions prepare you to praise God all day long.[39]

The word that is praise is meant to be extended and lived out in work that is praise. Actions that are praiseful, like a musical instrument, accompany and support hymns of praise. But they are more: they are signs that the singing of praise is genuine, not an empty-souled chanting of religious poetry. It is not by sounds but by fruits that we recognize the ring of authentic praise. These fruits are love-impregnated works that do the truth, that sing alleluia to the Father and hallow his name by arranging and orchestrating our lives in unison with his law of love. Thus the true word and work of praise are rooted in a heart that is praise, a heart that celebrates his goodness by striving to be good as he desires it, a heart that hymns his holiness by humbly bending its energies to serve him in accord with his thoughts and his ways of holiness. The inner self, the heart that gives itself to God, is a living song of praise, offering him the highest tribute, obedience to his commands and conformity to his desires. Obedience anchored in love is the sweetest-sounding praise that can arise to and delight the ears of God, for its music bespeaks an inner harmony that partially reproduces his own infinite harmony.

Always the realistic pastor conversant with the liabilities of his charges, Augustine illustrates this high moral teaching by examples from what some may deem the lowest common denominator of conduct. He does not urge upon his listeners a rigorous asceticism as a vehicle of praise but appeals to them to eschew greed, fraud, gluttony, and lust, capital sins and their progeny, ever tempting in the semi-pagan milieu that exerted powerful pressures on Augustine's workaday flock. Avoiding deadly sins and keeping the ten commandments are low-level moral activities only in comparison with the criteria for heroic virtues. For most of us, influenced by the sexual excesses and anything-goes mood of our partially decadent and nominally Christian society, steadily observing the basic laws of God and man and consistently saying no to the world and the flesh would seem to constitute a stern program of far-from-mean moral behavior. Such disciplined living ascends to the Father as sweet melody, praise in action.

> For a psalm is a song, not any sort of song but one backed up by a psaltery. Now, a psaltery is an instrument for supporting a song, like the lyre and harp and similar instruments that were devised to accompany singing. So a person who sings psalms does not sing with his voice alone, but he also uses an instrument called a psaltery that his hands pluck in concord with his voice. Do you want then to sing a psalm? Not only your voice should sound the praises of God but your works also should harmonize with your voice. After singing with your voice, you become silent for a while. Sing with your life in such a way that you are never silent. You are engaged in business and you are thinking about doing some cheating: in that case you have stopped praising God and, what is worse, you have not only stopped praising but you have gone on to blasphemy. Indeed when your good action praises God, it is you who are praising God by your action, and, when your bad action blasphemes God, it is you who are blaspheming God by your action. So sing with a pleasing voice that exhorts listeners to do good, but do not let your heart remain silent, do not let your life remain still. When you reject the idea of cheating in business, you are, in effect, singing a psalm. When you eat and drink, sing a psalm not by interweaving sweet sounds pleasing to the ear, but by eating and drinking moderately, frugally, and temperately. For this is what the Apostle tells us: "Whether you eat or drink or whatever you do, do all for the glory of God" (1 Cor 10.31). Thus if your eating and drinking are morally good, if you consume food to nourish the body and to give fresh vigor to its members,

while thanking him who gave you, mortal and frail as you are, this comforting sustenance, both your eating and drinking praise God. But if, yielding to a voracious appetite, you go beyond the due limit of nature and glut yourself with wine and get drunk, no matter how many praises of God your tongue sounds, your life blasphemes him. After your food and drink you lie down to sleep: while in bed do nothing shameful nor go beyond what the law of God allows. Keep chaste the marriage bed you share with your wife. If you want to beget children, keep your nuptial union free of unrestrained and lustful sense-pleasure. In your bed respect the dignity of your wife because both of you are members of Christ (1 Pt 3.7; 1 Cor 6.15), both created by him, both recreated by his blood. In acting chastely, you are praising God and, in so continuing, you will never stop praising him. Suppose that sleep comes over you — what shall you do then? When you are sleeping, do not let an evil conscience disturb your rest, and the innocence of your sleep praises God as well. So if you praise God, sing his praises not only by tongue but also by the psaltery of good works "because a psalm is good" (v. 1). You praise God when you are engaged in business, you praise him when you are eating and drinking, you praise him when lying in bed, you praise him when you are sleeping: when are you not able to praise him? Our praises of God will be perfect when we reach the heavenly city, when we become the equals of the angels of God (Mt 22.30), when no bodily necessity disquiets us in any way, when no hunger, no thirst disturb us, when no heat fatigues us, when no death puts an end to us. To achieve that most perfect praise let us now devote ourselves to praising God in good works.[40]

Our praise has to be wholehearted if it is to be truly full-throated. Full-blown praise cannot be voiced by a heart divided, one given over in part to a love and service of this world for its own sake. Serious sin introduces division into the heart, and servitude to the lower self clashes with our spoken praise of God. When we do sin thus, the potential Pharisee, the potential hypocrite, within each of us surfaces: our dispraise of God by action belies our praise of God by voice. But the God who bids us raise our voices up to him stoops down to us through Jesus. Sinners all, we have been redeemed by the saving blood of Jesus. "His blood be upon us and our children" (Mt 27.25), the people of Jerusalem cried out, dooming the Lamb of God, repeatedly falling face forward, to the hill of Calvary. Mystically and gently, with all the vengeance of forgiving love that repays evil with good and heaps coals of fire upon bitter enemies (Rom 12.19-20), Jesus continuously lets his blood fall upon us, the spiritual offspring of the people of Israel, to cleanse us of our iniquity and restore us to a Godly estate, so that in his name we can go on praising the Father in all our works, each of which flows forth from a renewed Jesus-heart. It is this heart, not the outward appearance, that is pleasing to the Father.

> So if praise in the mouth of a sinner is not attractive (Ecclus 15.9), it is not pleasing to God, for what is pleasing is attractive. Do you want your praise to be pleasing to God? Do not drown out your song by evil ways. "Let praise be pleasing to our God" (v. 1). What did the psalmist mean here? He meant this: you who praise God, live good lives. The praise of the wicked offends God. He pays more attention to the way you live than to the words you sing. Surely you want to be at peace with him whom you praise. How can you strive to be at peace with him when you are in discord with yourself? "How," you ask, "am I in discord with myself?" This is how: your tongue speaks one thing but your life bespeaks another. "Let praise be pleasing to our God." For praise may be pleasing to an individual when he hears himself praised in a dulcet voice rolling off polished and adroit turns of phrase. "But let praise be pleasing to our God," whose ears are open not to the voice but to the heart, not to the tongue but to the life of the person praising.
>
> Who is our God to whom our praise is to be pleasing? He makes himself sweet to us, he commits himself to us: and all this occurs thanks to his condescension. He condescends to commit himself to us not in order that we may give him anything but rather that we may receive much from him. How then does God commit himself? Listen as the apostle Paul tells us: "God," he says, "commits his love for us" (Rom 5.8). How does he commit it? Listen to what the Apostle himself tells us so that you can compare his words to the psalm: "God," he says, "commits his love to us." How does he commit it? "Because when we were still sinners, Christ died for us." Since God commits himself in this way to sinners, what then does he have in store for those who praise him? According to the Apostle, God so committed his love to us that Christ died for the wicked, not that they might stay wicked but that the death of the just man might heal them of their injustice. . . . [41]

With hearts purified by the way that is Jesus, with minds more open to the truth that is Jesus, with spirit more quickened by the life that is Jesus, we can boldly but realistically hope to praise the Father in every trivial action, in every casual encounter. God is infinite spirit, and we worship him in spirit and in truth (Jn 4.24). Not only his creative but his Fatherly presence touches us at every point and in every circumstance. In union with Jesus we can praise the Father who "is spirit" by externally earthbound activities. And since action is the outflow of the inner self, we

can become, as Jesus was and is, incarnate praise. In singing with our
hearts, we are singing with our inner selves. The most banal of events takes
on a sacred aura as we give our hearts to the Father in daily actions. Each
act becomes a note of praise, the whole of each life one great song of praise
to the Father through Jesus.

> My brothers, my sons, you are the fruit of the Catholic faith,
> you are holy seed from heaven, you are made newly alive in
> Christ, you are born from above! Listen to me or, rather, listen
> to the Lord speaking through me. "Sing to the Lord a new song"
> (Ps 149.1). "Look," you say, "I am singing." Yes, you are
> singing, you are singing clearly. I hear you. But be sure that your
> life does not belie the witness of your tongue. Sing with your
> voices, sing with your hearts, sing with your lips, sing with your
> actions: "Sing to the Lord a new song." Are you asking me to
> tell you what you shall sing of him whom you love? Undoubtedly
> you do want to sing of him whom you love. You are seeking to
> sing his praises. You heard the words, "Sing to the Lord a new
> song." Are you seeking to sing his praises? "His praise is in the
> assembly of the saints" (Ps 149.1). The singer himself is the praise
> that is sung. Do you want to express praise to God? Live what
> you express. You are his praise if you live good lives. For his praise
> is not in the synagogues of Jews, not in the frenzy of pagans,
> not in the errors of heretics, not in the applause of theatres. Are
> you asking me to tell you where this praise is? Focus attention
> on yourselves: you yourselves are to be this praise. "His praise
> is in the assembly of the saints." Are you asking me to tell you
> the source of the joy you experience when you sing? The psalmist
> tells us, "Let Israel rejoice in him who made him (Ps 149.2),
> and he finds out that the source of this joy is no one but God.[42]

Reflections

1. The spiritual side of man, transcending individual concrete objects,
travels spacelessly and timelessly over the contours of the universe. What
a powerful instrument is even my ordinary mind! Yet my spiritual side
is linked to an animal body. I am not complaining, Father: after viewing
the whole universe as good, you saw the creation of man as very good (Gen
1.31). But at first blush it is not easy to reconcile myself to the fact that
a mind open to infinities seems chained to a body that occupies a limited
space and a limited time and never stops clamoring for food and sleep.
The time for rest can be cut back sharply but the majority of men probably
spend about one-third of their lives in bed. Lord, only a slight fraction of
the clock seems left for prayer and praise. I would be dissembling if I did
not admit to letting chances for prayer and praise often slip through my
fingers. Withal, even were I not to squander a minute, I could budget but
little time for explicit rejoicing in your name. I am not one of those lucky

individuals up at all hours yet always energetic, who allot at most two to four hours a day for repose. Father, as I bow to your plan for me, impress on my soul the wisdom of St. Augustine's observation. Even while resigning myself to the iron necessity of sleep, I can praise you. How gracious you are, Father! Hours and hours lost in unconsciousness can serve as periods of praise. After a day in which I have neglected to praise you, I can, before closing my eyes, consecrate my hours of sleep to you as wordless, actionless songs, assured that you will welcome this mite as true praise. As I murmur, "Father, into your hands I commend my spirit," put my heart in your heart and count this literally thoughtless state as a segment of fruitful praise. Father, how wonderful you are! I do nothing yet through this nothing I can praise you as my all, I can further clamber toward possessing you in a life that will be all praise.

The rest you appoint for our frames, Lord God, is not an end in itself. We lie down only in order to rise refreshed for work. Man is *homo faber*, man the maker; as an older version has it, "Man is born to work as the bird to fly" (Jb 5.7). Father, you have made man "a little less than the angels," giving him charge over all birds and fish and land animals (Ps 8.5-8). So man tills fields, fishes in lakes and oceans, digs into the earth in search of metals and coal and oil, heals bodies, instructs minds, builds houses and bridges and dams, assembles automobiles and TV sets, synthesizes artificial elements and compounds, and in simpler occupations washes dishes, rakes leaves, cuts grass, and shovels snow. On another plane the abstract thinker and research scientist, loosely speaking, do work also. Father, you have made me a worker, a maker — I cannot not work — tying this natural drive to my supernatural bent to praise your name. As a son of man I am made to work; as a son of God I am made to praise you. Thank you for dovetailing the first with the second. Rightly motivated, united with Jesus, the work of man is also *opus Dei*, the work of God. As I write these lines, my hands are mystically raised up to you in praise. When I brush my teeth or shave, my heart is, in effect, chanting your praises. As I drive a car, my face is adoring your Face with accents of praise. Each place of activity can become, in union with Jesus, a sanctuary. This room in which I write takes on a sacred dimension and hue: it is haloed with your Fatherly presence. Occasionally in the past I thought, perhaps dreamed, of living in solitude, contemplating you apart from busyness and turmoil. I am not intended to lead such a privileged quasi-hermitlike style of life, yet, if I open my heart wider to understanding your heart, I need not envy cloistered souls, for every action can be electric with your life, every movement part of a ceaseless hymn to you. Wherever I am, I stand on holy ground. Whatever I do, I am offering praise to you. However engrossing the task, I can center my heart in your heart, silently worshiping you and inwardly singing your praises through the work of my hands.

Other men are my fellow workers and, as co-workers, co-praisers. A globe-girdling chorus of praise swells up to you, Father, not just from churches and chapels but from temples of activity in which men work, in kitchens, classrooms, shops, factories, fields, mines, ships, submarines, airplanes, and spaceships. How faithful these millions and millions are in their work and thereby devoted in their praise. When men recognize and seek to serve you, their work homages you with an aroma fragrant to your nostrils. Truck drivers, steamfitters, secretaries, cataloguers, seamstresses, jewelers, salesmen, chefs, waitresses, busboys, stevedores, drivers of subway cars, policemen, firemen, tool and die workers, stonemasons, bricklayers, plumbers, electricians, bookkeepers, accountants, bulldozer operators, sheepherders, cattlemen, horseraisers — from all these workers an unceasing song of praise rises to you, Father. Without them I could not survive; with the breakdown of the machinery they make and service I would be soon without food or water. Without them I could not worship you in a super-chorus of praise. Once more I beg you, Lord: open my spiritual senses to perceive this immense chant all about me. The highway patrolman insuring traffic safety is also praising you from behind his wheel. The cook whose skill puts a fine meal before me is praising your name. Every stroke of a broom, every finger-tap on a typewriter, every washing of a dish, every movement of a sewing needle, every pounding of a hammer, every sowing of a seed, every writing of a single word — each is a note in the polyphonic hymn of praise that ascends from earth to heaven, sounding the growth of man and the increase of your glory, Lord. How good you are, Father! Sensitive to my straggling efforts at explicit praise, you welcome the work of my hands and head as praise. As I praise you in official worship, give me a deeper love and respect for work, my work and the work of my brothers and sisters. As I work at whatever task, make my spirit of praise abound the more. Imbue me too with the zeal for work of my brothers and sisters. As we lift up hands and hearts in our choric chant of work, let me catch and be permanently infected with the unflagging zest for work of your servants in Jesus.

But Genesis 3.17 rings true today: "In the sweat of your brow you shall eat your bread." It would be pseudo-romantic to forget that work can be grimy and debilitating, and, over the years, life-destroying. Many jobs bend and stretch and pull the aching body to the verge of exhaustion. Worse, certain occupations slowly induce death. In some parts of the world miners still die of black lung disease, and in the United States job-related deaths of workers in their prime still go unreported in certain industries. Fortunately the chilling callousness of nineteenth-century buccaneer capitalism is now repudiated. After the Brooklyn Bridge was finished in 1883, Al Smith's mother somberly remarked that its construction would have been halted had the people of New York been aware of the deaths connected with the sinking of the caissons for the bridge's towers.[43] Yet even today job-related accidents kill around 15,000 American workers every year. Father, work glorifying your name is wrung from sacrifice, the sacrifice of erosion of health, pain, crippling disease, and death. Let me see that the sweat of renownless men giving themselves to their tasks is a sacrifice of praise invaluable in your eyes, a libation of mind and body daily poured out. If I obey your law of work, Father, the chains that constrain head and hands to a perhaps uninviting task become bonds of love as I learn more and more to forget myself and by that self-oblivion help release the inner freedom that is the fruit of your Spirit. More, while secular humanists try to cut the heart of the sacred even out of religious rites, your holy word urges me to ensoul the secular with the sacred. This desk on which I write becomes an altar from which a small sacrifice of praise ascends to your glory. Plugging away at my appointed piece of work not only changes the world somewhat but lifts up my inwardly changed spirit into your presence. My sacrifice of praise-in-work glorifies you, Father, with the glory of God that is, in St. Irenaeus's words, man alive with your life.[44]

2. Ours is an age inclined to be anti-institutional and, along with that, anti-traditional. A semi-idolatry of the novel seems a part of the temper of our day, erupting now and then in contempt for all that has gone before. One perceptive academic put his finger on ignorance of the past as one major reason for the flaky attitudes of young adult Christians: "The trouble is that most of them have not read the minutes of the previous meetings."[45] Ever-faithful Father, the people of your Church who blithely dismiss the lessons of the past are bound to trip themselves up. A neglect of the marvels you have wrought in me in days gone by has partly undermined my confidence. Now and then my resolve sags, I tend to buckle before defeatist ideas and feelings because I let my eyes stray from the feats of power you have done in and for me. "The minutes of the previous meetings" proclaim in capital letters your prodigal mercies. Surely I must live in the present, I must not lament water over the dam, but, no less truly, not for one moment must I lose sight of the past in which you wrote straight with crooked lines, cutting me free from traps in which my moral stupidity ensnared me, shepherding me along or back into paths of love. Feasting in memory on these wonders, as enchantingly as any cloistered monk or nun I can hallow your name in unGodly-looking tasks that an uncloistered world may rate bagatelles or nuisances.

Only by frequenting the Eucharistic presence of your Son can I progressively clarify my sense of the sacred. Only by being illumined by those invisible sacramental eyes, Father, can I relearn that you are all and without you all else is nought. In Augustine's words, "If you have God, what do you not have, and, if you do not have God, what do you have?"[46] Before the Blessed Sacrament I can best plumb the meaning of my work, seeing it rooted in the all of your love in Jesus. If I write poetry that outdazzles that of Shakespeare and Dante but have not charity, my art counts for nothing. If I have scientific genius that unlocks the most elusive arcana of nature but lack charity, I am as good as nothing. If I have the engineering genius to invent a cheap technique of tapping solar energy but am without charity, my creativity is worth nothing. If I am a super-skilled healer of bodies but destitute of charity, I still amount to nothing. Scrubbing a kitchen floor with charity praises you far more than the religionless construction of the most mammoth skyscraper of all time. Dashing off a note in Christian love honors your name more than a breakthrough in synthesizing life achieved by some irreligious scientists. It is your love in the spirit of Jesus that makes the most piddling piece of work a chant of praise charming to your ears. An outstanding artist inscribes his *pinxit* in a corner of his painting; so my work, next-to-worthless as it may seem, becomes valuable because it bears on its inner face the signature of your love. It is in terms of this love that you send forth your Spirit to renew the face of the earth through man — man plowing, man healing, man mothering, man contemplating, man building bridges, man exploring the moon and the planets, man praising you in activities that breathe forth the love in your heart. Your love translates the least work into a song of praise, builds up the city of God, the city of love, through a people at work praising your name. How then can I fail to love my work, for, in loving it, I praise your name, bodying forth the love and praise at work within you, Father, and your Son and Spirit.

3. Perfect praiser on earth, Jesus was also the servant perfect in the work that was implicit praise. This service-praise prefigured his supreme act of service, the highest sacrifice of praise that was his death on the cross. The sweat in the carpenter's shop, the fatigue on the dusty roads of Palestine, and the outward loss of face in washing his disciples' feet anticipated the bloody sweat in the garden, the horrible weakness on the road to Golgotha, and the obloquy of execution as a common criminal. The work of Jesus was, at least dispositively, redemptive praise. Father, thank you for re-presenting the one perfect sacrifice in the Mass. This supreme sacrifice of praise reenacted on our altars is prepared for by the work of men who cultivate the wheat and grapes, who knead the flour and crush the grapes for the bread and wine of the Eucharist. From morning to night, all around the globe, your name is honored among the Gentiles by the offering of the pure sacrifice of Jesus (Mal 1.11). Reflecting, witnessing to that sacrifice of praise, is the work of hundreds of millions of Christians all over the world. As the outcome of the power of the Jesus we feed upon in the Eucharist, our work seems a sacrifice of praise, quasi-Eucharistic. Along with and in Jesus our work that sacrifices ourselves to you, Father, uninterruptedly praises you.

Father, once more I beg you, "Let that mind be in [me] which was in Christ Jesus" (Phil 2.5). Plunge me again into the abyss of your infinite life, and teach me, as you commissioned Jesus, to empty myself. It is by the way of darkness that I will enter into light. It is when pressures, crowding in, make things look hopeless and myself helpless that I will bound ahead in reliance upon you. It is when human love, the life-blood of my soul, drains away drop by drop, that through your love I can inexhaustibly abound with new life. Some years back I learned of the special state of soul of a cloistered nun who early in this century founded a midwestern monastery. Though her fervent community loved and revered her, she usually experienced, surprisingly, not quiet joy but abjection. Jesus, her beloved, generally cast her into the depths so that she could absorb the wisdom of nothingness that his life and death teach. I shudder at the wintry, gloomy-looking pathways of such abasement. But, Father, if I can achieve emptiness of self in no other way, lower me gently into the frigid pit of desolation that is abjection. There ice will turn into fire, night into day, stony ground into a meadow of roses, sadness into joy unconfined. There I will be purified, and my work will rise a sacrifice of praise, ablaze with your love.

The living of your ordinary and great saints, Father, prolongs the sacrifice of praise of Jesus the worker, finely reproduced. Out of his own and others' experience the Trappist monk Father Raymond astutely observed: "There is a mysticism of action, a mysticism of prayer, and a mysticism of suffering."[47] Without attaining a high degree of prayer, self-sacrificing mothers and fathers "mystically" praise your name in their constant devotion to their children, especially the lame and retarded, and in the uncomplaining, resourceful performance of wearing duties. What a glorious sacrifice of praise goes up from these sanctuaries of service that are Catholic homes! Single-hearted, selfless labor in justice and charity accounts for the higher level of praise in the lives of many prominent saints. Mother Cabrini, the first United States citizen to be canonized, toiled tirelessly for the material and spiritual nourishment of Italian immigrants. The nearly nonstop activity of this tiny saint was a near-ceaseless song of love and sacrifice of praise. St. Francis de Sales, so fetching because of his unflappable gentleness, astonishingly, hardly ever lost the sense of your presence, Father, in spite of a tyrannous load of activities during a less bureaucratic era when a bishop frequently acted as his own chancery office and pastor-at-large in his diocese. While occasionally he felt the urge to fly to a hermit's solitude, he became through your favor all things to all men in his region, unremittingly offering you his work as praise, somehow, near-miraculously, within remaining, in the classic phrase, alone with the Alone, and banqueting on your countenance while he guided his flock and surrendered himself to tasks that sounded in your ears as the purest, undistracted praise. Here we cannot omit mention of St. Joseph, your vicar on earth, who, as remarked before, imaged so many of your Fatherly attributes. Reflecting your providence, he was a provider and therefore a worker, who spent long hours making or repairing plows, wheels, cabinets, yokes, chests, beams, buckets, stools, doors, troughs, and cups, each shaped and adjusted with accents of practical praise that rang like celestial music. How proud Jesus was to be known as Yeshua bar Joseph, Jesus, son of Joseph! At the side and feet of Joseph Jesus learned to fashion and smooth cradles, rakes, and tools of all sorts, to sing with his hands the sublime song of praise that is work done out of love of you, Father.[48]

My work becomes exalted praise once it is impregnated with the Spirit of Jesus. It can be only praise too because it imitates your unceasing work. As Jesus informed the Jews, you never stop working (Jn 5.17), you who uphold the frame of the universe and constantly bring new beings into existence. You are love: all your work is praise-filled. In helping, slightly, to shape the human world, I am joining in your one act of love and thereby praising your name. It is gladdening, not degrading, to be used as your instrument, for then I am, like Jesus, your servant, at the beck and call of your commands for making and remaking the world, a co-worker in love, a co-worker in praise. As your living tool I am fulfilling the highest of callings: mine is the supreme role of loving and praising you in work for the sons of God.

Praise

1. Father, how generous and thoughtful you are to me! These adjectives may be freighted with human connotations but, beause your kindness is so nicely nuanced and our English vocabulary of affection so comparatively impoverished, I beg you to be pleased with them. You stop at nothing in order to enable me to live by your loving imperatives, going out of your way to make it easy for me to obey. Praise to you, Father, for sharing your only-begotten Son, for adapting your justice to our condition. According to an adage accredited to Laurence Sterne, "God tempers the wind to the shorn lamb": you temper the force of your commands to our infirm spirits. "Give what you command, and command what you will," St. Augustine prayed.[49] I offer you praise, Father: this is your modus operandi, your style, to tailor grace to every opportunity and exigency, always giving what you command so that I can carry out whatever command you will. Glory to you, who call upon us to praise you all the time, then liberally count as implicit praise anything we do in union with your love. Again and again your heart, in effect, whispers, "Offer me all you do. Everything is priceless. All your actions are lovable in my eyes." How can my thanks and praise requite you for this comforting light that corroborates your Scriptural truth: "Whether then you eat or drink or whatever you do, do everything for the glory of God" (1 Cor 10.31). If I take a walk, I am praising you. If I read a newspaper for relaxation or passing information, I am praising your name. If I do push-ups or touch my toes, I am giving you glory. If I chat with a friend, I am lifting up my voice in praise of your goodness. Praise to you especially for uniting your command to praise with your law of sleep. Throughout his life your incarnate Son had to sleep; yet his slumber silently praised your name. Praise to you for the sleep of Mary; mystically her repose sang anew her *Magnificat* of self-naughting and praise. Praise to you for Joseph settling bone-tired on his nocturnal mat into sleep that praised you no less essentially than the beat of his hammer during the day. I praise

you for the miracles of energy you wrought in some of your saints who slept, if at all, only one or two hours a night; but no less too for your servants who became mystically married to your heart while relying on a reasonable amount of sleep — they praised you also from the moment they put their heads down till they bounded from bed. So I will praise you, Father, when at day's end I lie down, I will praise you throughout the night as your blessed sleep resurrects my powers, I will praise you as light pries open my eyes and, drowsiness ebbing and head clearing, I toss the covers aside.

Aboriginally cursed, the work that man has to do just to survive becomes what you bless him with. Praise to you, Father: the grueling burden of work becomes the pleasant yoke of praise. Thank you for hooking up with love and praise all the labor that makes our human world go round. As I write, as I straighten out my cluttered room, I am praising you in harmony with all fellow praisers from one end of the earth to the other. The varied voices singing the beauty of your countenance rise up and up, their musical poetry resembling the canticle of the three young men (Dan 3.56-88). Bless the Lord, all you workers of the Lord./Praise and exalt him forever! Priests of the Lord, bless the Lord./Housewives of humble heart, bless the Lord./Farmers and fishermen, bless the Lord./Teachers of wisdom, bless the Lord./Carpenters and plumbers, bless the Lord./Praise and exalt him above all forever! Father, I praise you too with workers in thousands of other occupations too tedious to list. All you workers in other occupations, bless the Lord: praise and exalt him above all forever! Let my insufficient praise empower me to see this human world as you want it to be: a worldwide basilica swelling with the praise of workers everywhere, a universe of man inspirited by God, a world of flesh in which the Word dwells, chant upon chant intermingling spontaneously yet artfully, song after song blending into a whole, a symphony of symphonies woven from the clicking of typewriters, the chopping of hatchets, the snipping of scissors, the whirring of motors, the hum of lawnmowers, the pounding of piledrivers, the drone of jet engines, each and all symbolizing the aspirations of workers whose stick-to-it-iveness helps create this divine-human world of praise-in-work.

I praise you, Father, for the little ones unassumingly doing the unglamorous jobs, farmers, factory workers, truck drivers, dockworkers, miners, and oil field workers, without whom we would be practically bereft of food, clothing, shelter, and heat. Praise to you for their taken-for-granted lowliness: they are so behind the scenes, so "under," so unacclaimed. Praise to you for the golden words of Jesus, "If any man wishes to be my disciple, let him deny himself, take up his cross daily, and follow me" (Lk 14.27). The strain and pain in work form our daily gibbet, a "sacrament" of praise offered every day by working men and women who exude sweat, occasionally pour out tears, and at times shed blood to feed and clothe us. Rain the unction of the Spirit of Jesus on their bruised bodies and spirits, lighten their burdens, enwrap them in your peace, stroke them with your joy. Lead me now, Father, to praise as they do, unpretentiously, steadfastly, punctually, make me enthusiastic in work, celebrating your name through the labor of heart and head and hands.

2. Much wisdom is packed in the reputedly Spanish proverb, "Take what you want, says God, take it — but pay for it."[50] Father, you have fashioned a moral world shot through with causal connections. If we recklessly grab the fleeting pleasures of foul actions, we pay by later manacling ourselves in evil habits. If we try, however falteringly, to do good, we pay first by denying ourselves — self-abnegation that fructifies in the joy of the self-discipline of the truly rational man. Praise to you for your law of compensation teaching me my follies by compelling me to taste their bitter fruits. Yet your mercy, in a way, overrules your justice or, better put, enlists your justice in the service of its sweeter ends. So often have I chased after the tawdry, succumbed to indolence in my work, missed the beauty of seeing you in unpleasant tasks. So often has my best been a feckless grin-and-bear-it worst without the grin, inwardly putting my nose to the grindstone with barely a spark of zest. Glory to you: the forgetfulness of your unexacting mercy annulled the effects of my listless performances, and, instead of permitting me to remain stuck in shoddy sub-mediocrity, you garmented me in your love, making me new and stronger after I sank into old and weak ways.

Father, transfuse me with your love; then will I praise you to the fullest. Generate anew the love within me; then will I praise you in the image of your Son. Send forth more of your Spirit; then will I praise you the more with fire. I praise you: through your love I can truly aspire rather than crazily ambition to be your co-worker. Through your love the least of my works can have preeminent, i.e., supernatural, import. The love of your cleansing Spirit covers a multitude of sins, sluggish, careless, half-hearted, slovenly ways of working verging on sloth. Without your love the most awe-inspiring of masterpieces in art, technology, or social groupings will be eaten away, defaced, made to crack and peel, and, withered by time, disintegrate into debris in a wasteland. Glory to you for determining that even in human flesh the fruits of work animated by love will last forever.

Praise to you, Father, for summoning me to lend hands to the making of a city of love while the pillars of a liberal-humanist world seem to be splintering and its foundations shaking. Glory to you, the prime Worker, the sovereign Lover, whose life leavens my output to supernatural increase. Let me go on in love, without panache or splash, trusting that my work is contributing to the ascending superstructure of your kingdom of love.

No seed shoots up overnight into a full-grown plant; between seed-time and harvest the farmer must wait for the new fruit. Praise to you, Father: teach me that the seed you sow needs time to develop, let me trust that at the right moment, neither too soon nor too late, you will bring to full flower in my heart the spirit of consecrated work. I can hasten neither the day nor the hour, but I can expect to grow at the unhurried pace you set, with waiting that is worship, with patience that is praise.

I praise you, Father, for your faithfulness; you never rouse an apparently sincere desire that you do not intend to push on to fruition, unless the soul presents some obstacle. Perhaps there's the rub, perhaps some self-indulgence has me clamped to the ground or so fettered that I can only crawl or roll forward. Send down your Spirit once again to enlighten me and arm me with fresh courage. Praise to you for the wind and fire of Pentecost that transformed shaky and vacillating men into bold and stout messengers of your word now perceived in full clarity. Let your Spirit "force" me, i.e., entice me, by infinite love and power to burn away whatever barriers lie astride the path to consecrated work.

Most generous Father, I praise you for the Mass that is always being offered somewhere in the world at every time of the day. In the Mass my spirit feeds on "the bread baked by the fire of Holy Spirit"[51] and drinks of the blood gushing from the divine heart, and my work is transubstantiated into a thing divine. Through Jesus your ordained priest offers your crucified Lamb to you for the redeeming of the world. The work of unordained Christians who are priests in the general sense becomes a holy sacrifice in union with the blood of the Lamb streaming down from the Mass. It was Jesus dead on the cross who gave you glory, Father, it is Jesus sacramentally sacrificed in the Mass who still gives you glory, it is Jesus steeping in his blood those who work in his name who proclaims your glory.

Praise to you, Father: let dying to self that faintly mirrors the death of Jesus be experienced in the uncertainty, self-doubt, dread of failure, blundering, and the need to force myself to do sustained thinking and writing here and now. "Man is made in the shape of a cross," St. John Vianney once said, somewhat paradoxically, for a cross seems made in the shape of a man. Surely in Jesus man at work can be stretched out on the cross. Work that demands catering to others, work that stings and bruises, work that is a thankless task, is carved in the form of the cross. Unite my work with the sacrifice of Jesus in the Mass — then gradually emptied of the false me, it will ascend as a holocaust of praise.

Praise to you, Father, for Paul's words that spur me to walk with a brisker hope: "I can do all things in him who strengthens me" (Phil 4.13). Like many another average Christian, in my earlier years I felt a vague longing for a life of seclusion. Only a very few can live in a strictly monastic or contemplative state but everyone in the body of Jesus can aspire to closest union with you. Praise to you for the example of Paul who in hunger or plenty, in near-destitution or abundance, served and rejoiced in you without let-up. In an apparently prayer-starved setting I can be wedded to your heart, I can gaze on your beauty in the rush and fever of activities. Praise to you: it is your energy that drives me to fly to your arms, to murmur and hear words of love, to praise you softly amid work that usually suffocates the inward self.

Father, all praise to you for your saints who heroically incarnate in a particular time and place and lifestyle the way and the truth and the life that is Jesus. If one picture is worth a thousand words, one saint is worth a thousand theological explanations of holiness. I confess that more than a few times the concrete possibility of the call to a life of holiness seemed to be a gossamer velleity, as far beyond my grasp as are possible planets tied to the outermost stars of our galaxy beyond colonization. Each saint enfleshing praise in ordinary work conveys fresh hope as well as light. Glory to you for being so munificent in sharing your holiness: how many unknown saints have climbed to the mountaintop, then vanished without leaving striking clues of their extraordinary love, saints disciplined and mortified, humbled and exalted by hard work for family and community. Perhaps the number of unknown saints equals or exceeds that of your recognized saints. In any case, your Church grows silently, unstoppably by the largely unremarked praise in the work of your little people, those who count for nothing in the eyes of the world (1 Cor 1.26-29). I praise you especially for St. Joseph, patron of workers, for his unerring practical judgment, his docility to every impulse of your Spirit quickening his consecration to you in work. Jesus was directed by words of practical wisdom from your alter-ego on earth, but he gained most from the sight of Joseph steadily, tranquilly, holily, ever spiritually at work. Though his work-style allowed perhaps little time for explicit prayer and praise, never for a moment was his heart apart from yours since his was bonded to yours by the praiseful company of Jesus and Mary. I praise you for concretizing in Joseph the beatitudes Jesus was later to preach. I praise you for Joseph poor in spirit, sweating for his bread, joyfully bearing the cross of unremitting labor. I praise you for Joseph the meek, who uncomplainingly endured complaining and discourteous customers. I praise you for Joseph the single-hearted, focusing in the multiple activities of his shop on one object, to love you with his whole heart and whole soul and all his strength. Praise to you for Joseph the working father; as he applied his fatherly hand to the task before him, he saw your Fatherly hand assisting and upholding his; he saw every chair or stool he shaped as also shaped by you, the product of your wisdom and love crafted through his hands; he saw himself as a worker in the image of you, Father, always at work in the maintenance and upbuilding of the universe.

Glory to you, Father, everlastingly the same, without shadow of change, yet living with infinite intensity. The more I work with and under you, free me more from agitation, make me like you, tranquil in the love that is yourself. Glory to you for the caducity of things, for the resistless law of change dooming all that is human to die and be buried under sand drifts heaped up by the howling winds of the desert. Yet out of consecrated work whose earthly products are bound to be remorselessly destroyed by time your eternal kindness forms fruits of love and power to last forever.

Thousands and thousands of years from now there may not remain a stone upon a stone of the building in which I am now living, the religious community to which I belong may vanish and be remembered, if at all, in recondite historical footnotes, the United States may disintegrate into a wilderness and its proudest works into rubble. For this prospect of ruin and oblivion I praise you, Father: in union with your work my little work arrayed with the love and power of Jesus will outlast the wrecks of time and remain imperishable fruit of praise to your name.

Notes

[1]Conf. 1. 1. 1.
[2]EP 144 (145).1; CC 40, 2088-89.
[3]S. 34. 2. 3; PL 38, 210.
[4]S. 34. 1. 2 and 2. 3; PL 38, 210.
[5]EP 144 (145). 17; CC 40, 2100-01. The expression, "the mass, the large group of holy martyrs," which occurs in the ninth sentence from the end of this selection, calls for some elucidation. This expression freely renders Augustine's *Massa* (translated as mass, without capitalization, to forestall confusion with the Eucharistic Mass); freely, because I have taken the liberty of adding in apposition the clarifying phrase, "the large group . . . ." In line with the usage of his day Augustine ordinarily referred to these martyrs as *Massa candida*, literally "the White Mass." They were called a mass because they were numerous: S. 306. 2. 2; PL 38, 1401 and EP 49 (50). 9; CC 38, 583; and described as white to underscore the brightness of their sacrifice: S. 306. 2. 2. Other sources do not agree with Augustine on the number of martyrs, the location, and the date of martyrdom. There were, by Augustine's somewhat vague reckoning in EP 49 (50). 9, more than 153 martyrs, while the Acts of St. Cyprian specified 300 martyrs. Augustine spoke of them as "the White Mass of Utica" (S. 311. 10. 10; PL 38, 1417), whereas the Roman martyrology put the place of death in Carthage. Two sermons preached by Augustine on "the birthday" of the martyrs were delivered on August 18, at variance with which was the Roman Martyrology's designation of August 24 as the day of their deaths. The two sermons given on the natal day were S. 330 (PL 38, 1455), delivered at Carthage, and EP 144 (145), from which the selection cited here was excerpted, which was delivered in the Basilica in Utica dedicated to "the White Mass" on August 18 in one of the three years 412-414. See footnote (a) in PL 38, 1401 and *Serm. Morin* 14; MA 644. In the opinion of Hugh Pope, O.P., *St. Augustine of Hippo* (Westminster, Md.: Newman, 1949), p. 67, n. 8, the martyrs died in 259, while an earlier scholar, Patrick J. Healy, in *The Valerian Persecution* (New York: Houghton, Mifflin, 1905), p. 201, puts their deaths, perhaps with greater probability, in 258, consequent upon Valerian's sweeping edict of persecution in that year.
[6]EP 144 (145). 13; CC 40, 2098.
[7]EP 144 (145). 13; CC 40, 2097-99.
[8]EP 148. 15; CC 40, 2175-76.
[9]EP 149. 7; CC 40, 2183.
[10]EP 85 (86). 1; CC 39, 1176-77.
[11]EP 30 (31). (*En. 2. S. 1*). 4; CC 38, 193-94.
[12]EP 60 (61). 1-2; CC 39, 765-66.
[13]Blaise Pascal, *Pensées*, text established by Louis Lafuma (Paris: Seuil, 1962), n. 201 (206), p. 110.
[14]EP 145 (146). 1; CC 40, 2105.

[15]EP 145 (146). 1; CC 40, 2105.
[16]EP 53 (54). 10; CC 39, 653.
[17]EP 137 (138). 3; CC 40, 1980.
[18]EP 137 (138). 3; CC 40, 1980.
[19]EP 145 (146). 1; CC 40, 2105.
[20]EP 53 (54). 10; CC 39, 653-54.
[21]EP 137 (138). 3; CC 40, 1980. As Augustine indicates in EP 120 (121). 13; CC 40, 1799, Crispina, a delicate woman of noble lineage and great wealth, was beheaded by sword on December 5. A member of Christian colony of Thacora or Tagora, she was martyred in 304 under Diocletian when Annius Anullinus ruled as procunsul of Africa. See The Acts of the Christian Martyrs, introd. and tr. Herbert Musurillo (Oxford: Clarendon Press, 1972), p. xliv.
[22]Only while engaged in a final revision of these pages did I come across a like and more frequent use of the analogy between gangsters and totalitarians in Paul Johnson, Modern Times (New York: Harper, 1983), pp. 261, 263, 356, 359, 360, 361.
[23]Catherine Doherty, "Dorothy Day," Restoration (February, 1981), p. 1.
[24]Jean Jacques Olier remarkably depicts St. Joseph as the sensible image of the Father, reproducing on earth the holiness, wisdom, prudence, and love of the Father for his Son. See Sentiments de Monsieur Olier sur la dévotion à saint Joseph (Paris: de Soye et Bouchet, n.d.), pp. 1-22. Passages from this work are reprinted in Charles de Koninck, La piété du Fils: études sur l'Assomption (Quebec: Presses universitaires Laval, 1954), pp. 199-204.
[25]James Patrick Derum, The Porter of St. Bonaventure's: The Life of Father Solanus Casey, Capuchin (Detroit: Fidelity Press, 1968), p. 271.
[26]Robert Ornsby, The Life of St. Francis de Sales (New York, Kenedy, n.d.), p. 19.
[27]Blaise Pascal, Pensées, n. 423 (277), p. 180.
[28]Maurice-Henry Couannier, St. Francis de Sales and His Friends, tr. Veronica Morrow (New York: Alba House, 1964), pp. 283-84.
[29]See The Chronicle (January-February, 1981), p. 2. This small publication carries facts and analyses beneficial to young mothers.
[30]St. Thérèse of Lisieux Her Last Conversations, tr. John Clarke, O.C.D. (Washington, D.C.: Institute of Carmelite Studies, 1977), p. 123, para. 13.
[31]Canticle of Love Autobiography of Marie-Sainte Cécile de Rome, R.J.M., tr. Mary St. Stephen, R.J.M. (Sillery, Quebec: Religious of Jesus and Mary, 1961), p. 89.
[32]This selection from a homily of St. Thomas on the Assumption is translated in the Proper Offices of the Augustinian Saints and Blessed, 2 (O.S.A. English-Speaking Provinces, 1976), p. 42. The original is found in In Assumpt. cont. 3. 7-8, Opera omnia, 4 (Manila, 1883), pp. 441-42.
[33]Elisabeth Stopp, Madame de Chantal (Westminster, Md: Newman, 1963), p. 45.
[34]Summa theologiae (Madrid: Bibliotheca de Autores Cristianos, 1961), 1. 50. 2 ad 4.
[35]EP 34 (35) (S. 2). 16; CC 38, 321.
[36]EP 34 (35) (S. 2). 16; CC 38, 321.
[37]EP 146 (147). 2; CC 40, 2122.
[38]S. 34. 3. 6.; PL 38, 211.
[39]EP 34 (35) (S. 2). 16; CC 38, 321.
[40]EP 146 (147). 2; CC 40, 2122-23.
[41]EP 146 (147). 3-4; CC 40, 2123-24.
[42]S. 34. 3. 6; PL 38, 211.
[43]William V. Shannon, The American Irish (New York: Macmillan, 1963), p. 152.
[44]Adversus haereses 4. 20. 7. Sources chrétiennes, 100 (2), in the critical edition, with translation, of Adelin Rousseau et al., Contre les hérésies (Paris: Cerf, 1963), p. 648.

[45]John M. Kruma, *Must Christians Go to Church?* (Cincinnati: Forward Movement Publications, 1981), p. 8.

[46]S. 311. 15; PL 38, 1120.

[47]Fr. M. Raymond, O.C.S.O., *Forty Years behind the Wall* (Huntington, Ind.: Our Sunday Visitor, 1979), p. 234.

[48]For an expert, fascinating account of a carpenter's work in first-century Palestine see Nan Shanahan, "A Carpenter of Nazareth," *The Carpenter* (April, 1965) [no pagination indicated].

[49]*Conf.* 10. 29. 40.

[50]This appears in one of the books of sermons written by Harry Elmer Fosdick, a Protestant preacher well-known a generation ago. Unfortunately I have not been able to locate the sermon in which it occurs, nor have I been successful in tracking down its supposed Spanish original.

[51]Matthias Scheeben, *The Mysteries of Christianity,* tr. Cyril Vollert, S.J. (St. Louis: Herder, 1946), p. 515. Scheeben's graphic figure seems to echo in part a like phrase employed by Augustine in a different sacramental setting. In addressing neophytes, i.e., those who had recently received the sacraments of Christian initiation, he said: "When you received the Holy Spirit, you were baked by his fire." S. 272; PL 38, 1247.

Chapter IV

Praise in Adversity

The human scene includes not only light but darkness, not only the smile of virtue but the pockmarked face of deep-seated sin. Augustine is no Pollyanna gushingly blinking grim facts of misfortune and malevolence. He boldly advocates that we continue to praise God in affliction and grief. The psalmist bids us proclaim his mercy in the morning, a period of well-being, and his truth in the evening, a period of sadness. Whether straitened by tribulation or expansive with gladness, as his children we must discern our Father both fondling and correcting us and therefore we should never let up praising him. Stripped of possessions, bereft of family, agonizing from head to foot, Job stands as a holy model of such praise: "The Lord gave, the Lord took away:...blessed be the name of the Lord" (Jb 1.31). His capsulized lesson-in-the-flesh urges us to praise God without pause, descrying in the bestowal of gifts his mercy that caresses to strengthen us and in their removal his truth that chastens us to keep from falling. Indeed in the very act of praising him we are healed: "Praise of the God chastising you is the healing of your wound."[1] Our praise too extols his plan for our progress toward spiritual adulthood, since through testing we are found not wanting but sound and strong. "Is it not better to be tried and proved than not tried and ultimately reproved?"[2] Trusting that he will thrust on us no backbreaking burden, we are to praise him in and for whatever happens for weal or woe all day long.

Praise in Tribulation

Because we are sinful in origin and actuality, the problem of evil is always with us. Some secular humanists who, with the naive credulity of the Enlightenment, believe in a sort of automatic human progress have been recently perplexed and dismayed by the pertinacity and progress of evil, for paradoxically, on their reckoning, evil seems to be advancing as fast as modern technology — witness the threat of a nuclear holocaust. Though theoretically untroubled by such a paradox, Christians can never suspend practical grappling with evil. Pain, economic reverses, character assassination — evils like these do not cheer us or initially invite us to lift heart

and hands in praise of God. Yet we have to go on praising God or at least
never give up trying to praise him in the midst of woes. In God's design
evils befall us to let us know the truth about ourselves, that we are sinners
in need of healing and purification. The divine teacher permits the rod
to fall upon our backs both to notify us that we have transgressed his law
and to rectify in part the disorder that is the fallout from our faults. If
affliction is the inescapable lot of every man, praise of God merciful and
just must be the inevitable response of every true Christian.

> "To proclaim your mercy in the morning and your truth
> throughout the night" (v. 3). What does it mean to say that
> the mercy of God is to be proclaimed in the morning and his
> truth throughout the night? Morning stands for the time when
> things are going well with us, night for the time when tribulation
> grieves us. What then does the psalmist tell us in these few
> words? He tells us this: when things are going well with you,
> rejoice in God because this comes from his mercy. But you might
> say, "If I rejoice in God when things are going well with me
> because this comes from his mercy, what am I to do when I
> am in sorrow and tribulation? When things are going well with
> me, this comes from his mercy. When things are going badly
> with me, does this then come from his cruelty? If I praise his
> mercy when things are going well, shall I reproach him for his
> cruelty when things are going badly?" Not at all. But when
> things are going well, praise his mercy. When things are going
> badly, praise his truth because it is not unjust for God to chastise
> sins. When he was praying, Daniel was in the time of night.
> For then he was being held captive with the other people of
> Jerusalem; his life was in the hands of his enemies. At that time
> holy men and women were suffering many afflictions; at that
> time he himself was thrown into a lions' den; at that time three
> young men were cast into a furnace. The people of Israel suffered
> these evils during their captivity; it was night. Throughout the
> night Daniel went on confessing the truth of God, in his prayer
> saying, "We have sinned, we have done wrong, we have
> committed iniquity. O Lord, you are glorious and we are shame-
> faced" (Dan 9.5, 7). He was proclaiming the truth of God
> throughout the night. What does it mean to proclaim the truth
> of God throughout the night? It means this: do not blame God
> for some evil you are suffering but attribute this to your sins
> and the amendment he is working in you. So we are "to
> proclaim his mercy in the morning and his truth throughout
> the night." When you proclaim his mercy in the morning and
> his truth throughout the night, you are always praising God,
> you are always confessing to God, you are singing a psalm to
> his name.[3]

Though its extent and implications have probably been somewhat exaggerated, a generation gap does exist between parents and children. As we were growing up, we expected our father and mother to embrace us and smile on us and pat us on the back. But almost as naturally we shrank from the punishment that our parents felt it necessary to threaten or inflict to rein in our wayward inclinations and, not unimportantly, to safeguard their own right to a peaceful existence. Usually it was only later on, after maturing, that we experientially penetrated to the kernel in the simple but significant truism that punishment helps mold character. Then we thanked and praised our parents for doing us the kindness of cracking our knuckles when we needed it. Analogously the awesome and consoling truth that God is our Father explains in part why he not only fondles but disciplines us. As we put aside childish ways, as we grow up spiritually, we slowly — O so slowly — come to see that physical and psychological afflictions, protracted pain after surgery, misunderstandings, slanders, frustrations are allowed by our Father to teach us littleness, to apportion to us some of his rocklike strength. So, St. Augustine urges, we are to praise him during tribulations: these are the stern means our Father uses to school us in his righteousness and love.

> The words, "in hymns," in the title of this psalm mean "in praises." Whether we are troubled and straitened or whether we rejoice or exult, we are to praise him who schools us in trouble and solaces us in joy. For the praise of God should never leave the heart or the lips of a Christian. So the Christian will not praise God in prosperity and curse him in adversity but will follow the course one of the psalms lays down: "I will bless the Lord at all times, his praise will be always on my lips" (Ps 33 [34].1). When you are rejoicing, recognize your Father caressing you. When you are troubled, recognize your Father correcting you. Whether caressing or correcting, he is schooling his child for whom he is preparing his inheritance.[4]

One of the outstanding exemplars of fortitude and trust in suffering is Job. After a catastrophic change in fortune including the loss of all of his property and the swift death of his children, after being smitten by a loathsome disease, Job goes on praising God who in his mercy and power is able to freely give and freely take away benefits. Most of us need not fear that God will so quickly divest us of possessions and bereave us of family as he did Job, for he fits the burden to the back. Yet it would be entertaining illusion, Augustine cautions, to presume that no tragedy or trial will cast its shadow over our path. It would be more foolish to hope that we will be spared of ills that beset every generation. For if we were without trials, our soul would go untested and, become flabby and shallow, be exposed to evils of the heart that grease the slide downward to everlasting reprobation. Thus if we are dispossessed of all we hold dear, if we are tormented in body and spirit, if our world falls apart and our inward self is apparently broken to bits, we are, in the spirit of Job, to bless the name of the Lord. All our Father does he must do from love and mercy, and as his children we must not respond by proclaiming his goodness in ongoing praise.

> You see then that you have the means for tasting delight every day. For your God will not desert you even if something sorrowful happens to you. For how sorrowful were the tribulations that happened to the holy man Job. How he was suddenly stricken with numerous woes, how all those things in which people believed, he found (though actually these were things in which he did not find joy) were snatched away when the devil tried him, how too his sons suddenly died. All the goods he was saving perished, and those for whom he was saving them perished; nevertheless, he who gave both goods and sons did not perish. And his sons themselves perished in this world so that he could recognize and reclaim them in the world to come. But this man had another sort of good in which he found joy, and in him was verified the verse that we just mentioned, "I will bless you every day" (v. 2). Did the interior light in his heart go out because the day on which everything perished shone with sorrows? Not at all. For he stood strong in that light and said, "The Lord gave and the Lord took away; it has been done as the Lord pleased; blessed be the name of the Lord" (Jb 1.21). So every day praise rose from this man who even praised God in his day of sorrow. The brief lesson for us is this: always praise God and with a sincere rather than an insincere heart say, "I will bless the Lord at all times and his praise is always on my lips" (v. 2).

> The brief lesson for us is this: know that God is merciful when he gives and merciful when he takes away. Do not think that his mercy has abandoned you. For either his giving caresses you lest you fall or he corrects you when you are overjoyed lest you perish. So whether you receive his gifts or his chastisement, praise him. Praise of the God chastising you is the healing of your wound. "Every day," he says, "I will bless you." My brothers, bless God every day without exception. No matter what happens, bless God, for he makes sure that nothing will happen that you cannot bear. Hence you should live with a certain fear when things are going well with you. You should not fall into the habit of thinking that you are never going to be tried. For if you are never tried, you are never proved. Is it not better to be tried and proved than not tried and ultimately reproved? "I will praise your name forever and forever more" (v. 2).[5]

Reflections

1. Father, you have made me, like other men, a creature of the morning, oriented toward happiness, ultimately toward the joy that is yourself. So much are we the children of your mercy, so much pointed toward joy that a comparatively small slice of sorrow can unhinge us and blacken every hour until day seems changed into night. So bountiful is your generosity that you let your sun warm and your rain refresh the unjust as well as the just. You refuse to withhold joy from those who hardly let a day pass without hurling insults at you and blaspheming your name. Only reluctantly do you temporarily allow ebony lines of suffering to be threaded into our lives. Temporarily: for all that you do, you who are purest joy, must issue in final joy for all hungering for your love.

Yet without sorrow I cannot grow. "All sunshine makes a desert," goes one Arab proverb. Anyone spared from all sorrows is liable to become utterly superficial, devoid of moral strengths, his life barren as the Sahara. Playboys and playgirls from jet-set circles probably live a largely care-free, and therefore carefree, existence that is flashy and fruitless. Misguidedly shielded from the suffering that is an ingredient in character, they apparently come close to lacking the slightest trace of sound self-knowledge. Thank you, Father, for depriving me of fortune that is misfortune. In struggle and sorrow I have caught sight of the truth about myself: I am weak, enervated in spirit, ashamed of my sins; I have to cling to you for help.

Once when queried about reasons for his success, Oliver Wendell Holmes responded, "Young man, at an early age I learned I was not God." Trials springing from my foolishness and moral blindness help strip away sheaths of pride masking my narrow range of mind, my unGodlike flabbiness as well. My sins also make my head droop in shame. You are truly my Father, beckoning me always to be buried in your bosom. But first let my sense of ingratitude press my brow to the ground. Father, through Jesus you are always by my side, urging me on, whispering words of love. Yet in return all too frequently I cold-shoulder you and as a result neglect to reach out to brothers and sisters with consistent love. How often I sin by omission. A disturbed brother is looking for someone to whom he can ramble on about his present preoccupations but I will not sacrifice the time to lend him an ear. I fail to live the beautiful lines of the prayer, "Lord, make me an instrument of your peace," ascribed to St. Francis Assisi. "Where there is hatred, let me sow love": when hate stings me, I am hardly ever quick to respond with love. "Where there is despair, hope": I inwardly withdraw and, instead of imparting hope, give way to discouragement. "Grant that I may not seek...to be consoled as to console": I cherish understanding but only stingily console others. In feeling abashed, I am coming to know myself: long on promises, short on delivery; given equally to skyey aspirations and mean faults; hurt if others blithely ignore me yet stubborn in my casual ingratitude to you. How I need you, Father! Through the night of sorrow teach me the truth about myself, that I am a sinner whom you love and call to be sinless like you (Mt 5.48).

Father, when the shades of night come down, your light reveals the refulgence of the self-oblation of your devoted ones. Prior to her husband Pierce's ordination in July, 1845, Cornelia Connelly made a vow of perpetual chastity, then the following year entered the religious life (she was foundress of the Society of the Holy Child Jesus), consecrating herself to the Lord "without reserves." The night descended on her in 1848 when Pierce unexplainably launched an attack on the Church and, recanting his previous renunciation of marriage, sued for the restitution of his conjugal rights, a demand that was upheld by a lower English court in 1849. Cornelia appealed, and had to force herself to remain day by day calm and trustful in spite of inner anguish and foreboding, until in 1851 a higher tribunal suspended the lower court's decision, a move that effectively reversed the earlier verdict. In the darkness of this harrowing experience, in which the husband whom she had loved so much and had sacrificed her marriage to satisfy betrayed and reviled her in outbursts that, in hindsight, seem partly demonic and partly pathological, Cornelia learned the existential meaning of self-oblation. Taking her at her word, Father, you taught her the cost of giving herself. The canker in the heart of her capricious husband tore him completely out of her life, and the loss of his spiritual love was a gaping wound that lasted till the grave. Her life as a religious was not exempt from sorrows, perhaps one of the cruelest being the animosity of a certain faction of her congregation directed at her in the years shortly before her death. She had always aspired to be another holy child, and from misguided critics in her institute was distilled the astringent truth that only through the agony of misunderstanding is a soul shaped as a tiny one like Jesus.[6]

Cornelia bore the night with saintly patience to win the day she now enjoys. In the final joy all the terrific suffering will be erased from memory, as Jesus informs us in a remarkable figure: "A woman about to give birth feels sorrow because her time has come, but, when she has given birth to her child, she no longer remembers her pangs for joy that a man has been born into the world" (Jn 16.21). A spiritual woman of my acquaintance, who reared six children, once shared with me the travail a mother undergoes. Nothing she heard from doctors or others afforded an inkling of the excruciating pain she experienced in delivering her first child after a labor of over twelve hours. Yet when the actual birth occurred and her infant girl was lifted up, never before did she thrill with such joy over the ultimate of natural miracles. By the time she first cuddled her little girl in her arms to feed her, all memory of the dread birth pangs had evanesced in the transcendent insight that the living God so loved her that he had sent her this child. So when a saintly soul breaks free of the body or a purified soul is released from the purgatorial furnace of mercy, he is swept up into an ecstasy of delight that expunges from memory all the long reaches of prior suffering.

Father, any night I am passing through, any suffering I shoulder, pales in comparison with the day ahead, the inheritance that is your infinite love, the ultimate miracle of entering fully into your unalloyed joy. Expel all fear of pain, make me patient during travail with the hope with which an expectant mother looks forward to her newborn-to-be: out of the darkness, the noonday; out of the labor, life, this fragile self transfigured into a Godlike being like you, leaping and bounding with a happiness beyond pain or loss.

2. However trite-sounding, it seems noteworthy that the ceremonial terminus marking graduation is called a commencement to underscore that formal education is only the beginning of what ideally should be a life-long development of the mind. But the large block of hours budgeted for simply earning a living rules out, save for a comparative few, leisure enough for sharpening strictly intellectual skills. Post-school learning for most consists of roughly on-the-job training. However, the realm of the spirit, Father, seems more democratic. Practically everyone hospitable to your word can continue learning in your academy of justice and mercy. In your school of the spirit open all year twenty-four hours a day you never stop teaching me my meaning in the meaning of your life revealed through Jesus. There is no incident that lacks import, no circumstance that cannot convey your truth and love. Unhappily I am an idle, doodling student, distracted by trivia, clowning around as the theme of a lesson sails over my head, often simply putting in time and occupying space instead of devouring the lights you unceasingly press upon my soul. How long-suffering you have been with me in my lassitude, how tolerant of my childish resistance. At least show me how to learn from my failure to learn. In 1913 the Prentice-Hall publishing company issued its first book, a volume on United States tax laws. Shortly after, Congress initiated the income tax, a move that made the book partly outdated and outmoded. Disconsolate as he was, Richard Prentice Ettinger said to his colleague and co-founder, Charles Gerstenberg, "All right, we made a mistake. Now let's see what we can learn from it." With that thumb-rule he handled mistakes gross and slight in the years ahead; humble analysis could turn a definite loss into future profit. It is no straining for a manifestation of humility to say that from one angle a good deal of my life has consisted of a string of errors. I have failed and failed. Train me, Father, to learn from sins of commission and omission, show me how to school myself through my unschooling. Once when about to officiate at a marriage ceremony I asked for her counsel for newlyweds, a mother of eleven ranging in age from two to twenty-four cheerily offered one hopeful note born of her own hard experience: "Tell them to keep on trying." No matter how obdurately I sometimes refuse to learn from my blunders, never let me stop trying: let every fall be a rung upward for fresh

effort, let every discouraging outcome spark encouragement.

Father, because you assure me, "I have loved you with an everlasting love" (Jer 31.3), at every moment your hand of love, I trust, rests upon me, caressing or correcting me. You never stop reiterating in divine action that is all tenderness: "I am loving you with an unending love." While you always speak as a Father, I frequently do not listen as a child. In discussing roadblocks to higher degrees with a young, extremely bright Ph.D. candidate in electrical engineering, I mentioned that it was tough for a person in his late thirties or early forties to knuckle down to the grind of classes to which youth smoothly adapts. His reply was just a bit bumptious but sage: "If that is the case, then I hope that as regards learning I always remain a child." Surely this is the ideal of the seeker after truth: to put aside arrogance and prejudice and to stand or kneel before each feature of reality with the wonder and receptivity of a child. Surely too this is the ideal of the seeker after the truth that is love. Father, I have begged for this already before, but even were I to ask a trillion times, it would not be enough: give me the heart of a child so that my spiritual ears can capture every least inflection and tone in the conversation in the Spirit that you desire to carry on with me. At every instant lights pour down from you but the point of much of your messages goes unscrambled because I have eyes but do not see and ears but do not hear. O Father, how I yearn for a childlike heart! To be a child again — this could be a velleity harboring a latent intention to shuck off responsibility. But you know that I want to be a full spiritual child for the first time in my life, with heart and mind maturely wide-open to your words. "Certain thoughts are prayers," Victor Hugo wrote. "There are moments when, whatever the posture of the body, the soul is on its knees." Whatever I am doing, however adult-seeming my status, however unchildlike my visage, let my soul be constantly on its knees, let my every moment be a childlike prayer shining with some of the reverence of the holy child Jesus, every breath silently crying out, "Abba, Father, I love you, make me more and more your child of love."

What delight thrills a father when he sweeps his child up into his arms. And how a child beams as his own dad hugs him. Father, you want to so father me with affection throughout the day, especially when I feel bruised. In the rays from your eyes I will come to grow glad also in your discipline, welcoming in each chastisement one of many complex disguises of your caress. This is the glory of the saint: a merest child, a toddler in the Spirit, he is gifted with immense capacity to know you, as Jesus knows you, in inexpressible intimacy (Mt 11.25-27).

3. Job of old had the inner self of a child, Father. Covered with sores, bereft of family, he bowed totally to your will, resigned to his tragic lot from your hands. It had to be that way, he said within, because you wanted it so. Yet at best he managed only a far-off glimpse of your love. Now I see that all that occurs has to be so not with an inflexible determinism, not because you could do no other than permit evil, not because you dangle

us like puppets on a string. All that transpires has to be so because you are all love, purest love. All that happens to me bears the imprint of your embrace and kisses. This life on earth is a warfare (Jb 7.11), its struggle and conflict balking complete praise here for the restive human heart. Yet much of your own peace filters into this valley somber under a leaden sky. Perhaps we can also describe this life as a marathon of hope, a phrase coined by the valiant Terry Fox. In 1977, after bone cancer had dictated the amputation of his right leg, and while recuperating and getting accustomed to his artificial limb, the young man made up his mind to run across Canada to help raise one million dollars for cancer research. In April, 1980, after rigorous training he left St. John's Newfoundland, vowing that he would not stop till he had dipped his artificial leg in the Pacific Ocean off British Columbia, roughly 5,200 miles away. In spite of his handicap he was able to average close to thirty miles a day. But he never reached his goal. Worn out after some 3,200 miles, he contracted pneumonia, then, after gradually sinking, died at the age of twenty-two on June 28, 1980. But his lion-heartedness captured the admiration of his countrymen who contributed twenty-four million toward cancer research. A life short but rich with poignancy and power; Terry Fox burnt himself out in a hopeless fight against death; yet his marathon was one of renewed purpose for the human spirit. In a life that did not go much beyond twenty he buoyed up more hearts than do thousands who last into their eighties. Terry Fox symbolizes your faithful who run the course of life. Each of us has to limp his way along. Most of us collapse far short of our goals, apparently partial failures. Yet even more than brave Terry Fox's run the race of the determined Christian is a marathon of hope. Humanly speaking, I seem fated for unsuccess, never accomplishing the projects set for myself in spirit and mind. But I can succeed by failing. Like the abrupt stopping of Terry Fox's run, my abortive effort can end in victory through your power and love. Father, disregard what may annoy some as a broken-record ring: make me a child of hope, undismayed by the bitter cold and smothering heat of contrary circumstances, unconcerned about storms that ordinarily garrot resolve. Lame I am but with hope in you I will jog on and on, staggering here and there, tottering now and then from exhaustion, never, never for a moment halting my running. So will I run the race, so will I triumph by not finishing, so will I win by losing.

A man greater than Job teaches the meaning of suffering. In the eyes of men the life of Jesus was cut drastically short. He was struck down in his prime, at the height of his mission, perhaps just when he was sowing grass-roots support that would eventually consolidate his power and make him the most formidable figure in all Palestine. How swiftly his foes ganged up on him, how suddenly their fury and cunning hurled him to his doom. Yet the cross was part of the glory of Jesus, a night in which his praise in submission assured an everlasting morning for his brothers and sisters. Shattered by enemies, he won victory for both friends and enemies. At the end of a life that was, by human calculation, unfinished, he could cry out in triumph, "It is finished." Jesus not only exemplifies obedience to suffering, but, in commending to you my spirit along with his, he implants his will to accept suffering. Father, how you comforted Jesus on the cross! In the measure in which I suffer I can share in your strength through Jesus. Always your power overflows to us through him, always light from your eyes equips us to walk in the darkness as if it were noon, always your consolation turns a cross from a dread burden into a yoke one with that of Jesus (2 Cor 1.3-7). Then feeble though I be, I can offer the very support of God to my brothers and sisters whose cup reeks with woe. Suffering sensitizes my soul so that I can somehow co-suffer with someone slumped over in anguish. Father, you are all in all: all the suffering I am given is aimed at making me like you in the Spirit of Jesus. You swathe me in consolation so that I can press to the lips of others the word with which you have made my soul at least resigned in pain.

Praise

1. Father, thank you for making me a child of the morning. How much joy you have showered upon me! Praise to you for my beautiful family, my most precious human possession. I praise you for the unpretentious, unstinting care of my dear mother and father, for the rosy glow of affection and security in our undistinguished-looking rowhouse in a low-middle-class neighborhood. Praise to you for the hidden glory and charm of this, for me, best of homes. What will I be thinking about on my deathbed? Only you see in your eternal present the thoughts that may grip my mind then, supposing there is time for reflection. If accorded one last opportunity to fondle a landmark of the past, the eyes of my memory would savor the quietly joyous days of my youth on a small street in north Philadelphia. Outwardly uneventful, this was inwardly the happiest period of my life, for it was a time of love, the air that my soul matter-of-factly breathed and fed on. I praise you, Father, for this little golden age in my life, so dull-looking, so bright with pleasures of the spirit.

Praise to you for the genuine friendship you have sown in my heart. Earlier in my life I seemed to be more enamored of ideas than of people, and only in recent years have I come to prize friendship as one of the supreme goods of nature. How many friends you have deputed to comfort me and set my heart aflame with their affection. How wonderful it is, Father, to be taken into the homes and hearts of others as one with them, as one of them, as one in them. What a joy it is to be befriended! Praise to you for this love from others that suffuses my spirit. According to William Ellery Channing, "A beloved friend does not fill one part of the soul, but, penetrating the whole, becomes connected with all feeling."[7] Loving and being loved, my spirit is multiplied; my friend lives in me, in every part of me, and I live in the one I love, through and through. "My love is my weight," Augustine wrote.[8] Love carries me to those I love almost as irresistibly as gravity pulls an unsupported body to the earth. But this spiritual-gravitational tendency never comes to an end. I want to so possess the ones I love that they possess me, blending their spirits with mine. Glory to you, Father: through love I am not one being but many, through love I am absorbed by others yet grow in integrity; through love my self increases its dimensions yet becomes more unified; through love I discover myself in the clasp of friends and read their souls as I hold them close in spirit.

Eugenie de Guerin said, "After God, there is nothing . . . as sweet as a friend."[9] Indeed, Father, without your friendship no other friendship could be enduringly sweet. So I praise you again for my gift of faith underlying my friendship with you. Rather than forsake this light let me prefer to drag out my remaining years in a Soviet slave labor camp in the Gulag. Without faith I would be more doleful than a shipwrecked man with all prospects of rescue gone, drifting, drifting, drifting in an endless sea, looking forward only to the "long sleep" of death, tempted hour by hour to win swift release by sliding off the raft and going to rest beneath the waves.

Praise to you, Father, for making me a priest, for enabling me to represent the death of your Son, then to feed on the sacrificial food that is Jesus. Glory to you for my office as a healer in the sacrament of penance. In the words of absolution the power of Jesus once again flashes down through my words to cleanse another heart. Through me Jesus gives the soul his kiss of mercy, wraps him in all his purifying fire. Praise to you for the fruits of this morning dignity: I am your priest, a priest of and because of Jesus, seeking to serve you in your people.

2. What a sub-world of darkness lies around us! The laments and groans of the sick and suffering everywhere pierce the air. Father, how can I praise you for this ponderous pain that tortures fellow men? Yet I will praise you not only in spite of but because of this suffering, for you are all love, all you will is from love, all that you permit finds its final answer in love. Through Mary my mother speed me in spirit to Lourdes, your stupendous shrine of healing. There before the Blessed Sacrament, in that small city of God where your presence is palpable,[10] I can praise you, without seeming grotesque, for the cancer, blindness, paraplegic bodies, lupus, arthritis, indeed all the diseases that tear down the human frame. There everything murmurs your name, everything points to your mercy. Praise to you for this mountain of sorrow that lifts up and reconsecrates my spirit to you. In the atmosphere of prayer of Lourdes the most wretched of suffering looks bearable and somewhat intelligible.

I praise you, Father, for the meaning inscribed in the suffering of Bernadette, the tiny seer of Lourdes. This select soul serenely endured a huge tumor on her left knee. Uncomplaining in love, freighted by tuberculosis, she dragged herself about in attending, so far as able, to the most menial and earthy needs of Sisters in the convent infirmary at Nevers. Hers was the ordinary way during those grimmest hours leading to the end; you allowed her to cry out, to weep in her pain, to submit to the use of narcotics that might alleviate the agony. Glory to you for her life-epitomizing sigh near her departure: "I love, I love!" Of St. Vincent de Paul it was once said that he was not a saint because he was charitable but that he was charitable because he was a saint. Bernadette loved because she was a saint and she was a saint because she loved. In her your holiness and love were two sides of the one divine energy. Praise to you for her littleness that enabled her to penetrate the mystery of penitence, which she first proclaimed as the visionary of Mary at the grotto. What a labyrinthine riddle is human suffering! Praise to you for this so-human saint who, while "charged with your grandeur," walked the beaten path, whose love of the cross partially illumines a crux that evades adequate analysis.[11]

Praise to you, dearest Father, for all in my life, sorrows as well as joys. If it is true that you fit the burden to the back, I must have an extremely feeble back. Praise to you for allotting me minuscule physical suffering, for attracting me to interior mortification, the subjugation of doughty pride, and at least an aspiration to self-oblation. Glory to you for showing me in Jesus how to draw the sting of inward suffering so as to transcend it. Without becoming a spiritual hypochondriac, I can capitalize on inconveniences, setbacks, putdowns as means of entering somewhat into ugly malignancies that torment the human heart. Then under the firm pressure of your gentle hand I can grow more like the holy child you want me to be.

When, after entering the convent, Bernadette was asked what she could do, she answered self-deprecatingly and discerningly, "Nothing very much."[12] These few words sum up what I have accomplished and what I am capable of doing, and nicely describe the amount of suffering I have undergone. Praise to you, Father; even the scantiness of my suffering conveys the central lesson you want to instill: I am nothing very much, practically nothing, i.e., really nothing at all. Secretly, in the recesses of the imagination of my old self, I have perhaps dreamed of performing feats of derring-do in behalf of the Gospel and of being beaten and tortured and of heroically enduring sundry hardships. Praise to you: my suffering has been only a mite, which, I beg you, join to that of Jesus and, in him, to that of a saint like Bernadette. Through his power and in her company it will impress more deeply the image of your love in my heart, an image after the soul of the holy child Jesus.

3. Just after the wasted frame of Bernadette succumbed to death, Father Dominique Peyramale, at first skeptical, then a fast friend, was moved to whisper toward the still nun, her face lit up in ecstasy, "Bernadette, your life is beginning."[13] Praise to you, Father, for the contractions, heaving pressure, distress, sweating — without travail there can be no birth, without suffering my heavenly life cannot begin. So overjoyed is the heart of a mother resting her eyes on her new son or daughter that, if she had to,

she would not flinch to re-agonize through her labor pains. Father, joy beyond all expectations will be ours when we see your Face — an ecstasy of ecstasies! Truly, "the sufferings of this present time are not to be compared with the glory that will be revealed in us" (Rom 8.18). At that transfiguring instant all anguish that went before will be sublated and swallowed up in super-joy. It may be wild surmise, but I am convinced that not one of the billions of the blessed would hesitate for a second to return to this world and pass, if need be, through a thousand earthly hells so long as they were assured of shortly recapturing your beauty. Husbands of wives who undergo natural childbirth are now admitted to the labor and delivery rooms. After Laurel's protracted delivery so enfeebled her that she could not embrace her second boy, her husband Bob picked up the child and held him in his arms for a long time: this boy was his, the fruit of his love, to be fondled as his very own. Praise to you, Father: the transport of the soul receiving the vision of your Face resembles not only the mother's joy but the joy of being held by you. What rapture that will be, when in union with your Son and Spirit, you envelop me in your arms, pressing your cheek to mine as you murmur, "I am your Father, you are my very own, the fruit of my love that I have waited for so long — I will never let you go."

Everything other than you who are changeless mercy can wither and decay and be blown away like dust in the wind. Into your hands alone I place my trust, in you I am "saved by hope" (Rom 8.14). I praise you, Father, for daily testing, daily experiences of being checkmated, daily recognitions of powerlessness, confident that my trials along with the groaning of all creation will upflow into a golden transformation.

Send your love streaming into me. Then I will care for nothing but your will, then I will do as I please (for all I do in love will be according to your pleasure), then I will be living more of the deathless self-sacrifice central to your life. This is the core of the true pangs that must anguish me before I enter into your joy: I must daily give myself to you, Father, so as to become one with the threefold self-giving that is your life with Son and Spirit, I praise you: one day, I hope, you will whisper to me, "Your life is beginning." In anticipation of that eternal new birth let no hour wing by in which I do not fasten mind and heart on the first and lasting moment of never-ending life.

God Draws Good Out of Evil

St. Augustine's claims are not pious effusions, bordering on the irrational, of a man of blind faith ready to leap into the dark and absurd because God so wills it. Underpinning the valorous practice of praising God amid woes of body and spirit is a faith illumined by understanding that prayerfully ponders the providence of a Father whose merciful law programs seeming happenstance for the good of world order and permits evil only so as to extract good, or even a greater good, out of moral evil. A superficial appraisal of natural events inclines 'the shortsighted to deliver the lower zone over to the reign of chance. The fact that rain falls into the sea while leaving desert regions parched apparently indicates essential disorder in the inferior portion of the cosmos. But this is only appearance feeding misconception, for life in the sea as well as that on land requires rain. Indeed the planning of God extends to the tiniest of insects like the gnat whose stinger is even marvellously constructed. So the providence of God gathers all things in its sweep, from angels to worms, building each thing down to its smallest specification, orienting all things and events in a universal order.

More mysteriously and, ultimately, more gloriously, moral evil also does not escape the divine order but through omnipotence in the ministry of divine mercy subserves the efflorescence of good. Over the centuries the fact of evil has been construed as an insurmountable obstacle to a God both all-good and all-powerful. Either he will not or cannot eradicate evil; either he is not all-good or he is not all-powerful. Grasping the very nettle of the objection, Augustine counters by arguing that evil is explicable only because God is both infinitely good and omnipotent. Since he is all-good, he ordains evil to good; since he is all-powerful, he is able to bring good out of evil. To resort to a phrase long a staple of spiritual literature on trust, *etiam peccata*, even our sins, contribute to the ripening of moral personality and the perfection of the universe. Strictly speaking, not sins as sins but souls as souls are necessary for the perfection of the universe. In other words, God positively wills human nature and permissively provides for the evil that in the long run issues from twisted hearts. "For those who love God all things work together unto good" (Rom 8.28). In Augustine's reading of this most consoling of texts, God employs faults to make us humbler and wiser. When we tend to be cocksure of our moral invincibility and smug in the illusion that we are impregnable against serious lapses, God allows us at times to topple into sin to school us in our self-nothingness and our need for total reliance on him. When we sin, the mask drops off, pretenses are pulverized, we are exposed for what we really are: barren, feckless — moral nonentities. In our degradation we grope to find ourselves, and from shame emerges a clearer-eyed humility. Like the bumptious Peter, we learn self-knowledge out of the depths of denial of Christ. After we turn our face away from the Lord, he turns his face toward us, and in repentence we rise anew, stronger through weakness, better for having been worse. Keenly conscious of our caducity, purged of arrogance, we empirically share in Augustine's acute perception of each man's infinite capacity for evil: "Any sin any one man commits any other man can commit — once he cuts himself off from the Ruler who made him."[14]

Initially the universe in whole or part strikes the mind as a world of order. The very writing or reading of this line would be impossible without the multi-billioned-celled operation of a human brain underlying the movement of hand or eye. Yet nature is far from a perfectly mathematicized harmony. Various agents apparently work at cross-purposes, with the result that the lower zone of the universe may seem disorderly, even radically indeterminate. An avalanche buries a party of mountain-climbers; a volcano erupts and wipes out villages and makes soil infertile for generations; an earthquake destroys the lives of thousands. Again, like a society grossly lacking in social justice, nature seemingly distributes its bounty inequitably, some inferior regions being blessed with a balanced climate and an abundance of water, others being so deprived that they become arid wastelands. But it is illusion to conclude that chance is king of earth, to think that the lower zone is through-and-through disorderly. A small insect could not fly or leap about for a moment were it not superbly ordered in all its parts. So too the universe itself would fall to pieces were it not basically ordered in all its parts. A supernatural perspective helps account for the deprivation suffered by an area with a deficient water supply. The inhabitants adapt to the limitations, many of them preferring their less endowed area to areas more naturally wealthy. Moreover, hard circumstances firm and help mature the soul. So not chance but order reigns in nature, with minor-degree disorders serving to strengthen a too easily spoiled human spirit.

"Fire, hail, snow, ice, storms, winds that carry out his word" (v. 8). Why does the psalmist add here the words, "that carry out his word"? Many shallow individuals, who are incapable of studying creation and discerning that the universe in its various parts and overall design executes its movements at the behest and command of God, think that God directs all superior things but that he despises, spurns, abandons inferior things so that he neither takes care of them nor directs nor regulates them. They hold rather that chance determines how and whence inferior things operate. The individuals making these claims influence others with whom they sometimes discuss these matters (but do not let them discuss these things with you; that is, do not listen or assent to their claims for these are execrable blasphemies in the eyes of God). They argue, for instance, "If God caused rain, would he cause the rain to fall into the sea? What kind of providence," they say, "is this? Getulia is thirsty, and rain falls into the sea." They think that they are stating their case shrewdly. But in response we say to them: Getulia is indeed thirsty but you are not thirsty. It would have been profitable for you to say to God, "Before you my soul is like land without water" (Ps 142 [143].6). This is clearly put in another place: "My soul thirsted for you; and in how many ways my flesh also" (Ps 62 [63]. 2). And in the Gospel the Lord tells us, "Blessed are those who hunger and thirst for justice for they shall have their fill" (Mt 5.6). For the man who argues along these lines is already filled. He deems himself learned and refuses to learn; therefore he does not thirst. For if he did thirst, he would be willing to learn and would recognize that the providence of God directs everything on earth and would marvel at even the arrangement of the members of a flea. In your charity give me your attention. Who arranged the members of a flea or a gnat so that they would have their proper order, their proper life, their proper movement? Take a look at one small animal, the tiniest you wish. If you examine the order of its members and the animation of life whereby it moves, notice how for its own good it steers clear of death, loves life, seeks pleasure, avoids pain, exercises various senses, and thrives in movements suitable to it. Who gave the gnat the stinger that enables it to suck blood? How narrow is the tube through which it sucks in blood! Who arranged all this, who made all this? You are awestruck when you examine the least of things: then praise their great Maker. Hold fast then to the truth, my brothers, do not let anyone shake you from your faith or from sound teaching. He who made the angel in heaven made the worm on earth; but he made the angel to dwell in heaven and the worm to dwell on earth. Did he make the angel to creep in the mud and the worm to move about in heaven? He assigned inhabitants to their proper regions; incorruptibles he assigned to incorruptible regions, corruptibles to corruptible places. Ponder the whole universe, praise the whole universe. If he arranged the members of a worm, does he not then govern the clouds as well? And why does rain fall into the sea? Individuals favoring chance argue as if there were nothing in the sea fed by the rain, as if God did not make the fish in the sea, as if he did not make the animals in the sea. Observe how fish swim to sweet water. "And why," the defender of chance says, "why does God give rain to fish, and at times no rain falls on me?" This is why: so that you may realize that you are sojourning in a desert and that this life is a pilgrimage; and that, as this present life becomes bitter to you, you may yearn for the life to come; or that you may be punished and chastised and corrected. And how does he distribute the goods proper to each region? Take the case of Getulia since we have spoken of it in our own land. God sends rain nearly every year, and every year he gives us wheat. But the wheat cannot be stored here; it quickly rots because it is given us every year. In Getulia because wheat grows only rarely, the people have it in abundance and store it for a long time. But do you perhaps think that thus God forsakes men in Getulia or that they do not praise and glorify God with joyful hearts there also? Take a Getulian from his homeland, set him among our lovely trees. He would want to flee from here and go back home to his barren Getulia. Thus to all places, regions, and times God has assigned and determined things proper to them. It would take a great deal of time to pursue a more thorough inquiry into all these matters. Who would be able to explain all this adequately? Nevertheless, those who have eyes see a great many of these wondrous things. When they see them, they are pleased; when they are pleased, they praise not really the things themselves but him who made them: so it is that all things praise God.[15]

The enormous fact of evil has been constantly brandished in the face of Christian believers as the source of an apparently unanswerable objection to the reality of a traditional God.[16] Abstractly, a God both infinitely good and all-powerful seems tenable, but, concretely, in view of the evil that persists all around us, such a God seems to be as paradoxical as a square circle. If God is all-good and yet evil exists, he must be powerless to stamp out evil. If God is all-powerful yet evil continues, he lacks the desire to abolish all evil, i.e., he cannot be all-good. In brief, a God both all-good and all-powerful could not tolerate evil; and if evil somehow came into existence, he would destroy it. However, Augustine argues, only in virtue of a God both infinitely good and infinitely powerful can we make sense out of the riddle of evil. God is so good and so powerful that he permits evil only in order to draw good out of evil. Since he is all-good, he appoints a good end for all agents and events, both good and evil. Since he is all-powerful, he is able supernaturally, miraculously, to derive good from evil. God as all-good desires only good, and his infinite power at the service of his goodness enables him, beyond the limits of natural moral causation or the law of consequences, to bring good out of evil.

All things have been created by the supremely, equally, and unchangeably good trinity. These things are not supremely, equally, and unchangeably good, but they are nonetheless good, even taken individually. Indeed when viewed as an ensemble, they are very good (Gen 1.31), because the wonderful beauty of the universe is constituted by all things.

In the universe even what is called evil, when exactly ordered and situated in its proper place, sets in relief the value of good things, which are the more pleasing and praiseworthy when compared with evil things. Since he is all-good, the all-powerful God, who, as even pagans recognize, possesses supreme power, would not in an way permit any evil whatsoever in his works if he were not so all-powerful and good that he could produce good even out of evil.[16]

Yet this solution provokes another, a subtle difficulty: if everything in the universe subserves its perfection, then even our sins are necessary for the perfection of the universe. Surely a paradoxical consequence — without moral evil the universe could not achieve its total moral goodness. However, Augustine shrewdly points out, sins as such are not necessary for such perfection. Rather, souls as souls are necessary for the perfection of the universe. But since some souls will sin, provision must be made for evil in the universe. Evil is permitted, i.e., only reluctantly admitted as a side effect of the fact that some souls can and will commit sin. Thus it is not because of but in spite of sins that the universe achieves moral perfection. In themselves sins are moral evils, they are literally no good, they contribute nothing directly to the good of individuals or of the whole universe. Evil as such adds up only to evil. On the natural plane we can no more get good out of evil than we can get blood out of a stone. But while not directly willing evil, God does permit it, i.e., he makes a place for it in his plan. Since his plan aims at good, all the evils permitted in the universe are ordained by God toward the good or perfection of things. Because he is so loving and powerful, God is able to take what is naturally bad and rotten and, supernaturally, over the long haul, make evil indirectly serve good purposes. Evil stubbornly persists; it is concretely ineradicable until the Day of the Lord. But God will not, cannot, be defeated by evil: so he capitalizes on the unpromising raw material that is evil and all-powerfully converts it to the good of the universe. This ordering of evil to good is worked, we said, over the long haul. Strictly, the complete picture of the supernatural orientation of evil to good will not become evident till the end of the world. Now we see in a glass darkly; we must wait till the final judgment to see in all their intricacy, in the full blaze of the divine light, the infinitely delicate divine operations that spin a peerless final pattern of nature and history not only out of good materials but out of stuff that is tarnished and stained and sleazy.

> But still someone who has not quite grasped what we have said may pose an objection along these lines: "If even our unhappiness completes the perfection of the universe, something would be missing in this perfection if we were always happy. Consequently, if the soul arrives at unhappiness only by sinning, even our sins are necessary for the perfection of the universe God made. How then in justice does he punish sins without which his creation would not be full and perfect?" My answer is this: neither sins in themselves nor unhappiness in itself is necessary for the perfection of the universe, but souls as souls are necessary, which, if they so will, sin, and, once they sin, become unhappy. For if unhappiness persists after their sins have been removed or if unhappiness also precedes sins, then the order and the government of the universe are properly called defective. Again, if sins occur but no unhappiness ensues, injustice no less sullies the order

of the universe. However, when the sinless gain happiness, the universe is perfect; and when sinners receive unhappiness, the universe is nonetheless perfect. So long as there is no lack of the souls themselves for whom unhappiness is consequent upon sins or happiness upon their virtuous living, the universe is always full and perfect as regards all natures. For sin and punishment of sin are not natures but states of nature, the one voluntary, the other penal. But the voluntary that is expressed in sin is a dishonorable state. This is why punishment is used to put order into it (in such wise that it is not dishonorable to be such) and compel it to harmonize with the beauty of the universe, so that the punishment of sins repairs the disgrace of sin.[18]

Still the statement, "God draws good out of evil," has to be qualified: it is for those who love God that evil works toward ultimate perfection and final glory. The plan of God is one of love, and only for those who love him do "all things work together unto good" (Rom 8.28). In the context of love, in the framework of seeking God, our falls make us humble, our follies make us wise. The historian Edward Gibbon half-cynically, half-realistically somewhere remarked that history is "little more than the register of the crimes, follies, and misfortunes of mankind."[19] Even those with a smattering of history are at times appalled by the horrors and moral stupidities perpetrated by predecessors. How, we at first think, how could men stoop to such depravity, how could rational animals become frightfully vicious in pursuit of a few fleeting trinkets of power and wealth? Why, we muse, do not our contemporaries inclined to similar moral madness profit from the disasters of the past? This is a slippery question; let it suffice to say here that even our detailed knowledge of history seems to be somewhat objective and "theoretical," something more apart from us than a part of us. Our own moral blunders and vices, however, are on the concrete, experiential plane: through them iron enters our souls. Their harsh consequences are burned into our hearts. Their point is hammered into our spirits never to be completely forgotten. When we fall into sin, we go down into the depths of self-knowledge, abashed by our disagreeable inclinations, shocked by our meanness and perversity. Secretly we had boasted of our own strength; inwardly we had slipped into a kind of presumption; implicitly we counted on our inner resources to combat and defeat sin. Now after our fall we see ourselves as we are: halting, weak-kneed, helpless to stem the ferocity of the lower self. We see concretely that we are self-seeking, callous, cruel, and nasty, we see concretely the truth that original sin sinks deep, tenacious roots in each individual, i.e., in each of ourselves. It is we who spoil ourselves by our own devices and inflict wounds on ourselves by our own desires. Yet the damage we do we cannot undo. All our hopes for self-acquired moral maturity, we painfully observe, have played us false. The shambles we have made of ourselves

and the muddle we now wallow in throw glaring light on our vain preten-
tions. Now we know: we are sinners, sinners unable to pull ourselves out
of the sad mess we have made. From the bottom of the pit we have dug
for ourselves we cry out to the Father for mercy. The prince of the apostles
had to gain self-knowledge and the grace of divine mercy through the shame
attending his denial of Jesus. Swaggering a bit, he had bragged to Jesus,
"I will lay down my life for you" (Jn 13.37). But as Jesus was being vilified
and sentenced to death by a kangaroo court, Peter, vehemently repudiating
any association with him, turned his back on his master. The man who
boasted that he would die for Jesus could not muster enough courage to
admit that he was a companion of Jesus. The triple denial was a moment
of spiritual catastrophe for Peter. The petty kingdom of ego shaped by his
conceit and self-sufficiency came crashing down around his ears, and in
the ruins of his false world he came to contempt of self. The agonized,
gentle look of Jesus began the healing of his wounds, and he wept and
wept in compunction until his triple avowal of love compensating for his
threefold denial staunched all tears save those of love.

> This is why the Apostle, after he had said, "We know that for
> those who love God all things work together unto good," added
> the words, "for those who are called according to his purpose"
> (Rom 8.28), for he was aware that some men love God and do
> not persevere in this love till the end. He is referring to those
> individuals who do persevere till the end in their love of God:
> this also includes men who, after wandering for a time from this
> love, return to God and thereafter continue till the end in the
> love that they embraced in the beginning. In order to show what
> "to be called according to his purpose" means, he added also
> what I have already cited above: "Because those whom he fore-
> knew he also predestined to be conformed to the image of his
> Son so that he might be the first-born among many brothers.
> Those whom he predestined he also called" — that is to say,
> according to his purpose — "and those whom he called, he also
> justified; and those whom he justified, he also glorified" (Rom
> 8.28-30). . . . Thus all those who in the super-provident plan of
> God are foreknown, predestined, called, justified, glorified, I do
> not say before even being reborn but before even being born,
> are already sons of God, and in no way can they ever be lost.
> These truly come to Christ because they come in the manner in
> which he himself speaks of it: "All that the Father gives me will
> come to me; and him that the Father gives me will come to me;
> and him who comes to me I will not reject" (Jn 6.37). And shortly
> after, he says, "This is the will of the Father who sent me that
> I should lose nothing of what he has given me" (Jn 6.39). Thus
> this perseverence in love till the end is also given by the Father;
> and it is given only to those who will not be lost, since those who

do not persevere will be lost. For those who love God in this way all things work together unto good. This means all things without exception so that if some individuals go astray and off the track, even this misdirection causes them to progress in love because they come back humbler and wiser. For they learn that in the very way of justice they should rejoice with fear, not arrogating to themselves credit for the strength enabling them to trust to remain firm, not saying in their abundance, "We will not be moved forever." (Ps 29 [30].7). This is why they are told, "Serve the Lord with fear, and rejoice in him with trembling, lest at any time the Lord become angry and you perish from the way of justice" (Ps 2.11-12). The psalmist does not say, "And lest you not come into the way of justice," but he says, "lest you perish from the way of justice." And what does this show but that those already walking in the way of justice are warned to serve God in fear, that is, not "to be high-minded but to fear" (Rom 11.20). This means: they should not be proud but humble. Hence he says in another place, "Do not set your mind on lofty thoughts but agree in thought with lowly folk" (Rom 12.16). Let them rejoice in God but with trembling, let them boast of nothing since we know nothing of ourselves, let him who boasts boast in the Lord. Such boasting in the Lord is necessary to avoid perishing from the way of justice, in which they have already started to walk, by giving themselves credit for walking in this way.

The Apostle also uses these words where he says, "Work out your salvation with fear and trembling." And explaining why he speaks of "with fear and trembling," he says, "For it is God who of his good pleasure works in you both the willing and the accomplishment" (Phil 2.12-13). The man wont to say in his abundance, "I will not be moved forever" (Ps 29 [30].7), did not have this fear and trembling. But because he was a son of the promise rather than of perdition, when God abandoned him for a short time, he experienced what he himself was and said, "Lord, in your good will you gave strength to my honor: you turned your face from me and I became troubled" (Ps 29 [30].8). See, he is wiser now, and, because wiser, humbler. He remained steadfast in the way, at length seeing and recognizing that God in his good will gave strength to his honor. It was this strength in the abundance as God had accorded it that he formerly ascribed to and claimed for himself, instead of giving credit to God who had bestowed it, and so he said, "I will not be moved forever." Thus he became troubled, and in his trouble he discovered who he was and in his humility he became wiser and learned on what to rest his hope not only for eternal life but also for holy living and perseverence in this life. This sort of expression could be found in the mouth of the apostle Peter also inasmuch as he also had said in his abundance, ''I will lay down my life for you'' (Jn 13.37), impulsively attributing to himself what was to be later bestowed on him by the Lord. For the Lord turned his face away from him, and so troubled did he become that for fear of having to die for him he denied him three times. But once again the Lord turned his face toward him, and Peter washed away his sin in his tears. For the words, ''He looked at him'' (Lk 22.61), can mean only this: he turned back toward him the face that shortly before he had turned away from him. He had become troubled; but because he learned not to trust in himself, even this sin reaped profit for the good of his soul through the working of him who makes all things work unto good for those who love him. For he had been so called according to his purpose that no one could snatch him from the hand of Christ, to whom he had been given.[20]

Reflections

In your wisdom, Father, you created not a world of immobile forms but a universe of change that includes minor disorders. Every year blizzards, tornados, earthquakes, and floods wipe out thousands of insects and smaller animals. The Japanese beetle and other insect pests cause yearly damage to crops amounting to more than one billion dollars in the United States alone. Houseflies can spread typhoid fever and other infections, and rat fleas, the bearers of the Black Death that killed one out of three Europeans in the mid-fourteenth century, still menace parts of southeast Asia. Yet chance and other disorders, however devastating their short-range consequences, subserve your grand system of nature. There would be no disorder if agents fashioned by your consummate art were not masterfully designed. Even from within the constricted purview of the science of his day St. Augustine was able to note structures within the flea and gnat. The further modern science progresses, the more order it descries. Like other insects, the common housefly, which the untutored eye takes to be grossly organized and rather simple in frame, is delicately constructed. It has a complicated head, with compound and simple eyes, antennae, specialized mouth parts, a three-segmented thorax, three pairs of legs, thin but tough wings, an abdomen containing internal organs like the heart, and complicated respiratory, circulatory, digestive, and nervous systems, the latter equipping it with a well-distributed variety of sense organs. Let these few items be deemed enough to point up the striking order of each specific entity, each a small sub-world in itself.

Contrary to empiricists, we have achieved exact explanations of features of the material world. Yet this scientific fruit gathered by analyses over the centuries seems dwarfed by the numerous unsolved puzzles that overhang acquaintance with your universe, Father. It seems unlikely that we will ever fully explain the outer reaches of the Milky Way, not to mention the complex structure of billions of other galaxies. Too, much about our planet, tiny in comparison to a star, seems destined to be almost indefinitely cloaked in obscurity. In most living species a balance is constantly struck between male and female members: what controls this near-invariable equal distribution of the sexes? Again, realistic philosophers of nature lay inescapable physical evil at the door of primary matter, an elusive proto-passive factor constituting all beings of nature: why must matter be the source of the iron determinism that issues in breakdown and decay?

Nothing will stop the human intellect from posing such questions, content to glean a few new bits of light. But at some point in the pursuit of analytic answers every individual has to pause and take the universe as it is, staggering in its complexity, steeped throughout in patterns whose basic lines fade away into mysteries. As I set myself astare in astonishment at the universe, Father, teach me to adore you in the wonders of nature. Teach me to accept the brute fact that I am a vulnerable being of nature. I can be struck by lightning, bitten by a disease-bearing insect, clawed by a bear, sucked under ocean waves during a seizure of cramps. Since you desire that I grow in union with you in this sluggish body, show me that its upsets and ills can work a sort of reparation. Father, how astutely inventive you are! You saw how I recoil from prolonged external mortification; so you built means of penitence within my very physical frame. My body, undoubtedly a thing of beauty, is a source of distress. Even as I write, my energy is gradually ebbing till I nod or become foggy. With weariness word-fluency gives way to slurring of syllables and at times freshly minted Spoonerisms. So often I feel dull-brained from fatigue. I accept this cross of nature, which, I beg you, will help cleanse me of my sins through the precious blood of Jesus.

2. Father, without your love-in-power and power-in-love our world seems meaningless, worse than "sound and fury signifying nothing," a farcical tragedy that looks at times like the worst of all possible worlds. For if you permitted evils that would go forever unchecked, then you would wear the visage of a fiend, and the life of man and each man would seem to be a devilish drama that makes room for good only in order to bring about greater evil. But you are not boxed in by evil, compelled to sit on the sidelines with hands tied while evil inexorably tramples upon good. In touch with every pulsation of the universe you control all by your boundless love. So the world is not a quasi-Satanic travesty but a universe of divine love, a tragedy whose denouement is joy. Because of your love, Father, light conquers darkness; through your power you miraculously draw good out of evil. The panorama of all life and history lies outside my ken. Only in the everlasting super-sunlight of your wisdom in the grand assize shall I grasp the whole of your plan, seeing evil yoked to the production of good in your transcendent design.

Here and there in this life, especially in the careers of your saints, can

I bring within focus the fruition of good from evil. Contrary to the tears and pleas of his mother Monica, whom he tricked just before departing, Augustine set sail from north Africa for Rome in the autumn of 383. In her eyes, his quest for greater prestige in Italy portended harsher bondage for his spirit. But this move proved to be the first in a chain of events that would lead Augustine into the Catholic Church.[21] Father, you turned his search for worldly power into a joyous submission to your way. Your law that uses evil to produce good has to be continually at work also in your holy Church, but the lines of its operation seem more cloudy. The disastrous break-up of western Christendom at the Reformation became the source of a new outburst of spiritual vigor. Nearly two centuries later the French Revolution turned out to be a curious mix of freedom and new tyranny, release from oppression and fresh atrocities. The avaricious seizure of religious houses that ensued, you used to further detach religious communities from earthly posessions. May I surmise too that the loss of papal temporal power in the nineteenth century, however unjust, has been converted into a boon by your ingenuity? For in an era still tormented by the collective egoism called nationalism the vicar of your Son Jesus now stands out as a transnational figure appealing to men of every political hue. Though challengeable in part, these conjectures perhaps indicate how your loving power unfailingly confounds forces of evil by causing deserts to bloom with fruits of every kind.[22]

As Augustine shows, you fashioned as a necessary part of the universe not sins as sins but souls as souls, most of whom cannot go a day, some not an hour, without sinning. Strictly, our sins unhinge parts of the world and smash its gears and motors. In spite of sins but because of your mercy a world of sinful souls still moves upward to its perfection. How tolerant, how forbearing you are, gracious Father! A universe swamped by darkness climbs closer to full light because your forgiving love unstoppably sweeps even the unloving into your arms.

Yet, merciful Father, you are a God of justice. The ancients untouched by your revealed truth worshipped gods whom at times they tried to cajole and placate, regarding them as, in effect, superhuman beings made in the image of man. Today in a world of technological brilliance and moral decadence some who call themselves followers of your Son strangely characterize you as a finite being, a God of persuasion who is all kindness and nothing else, a charming Mr. Nice Guy radically helpless in the face of sin. But a finite God trimmed to suit the appetites of contemporary man is defeated by the wickedness of men: he is the sovereign of a world that makes no ultimate sense. Because you are God, Father, you have to be infinitely just, imposing the order that is punishment on what is out of kilter.

Spiritual dullness that is increased by the pressures of a sensate culture tends to conceal the truth limned by Augustine: the punishment of a sin is contained within the sin itself. When we sin and sin, we forge links in a chain that gives us, we sink into blindness, our egos swell grotesquely. Father, in your plan the pleasures of the sinner become the very instruments of his punishment. An alcoholic who enslaves himself to the bottle looks disgusting. But had I only some of your perception you share with your saints, I would see every habitual sinner as a pitiable slave strewing disorder wherever he goes. The sinner who plays at being god lives like a beast.[23]

Father, what a trail of disorder I have recklessly left behind me in my life. Always, it seems, you have dispensed your sanctions mildly, so caringly. Often I have let dribble through my fingers chances of offering up small setbacks for my numerous sins. Lord, your eternal eye holds in one intuition the whole course of past, present, and future: let my present offering transmute lost opportunities into gold of reparation for pruning away disorder in my spirit.

Father, in your liberality stretch, so to speak, the value of my meager store of reparation to compensate in some way for the horrible evil that every day seems to mount higher and higher, a stench in your nostrils. Perhaps the passage of years has inclined me more and more to notice the unlovely underside of the human scene. Sin seems to be everywhere, everywhere proliferating, everywhere polluting cities and homes, everywhere choking and suffocating more souls, everywhere creeping ahead even into sacred enclaves professedly consecrated to your name. A couple of years ago I accidentally encountered an attractive young woman in her early twenties, so slight and baby-faced she seemed no more than eighteen, about to attend an Alcoholic Anonymous meeting on the Villanova University campus. During our brief conversation she related that for a few years she had been living an illicit union with a self-styled born-again Christian (who during her absence thought nothing of having an affair with a married woman). Though from a good Catholic family that had sacrificed to finance her education, she had repudiated her faith. This came as a minor shock to me: here was the overgrowth of evil, a frightful instance of the blighting of the young and innocent in a corrupt age.

Father, I have contributed more than a modicum to the evil of our time, and some of the evil of others has left its mark on my spirit. In this apparently all-encircling dusk I turn to you in hope. Once more open my spirit to the Spirit of Jesus constantly flowing down from your bosom to heal me. The visitation of your mercy in Jesus is the greater good occasioned or incidentally elicited by evil. Your promise of continuous forgiveness in him is the light of joy that drives back the gloom. Come, Father, never wearied in your love, come and empower me, your child, to raise my arms to you with the confident beseeching of your saints. Then press my lips to those of the crucified Jesus so that his saving death may be my saving death to sin.[24] No matter how often I die in sin, as often as I die to sin in him I can come alive again in the power from your love.

3. Father, each of your revealed words can pierce the soul like a two-edged sword, its very cutting healing it with your priceless love. In par-

ticular, Romans 8.28 seems to penetrate my spirit with maximum force and fruit. At one stroke this great text solves problems that persistently worry and weary the spirit. The magnificent truth that you derive good from evil exorcises demons of doubt and gives moral meaning to history. A year or two ago I came across humorous portions of a volume entitled *The Incomplete Book of Failures*, which recounted such minor disasters as a Portuguese-English phrase book compiled by a Portuguese whose command of English seemed sadly and hilariously wanting. Yet, seriously, a large slice of history may be described as an incomplete book of failures. From one angle the story of man resembles a bitter and sick comedy, a series of nasty practical jokes. Gross social injustice continues to condemn many humans to a subhuman existence. For example, the lack of basic foods and medical care in certain African countries dooms 80 percent of their children before the age of two. Even efforts to aid such nations are not always untainted by power motives to stem the influence of Communism among the economically disadvantaged. Too, terrible to relate, the best become corrupted: the ranks of your Church are winnowed by false ideas that "free" men for sycophantic crawling before the overlords of secularism. Other Christians end up as burnt out cases; wounded by institutional injustice, battered by reverses, they fold up, becoming torpid and cynical. How high has risen the tide of evil, how low have sunk the spirits of the army of light. Among the legions of darkness: cocksureness, a feeling of irresistible movement forward. Among the regiments of the just: disarray, sapping of incentive, steady erosion of loyalty, apathy, a foreboding of final defeat. But your promise scatters all gloom. Re-viewed through your guarantee, a hapless world shines with hope. In spite of itself evil will spawn good, the wickedness of human hearts will serve the goodness of your heart lavishing itself upon man.

Not for all, Father, but only for those who love you do all things work together for good. Unhappily some love the darkness more than the light; some rebel against your thoughts and ways. This is the mysterious upshot of your omnipotent love: you cannot share your everlasting yes with those who recalcitrantly cry no. Where idolatrous self-love shuts out your love, even you cannot extract good from evil. Now I see a little less hazily that it is love that works the miraculous harvesting of good from evil. The more steeped I am in love, the more the evil of my past can produce fruits of your Spirit. With your love I can strike back at evil with good, I can avenge a look of scorn, a sneer, a jeering word, with a look and inward embrace of love. In the pain of being spurned or hooted at, in the very moment the tongue of hate stabs my soul, I can shoot arrows of love into the heart of my assailant. Through love I can heap burning coals on my adversary. Through love I can gladly give food and drink to my famished enemy (Rom 12.20). Through your love I can help roll back and vanquish evil, for evil is defenseless before the weapons of love. Your secret is love, your name is love. So through the Spirit of Jesus, in some sense I am to be love, my name is to be love.

It is factually inevitable, Father, that I will fall, but, if I humbly seek your healing, I can grow in the likeness of Jesus. "Is it I, Lord?" (Mt 26.18), I ask, and, though you sorrowfully nod yes, I can rejoice in the privilege of prostrating myself before you. Abandonment to your mercy is the royal road to total love; surrender to your infinite pity even in the pit of degradation is the narrow but swift way to your sweet embrace. Peter, Augustine, Mary of Egypt, Margaret of Cortona, and John of God, among others, traveled this glorious road to the highest holiness, for your mercy minted their brass and clay into the purest gold. Though never apparently notorious sinners, practically all the rest of your saints converted the scraps and shreds of their faults into the currency of divine life. I simply cannot get over the charm of your plan, which bids me lift up my heart by profiting from day-in-and-day-out faults that drag me down.

Now and then, Father, I feel drawn by your invitation, "Be holy as I am holy" (1 Pt 1.16). At other times, however, the thought of becoming a saint fills me with dread. How can I muster courage to trudge upward over the rocks to the summit, how can I withstand snow and ice and biting blasts of mountain winds? But as I ruminate on Romans 8.28, your unparalleled promise pulls me out of my slough of despond, braces my shoulders, and sets me plodding uphill slowly, slowly, for even my backslidings are fresh fuel for causing my spirit to blaze with single-hearted love.

Yet much of the old self lurks within, ready to bamboozle me. A well-known line puts down the later Bourbon kings of France in perhaps too harsh terms: "They learned nothing and they forgot nothing." They were blind and deaf to the outcries of the oppressed and to the seething of revolt: they learned nothing. They luxuriated in past glories won by the force and cunning of forebears: they forgot nothing. Much of this syndrome, which few escape, lingers on in me. At certain junctures I seem to have learned nothing. A downturn in an emotional cycle, an unpleasant encounter, upset over another scandal — any one of these can make my spirit droop. At these times also I seem to have forgotten nothing. Instead of remarking the dissension and turmoil in the Church throughout history, I lopsidedly focus only on its past glories. Come, infinitely patient Father, tutor me anew in the meaning of your master-formula that resolves all problems, showing me how to forget everything but your divine pity, to learn everything in the perspective of your never-failing mercy.

Deepen my trust, not merely fiducial trust, which satisfies only an affective or emotional yearning for assurance about salvation, but trust grounded in faith and poised to minister in love. During a long, zigzag journey I have probed for my identity, sought to unlock the secret of my spiritual self. Such self-knowledge in its plentitude, I now see, lies beyond my grasp on this side. I can perceive only the contours, perhaps the silhouette, of my innermost core. So you call me to absolute confidence in the outpouring of your goodness day by day, hour by hour, indeed minute by minute. Father, I must remain a little one, like an infant in its mother's arms, lovingly passive, waiting for, completely dependent on, the stroking impulse of your kindness. Yet I must also act, searching for you in every event, person, and situation. Through trust theory will be translated into practice, idea clothed in fact: I will sin yet love you and rejoice in you in all circumstances. I trust you: there is no gift that you will deny me so that, everywhere caressed by your love, I can repeatedly respond with love. I trust you: you will give me all for all, all your gifts for all that happens, your way of love that amid the most racking of pains bedews the soul with consolation and sets it throbbing with secret songs of joy.

Praise

1. Some scientists of the late nineteenth century were of the opinion that all the basic laws of physics had been discovered, and all that remained was to refine measurements and add decimal points. However, as they approach the end of the twentieth century, scientists are stressing the constricted ambit of their metier. Allowing for exaggeration, the statement of one scientist seems noteworthy: "The greatest single achievement of science in the most scientifically productive of centuries is the discovery that we are profoundly ignorant: we know very little about nature and we understand even less."[25] Surely every advance of the human mind adds to your glory, for the human spirit images your creative intelligence, but I praise you for what the simple of heart have always vaguely guessed, for what sophisticated thinkers now readily acknowledge: the universe in its complexity can never be totally scientized. Its order seems overpowering even in some of its nearest features. I praise you for the sun that pours out four million tons of thermonuclear energy every second. Some may balk at this mathematical-physical proposition as a dry abstraction stifling poetic musings. No; the more precise the prosaic proposition, the more poetic awe before the sun is reinforced. I praise you, Father, for a planet that teems with life, life that hangs on in hostile environments — vegetation that thrives in rocks buried deep beneath antarctic ice, cells that live in sponges close to the boiling point of water, and species that feed on pure sulphur. I praise you for the life-support systems, for soil, air, and water making each breath possible, for foliage and plankton in the sea that supply oxygen to fuel my body. Special praise to you for the human body, the most magnificently organized piece of matter in the cosmos. Each breath I take, each word I utter, and each glance I make depend on a trillionfold interlocking system of parts subserving the subsystems of my organism.

I can learn to sing your grandeur in the whole of your universe, Father, by saluting you in the least things. A Trappist monk in charge of the pigs was once fascinated by the eyes of a piglet, and in this he praised you. Let me praise you in every corner, in every speck, of your creation. Empiricist philosophers bizarrely reject the massive empirical fact of order: what we call order in nature, they insist, is a device our minds invent for cataloguing heaps of random particulars. Let my praise of your order serve as partial reparation for this denial of the undeniable, this sort of sin against the light of reason.

Father, I praise you also for all the odd phenomena of chance, for chance presupposes order; well-desiged automobiles could not collide unless they were purposefully driven. I praise you for disruptions that visit misfortunes upon men, which manifest, albeit the hard way, the out-workings of your laws of nature. I praise you even for the deserts which arise because of the overgrazing of lands, for the side effects of DDT, strontium-90, and acid rain on food chains, for the pollution of air and water. Checked by the dire consequences of our infinitely expansive avarice, we learn that basically this is not our but your world, the misuse of whose finite resources punishes the misuser. I praise you, Lord, for this earth, this garden of gardens in the universe, a unique diamond sparkling with countless facets. Glory to you: in spite of human potential for despoliation you will never permit monsters of rapacity to utterly deface the planet and turn it into a conglomerate of junk heaps and garbage dumps. Your love will always preserve earth as a home for the race for whom through Jesus' death you evidenced the ultimate in love.

Plotinus, the celebrated Neo-Platonic philosopher, was ashamed of his body, in his eyes a transitory strait jacket, a prison-house the soul of the sage strove to escape from. In death the godly self within, he thought, throws aside its material raiment to mount to the realm of the divine above matter. Now and then I tend to become embarrassed by my body. Unlike Plotinus, who lacked the gift of faith, from my first toddling you readied me for your truth. Praise to you, Father, for sparing me from contempt for my body; since your Son became man, every body can be a shrine of the divine. I am not blue-penciling some earlier remarks; at times my body is a source of affliction, constantly nagging for attention. But now I realize that its blessings far outbalance its burdens. How glorious it is to walk or talk or see the grass bend in the breeze or watch the sun go down. Occa-sionally I muse to myself: suppose that my whole life from birth to death came and went within one week, with birth on Sunday, maturity on Wednesday, hasty decline on Friday, and death by Saturday midnight.[26] Would I not praise and praise you during those speedily vanishing seven days? You have endowed me not with days but with decades of years: how much more then should I chant your praise in my body for my body.

At the root of some of my discontent is my ingratitude. Though nothing of myself, I act like a spoiled child, yammering for the best of everything. Father, I praise you: in G. K. Chesterton's phrase, I am a might-not-have-been who actually is. Life is not a necessity but a luxury bestowed by your liberality. So I praise you for my body, for, however cumbrous its matter, it is blessed with the gift of existence. Frail and ephemeral, it is the vesture of earth your hands have lovingly woven for me, the garment of flesh in which I am to proclaim your glory, the yoke whose abrasiveness is softened by the crucified body of Jesus. In his body the weakness of mine shows forth your power.

Glory to you, Father, for a chemistry of love drawing good out of evil. You permit evil to be a part of the human atmosphere, an ineliminable spiritual pollutant potentially more destructive to souls than high concentrations of DDT and strontium-90 are to human bodies. Yet at every instant your goodness and power point chunks of evil toward the making of some good. Praise be to you; evil seems to smear everything and contaminate everyone, but every bit harbors a really possible good, for through your love dark is the womb of light, night the seedbed of day. Father, I thank you for your martyrs who in faith and fortitude bared their bodies to sword and fire. Yet much of the weal to come from woe seems beyond human reckoning. How many horrors of our day seem irretrievably rotten, incapable of yielding but a marginal good. At first I hold back, questioning how I can praise you for the slaughter from the warfare of the Soviet Union and its satellites; for organized crime's empire of racketeering, drugs, prostitution, extortion, and professional murders; for the apparently unbridgeable chasm between the very wealthy and the destitute around the world; for the entrenched crookedness in big and small business; for the millionfold systematic extermination of human beings under the name of abortion, crusaded for by men and women who pride themselves on their dedication to human progress. What good can evidently sprout from deadly evils like these? Glory to you, Father, for the great hope to which we have been called (Eph 1.18). In the most God-hating and sanguinary of centuries I trust that you will reshape all the hate and blood, using them to fashion in the end a new heaven and new earth, bliss untold for the countless elect whose love will have responded to yours.

I praise you, Father: bending down to my misery, you urge me to stop simply wringing my hands, to engage in the never-ending battle against the armies of the night whose high command is centered in hell. In the majesty of your mercy show me how after an initial shudder of revulsion to look with eyes warm with your compassion upon wayward brothers and sisters. Some Catholic acquaintances of mine visit and converse with, entertain and console the hapless residents of a nearby state mental hospital. Stock my soul with like pity and understanding for sin-ridden men and women whose habitat of spirit sometimes seems roughly equivalent to a moral madhouse. Glory to you for sharing your mercy: where there is sin, I can bring your forgiveness; where there is moral insanity, I can offer a soul-look of mercy. "Blessed are the merciful, for they shall obtain mercy" (Mt 5.7). By extension this beatitude may also be taken to mean that when I give mercy, I spread the kingdom of mercy and obtain mercy for others. Let my mission of mercy begin at home, let this heavenly dew fall first on those with whom I rub shoulders day by day. You have appointed me your minister of mercy to touch this brother, that sister, with a kind word, a pleasant hello, a silent prayer, each speeding to the other with its message of mercy from your heart.

Father, strike from the foregoing lines any least hint of condescension. I too am a gross sinner, but, and this is my point, in spite of my need for mercy I must try to pour out your mercy on others.

As I praise your mercy, cause the spirit of mercy to shoot up higher in my soul so that, anticipating the Day of the Lord that for your own will be a day of triumphant mercy, making each day a celebration of your all-powerful mercy that brings good out of evil.

3. Endless praise be yours, Father, for your wisdom that defangs hate by love, that overcomes evil by good. Praise to you for the unwisdom of your wisdom, for the folly of your plan. Your plans are not ours, your ways are not ours (Is 55.8-9). your infinite love pursues and traps and carries home rejoicing every possible soul with every possible wile, which turns to its advantage every opportunity initially fair or foul.

Recently I heard of a woman who loves with a love few would think possible. Her spouse is a middle-aged man rather plain and unprepossessing, remarkably unremarkable, an individual whose spiritual attributes could hardly be called outstanding. Yet consumed with love for him, she centers her inward attention and prayer on him for several hours daily, unfailingly esteems his conduct near-flawless, hangs on his every word, and showers affection on him — in a word, she deems him wholly adorable, fully lovable. Her invincible love counts every failing insignificant and fuses her heart with his, a heart set on fire by hers. Such unusual love opens a window on your super-love for me, Father. Selecting me as a particular object of your measureless mercy, you have attired me in your gifts, robed me in a bit of your holiness. I praise you for invincible love that lets not one of my sins stand in your way.

I praise you, Father, for the love with which you burningly enfolded your Son at every stage of his earthly existence. How delighted you were as he was nursed at Mary's bosom, as he threw his tiny arms and legs about, as he crawled and ventured his first steps, as he spoke his first word. I praise you for gracing me with a like love. All events of my life you have appointed for my good, each an opportunity for you to enwrap me with a fiercer divine passion. You held me close in love when my dear mother suckled me, when I smiled and laughed, when I started to crawl, then walk, when I blurted out my first word. In those childish scenes, in your love or in the love that is you, you caressed me as if I were your only son. With this same love you have environed me in every circumstance of my life. When my sins distanced my soul from you, you watched and waited, then consumed me anew with your restoring love. Praise to you: no barriers can block the flood tide of your love. As you use sins that hamstring me in order to accelerate my pace toward you, cleanse me especially of human respect. How fawningly I angle for the good opinion of others, how greedily I grasp at — and sell a little piece of myself for — a passing nod of approval or a pat on the back. Bent down by the dead weight of faults, looking hopeless, I run to you: only say your word of love and my soul shall be healed.

I praise you, dearest Father, for saving me from false faiths that befuddle, then destroy souls. How many have been duped by a pseudo-mystical faith in progress. Among the most pitiable was the Marquis de Condorcet, whose *Sketch for a Historical Picture of the Progress of the Human Mind* ironically deemed modern historical progress automatic, this being penned in 1793-94 while he was hunted (prior to imprisonment and quick death, possibly by poisoning himself) during the Reign of Terror. Today some Christian theologians profess pseudo-mystical faith in revolutionary Marxism, a system that has murdered more human beings than any other in history. Glory to you; only your infinite power can pull men out of the sinkholes and quicksand their wickedness plunges them into; only your divine love can do the impossible. From the blindness of the apostles of progress, from the duplicity of prophets of Marxism preaching hate as the path of love and surrender to the devil as the route of God, you will extract good by means past imagining, by love beyond utterance.

Father, increase my distrust of self; keep me from slipping into a subtly cultivated presumption. The debauched King Louis XV of France once cautioned a somewhat wayward minister of state, "Watch out, your soul is in danger." The official was bold enough to come back with, "But what of your soul, my lord?" Louis XV replied, "Oh, it's different with me. I am the anointed of the Lord."[27] A curious spiritual vacuity here — Louis XV was not aware that, however civilly anointed, a libertine could not be of the Lord. I praise you: rid me of all self-importance, every taint of self-trust so as to recognize that I can become quietly more vicious and correspondingly more smug in the appalling deception that as an anointed of the Lord I am so incongruously privileged that I can rupture my bond to you without ill-consequence. Praise to you Father of the hopeful: even pulling the wool over my eyes can beget good — light from your eyes pinpoints this fragment of darkness and impels me to my knees to beg your healing that changes humiliation into humility.

A Basic Law of Christian Living

From a broader perspective the miraculous production of good out of evil becomes a basic law of Christian living. Out of the crucifixion of Jesus, the most execrable act in history, came the redemption, the turning point in all history. In being victimized by sin and death, Jesus was victorious over sin and death. The cross of the Lord functioned as a kind of trap for Satan, and the bait that snared him was the death-in-love of the Lord. The members, not being greater than their head, submit to the same stringent but gentle pattern. The Church is also bound to be betrayed, scourged, spat upon, and crucified. Ferocity purposed to wipe out the name of Christ swells its ranks, for the blood of martyrs, in whom Jesus dies a second time, further broadcasts the seed. Physical blows make the Church more patient, perverse teachings deepen her wisdom, and reparation for enemies displays more mettlesome brotherly love. Within the Church the foul lives of some internally persecute the hearts of the just. Yet these sorrows become springs of consolations mediated by the charity of fervent Christians reclaiming the wandering sheep. From a natural standpoint the whole of history is a river flowing unendingly into the sea, and individuals are nothing but drops of rain that, falling into the river, are borne away to vanish in the abyss. Each person is only a drop in the bucket, insignificant-seeming, flourishing briefly only to be swallowed up in the sea, leaving little or no trace. But in a supernatural scheme the Father cares "for each one as if each were all, and for all as if all were but one."[28] In the priceless microcosm that is each individual the law of the blossoming of the good fruit from the bad tree also obtains. Some of Augustine's comments on the inner persecution that true Christians suffer were no doubt excerpted from his own experience. Lovingly defending his flock from heretical and pagan wolves, his tortured soul grew in patience, wisdom, and compassion. Further, the rule enunciated by Romans 8.28 is probably even more remarkably attested by Augustine's instantaneous turn from the flesh and darkness into purity and light. The *Confessions*, his unequalled part-autobiography, is in one sense a sacrifice of praise celebrating the transcendent design that exploited the squalid and supine in him to transfigure him into a gloriously free new creature.

Through Satan working directly or indirectly in the traitor and enemies of Jesus, the Son of God was put to death on the cross, a death that seemed to destroy his mission. Yet the devil's apparent victory was his actual defeat. In maligning and killing Jesus, the father of lies and lord of murder assured the triumph of him who is the truth and the life.

> But if Jesus had not been put to death, death would not have died. . . . The victory of our Lord Jesus Christ was accomplished when he rose and ascended into heaven. . . . The devil exulted when Christ died, and the devil was vanquished by the very death of Christ: he fell for the bait, as it were, in a trap. He was rejoicing over this death as if he were prince of death. But the very thing he was rejoicing over was responsible for setting the trap. The trap of the devil was the cross of the Lord; the bait that ensnared him, the death of the Lord.[29]

The psalms are in one sense wedding songs, hymns of love and joy sung in honor of the wedding of the Word with human nature and of Christ with his Church. The nuptial union of the Son of God with human nature was celebrated in the bridal chamber that was the womb of Mary, the mother of Jesus. By extension the union of Christ with his mystical body is also called a marriage. In this second case those united to the wedding banquet themselves make up the bride of Christ, so that Christians chanting the psalms are singing honor to their own marital union. It is the beautiful or handsome bridegroom who cleanses and beautifies his bride by his sacrifice. Jesus suffering and dying on the cross to make his bride beautiful was outwardly most unbeautiful, a mass of wounds, a criminal deservedly, in the opinion of many, battered and bloodied. Nonbelievers scorn the cross as a stumbling block or stupidity and the crucified one as a worthless reject. But inwardly Jesus was beautiful in his crucifixion, which marked the crowning point of a life shining with beauty at every juncture. The Word made flesh is the super-amazing miracle of the mercy of God. Supremely just, perfectly attuned to the will of the Father, he was beautiful at every stage. All-beautiful as God, the God-man was beautiful as an infant and young boy, beautiful in preaching the kingdom, beautiful in his death, beautiful in his resurrection. Thus the eyes of faith perceive Jesus nailed to the cross not as uncomely and revolting but as beautiful and captivating, a priest-victim of love who comes as the adorable bridegroom to wed his bride, the Church.

> The introduction continues, ''For the things that will be changed, to the sons of Korah, for understanding, a song for the beloved'' (v. 1). For the beloved was seen by his persecutors but they lacked understanding. For ''if they had known him, they would have never crucified the Lord of glory'' (1 Cor 2.8). He was seeking understanding in eyes other than theirs when he said, ''He who sees me sees the Father also'' (Jn 14.9). Let the psalm then hymn the beloved, let us rejoice in the marriage feast, and we will be among those who are invited to the marriage feast. Indeed the very individuals invited are the bride, for the Church is the bride and Christ the bridegroom.

> It is customary for rhetors to sing to bride and groom certain nuptial songs called epithalamiums. All the verses sung in this setting are sung in honor of bridegroom and bride. Is there perhaps no bridal chamber in that marriage to which we have been invited? Why then does another psalm tell us, ''He has pitched his tent in the sun and he comes forth like a bridegroom from his bridal chamber'' (Ps 18 [19].5)? The nuptial union is that of the Word and flesh, and the bridal chamber in which their union is realized is the womb of the virgin. For the flesh itself was united to the Word; hence it is also said, ''Henceforth they are no longer two but one flesh'' (Mt 19.6; Eph 5.32). The Church was taken from the human race in order that the very flesh united to the Word might be the head of the Church and that all believers might be the members of that head. Do you want to see who has come to the marriage feast? ''In the beginning was the Word, and the Word was with God, and the Word was God'' (Jn 1.1). The spouse loved by God should rejoice. When was she loved? While she was still defiled. ''For all have sinned,'' says the Apostle, ''and fallen short of the glory of God'' (Rom 3.23). And again he tells

us, "Christ died for the wicked" (Rom 5.6). Christ loved her while defiled to make sure she would not stay defiled. He did not really love her in her defilement because he did not love defilement. For if he had loved this, he would have kept her that way. He wiped away her defilement and formed beauty in her. What was she like when she came to him and what is she like after he remade her? Let the Lord himself come to us in the words of prophecy. Truly, let the bridegroom come forth to us. Let us love him; or rather, let us not love him if we find anything defiled in him. See, he found in us much that was defiled, and he loved us; yet if we find anything defiled in him, let us not love him. Consider the fact that he was clothed in flesh so that it was even said of him, "We beheld him, and he was neither attractive nor comely" (Is 53.2). But if you consider also the mercy at the root of his being made flesh, he is beautiful in that respect also. But the prophet was assuming the role of the Jews when he said, "We beheld him, and he was neither attractive nor comely." Why did he seem unattractive and uncomely? Because those so describing him lacked understanding. Yet for those who do understand, the verse, "And the Word was made flesh," (Jn 1.14) expresses an exceeding beauty. One of the friends of the bridegroom said, "But God forbid that I should boast save in the cross of our Lord Jesus Christ" (Gal 6.14). It doesn't amount to much for you not to be ashamed of the cross if you do not also boast of it. Why then was he neither attractive nor comely? Because Christ crucified was "a stumbling block to the Jews and a foolishness to the Gentiles" (1 Cor 1.23). But why was he comely even on the cross? "Because the foolishness of God is wiser than men, and the weakness of God is stronger than men" (1 Cor 1.25). For us who are believers the bridegroom should appear beautiful in all circumstances. He is beautiful as God, the Word with God. He was beautiful in the womb of the virgin where, without forfeiting his divinity, he took on humanity. The Word born as a babe was beautiful because when he was an infant, when he suckled the breast, when he was carried about, the heavens spoke, angels proclaimed his praises, a star guided the Magi, he was adored in the manger, he who is the food of the meek. So he is beautiful in heaven, beautiful on earth; beautiful in the womb, beautiful in the hands of his parents; beautiful in his miracles, beautiful in his scourging; beautiful in inviting us to life; beautiful in being unconcerned about death; beautiful in laying down his life, beautiful in taking it up again; beautiful on the cross, beautiful in the tomb, beautiful in heaven. Listen then to this song with understanding and do not let the weakness of the flesh turn your eyes away from the splendor of his beauty. The supreme and true beauty is justice; and you will not see him as beautiful when you perceive him as unjust: but if he is everywhere just, he is everywhere beautiful. Let him then come to us to be beheld by the eyes of our mind, let him come to us as depicted by the prophet praising him.[30]

G. K. Chesterton was once asked, "What would Jesus Christ do if he were alive in the world today?" The great Catholic apologist paused for reflection, then replied, "He is alive in the world today." A perspicacious reply, stressing a point that Augustine dwells on again and again: Jesus is alive, he is still with us, his life goes on in and with his Church. Not only does Jesus continue to live in his body, but his body, the Church, continues to relive his life. Century after century the Church reenacts especially the passion and death of Jesus. In every century, from the very beginning till the present day, her members have been somewhere reviled, hated, assaulted, scourged, tortured, and killed. Through this ongoing life from death the Church draws the impetus for steady growth. Everywhere Christ lives and dies in his members, and everywhere the redemptive fruits of suffering and death go on increasing. The enemies of Christ understandably believed that following quickly on his death at their hands would come the obliteration of his name and teaching. To their consternation the opposite ensued: his death and resurrection ignited the hearts of his disciples, his downfall and return to life spurred them to heroic endeavors. So with the Church of Jesus: the more barbarous the attempts to stamp her out in accord with the expression of Voltaire, the famous Enlightenment adversary of Christianity, "Écrasez l'infame" — "Crush the infamous thing" — the more confident her implacable foes are in her imminent decline and demise, the more vigorously the Church of Jesus thrives, the higher leaps up her hope not just to survive but to bound ahead. The Church's paradoxical-appearing endurance and progress stem not from human genius and initiative but from the energy that is divine power and love. In taking on human flesh, God emptied himself, he became poor. Yet, Augustine perceptively observes, in his poverty lies our richness, in his weakness our strength. The Church grows stronger because it is weak with the weakness of God; its doctrines illumine souls because it is foolish with the foolishness of God (1 Cor 1.25).

> The solemn feast of the martyrs has dawned. Christ, the king of martyrs, while ordering his soldiers to fight, did not spare himself but was the first to fight and the first to conquer, in order to spur on by his example, support by his power, and, in line with his promise, crown those fighting in his name. To give glory to the passion of Christ let us focus on some ideas in this psalm bearing on his passion. I have called to your attention a number of times and I do not regret reiterating what it is profitable for you to remember, the fact that our Lord Jesus Christ speaks often

of himself, that is, in his own person as our head and often also in the person of his body that we and his Church are. But these words come from the mouth of only one man; in this way we understand that head and body form a single whole and are not sundered from one another, as in that marriage about which we are told, "They will be two in one flesh" (Gen 11.24; Eph. 5.31). If then we recognize them as two in one flesh, let us also recognize then that they are two in one voice. . . . "My enemies spoke evil of me: when he dies, his name will perish also" (v. 6). This refers to the person of our Lord Jesus Christ, but see if this verse applies to his members also. In fact, these words were spoken when our Lord himself was walking in the flesh here on earth. For when they saw that the people hearkened to his authority and took his miracles as evidence of his divinity and majesty, when the Jews saw this. . .when they saw the people running after him, they said, "When he dies, his name will perish also." That is to say, when we have slain him, his name will no longer exist on the earth; once he is dead, he will no longer seduce anyone; his very execution will make men understand that they were following a mere man, that in him there was no hope of salvation; and they will forsake his name, and it shall exist no more. He did die and his name did not perish, but his name was sown as seed. He did die but he was the grain whose dying caused wheat to immediately spring up (Jn 12.25). Thus when our Lord Jesus Christ was glorified, people began to believe in him much more deeply and in greater numbers, and his members began to hear what their head was hearing. So our Lord Jesus Christ reigns in heaven and in himself laboring in us on earth. Still his enemies said, "When he dies, his name will perish also." This is the source of the persecution the devil has aroused against the Church to destroy the name of Christ. It would be wrong to think, brothers, that these pagans, when they were savaging Christians, did not intend to obliterate the name of Christ from the earth. In order that Christ might die again not in his head but in his body, the martyrs also were slain. The holy blood the martyrs poured out worked to spread the Church, and the death of the martyrs worked to increase the sowing of the seed. "Precious in the eyes of the Lord is the death of his just ones" (Ps 115.6 [116.15]). More and more have Christians multiplied, and what their enemies said, "When he dies, his name will perish also," has gone unfulfilled. Yet even now this claim is still being made. The pagans sit down and count the years till Christianity becomes extinct, they listen to their enthusiasts saying, "The time is coming when there will be no more Christians, when once again idols will have to be worshipped just as they were worshipped of old." They are still saying, "When he dies, his name will perish also." To the pagans I say, you have already been defeated twice — now this third time at least learn the truth: Christ died but his name did not perish. The martyrs died but the Church multiplied the more. The name of Christ grew among all nations. Christ foretold his own death and resurrection; he foretold the death of his martyrs and the crown they would win; similarly he foretold the future of his Church. If he spoke the truth twice, would he lie the third time? Pagans, all that you believe against him is baseless. It would be better for you to believe in him and so come to "understand the needy and the poor" (v. 2). For, although he was rich, he became poor, so that you might become rich through his becoming poor" (2 Cor 8.9). . . . Rich with God, Christ was poor with us; rich in heaven, poor on earth; rich as God, poor as man. Does it trouble you to see a mere man, to look upon flesh, to behold death, to deride the cross? Does this trouble you? "Understand the needy and the poor." What does that mean? It means this: understand that beneath the weakness laid before our eyes divinity lies hidden. He is rich because his nature is such; he is poor because your condition was such. But nevertheless his poverty is our riches just as his weakness is our strength, his foolishness our wisdom, his mortality our immortality. Think about who this poor man is: do not reckon him poor by the poverty of others. He who became poor came to enrich the poor. So open your heart to faith: receive this poor man so that you may not stay poor (1 Cor 1.25-30).[31]

The enemies of Jesus are not only without but within his Church. Though the name Judas, one of the most opprobrious in history, is eschewed by all, his unspeakable treachery seems duplicated to some degree by self-willed members of the Church who revile and spit upon her leaders and institutions and finally abandon her morally, if not juridically. In certain circles since Vatican II deprecation, scorn, and even hatred of the Pope are systematically cultivated under the trendy labels of pluralism and absolute freedom of thought. These mini-Judases are sowing the punishment they will reap. But more importantly, God will not be overcome by a disloyalty and a betrayal whose spirit is born in hell. Out of the wickedness and the suffering and wreckage it causes, he will bring the fruits of his mercy and peace.

"And they entered in to see" (v. 7). What Christ suffered the Church also suffers, what the head suffers the members also suffer. "Is the servant greater than his lord or the disciple than his master?" (Mt 10.24). "If," he said, "they persecute me, they will persecute you also" (Jn 15.20). If they have called the master of the household Beelzebub, how much more will they blacken members of the household? "And they entered in to see." Judas indeed was close to our head, in the presence of our head he entered in to see, that is, to spy on him; not in order to search for what he should believe but to discover a way to betray him. Notice that he was entering in to see, and the Gospel presents an example of this in the case of our head. What happened to the members after the ascension of our head? Doesn't the apostle Paul tell us, "Because of false brethren secretly brought in who stole in to spy on our freedom" (Gal 2.4)? So these individuals were also entering in to see. For they are hypocrites, wicked imposters, who, making themselves one with the brethren by a fake charity, seize upon all the actions, all the words of the saints, and try to set snares for them in all circumstances. And what happens to these hypocrites? Look at the words that follow: "Their heart speaks vain things (v. 7), that is, they speak with a fake love. What they say is vain, neither true nor genuine. And because they are hunting for material for accusation, what does the psalmist say? "They gathered wickedness to themselves." By working up calumnies, his enemies view themselves as powerful because they have accusations to make. "They gathered wickedness to themselves" (v. 7). "To themselves," he says, not "to me." Just as Judas gathered wickedness to himself and not to Christ, so too the imposters in the Church gather it to themselves and not to us, because concerning them we are told elsewhere, "And wickedness lied to itself" (Ps 26 [27].12). "They gathered wickedness to themselves." And because they went in to see, "they went outside and talked about it (v.7)." The person who went in went outside to talk about it. Would that he had stayed within and spoken the truth, then he would not have gone outside to say what is false. He is a traitor and a persecutor, and, once he goes outside, he speaks as such. If you belong to the members of Christ, come within and cleave to the head. Put up with the weeds if you are wheat, put up with the chaff if you are grain, put up with the bad fish in the nets if you are a good fish (Mt 13.30). Why did you flee before the time of winnowing? Why did you uproot the grain along with yourself before the time of harvest? Why did you break the nets before you reached the shore? "They went outside and talked about it."[32]

In another place Augustine traces this internal dissension and discord to the archenemy of man, the brilliant spirit who has been a liar and murderer from the beginning (Jn 8.44). Not only has God promised that the forces of hell would not overrun his Church (Mt 16.18) but he also turns all the weapons with which Satan besieges the Church into instruments for fortifying his people anew in wisdom and love. God is so loving that all the horrific armory of hate becomes the machinery of love. It is as if the fragments of bombs destroying a city were recycled to build a bigger and more handsome city. Furthermore, at times the haters and the persecutors themselves are changed into faithful and docile members of the people of God. The prayers of persecuted Christians call down a rain of fire, a shower of love, that burns away wickedness and converts more than one ferocious Saul into a zealous Paul. The Church is on the march, Augustine concludes, "amid the persecutions of the world and the consolations of God."[33] We must not, he suggests, be disheartened by Satan-instigated persecutions, which have been vexing the Church since the days of Jesus and the first apostles, which indeed have fallen upon good men since the time of Abel. Expecting them, we can meet them bravely, for in faith and hope we expect, in addition, the staying and enabling hand of the Father working through Jesus. The consolations of God are more powerful than the persecutions of the world. Because divine, not merely human, they find their soil in and sprout constantly, wondrously, up from the disconsolations heaped on the people of God by tools of the ancient serpent.

> But when the devil saw that the temples of the demons lay abandoned and that the human race took the path bearing the name of the mediator who sets men free, he moved heretics, while wearing the badge of Christianity, to combat Christian teaching, as if without censure they could indulge in a false spirit of freedom in the city of God just as philosophers espousing various conflicting opinions indulge in a false spirit of freedom in the city of confusion. Thus in the Church of Christ certain individuals maintain vitiated and depraved views and, when corrected and bade embrace sound and right teaching, mulishly resist and refuse to right their pestilential and deadly doctrines but rather persist in defending them. These men turn into heretics and, after leaving the Church, range themselves among her active enemies.

> Even so, true Catholic members of Christ profit from their evil ways, for God uses evil men for good, and for those who love him all things work together unto good (Rom 8.28). For God uses all enemies of the Church, whatever the error blinding them or the malice depraving them, for the good of the Church. If they possess the power of doing her bodily harm, they exercise her in patience. If they oppose her sheerly by false opinions, they develop her wisdom. Since she is meant to love even her enemies, she shows them loving kindness and deals charitably with them by persuasively presenting her teaching and by warning them of chastisements consequent upon disobedience of God's law.

Hence the devil, the prince of the city of evil, although he stirs up his minions against the city of God journeying through this world, is not allowed to inflict harm on her. Undoubtedly divine providence accords her the consolation of prosperity that keeps her from being broken by adversity, and the disciplined adversity that keeps her from being corrupted by prosperity. Thus one balances the other in line with a like point made by the psalmist: "Amid the many sorrows in my heart your consolations made my soul rejoice" (Ps 93 [94].19). The Apostle's words jibe with this: "Rejoice in hope, be patient in tribulation" (Rom 12.12).

What the same teacher also says, "All who desire to live piously in Christ suffer persecution" (2 Tim 3.12), we have to realize, will not go unfulfilled in any period. Even when enemies, without, cease savaging us and peace reigns, a peace that brings much consolation, most of all to the weak, there are some, indeed many within the Church whose degenerate ways agonize the hearts of those living devout lives. For through them blasphemy is heaped on the Christian and Catholic name (Rom 2.24). The dearer this name is to those desiring to live devout lives in Christ, the more they lament the fact that the influence of these evil men causes it to be less loved than their devout hearts would have it. Again, the heretics themselves, although they are regarded as having the Christian name and the Christian sacraments, the Scriptures and the creed, also inflict great sorrow on the hearts of the devout. For a large number of individuals who want to become Christians are driven to hold back from conversion because of dissensions due to heretics. In addition, many who bad-mouth the Church find fresh material for blasphemy of the Christian name since the heretics too in some sense bear the name of Christian. Because of the depraved lifestyle and errors of men of this ilk all who desire to live piously in Christ suffer persecution even if no one assaults them or does them bodily harm. They suffer this persecution in their hearts but not in their bodies. Hence the word of Scripture tells us, "Amid the many sorrows in my heart." It does not say, "in my body." Furthermore, because, as we know, the promises of God are unchangeable and because the Apostle tells us, "The Lord knows those who are his" (2 Tim 2.19) — "Those whom he foreknew and predestined to be conformed to the image of his son" (Rom 8.29), none of whom can be lost — the psalm therefore goes on, "Your consolations made my soul rejoice." For the very sorrow that the hearts of the devout experience when persecuted by the vicious ways of evil or false Christians fructifies their afflicted spirits because it flows from charity, the charity that makes them unwilling to have sinners lose their souls, the charity that does not balk the salvation of others.

Finally, great consolations also spring from their conversion, which fills the souls of the devout with a joy as great as the anguish caused by the prospect of the loss of their souls. So in this world, in these evil days, not only from the time Christ and his apostles walked the earth but even from the time of Abel, the first just man who was slain by his wicked brother, and from our own era to the end of the world the pilgrim Church continues her march forward amid the persecutions of the world and the consolations of God.[34]

Without the Church, without the transcendent plan of the Father embodied in the Church of Jesus, each individual life may look so brief as to appear paltry and, ultimately, senseless. Each individual life is a raindrop falling into the stream of human history, coming and going, quickly caught up in the flow and quickly disappearing. Where are the billions who lived and died since the beginning of the human race? From an earthly standpoint they are gone, utterly gone, lost sight of in the sweep of human time. The names of a comparative few are inscribed on the rolls of world history but these become more and more obscure even to scholars of a particular era. From the angle of nature man seems doomed to swift extinction in a torrent that never stops flowing, that goes on and on, while the individual drops of human existence that collectively and cursively compose it come and go. The life of each person is a tiny strip of light between two unbounded domains of darkness. But Jesus drank from the torrent, i.e., took on the lowliness and nothingness of the human condition, and by his divine love his lowliness was exalted, his nothingness became fullness of glory. In him each Christian drinks of the torrent, and his fleeting span, naturally no more than a drop in the bucket, supernaturally leaps up as a fountain of everlasting life.

> "He shall drink from the torrent by the wayside; therefore he shall lift up his head" (v. 7). Let us consider the Lord drinking from the torrent by the wayside. First of all, what is the torrent? It is the onward flow of human mortality. For just as a torrent is formed from drops of rain, overflows, rumbles, and runs till it runs down, that is, finishes its course: so is the whole course of mortality. Men are born, live, and die, and, when some die, others are born, and, when in their turn these die, still others are born. They succeed their forebears, flourish, then depart the scene, not one of their lives lasting. What remains stable here? What does not flow? What is not on its way toward the abyss like a stream formed from rain? A river suddenly formed from rain, from drops in showers, flows into the sea and is no longer seen, no more than it was seen before it was formed from rain. Similarly this human race of ours is formed from hidden sources, and it goes on flowing, at death making its way back

to the hidden source whence it emerged. This in-between span emits its sound, then passes away. This is the torrent he drank from, a torrent he did not disdain to drink from. Indeed for him to drink from the torrent was to be born and die. This torrent has two main features, birth and death. Christ took these upon himself: he was born, he died. In this sense "he drinks from the torrent by the wayside." "He rejoiced like a giant to run his course" (Ps 18 [19].6). So he drinks from the torrent by the wayside because "he did not stand in the way of sinners" (Ps 1.1). Because he drinks from the torrent by the wayside, he then lifted up his head. That is to say, because he was humbled, he "became obedient to death, even death on a cross; therefore God exalted him from the dead and gave him a name that is above every other name, so that at the name of Jesus ever knee shall bow in the heavens, on earth, and under the earth, and every tongue confess to the glory of God the Father: Jesus Christ is Lord" (Phil 2.8-11).[35]

It is in Jesus exalted because crucified, elevated because abased, that the most meaningless becomes the most meaningful. Jesus was brutalized and executed by his enemies, one more innocent victim swallowed up in the tidal wave of injustice. Jesus assumed flesh like ours, lived and especially died as a man, to show that a drop in the bucket, each evanescent human life, has infinite worth, God so loves each particular "world" or center of individuality that he gave his only Son (Jn 3.16). Jesus enfleshed the infinite love and care of the Father who embraces each as if he were the only man in the whole universe.

And you sent down your hand from above (Ps 143 [144].7) and drew my soul forth (Ps 85 [86].13) from the deepest of darkness when my mother, your faithful one, wept to you for me more than mothers weep over the dead bodies of their children. For by the faith and spirit she received from you she saw that I was dead, and you heard her, Lord, you heard her and you did not despise her tears when they fell from her eyes and watered the earth beneath everywhere she prayed. You heard her, for how else can I account for that dream with which you so consoled her that she agreed to live with me and share the same table with me in her home? Formerly she had refused to do this as a sign that she repudiated my blasphemous errors. In her dream she saw herself standing on a wooden rule, and approaching her a young man, radiant, joyful, and smiling upon her while she was grieving and weighed down by grief. When he asked her the reason for her sorrow and daily tears (he asked, as is usually the case, not to learn from but to teach her), she answered that she was bemoaning my state of perdition. He ordered her to be at

peace and directed her to pay careful attention: she would see
that, where she was, there I was also. and, when she looked, she
saw me standing beside her on the same rule. How else can I
account for this unless your ears were inclined to her heart? O
good and all-powerful Father, you care for each one as if each
were all, and for all as if all were but one.[36]

The infinite goodness that is at once infinite power sustains the entire
universe, harnessing all its energies toward the achievement of the good
of the whole universe. So tender is his goodness, so august his power that
God can, as it were, bring to bear all of himself on each individual: he is
wholly there as if the object of his affection were all there was. Touched
by his mercy, turned right side up by his liberating power, a person
experiencing conversion can only break forth in joyful weeping and songs
of praise that bespeak the self-giving of his heart responding to the self-
giving of the heart of God. After relating his miraculous conversion,
Augustine penned the words that follow in praise of and thanksgiving for
divine mercy. This passage may be taken as a model for exultant praise
not only vis-á-vis relatively major conversions but also vis-á-vis minor
conversions, switch points at which the struggling spirit makes small
advances. It is a passage too that may be prayed at any time of compunction
that moves us bewail our misery and sing the Lord's mercy.

"O Lord, I am your servant. I am your servant and the son of
your handmaid. You broke my bonds, I will sacrifice to you
the sacrifice of praise" (Ps 115.7 [116.16]). Let my heart and
my tongue praise you and let all my bones say, "O Lord, who
is like to you?" (Ps 34 [35].10). Let them say this and do you
answer me and say to my soul, "I am your salvation" (Ps 34
[35].3). Who am I and what am I? What evil was not lodged
in my acts or, if not in my acts, in my words or, if not in my
words, in my will? But you, O Lord, are good and merciful,
and your right hand fathomed the depth of my death, and from
the bottom of my heart you dredged up an abyss of corruption.
As a result my life now lay wholly in not willing what I willed
but in willing what you willed. But during those long years where
was my free will, and from what nethermost hidden deeps was
it called forth in that instant in which I bent my neck to your
easy yoke and my shoulders to your light burden (Mt 11.30),
O Christ Jesus, "my helper and my redeemer" (Ps 18 [19].15)?
How sweet it suddenly became to be deprived of the sweetness
of these follies. Now it was a joy to jettison things I was afraid
of losing. You cast them aside, far from me, you who are the true
and supreme sweetness, you cast them aside and in their stead
entered into me, sweeter than every pleasure but not to flesh

and blood; brighter than every light but deeper within than any secret; loftier than every honor but not to those lofty in their own eyes. At last my mind was free of gnawing cares — currying favor and amassing wealth and wallowing in the passions and scratching the scab of lust. And I spoke intimately with you, my light and my riches and my salvation, my Lord God.[37]

Reflections

1. Thinkers of genius like Aristotle and Newton deeply plumbed the workings of nature and man. Penetrating also, albeit on a lower level, were the analytical insights of a James Clerk Maxwell in electromagnetic theory and a Werner Heisenberg in quantum mechanics. Shakespeare incomparably sang the exquisite poetry of human living. Scientists and artists move about in the same universe as their contemporaries but their profoundly discriminating minds lay bare worlds within the world. In the supernatural realm your saints are geniuses of grace, souls of peerless understanding who experience, sometimes in ways incommunicable, worlds within the supernatural world every Christian believes in and tries to live in. Occasionally some, like St. Angela of Foligno, were so suffused by your presence that they could not think of anything but you, Father. Come, make me stupid with your unwisdom to see through the idolatries of the clever of this world. Thus witless and ignorant, I will divine your love everywhere at work. Let me unlearn my pride and covetousness. Cut away my shortsightedness, dispossess me of fleshy security. No more half-measures, no more oscillating between yes and no: hollow out of my spirit meretricious wisdom to ready me to see the beauty of Jesus in the individual and social life of his Church.

Father, how beautiful you are in yourself, how beautiful in your Son, how beautiful in every smallest circumstance of his earthly span. You give all to your only Son in the interior of your life, and in this most mysterious of generations your beauty becomes mirrored in his beauty. You are the first to know the beauty of the Son, he the first to know your beauty. Give me more light to know, in some measure as you do, the beauty of your and my Jesus, the same yesterday, today, and forever (Heb 13.8), the same all-enchanting one whose life our hearts and minds relive by your Spirit. Parents admire with affection and awe the newborn child you have wrought through their love. "Oh, he's beautiful, so beautiful," the delighted mother softly cries as she squeezes the tiny life closer. With like love and wonder Mary and Joseph first laid eyes on the fruit of the love of the Spirit. Moreover, in your light, Father, they saw the light radiating from Jesus, the light that was Jesus himself. Unite me to the mystery of Jesus' infancy. Beautiful as a babe, he was infinitely more beautiful as the God-man, Father in each little gesture that bore, within, all the might of eternal action. The exteriorly colorless years of the hidden life interiorly glowed with silent glory. Every situation harbored its spiritual beauty: Jesus stammering out his first words to the gleeful clapping of his parents; Jesus working smoothly alongside Joseph, taking pleasure in his craftsmanship, and even more in the serenity of his craftsman father; Jesus comforting and supporting Mary in the years after Joseph's death. These hidden years were beautiful in their utter surrender to your holy will. How sublime yet plain was his preaching that moved the deeps of the human heart as no man has ever done. How beautifully he stood in silence under the barbs and taunts of his enemies, swine who trampled upon his pearls. Beautiful too was his sacred anger that erupted against whited sepulchres full of dead men's bones. Most beautiful of all was Jesus in his passion and death: no love of man for man could flame forth more intensely than that from the heart of the God who laid down his human life. Subhuman brutality, unspeakable ferocity savaged the frame of this dearest of men. Yet his suffering and death were supremely beautiful because he shouldered your yoke of love. The face impressed on the Shroud of Turin excites pity, sympathy, and gratitude but also a shiver of repugnance. But in your light this is the most beautiful of faces: beautiful in its bruises, beautiful in the swollen nose and the puffy eyes, beautiful in the marks of thorns that pierced the skull, beautiful in its misshapen features, because each wound, welt, and scratch bespeak immeasurable love streaming from your heart. What towering beauty in Jesus's rising from the dead — the stone rolled back and a burst of blinding light signaling triumph over sin and death. How glorious too his final return to you, his earthly work finished. But Jesus was beautiful in his resurrection and ascension only because he was beautiful on the cross. Nothing was more lovely than the beaten and broken Jesus on Calvary. Defiled, abjection incarnate, every scrap of human dignity torn off, Jesus was beautiful because he embraced the cross with unparalleled sacrificial love.

If Jesus is beautiful, the Church wholly one with him must be beautiful too. One, Catholic, apostolic, holy, she is all-beautiful. Hundreds of millions assent to her pure doctrine, pay allegiance to Pope and bishops, drink deep from the seven streams of sacramental life. The sun never sets on the worldwide kingdom of faith and love stemming from the heart of Jesus. Remarkably she is the one and the same Church that sprang from the side of Jesus on the cross, spread like wildfire through the ancient world, and, while weathering disasters, has never stopped growing in every age since. The Church is especially prepossessing in her saints, masterly works of your divine artistry, Father, whose variegated heroism never ceases to astound. In every time and clime countless Christians have become holy in a more modest manner. Not souls of predilection, these generous lovers of their faith, refusing to be cowed or seduced by hedonism, have spent themselves body and soul for others, ever loyal to you and the Church of Jesus.

Unfortunately the beauty of the Church on earth seems blemished by ambition, intrigue, politicking, self-seeking, and worldliness that creep into every level from the top rungs of administration down to the smallest organization in a financially woebegone parish. It is incongruous too that, though I recognize myself as a sinner in need of radical purgation who wants to be counted a member of the Church, I find it hard to accept a Church soiled by so many sinners. Light, more of your light, Father, so I can truly believe that your basic law of the best out of the worst is at work here. Not a Church of the perfect but a Church of limping stragglers, chronic backsliders, the irresolute, and the backboneless glorifies you the more by her beauty because this actual Church of sin-ridden creatures of flesh and blood can continually beg only for your pity. A Church of the weak hymns your strength, a Church of the miserable shouts from the housetops that you are limitlessly merciful. "Indeed the Church walked in the dark in the time of her pilgrimage, all the while groaning amid abundant wickedness."[38] Out of that walk in the dark you raise up children of ever-lasting light. Too only a less-than-perfect Church is able to progress. Just as a child growing is beautiful to behold, so the Church is beautiful in its steady inner increase over the centuries. "The temple of God is still being built."[39] "Even now the house of God is being constructed."[40] Every fresh soul united to the body, every new stone put in place, makes the Church more inviting, brings her nearer to that beauty without spot or wrinkle that you will unveil on the last day.

How can the Church be other than essentially beautiful if the Son and the Spirit fill her with light and life? How can the Church be other than magnetically attractive since she is genuinely Jesus himself? It is the beauty of Jesus shining in the members that draws our hearts to Jesus our head. "Just as they saw Christ and believed what he foretold about his body, the Church, so we see the body and we believe what she teaches about the head."[41] Jesus is there, his Spirit enlivening every part of the Church, present by grace in the holy and good, present but not by grace in the sullied and sick, there in all his charms, all his ravishing love. Jesus forms "one flesh"[42] that includes all of us who are his members; each and all are beautiful in him because "we ourselves are he himself."[43] Each of us can claim to speak all tongues because we are one in the oneness of all peoples.[44] Father, let me proclaim in every tongue the beauty of Jesus in his Church, his loveliness in all Catholics, especially those I encounter day by day.

2. Jesus lives! He lives! He lives! In his Church he lives now, as he lived in Palestine, under suspicion and attack, beset by foes bent on killing him and effacing every trace of his name. As you permitted Jesus to anguish and die, so, Father, you allow him in his Church to be trampled under the heel of enemies in every age. Today only you know exactly how many of the close to one hundred million Catholics trapped behind the iron and bamboo curtains have laid down their lives out of love of Jesus. Many of those who have not been shot to death or hanged or forced to rot away in filthy jails have slipped into a religious underground, bearing the witness

that is dry martyrdom. They have to endure in silence the barbarity and lies of perhaps the most anti-God, inhuman system fabricated in this century, the official suppression of all they hold sacred, all the stench of men usurping the place of God, all the bogus propaganda about serving the people that masks the power-drive of a self-serving Communist elite. Most exercise patience not under the knout but in the civilized serfdom that is the daily grind in totalitarian society. In the free world too followers of your Son have to suffer for their faith. The United States has been indisputably one of the least repressive societies in history, but a persistent bias, at times virulent, against Catholics has stained American history. To this day various business and academic doors remain barred to Catholics. Catholic elementary and secondary schools are still unjustly denied proper public funding. A secular humanistic outlook dominating large segments of the media constantly snipes at Catholic values. The leading role played by rank-and-file Catholics in the near-miraculous surge of the pro-life movement since 1973 has brought ugly anti-Catholic bigotry once more to the surface.

"Unless a grain of wheat falls into the ground and dies, it remains alone; but if it dies, it bears abundant fruit" (Jn 12.24). Jesus, the supreme example of this law of garnering supernatural life, had to die to generate the new life of love. So we have to suffer to be one with him, to rise up anew in the love he won for us by his suffering. So at every moment Jesus is suffering in us and we in union with him; at every moment his Church is sowing the seed of Jesus-suffering that fructifies in love. So the Jesus-pain of the martyrs means fresh fruit for the Church. Father, the sacri-fice-in-love of Jesus transmutes a grim human fact into the glorious divine fact of your love. His body is bound to agonize yet bound to grow ever stronger, ever more lustrous in love. You have made the Church of Jesus the only institution that will outlast all the wrecks of time. Bonded to your heart in the heart of Jesus, the Church cannot die because she dies daily in and through him.

How I quail at the prospect of suffering, how I buckle or feel dispirited if thoughtless companions or strangers subject me to ill-usage. Sweep away my childish fears, teach me that suffering, the way of Jesus, must be my way to greater love, so that I can, without rashly seeking it, welcome any suffering of body or spirit, whether persecution or merely a passing head-ache. At every moment of suffering let me feed at the banquet of his heart where in his suffering and death Jesus is at once host and food. "The banquet table is great when the Lord of the banquet is the food of the ban-quet. No one feeds his guests on himself, but Jesus the Lord did just this: he who invites us is our food and drink. Thus the martyrs recognized what they were eating and drinking, and they were able to render the very same in return."[45]

Your Church suffers from within also, not so much from those whose devotion is choked by the thorns of the world and the flesh as by those who reject authority. The tormented, scheming, deceiving Judas was the prototype of many in the centuries to follow who would lacerate the body of Jesus. Whatever their indecipherable intentions, heretics and apostates have split and wounded the Church over the centuries: Tertullian, Marcion, Arius, Pelagius, Nestorius, Eutyches in the ancient world; Luther, Zwingli, Calvin, John Knox, who helped dismember Christendom into warring camps toward the beginning of the modern world. But sadly and strangely the Church of Jesus has been plagued by dissidents who have obstinately refused to be separated from the body. Only you, Father, know all the shocking details of all the outrages inflicted since Vatican II on the Church by so-called free spirits, i.e., irresponsible individuals enslaved in the worship of themselves. In certain quarters doctrinal unity seems shattered. Self-proclaimed demythologizers commonly voice skepticism about or openly disavow Catholic teachings such as the strictly real divinity of Jesus, his physical resurrection, his real presence in the Eucharist, consecration as the essence of the Mass, the infallibility of the Pope, the virginity of Mary, and even the immutability of the nature of God. Some moral theologians are boldly advocating a relativism that, on subjective grounds such as creativity, endorses fornication, adultery, and regular homosexual activity. Some left-wing Catholics serve as apologists for Marxist tyranny under the banner of theology of liberation, and one American missionary community formerly famous for its work in the field afar has lavished praise, in its publications, on Castro's Cuba and Soviet Russia. Certain professors in Catholic academia teach and live as anti-Catholic Catholics. On the liturgical level practices not simply offensive to the artistic eye and ear but repugnant to the Spirit crop up month after month. On one Palm Sunday one madcap liberal priest drove a jeep up the middle aisle to dramatize Christ's entry into Jerusalem; such insanity is only an extreme case of the irreverent, who-cares temper that has travestied the liturgy.

Why this outbreak of dissension, immoral teaching, and counter-sacred flamboyance in matters liturgical? The reasons for these ills may lie forever beyond human comprehension, but I am confident, Father, that the fruits you reap from each blight will superabound in goodness. Rebellious outbreaks and the debasing of the liturgy chillingly but tellingly remind me that the Catholic Church is your Church, divinely conceived, divinely fed, divinely protected against misguided and reckless men. Give me the tenderness of your heart as I level strictures on doctrinal, moral, and liturgical depredators. Hold my tongue from deriding them, and in your love let me pray for the healing of their disloyalty. Let me beg of you overpowering anointing unto forgiveness especially for those vindictive spirits who never tire of lobbing insults at orthodox bishops. Consume them in your fire, and they will be converted from recalcitrant children into child-like servants in spirit and in truth. Further, the more your holy teachings are pooh-poohed, the more lovable they should become to me. Let doctrinal sloppiness goad me to fiercer adherence to the least regarded of your words. Bathe me in your purifying truths so that I may live more intimately with and in you.

We are locked in conflict with spirits of wickedness in high places, who spread their confusion through the length and breadth of the world and sow pockets of darkness in the kingdom (Eph 6.17). How did these towering spirits fall in the greatest of cataclysms in the spirit world? Their primordial sin was a disobedience rooted in pride. Playing God, they would achieve their glory on their own, disdaining to generously lower themselves to the secret exigencies of your plan, Father.[46] Wanting their own way, the fallen angels thirsted for novelty, opted for alternative thought-styles, staked all on salvific variety, defended a kind of pluralism with coruscating but essentially flawed logic as they clashed with the unalterably God-centered Michael and his legions. It does not appear to go too far to say that some theologians' partial breakaway from Catholic doctrine seems tinctured in part with the no the devil and his angels hurled in the face of God. Influential errors of a false pluralism may be remotely traceable to the guileful prince of darkness.

The Church militant is always infested with fifth columnists, a disaffected band within undermining the people of God in the name of relevance or freedom or some other glittering idol of the Zeitgeist. However, Father, you capitalize on the assaults of the enemy to bulwark the body of Jesus. The more warped the errors, the faster her growth in wisdom; the heavier the pounding, the more luxuriant the flowering of patience; the more bemusing the hugger-mugger, the more consoling the ensuing peace; the more fragmented the disorder, the more entrancing the joy. To counter the derisive attacks on the Church in the Enlightenment you raised up John-Mary Vianney, a man somewhat slow of wit, hardly gifted in dialectical fencing, severely limited as a pastor, endowed "only" with the wisdom of your foolishness and the strength of your weakness, a saint through whose helplessness radiated your glory. So it is in every age: you use the weak to overthrow the strong, the little to topple the mighty, nobodies to reduce to nothing those who rate themselves somebodies. The holiness of these simple ones helps thaw the hearts of malevolent foes of your Church and transform lackeys of Satan into earthly "angels," transmitters of your light and love.

No one but you, Father, who fathom the human heart, can discern why many contemporary thinkers have exalted change. Change, change, change! goes up the impassioned cry that at times verges on quasi-religious enthusiasm. Everything, we are told, is changing but change itself; the only absolute is change; and everything else is relativized in change. Only academic word-spinners insulated from things can celebrate the sovereignty of change. In the real world where the arrow of time moves remorselessly on, change portending decline and death evokes fear and dread. If change reigns, the universe is meaningless. Where all is flux, death is the end for all. After the most august of emperors dies, millenia pass, and his dry bones bleach unrecognized in the shifting sands. In the grand sweep of history no one knows, no one cares about the careers of ordinary individuals. A human being lives, then shortly drops into the grave till in the slow unwinding of the eons he is utterly forgotten, his remains totally gone. In Augustine's figure, each of us a droplet in the never-ceasing river of life that is soon swallowed up in the sea. Eventually all higher ife on our planet will become extinct, and in this long perspective all the glories of the human spirit, all the heroic quests to realize ideals will seem worth next-to-nothing, vanishing alike with the grotesque and vicious in the unrelenting roll of matter.

In 1929 at the age of sixteen Albert Camus, the well-known French existentialist, and a friend noticed a crowd in Algeria gathered about the body of a young Arab crushed to death under the wheels of a bus. Camus, pointing to the sky, said, "You see, heaven is silent."[47] If there is no heaven, i.e., no world outside time, then every death seems as senseless as the death of the small Arab boy: each of us is eventually crushed beneath the wheels of change. But, Father, you are not silent, you have uttered your Word, you did not spare your only Son from the most ghastly, the most liberating of deaths. The absurdity of flitting human existence becomes shot through with light and love through the death of Jesus. The drops of water that are human lives are mingled with his precious blood. My meaningless exit is turned into a life-sharing, a life-receiving death offered to you in union with your Son's as a sacrifice of praise.

On one teacher's desk sits a plaque from a friend inscribed with the simple, powerful words: "You are loved." The crucifix never ceases speaking its mute witness to me: You are loved! I am loved by you. Father, with an everlasting love, loved by the very love with which you joined yourself to Jesus crucified, loved by the love that lit up the absurdity of Calvary, loved by the love with which you love your Son and Spirit and they love you. As one poet put it, "The dark itself is starry with His grace."[48] The midnight that begloomed Good Friday afternoon was illumined by his wounds. The sunset of Messianic dreams inwardly marked the start of the sunrise; more, it was the beginning of the noonday brightness still warming hearts and minds. Father, when I gaze upon a crucifix or kiss its corpus, I experience, however so slightly, the touch of your mercy. Show me how to feel your sustaining hand at every moment, during upset, desoltaion, depression, hollowness. Out of those depths let me cry out with fullest confidence to see the light streaming from the starry scars of the dead Jesus, my sun, my all, whose sacrifice tells me I am loved.

The weight of love in the cross unburdens me of some of my selfishness. Its bitterness makes life sweeter, its pain brings spiritual pleasure. The tree on which Jesus hung captive releases me from thralldom, freeing me to live not for the moment from which I can grab passing satisfaction but for the moment melded with the everlasting moment of your love. In terms of physical comforts big-city slum dwellers of today live more royally than did seventeenth-century monarchs in the cold, fetid palace of Versailles. So, living by your life, Father, my soul luxuriates in a more royal inward life than geniuses of the pagan past. Now I can see through the tinsel and trumpery of wealth, power, bubble reputation, applause. What is stronger than your gentleness, Father, what more lovely than trysting with you, what more transporting than your embrace, what more overjoying than the comfort of the Spirit of Jesus?

Praise

1. Despite poetic aspirations in youth I have lapsed into a utilitarian spirit, with scant eye for the beautiful. Hurrying along in busyness, I miss the splendor of a sunset, the quiet of a meadow, the delicately balanced diving of a robin, the charm of a starlit night sky. Father, I may never escape this shrunken natural outlook but, I beg you, still any activism that may blur my spiritual vision. Take me out of myself to capture your beauty in every scintilla of the life of Jesus and his Church.

I lift up to you Jesus, your all-beautiful Son. In and through him may the shabby and soiled in me fade, ceding place to the lovely and the pure of your quintessential beauty. Let me praise you, Father, as I praise Jesus in a few events of a life that is all mystery, all love. I praise you, Jesus, newborn in the cave, joining my voice to the exultation of armies of angels: "Glory to God in the highest and on earth peace to men of good will" (Lk 2.14). Beautiful beyond compare, Jesus, were you in the rough feedbox, beautiful in your Godly strength, beautiful in your human weakness, beautiful in the apparent paradoxes that poets have never ceased singing and sages never stopped pondering. How can the finite be united but not blurred with the infinite, how can the infinite be compressed within a finite infant? Miracle of miracles this: I praise you, wonder of wonders, most tremendous of miracles and most beautiful of beings ever to walk this earth. Every moment of your earthly span was charged with this essential beauty. I see and praise you astounding the doctors of the law in the temple with your brilliance, adroitly but not smugly fielding every question, putting your finger on the nub of each difficulty, then unriddling it with lightly worn learning and acuity. As that puzzling scene disappears, I praise you for the outwardly uncircumstantial years in Nazareth where, Light of Light though you were, you subjected yourself to the ideas and decisions of Mary and Joseph. How indescribably beautiful was the peace reigning in your home. Three different individuals dwelt in perfect concord, a foretaste of the unbroken harmony in diversity that is certainly not the least of the joys of heaven. Then Joseph was gone, the long years of preparation came to an end, and at the signal from the Father and the anointing of the Spirit you took to the dusty roads of Palestine. I praise you for your words, simple but none more forcible, none more engaging, none more catching, none more holy, none more human, none more divine. I praise you for your works, the numberless healings, the miracles that defy description. O Jesus, how can I praise you enough for opening this door to the Father, stunning and attracting men by this downrush from the divine. How awesome you were in your power, so convincing in your discourse, so commanding in your authority, yet so, so approachable in your gentleness that welcomed all open hearts with the innocence of a tiny child. But offspring of hell besieged you and hemmed you in and, lion of Judah though you were, you submitted like a lamb to the slaughter. As you agonized in the garden, you allowed your spirit to be constricted, choked by the moral pestilence from Adam's fall to the last fault prior to the crack of doom. You became sin (2 Cor 5.21), more repulsive than all the most forbidding lepers in history. A nauseating sight were you debased to, a spiritual abomination. I praise you, for, when blood oozed out of you like drops of sweat, you were welcoming the chalice from the Father's hands. Then in closest union with the Father you rose to go to be arrested by your devil-filled foes. I praise you for your love and humility in those dread scenes. In your ultimate self-oblation you became a sort of nonperson, a mere thing to be knocked and kicked around. How beautiful in abasement were you as your face thrice struck the ground, how beautiful as you were disrobed and exposed to the gawking and jeering of the multitude, how beautiful in the jolting of your frame as you said yes to the nails being driven in, how beautiful as you were raised up on the gibbet. I praise you: nothing has ever been more beautiful in the Father's eyes than your suffering and death on the cross. You reigned indomitable in abjection, triumphant in defeat, conqueror of the enemies of God and man, unexampled lover of God and man. Praise to you for rising glorious in your wounds, each scar an emblem of victory. Praise to you for your ascension: your heart was torn as you left the disciples you loved so much, but, obedient to the last to the Father, you went up beautiful in glory to sit at his right hand.

Your mystical self lives on in your Church. I praise you for the Church indefectible. Assailed within and without, mocked and scourged and crucified over and over, your Church endures, thrives, and, wracked by dissension in one region, grows by leaps and bounds in other lands. I praise you, Jesus, for this superb instrument of your love. In the fleshly robes of imperfect, always sinful men you dispense the bounties of your mercy, laying healing hands on the wayward, sending your Spirit on children, anointing the sick, merging man and maid into holiest oneness, consecrating new priests, and feasting all in the banquet that is yourself. I praise you for being indissolubly one with your people, for making the invisible visible in countless ways all over the world, for manifesting in your Church the deathless presence of the Father. Praise to you, Jesus, ever present in your Church: he who sees you sees the Father, he who sees your Church sees the Father.

2. Praise to you, Father, for the rapid expansion of the Church during her early centuries. Only your Spirit who deciphers the deeps of your Godly

nature descries all the factors that triggered her swift spread. How scattered and flimsy seemed the forces of the little band of Christians in the first century, some 20,000 in all. But praise to you for the promptings of your Spirit, for in a few centuries the cultural outlanders had gained status in and control of the Roman empire. They were despised as otherwordly *exaltés* and nonconformists, smeared as orgiasts, persecuted as subverters of all that was sacred to Rome. Praise to you for employing scorn, insults, ostracism, and periodic bloodbaths to gradually overcome her haters and to change their temples into churches, their pagan festivals into holy days. Glory to you for your wisdom that seizes upon what some existentialist wise men bewail as absurdity and transmute it into a vehicle of your love. The weak are sent to the wall, the powerless are exploited, those who resist the world-system are slandered and denounced. Praise to you, Father, for allowing the absurdity of the triumph of evil to issue in the victory of the good. In the slow workings of your law of suffering in love, the foolish outwit the cunning, the lamb bests the lion, the lowly master the exalted, the persecuted bury their persecutors. Glory to you Father for this law of life from death; from it springs healing for the mind tortured by the spectacle of the absurd, through it peace and joy blossom on the tree of suffering.

Father, in your generosity you use not only your saints but anonymous plodders wholly committed to your Church to bring joy out of suffering. I thank you for a nun who, as I write, is slowly dying of cancer, a hardly uncommon occurrence, but the cancer now infecting her liver began in her face so that her nose had to be removed. Her new nose, reconstructed from flesh of other parts of her body, left her looking blotched and unpleasing. Not despondent but cheerful about her misshapen face, she went about her duties with vigor and gusto, exempt from almost all self-pity. I praise you, Lord, for this brave nun, consecrated to you especially in her suffering, whose distorted features magnify the beauty of your Church. I praise you too for the fidelity of a west Philadelphia woman stricken by family woes. After her husband deserted her, she raised her six children single-handed. A few years ago a twentyish son was killed in an automobile accident. Just a few weeks prior to this writing, a son addicted to drugs plunged to his death from a downtown hotel room. Fighting back her tears, she courageously did the readings at the second son's funeral Mass; an object of pity in her grief but an example of fortitude and self-surrender in her broken heart. Praise to you: you accept her brokenness to make your Church more whole, her wounds to help heal the lacerated body of Jesus, her fidelity to motherhood to help stem the tidal wave of selfishness that has wrecked many Catholic homes.

As I praise you for these living images of your law that draws light from the darkness, heal me of a spirit of complaining that conflicts with the law of suffering-in-love. I praise you, Father, for your meek and tranquil saints, serene in nearly all their troubles. Because of your liberality I cannot,

I must not be a whiner over niggling setbacks, reverses, and pinstabs. As I sing your praises, because I hail the glory of your name, keep my lips sealed and my heart open to the cross as paltry problems surface. With so many hours slipping away swiftly as seconds, let my praise of your strength empower me to pounce on every slightest misturn as an opportunity to upbuild your Church in redemptive suffering.

3. As I sorrowfully ponder the scandals of Church history, I have to cry out my praise and thanksgiving. Blessed be your name, all-kind Father, for the treasure of steadfastness in faith and for the extra grace that has saved me from becoming a second and perhaps worse Judas. You forgive all who respond to your pursuing love with the briefest spark of love: teach me to understand the catastrophe that was Judas, largely a shadowy figure through most of the Gospel portrayal. How could a soul so high fall so low, how could a confidant so trusted sell out the Son of God to enemies? Throw light on this most tragic of figures; show me too why other defectors throughout the centuries have learned little or nothing from the dread tale of Judas. For what motives only you know, other betrayers jettisoning your doctrines passionately decried the Church of Christ as the harlot of Babylon and bawled out half-truths that convulsed and split Christendom. I praise you for raising up new gifted souls to replace those who choose to blaspheme the ancient faith. Glory to you for the fidelity of the hundreds of millions whose example firms my heart to be faithful in word and work. Source of all light, never let the light within me go out; anoint me more and more with the oil of your charity. Pull me back instantly from the least temptation to play the rebel and traitor. Make my soul faithful, ever grateful for your holding me in your arms.

Father, teach me how to utter words of praise concerning disasters within your Church. Since Vatican II the dark heart of man has spewed forth arrogant dissent, contempt for authority, and childish exhibitionism in the liturgy. Father, let me praise you for the rocklike loyalty of so many of your faithful in the face of breakdown and decline. I praise you for the new legions of the Church militant mobilizing to fight your fight of justice with the weapons of meek courage and humble tenacity. Praise to you for rallying your little ones, who in the feebleness of your power shine with light that disperses self-blinded academics; little ones whose lowliness upends the new Pharisees who, like the old, seek only their own glory. As I laud you for these contemporary defenders of the faith, spur me to pray for a like unyielding stance in the face of evil in high places, to pray with the intensity and aching need of the blind man who yelled after Jesus, and with him to beg, "Lord, I want to see" (Lk 18.35-43), to understand my faith in the deepest moral and mystical way, to live my faith uncompromisingly, uncomplainingly giving no quarter to self-indulgence, stifling faintheartedness, and leveling fears of criticism and insult.

I praise you too, Father, for wayward minds that have become, in fact, heretics, who have disinterred ancient errors, now labeled avant garde, all the while battling by every legalistic strategem to go on wearing the mantle of Catholic scholars. I praise you for your tolerance of these disquieted spirits who try to dress up the wildest theories in the garb of Catholic truth. In the past I lumped person and position, tending to deem the man as objectionable as his erorr. Praise to you for encouraging me to follow now the loving directive of Augustine: "Love men, slay errors. Hold on to the truth without pride, fight for the truth without cruelty. Pray for those men whom you rebuke and refute."[49] Grant me a brotherly sympathy for psuedo-Catholic minds that put reputation for originality ahead of fidelity to your word. Father, what have I that I have not received (1 Cor 4.7), and, if I have received how can I refuse to help those who have junked what they once received? Let me never stop praying for the lost sheep of the house of theology, wise according to academic credentials but unwise in their faith-repudiating claims, wealthy in learning but destitute of loyalty to the Church. Praise to you for the light with which you will invade their minds, the fire with which you will melt their hearts.

4. I praise you, Father, for your plan that permitted some of the highest angels to fall. How could, how did it happen? Angels are totally concentrated on their goals, not at all ruffled by the tug of passions, minds and wills so originally suffused with light as to seem absolutely infallible and impeccable. Yet, calamitously, these luminous spirits hurled themselves to their doom. Though this blotch will forever disfigure part of your creation, I believe that, without discerning how, this almost unthinkable wreckage does add to your glory. Praise to you for your Spirit that led doctors of your Church to underscore the radical sin of these blackened but still puissant spirits: pride. This is the root sin of human failings. The glory of man is his spirit, the abomination of man is his pride of spirit. Praise to you for the healing humility of your Son who emptied himself of the glory of the Godhead. Thank you for pardoning my numerous falls; how often, while aspiring to be lowly and meek as a lamb, I have inwardly roared like a rampaging bull. I praise you for the insight of Augustine making it plain that I cannot escape seeking and imitating you. If I do not share in your attributes by humility, I have to perversely ape your power through pride.[50] I praise you for the power in the powerlessness of lowliness, which Augustine describes: "So if strength lies in humility, do not be afraid of proud men. Humble individuals are like a rock. A rock is, we see, beneath us but it is solid. What about proud men? They are like smoke. Although they rise high, they fade away."[51] Never let me leave off praising you; when I become nasty in my pride, let my praise of your mercy set me once more on the rock of humility.

It is on this rock that my hope is built. I cannot but praise you, Father, for the cosmos and its incessant change, but without you I am bound to be sucked into the flux and, gyrating in its whirlpools, so despair that I may be in danger of sinking and dropping out of your sight forever. I raise my eyes constantly to your changeless life that outlasts all change. Praise to you for leading me to grasp at least abstractly the transience of life. Now stamp this truth fully into my soul, and never will I forget in my every word and work that my life is inching away like drops of water through a sieve. I praise you; my frame is made of dust, and each fugitive moment, each bit of dust lost in the atmosphere can be currency of eternity, seed that will bring forth its harvest in your eternal day. With the poet Keats I may say, "My name is written on water," but in your mercy, I hope, is waiting my new name (Rev 2.17), my secret mystical identity, in the Book of Life stored in your heart.

"Love never fails," (1 Cor 13.8), it goes on and on. Glory to you, Father: it is your love, the love that is you, that threads and gives meaning to human history and indeed meaning to the cosmos itself. A few years ago American and Spanish anthropologists discovered in Santandar, in the north of Spain, a religious shrine that went back some 14,000 years. Throughout the millenia men have sought and propitiated you, at times in partially distorted and coarse ways, but nearly always through the urging of your love. When tribesmen beseeched you, it was your love that moved them to raise their arms in supplication, to cast themselves down in adoration, and to burn sacrifices fragrant in your nostrils. When men of old quaked in your presence, it was your love that, concealed in their reverential fear, held them close to you. All praise to you for leaving aside fragmentary expressions and finally disclosing yourself in Jesus as absolute love. It is your love that steadies me when I feel kicked around like a soccerball in a scrimmage, unable to make sense of the to-and-fro and the give-and-take. I praise you, healing Father, for laving my fevered brow and soothing my roiled feelings: in your love are my health and peace. I praise you, my everlasting lover: one day not so far off my earthly remains will be lowered into a little plot of earth, there to moulder till the last day. But as my body dissolves into a cloud of dust, I will go on living, sustained by your love in Jesus that conquers the grave. Praise to you: in a small measure I bathe in, I am anointed and caressed by, that love. Gracious God, how can I praise you enough? You love me!

Life a Sacrifice of Praise:
Weakness Transmuted into Strength

Though it would be folly to entertain the hope of duplicating Augustine's super-genius and the masterly literary grace with which he portrayed his life, his story as a sacrifice of praise magnifying the law of divine mercy that causes minuses to add up to pluses is meant, in substance, to be the drama of Christian Everyman. For every believer who strives unfailingly, even while many times failing, to love the Father, divine power derives supernatural benefits from the moral "cussedness" of things. Omnipotence as the handmaid of boundless mercy takes junk, worn-out parts, and worthless odds and ends, then reshapes them and reassembles them into a sturdy fabric. God, so to speak, takes a scrap heap of parts of smashed Volkswagens and converts them into a brand-new Cadillac. Through infinitely empowered wisdom, out of wretchedness comes vibrancy; out of destitution, abundance; out of the damaged beyond repair, the intricately beautiful (yet only partially in this life, for the perfection of the grand design of all history is reserved for the Day of the Lord). Each of us blessed by infinitely ingenious mercy is invited to respond with a sacrifice of praise. This sort of sacrifice, which Zaccheus held in his patrimony and the poor widow in her purse (Lk 19.8; Mk 12.42), lies within, needing no costly incense: the altar is our own conscience or heart. When this sacrifice of praise vaults to the self-surrender spoken of earlier, confession becomes a veritable interior holocaust. The ardent praiser begs to be denuded of ego and to have all of self transmuted into God through a whole-burnt offering. "Let my whole heart be enkindled by the flame of your love. Let nothing of myself continue in me, let nothing of self-regard remain. Let the whole of myself glow within you, let the whole of myself burn within you, let the whole of myself set on fire by you love you."[52] What a superb disclosure of the interior self-oblation of the soul of Augustine! Momentarily unveiling his inner countenance, the secret of his indefatigable zeal, he rouses each of us to a like self-immolation that is the acme of praise. Plunged into the heart of God, set ablaze and consumed by his love, each of us is to be a living flame of love, a whole-burnt offering of praise, enlivened by the fire of God alone. Thus we render to God the things that are God's, i.e., what bears the interior image of Christ the king — our interior self, to be constantly rekindled in our holocaust of praise.

It might be disingenuous not to concede that our praise of God falls far short of the perfect. Not infrequently it is distracted, perfunctory, and listless, for we praise God in this life, i.e., as staggering under the frightful load of the body. A candid yes to frailties and heartbreaks equips us to discern that God is hammering our trumpet of praise into shape so that it will emit sharper, more mellifluous tones. This is the hard but solacing truth learned by the stalwart Apostle: "Power is made perfect in weakness" (2 Cor 12.9). Weakness itself, accepted docilely, is a fountain of power-filled praise when united to the sufferings of Jesus, who, in being crowned with thorns and crucified, offered himself as a victim of praise to the Father. As we embrace the self-emptying of the cross, our feebleness is more and more endowed with his power. Lifting up our hearts in praise, we grow in vigor and, rocketing far above the cedars of Lebanon, dwell in the sanctuary of the Most High, where we drink in his plan of love. In the center of this plan is etched the figure of the Crucified who laid down his life with measureless generosity, to experientially proclaim the good news of mercy, to teach that out of brokenness comes strength; out of death, life; out of nothing, all. So joyously, as a living holocaust, we sing the wonder that is himself until our praise, prostrate before mysteries that slip through the meshes of our equations and formulas, fuses somewhat with that of a Paul, his soul whirling before and enrapt by unfathomable wisdom: "O the depth of the riches of the wisdom and knowledge of God! How inscrutable are his judgments, how unsearchable his ways!" (Rom 11.33).

The life of man is the response of his heart to the beckoning of the Father and the gifts that God showers upon him. What sort of response does God require of those called to be his sons and daughters and, from another angle, his spouses? The return the Father wants from his dust-born but glory-destined offspring is simply this: a sacrifice of praise. We need not be wealthy, talented, creative, innovative, tireless, energetic, enterprising, or resourceful in the line of nature. It is in the heart, it is in the depths of the soul, that our sacrifice of praise goes up to the Father, a sacrifice rooted in love, a sacrifice that need be no more valuable-looking than offering a cup of cold water to a little one who is a disciple of Jesus. In other words, it is a sacrifice that not only ascends to heaven but descends from heaven: the power and the impulse to offer it are pure gifts of God. Thus our sacrifice rises as a pleasing fragrance before the All-High, for only the gifts of God can fully satisfy him. The peace and concomitant sweetness that men of good will experience are their share in the fragrance that delights the heart of God.

> Tell us then, Lord our God, what tribute you demand of your people, your Israel. God tells us, "Offer to God a sacrifice of praise" (v. 14). Let us also tell him, "O God, in my heart I make vows to you: I will offer you a sacrifice of praise" (Ps 55 [56].12). I was afraid that you would demand of me something outside my power to give — I am thinking of some personal possession I no longer have perhaps because a thief stole it. What do you demand of me? "Offer to God a sacrifice of praise." Let me turn inward to myself where I will find what I am to sacrifice. Let me turn inward to myself; within myself I will find a sacrifice of praise: my conscience will be your altar. "Offer to God a sacrifice of praise." We need not worry about things to offer, we don't have to travel to Arabia in search of frankincense, we don't have to examine the wares of a money-loving dealer. God asks of us a sacrifice of praise. Zaccheus carried his sacrifice of praise in his patrimony (Lk 19.8), the widow in her small purse (Mk 12.42), some impoverished host or other in his wine jar. Think of some other individual who carried nothing in his patrimony or purse or wine jar: still he carried the sacrifice of praise wholly in his heart. Salvation came to the house of Zaccheus; and the widow gave more than all those wealthy donors. An individual who offers a cup of cold water shall not lose his reward (Mt 10.42); but there is too "peace on earth to men of good will" (Lk 2.14). "Offer to God a sacrifice of praise." O what sacrifice is there: it is gratuitous, the gift of grace! Indeed, Lord, I did not buy what I am to offer you but you gave it to me, for without you I would

not have had even this. "Offer to God a sacrifice of praise," and this is the immolation of the sacrifice of praise: to give thanks to him from whom you have whatever good you have and by whose mercy you are forgiven whatever evil, evil of your own doing, you have. "Offer to God a sacrifice of praise and render to the Most High the homage of your prayers." The Lord delights in this fragrance. "Render to the Most High the homage of your prayers." (v. 14).[53]

This sacrifice of praise is to be lifted up in all circumstances, especially in those characteristic of what moderns call the human condition: man is beset by ills of every sort, oppressed by hardships, disconcerted by reverses, stung by the past failures that seem to streak even remarkable successes. We have already touched on the misery of man, the ineliminable sorrow that afflicts everyone in body and spirit. As previously noted, man's stupendous technological achievements do not soften but in the long run sharpen his awareness of the slings and arrows of misfortune and, worse, the poisons that flow from human iniquity. Yet even where these ills are mitigated, the woe and agony reduced, the evils brought under control, still the heart of man is embittered by tribulation. He is an alien, a dweller in a foreign land, a sojourner on the march toward a homeland beyond the skies in which the food and drink of the spirit are the justice and the wisdom of God. The very fact that man is seeking and searching entails trouble and sorrow: nothing short of the superhuman can still the restlessness of the human heart. Yet man's response to God's wooing can issue in partial satisfaction on this side. Call on the name of the Lord, the psalmist inspired by the Holy Spirit urges. Man calls upon divine power when he praises the Lord for promising, drawing, and gracing him in his ascent to the heights of the divine. The tribulation of exile elicits a sacrifice of praise.

"And call upon me in the day of your tribulation: and I will deliver you, and you shall glorify me" (v. 15). For you should not count on your own powers; all your own resources are nothing but liars. "Call upon me in the day of tribulation: I will deliver you and you shall glorify me." This is why I have allowed a day of tribulation to befall you: perhaps if you did not experience tribulation, you might not call upon me. But when you experience tribulation, you call upon me; when you call upon me, I will deliver you; when I deliver you, you will glorify me, and thus you will no longer wander away from me. No longer fervent in prayer, a certain individual had grown sluggish and cold, prompting him to say, "I found tribulation and sorrow at my side, and I called upon the name of the Lord" (Ps 114 [116].3). He found he could profit from his tribulation. The gangrene of his sins had rotted his soul, he had gone on without feeling; then the tribulation served to burn and cut away the diseased parts. "I found," he says, "tribulation and sorrow at my side, and I called upon the name of the Lord." And indeed, brothers, everyone undergoes tribulations. Look at the number of tribulations afflicting the whole human race. One person bemoans the financial loss he has suffered; a second mourns the loss of a loved one; another grieves over being an exile from his country and yearns to return home since he finds his foreign sojourning intolerable; hail ravages the vineyard of still another, causing him to lament that all his hard work and toil were spent in vain. Is there a single moment when a man cannot be plunged into grief? A friend suddenly turns into an enemy. Is any misery greater than this possible in the whole of mankind? Everyone weeps and grieves over tribulations such as these; and in all these troubles they call upon the Lord, and they do well to do so. Let them call upon the God whose power will either teach them how to bear their afflictions or to heal those they have borne. In his wisdom he does not let us be tried beyond what we can bear (1 Cor 10.13). Let us call upon God even in such tribulations. However, notice that this sort of tribulation finds us; yet there is another sort of tribulation that we ought to seek and find. What is it? This is the very happiness of this world, an abundance of temporal goods. Still, strictly speaking, these do not make up tribulation; rather, in fact, they are consolations that relieve our tribulation. Which tribulation are we referring to here? This tribulation is our sojourning in exile. For the very fact that we are not yet in the presence of God, the very fact that we are living in the midst of trials and anxieties, the very fact that we cannot be immune to fear — all this goes into the making of tribulation, all this is the case because we still do not possess the security promised us. An individual who does not find this tribulation in his exile has to be someone who simply gives no thought to returning to his homeland. No doubt about it, brothers, this life of exile is tribulation. Surely we do good works now when we tender bread to the hungry, when we open our homes to the stranger, and when we do similar deeds. Yet even in these cases there is tribulation. For we find those individuals miserable toward whom we show mercy; it is the miserable condition of these miserable men that makes us compassionate. How much better off you would be there where you find no hungry person needing your food, where you find no stranger needing hospitality, no naked person needing clothing, no sick person needing your visit, no litigant needing your help in settling his case. There everything is supremely good, everything is true, everything is holy, everything is everlasting. There our bread is justice, there our drink is wisdom, there our garment is immortality, there our home is an eternal dwelling place in heaven, there our strength is immortality. Does sickness creep up on you? Does fatigue close your eyes in sleep? On the other side there is no more death, no more litigation: there reign peace, rest, joy, justice. No enemy gains entrance, no friend deserts us. What kind of rest will we have there? If we consider and ponder where we live now and where he who cannot lie promised that one day we will live, his very promise makes clear what a state of tribulation we live in at present. Yet unless he searches for it, no one becomes aware of this sort of tribulation. You are in good health: ask yourself if you are in misery, for it is easy for an ill individual to feel miserable. When you are in good health, ask yourself if you are in misery for the reason that you are not yet in the presence of God. "I found tribulation and sorrow, and I called upon the name of the Lord." So "offer to God a sacrifice of praise." Praise the God who makes promises to you, praise the God who calls you, praise the God who exhorts you, praise the God who helps you, and realize in what sort of tribulation you are stuck. Call upon him, and you will be delivered; you will glorify him, and you will abide forever.[54]

Praise like this must well up from within, from the heart, pouring itself out in self-surrender. At least in desire the heart wants nothing but what God wants because the heart truly seeking him comes to know that it is nothing of itself, has nothing of itself, is worth nothing of itself. Through the touch of Jesus the person reaching out to God recognizes that he is utterly insufficient. Because he has all from and owes all to God, he gives himself to God in humility and love so far as he can. Disencumbered of the debris of self, he is not a zero but a heart on fire, a small holocaust, a living sacrifice of praise responding with his all to the all-giving of God. In one respect it is his share in the giving of God that sets his heart ablaze and makes him burn with pure love and stark trust, endeavoring to detach himself from all because wholly attached to God, wholly consumed in his love that is divine self-giving.

"I will confess to you, Lord, with my whole heart" (v. 1). . . . Let us then listen to this confession. But first I remind you that, when the Scriptures speak of confessing to God, the word "confession" is used in two senses: confession dealing with sins or confession meaning praise. But while everyone knows about confession of sins, few notice that confession also means praise. Indeed so well known and so fixed in our minds is confession of sins that whenever we hear the words, "I will confess to you," or "We will confess to you," in any passage of Scripture, right away our hands start beating our breasts. Such a gesture indicates that men ordinarily take confession to mean only the confession of sins. But surely our Lord Jesus Christ was not speaking as a sinner when in the Gospel he said, "I confess to you, Father, Lord of heaven and earth" (Mt 11.25). Going on, he specified the object of his confession, thus enabling us to understand that he was making not a confession of sins but one of praise. "I confess to you, Father, Lord of heaven and earth, because you have hidden these things from the wise and clever and revealed them to little ones." He praised the Father, he praised God because he despised not the humble but the proud. And here we are going to hear this sort of confession, one of praise of and thanksgiving to God. "I will confess to you, Lord, with my whole heart." I place my whole heart on the altar of your praise, I offer a holocaust of praise to you. A holocaust is said to be a sacrifice in which the whole of the victim is burnt. For the Greek word "holon" means "whole." Look how the individual who says, "I will confess to you, Lord, with my whole heart," is offering a spiritual holocaust. "Let my whole heart," he says, "be enkindled by the flame of your love. Let nothing of myself continue in me, let nothing of self-regard remain. Let the whole of myself glow within you, let the whole of myself burn within you, let the whole of myself set on fire by you love you." "I will confess to you, Lord, with my whole heart, because you heard the words of my mouth." What does "my mouth" mean but my heart? For in the heart we have a voice that God hears, one that the ear of man knows nothing of. Surely the accusers of Susanna cried aloud but they did not lift their eyes toward heaven, while she kept silent but cried aloud from the bottom of her heart (Dan 13.34ff.). That is why she deserved to be heard as they deserved to be punished. This mouth then lies within: therein do we pray, from there do we pray. And if within we have readied a lodging or home for God, therein do we speak to him, therein does he hear us. "For he is not far from any one of us: in him we live and move and have our being" (Acts 17.27-28). Only sinful ways, nothing else, put you far from God. Tear down the wall of sin between you and God, and you become present with him to whom you pray. "You heard," he says, "the words of my mouth: I will confess to you."[55]

God hears our petition and praise or our praise-in-petition and petition-in-praise when we say our vows to him in the strict sense, i.e., when we utterly devote ourselves to him, when we give all of self to him. We return to God the image he has created in us, our spiritual self. More, we return to him the image he has recreated in us, the very sharing in the self of Jesus, his perfect image. Our sacrifice of praise renders to God the things that are God's.

"I will render my vows to the Lord" (v. 18). What vows are you going to render? What victims have you vowed to offer? What incense have you offered? What holocausts have you sacrificed? Are you referring to what you said a few lines back: "I will take the cup of salvation and I will call on the name of the Lord, and to you I will sacrifice a sacrifice of praise" (v. 13)? To the man who is giving some thought to what he ought to vow to the Lord and what vows he should render to him, I say: vow yourself, render yourself. This is what God requires, this is what you owe him. After looking at the coin of tribute, the Lord said, "Render to Caesar the things that are Caesar's and to God the things that are God's" (Mt 22.21). You render his own image to Caesar; then render his own image to God.

It is this likeness to God that draws us close to him, that makes us one with him no matter how physically removed he may seem, no matter how distant and silent he may appear when we raise our hearts to him in prayer. Because God is eternal, a thousand years seem to him as one day (2 Pet 3.8). Because he is love, for those like him in love a thousand miles apart are as one foot. We image him in love when we spread his love to others, especially, as remarked earlier, when we love our enemies. Then we are, if we dare use an old colloquialism, spittin' images of the Father, we are truly his children, his beings and agents of divine love. The love that burns in our hearts replicating the never-ceasing fire in the bosom of the Father is the coin of tribute we pay to him as Lord of the universe and master of our lives. A share in his love brings with it a share in his joy. Flames like those in the heart of God warm and exhilarate the soul, making it sing and shout with a holy gladness that no mere human good can elicit.

"This people honors me with their lips but their heart is far from me" (Is 29.13; Mt 15.8). Thus not place but unlikeness puts a person far from God. What does unlikeness mean here? It means an evil life and evil habits. For if good habits draw us near to God, evil habits draw us away from him. Thus one and the same man, while occupying the same physical place, draws near to God by loving God and draws away from God by loving wickedness. He never takes a single step yet he can both draw near to and away from God. In the journey of this life our affections are our feet. According to the object of his affections, each individual draws near to or away from God. When we judge things unlike, don't we ordinarily say, "This is far from that"? When we are comparing two men, two horses, two articles of clothing, and someone says, "This article of clothing is like that, it is the same sort as that," or "This man is the same sort as that," what words are used by a third person who disagrees with these opinions? He says, "Not at all; this is far from that." What does this mean: this is far from that? It means: this is unlike that. Two men are standing next to each other yet this individual is far from the other. But two individuals equally evil in life and habit, whether one lives in the east and the other in the west, are next to each other. And similarly two good men, whether one lives in the east and the other in the west, are in each other's presence because they dwell in God. Contrariwise, one good and one evil man, even though bound by the same chain, are greatly distanced from each other. Thus if unlikeness draws us away from God, likeness draws us near to God. What likeness are we talking about? It is the likeness according to which we have been created, the likeness our sins destroyed in us, the likeness we regained by forgiveness of our sins, the likeness interiorly renewed in our heart. So the image of our God, like the image engraved on a coin, is stamped anew on our soul, and so again we gain entrance to his treasures. Now, brothers, why did our Lord Jesus Christ choose to use a coin to show to those testing him what God wants from us? When those bent on trapping him in false accusation sought the advice of the teacher of truth about the tax for Caesar and, to put him to the test, asked whether it was lawful to pay the tax to Caesar, what did he reply? "You hypocrites, why are you putting me to the test?" He said, "Whose image is this?" They answered, "Caesar's." He then said to them, "Render therefore to Caesar the things that are Caesar's and to God the things that are God's" (Mt 22.18-22). It was just as if he had said: "If Caesar requires his own image on a coin, doesn't God require his own image in man?" Inviting us to live according to this likeness to God, our Lord Jesus Christ commands us also to love our enemies and proposes God as our model. He tells us, "Live as does your Father in heaven, who makes the sun rise on the good and the evil and makes the rain fall on the just and the unjust" (Mt 5.45). He bids us, "Be perfect as your Father is perfect" (Mt 5.48). When he says, "Be perfect as he is perfect," he invites us to live in his likeness. Thus if he invites us to live in his likeness, this point becomes plain: when we did not live in his likeness, we drew away from him; unlikeness put us far away from him. Likeness made us draw near to him so that we realize in our lives the word of Scripture: "Draw near to him and receive his light" (Ps 33.5). Addressing men far from God and living evil lives, this psalm says, "Come, let us rejoice in the Lord." Where are you running off to? Where

are you withdrawing to? Where are you departing to? Where
are you fleeing to as you pursue joy in this world? "Come, let
us rejoice in the Lord." Why run off in pursuit of joy to a place
lacking true joy? Come, let us rejoice in him who created us.
"Come, let us rejoice in the Lord."[57]

The image of God engraved in our souls is far removed from perfection so that the joy not of this world it brings is mingled with hardship,
tiredness, and distress. However bright our certitude about God's presence,
however gripping the touch of his power, however piercing the darts of
his love, we still trudge along as creatures of earth and time, weighed down
by sins and buffeted by storms. It is by faith that we are patient in trouble,
it is in hope that we rejoice. Strong though be the divine light and love
within our hearts, we lift up our sacrifice of praise with hands trembling
from the fatigue and hurts of the journey in exile.

> Listen: the psalm is sounding in your ears. It is the voice of a
> man — it is your voice if you so listen — exhorting his soul to
> praise God and saying to himself, "Praise the Lord, my soul"
> (v. 2). For at times in the tribulations and trials of our present
> life our soul is, will or no, distressed. Another psalm speaks of
> this disquiet in the words, "Why are you sad, my soul, and why
> do you distress me?" (Ps 42 [43].5). To do away with this dis-
> quiet the psalmist suggests joy, a joy not yet possessed in reality
> but in hope, and says to the soul disquieted and anxious, sad and
> grieving, "Hope in the Lord, for I shall again confess to him
> (Ps 42 [43].5). It was in confession that he laid the foundations
> for the hope whereby he raised himself up. It was as if his soul,
> distressed by sadness, said to him, "Why do you tell me, 'Hope
> in the Lord?' The awareness of my sins holds me back from
> hoping. I know what sins I have committed yet you tell me, 'Hope
> in the Lord.' " True, you have committed sins. Nevertheless, what
> is the source of your hope? It is this: "for I shall confess to him."
> Just as God detests an individual who justifies his sins, so he helps
> the man who confesses them. So once we have received this hope,
> a hope that cannot exist without joy, although we find ourselves
> in the midst of the trying circumstances of this life, full of storms
> and tempests, this hope lifts up our soul because it rejoices in
> hope in the way the Apostle tells us, "Rejoice in hope, be patient
> in tribulation" (Rom 12.12). In a certain sense this sends the soul
> soaring up to God so that it may praise God; and so it says to
> itself, "Praise the Lord, my soul."[58]

The soul is to praise God in the human condition with its bodily and
temporal limitations. The very act of praising a God without limits makes
us aware of our incapacity. The infinite love we praise is infinite power
while we praisers are feebleness and infirmity. Again, as we concentrate

on praising him by standing or kneeling at attention, we sadly note that we are not fully concentrating. Our attention flickers, our minds flit from one irrelevancy to another, we daydream, we vaguely check our watches, we feel empty while supposedly putting ourselves in the presence of the Father. Instead of fixing our hearts on him, we are frequently distracted by personal and business cares. Variations in the body, a short attention-span, a shifting of moods that hinders intimate communing with the infinite — all these drawbacks are inescapable, part and parcel of a life that is, in one sense, a death. The spirit is burdened by a corruptible body, that is to say, it cannot live a wholly supernatural life untrammeled by weariness and worry and inconstancy so long as the soul dwells in its natural state. Still we must suppress all risings of disgust and frustration, for we are not bade to praise God perfectly or to always sing with the richest quality. We are asked to praise God in our life as it is, however soulless in execution and near-blank in results our efforts at praising may sometimes seem.

And what is our situation, brothers? We do praise the Lord, don't we? Don't we sing a hymn every day? As far as they can, doesn't our mouth sound and doesn't our heart give new birth to the praises of God every day? And just what is it that we are praising? What we praise is great but our power of praising is feeble. When will the praiser match the eminence of the one praised? See, a man stands in worship and he sings a long hymn to God, but often while his lips are moving in song, his thoughts are flying off in every imaginable direction his desires can take them. Thus our mind stood in a certain fashion to praise God, but our soul scurried hither and yon, pulled here and there by various desires and business worries. From above, so to speak, the mind sees the soul scurrying hither and yon and tries to still the restless-ness due to its anxieties. So it speaks to the soul, "Praise the Lord, my soul. Why are you concerned about things other than him? Why are you preoccupied and worried about things of earth that pass away? Stand beside me and praise the Lord." And the soul, heavy-laden, so to speak, and too weak to stand properly erect, replies to the mind, "I will praise the Lord in my life" (v. 2). What does "in my life" mean? It means this: now I am in my death. Begin then in this wise: exhort yourself and say to your soul, "Praise the Lord, my soul." Your soul will reply to you, "I praise him as much as I can — slightly, poorly, feebly." Why? This is why: "While we are in the body, we are exiled from the Lord" (2 Cor 5.6). Why do you praise the Lord in this way and not perfectly and constantly? Scripture has the answer: "For the corruptible body burdens the soul and the earthen house weighs down the mind pondering many concerns" (Wis 9.15). Take away from me the body that burdens my soul and I will praise the Lord. Take away from me the earthen house that weighs down the mind pondering many concerns, and then I will draw these many concerns into one focus, and I will praise the Lord. For while I am in this condition, I cannot praise him, I am burdened by the body. What then shall I do? Shall I remain silent, shall I not praise the Lord because I cannot praise him properly? Not at all. "I shall praise the Lord in my life."[59]

From another soul be the very liabilities that oppress the human spirit can serve to bolster the soul. The blows of the hammer that God lets fall upon us can shape the trumpet of the soul that sounds the praises of God. The hammer struck Job again and again, but even in the misery that mocked his faith, even in conversation with false friends and his misguided wife, he steadfastly refused to blaspheme and to shake his fist in the face of God. Faith and patience turned hammer-blows into means for disembittering his soul and purifying his praise of God. Paul too reeled under reverses and sufferings, one of which, in particular, he prayed to be relieved from. God answered his prayer not by removing the suffering but by making the back of Paul stronger to bear the cross or, more precisely, by using the suffering itself to make him stronger. In the weakness of man the strength of God shines forth. In God weakness is converted into strength, weakness becomes, miraculously, strength. The very hand of Jesus that holds the hammer becomes a hand of comfort, consolation, power, and fresh bridal love. Clung to in faith and affection, the divine hand wielding the hammer is a hand that heals, renews, fortifies the spirit of man.

> Let us see next what the psalm adds about other musical instruments, which we may regard as religious symbols: "Praise the Lord with ductile trumpets and the sound of the trumpet of horn" (v. 6). What do "ductile trumpets" and "trumpets of horn" mean? Ductile trumpets are made of brass, and it is hammering that shapes them. The fact that they are hammered implies that they are beaten. You will be ductile trumpets beaten and lengthened for the praise of God if you grow spiritually in tribulation. Tribulation is the hammering, growth is the lengthening. Job was a ductile trumpet. He was suddenly struck by heavy losses and the deaths of his sons; he was shaped into a ductile trumpet under the hammering of this great tribulation, a trumpet that sounded: "The Lord gives, the Lord has taken away. He has acted according to his good pleasure. Blessed be the name of the Lord" (Jb 1.21). How richly this trumpet sounded! What a sweet sound it emitted! This ductile trumpet still feels the hammer. He is delivered over to the power of Satan in order to be stricken in the flesh. His flesh is stricken, it starts to rot, it swarms with worms. His wife, doing the devil's work like a second Eve, tries to tempt rather than console her husband and suggests that he blaspheme God; but he rejects her advice. Adam in paradise complied with Eve (Gen 3.6), Adam on the dunghill repudiated Eve. For Job was sitting on a dunghill while his body was running

from sores and rotting from worms. Job rotting on the dunghill
was sounder than the man healthy in paradise. His wife was Eve
but he was not Adam. He answered Eve who was ready to trick
and tempt him. (We have heard how this trumpet was hammered
into shape. The devil struck him with a horrible disease from head
to foot, he was rotting from worms, he was sitting on a dunghill.
We have heard how he was hammered into shape; let us now
hear how the trumpet sounds; let us, if this meets your pleasure,
hear the dulcet sounds of this ductile trumpet.) He said to her,
"You spoke like one of those senseless women. If we have received
good things from the hand of the Lord, shall we not put up with
evils from him?" (Jb 2.10). O what a powerful sound! O what
a sweet sound! Is there anyone asleep whom this sound will not
arouse from sleep? Is there anyone in whom this sound will not
arouse confidence in God enabling him to march into battle
against the devil, assured of gaining victory not by his own power
but by that of the God who proves him. For it is God himself
who does the hammering; the hammer cannot act on its own.
Indeed the prophet referred to the future punishment of the devil
when he said, "The hammer of the whole earth has been broken"
(Jer 50.23). He took the hammer of the whole earth to mean the
devil. When this hammer is put as a tool in the hand of God,
that is, when it is put under the power of God, ductile trumpets
are hammered into shape that they may sound forth praises of
God. See how, I dare say, my brothers, even the Apostle was
pounded by this hammer. "To keep me from being puffed up
by the grandeur of my revelations," he says, "there was given
me a thorn of the flesh, a messenger of Satan, to buffet me" (2
Cor 12.7). Look at him being pounded by the hammer; let us
see what sound he emits. He says, "Three times I entreated the
Lord to rid me of it. And he said to me, 'My grace is sufficient
for you, for power is made perfect in weakness' " (2 Cor 12.8-9).
The divine Artisan says, "I want to make this trumpet perfect,
but I cannot make it perfect unless I hammer it: in weakness is
power made perfect." Now listen to the ductile trumpet itself
emitting fine sounds: "When I am weak, then I am strong" (2
Cor 12.10). And the Apostle himself, clinging, so to speak, to
Christ, clinging to that right hand that holds the hammer to
lengthen the trumpet, puts himself in that right hand and thus
also strikes with the same hammer when he says of certain
individuals, "These I have delivered to Satan that they may no
more blaspheme" (1 Tim 1.20). He delivered them to the hammer
to be pounded into shape. They sounded cacophonous before
hammering lengthened them. Once hammering lengthened them
and made them ductile trumpets, perhaps they threw off their

blasphemy and sounded the praises of the Lord. Men such as
these are ductile trumpets.[60]

Out of infinite love God did not spare his own Son from the most
horrible of suffering and the most repulsive of deaths. Because perfect, Jesus
needed no hammering, but, because perfect servant, he allowed himself
to be hammered to the cross as the perfect victim of praise so that the beating
inflicted on him might reshape our soul into fit trumpets of praise. His
death was the greatest sacrifice of praise. In the dark night of his passion
Jesus shone with the greatest splendor. Like him, each of us is meant to
become great, i.e., fulfilled in the eyes of the Father through suffering. In
weakness we learn strength; in helplessness, the greatness of divine help;
in the dumbness pain causes, the power of praising as a victim. Surely
no human praise can do justice to the magnificence of God. All our finite
praise has to fall short of a Father limitless in being and love. Yet in union
with the greatness of Jesus our suffering does really praise him, and the
inadequacy of the praise in any single hymn of life only spurs the true
praiser to go on offering himself, to go on praising a Father whose heart
is pleased and who swells with pride, so to speak, when his children tender
their little gifts.

"For the Lord is great and highly to be praised" (v. 4). Who
is "the Lord" who is "great and highly to be praised"? He
is none other than Jesus Christ. You surely know that he appeared as a man; you surely know that he was conceived in the
womb of a woman; you surely know that he was born from the
womb, that he was nursed, that he was carried in his parents'
arms, that he was circumcised, that a victim was offered for
him, that he grew up. Finally, you know that he was struck
in the face, spat upon, crowned with thorns, crucified, died,
was pierced with a lance. You know that he suffered all these
torments. "He is great and highly to be praised." Do not despise
the little in Jesus, understand the great in him. He became little
because you were little; understand the great in him, and in
him you will be great. For in this way a house is built, in this
way heavy stones become part of the structure of the house:
the stones used in building the house grow in number. Grow
then by understanding that Christ is great: he is little yet great,
great beyond measure. The psalmist has run out of words. He
wanted to say how great Christ is. Even if he were to keep on
saying all day long, "He is great, He is great," what would
he be saying after all? If he says all day long, "He is great,"
he would have to come to an end at some point because a day
comes to an end, but the greatness of Christ is before any day,
beyond any day, without any day. What then would he say after
all? "For the Lord is great and highly to be praised." For what

words can a little tongue speak in praise of one so great? In saying "highly," the psalmist uttered one word only, yet he showed how much the mind can and cannot conceive. It was as if he said, "What I cannot express in speech, reflect on, and after you have reflected, the yield of reflection will prove too little." Can the tongue of anyone express what the mind of no one can express? "The Lord is great and highly to be praised." Let him be praised and preached, his glory proclaimed and his house built.[61]

The mind of God is in itself all light but for a tiny mind seeing through a glass darkly much of God's intellect looks dim. Similarly the working out of the divine economy is in itself all light but for shortsighted human wisdom not a little of his planning looks dark. Yet as we offer self as a sacrifice of praise, tribulation sharpens our spiritual sensibilities so that we can at least make this much sense of a world of nature and man threaded through and through with contingency: all the pomp and pageantry of this life wither, fading as quickly and unceremoniously as the grass of the field. Even as we reach out to pluck the fruit of this life, it seems snatched out of reach, or our outstretched hands become paralyzed, signaling that we ourselves shall soon depart the scene. Through our sacrifice of praise we lift up our hearts far higher than the cedars of Lebanon, vouchsafed in faith and trust a slight glimpse of the depths of wisdom of the Father, peripherally but truly drinking of the light and love that awaits us when we adore and praise and rest and bound with joy in the sanctuary of God.

Thus we are told, "I will voluntarily sacrifice to you" (v. 8). Despite all things fix your eyes on him alone. And these things he has given you are good because their giver is good. For, no doubt about it, he gives these temporal goods, to some for their benefit, to others for their harm, according to the height and depth of his judgments. Before the abyss of these judgments the Apostle trembled in awe when he said: "O the depth of the riches of the wisdom and knowledge of God! How inscrutable are his judgments and how unsearchable his ways! For who will penetrate his ways and who will comprehend his counsels?" (Rom 11.33-34). He knows when to give, to whom to give; when to take away, from whom to take away. Ask in the present for what will profit you in the future, ask for what will benefit you for all eternity. But love him gratis because from him you will find nothing that he gives better than himself; or, if you do find something better, then ask for that. "I will voluntarily offer sacrifice to you." Why is it offered voluntarily? Because it is offered gratis. What does "gratis" mean? It means: "And I will praise your name, Lord, because it is good." I praise your name for no other reason than this: it is good. Does the psalmist say, "I will praise your name, Lord, because you give me fruitful lands, because you give me gold and silver, because you give me vast riches, a large amount of money, a very lofty status?'' Not at all. But what does he say? "I will praise your name, Lord, because it is good." I find nothing better than your name: therefore "I will praise your name, Lord, because it is good."[62]

Many years ago Pete Retzlaff, a wide receiver with the Philadelphia Eagles, when hobbling with a sprained ankle, remarked to a reporter, "A little pain is good for a man." In a Christian setting the good of suffering underlined by a wise professional football player is humility. A prolonged virus, the acute pain caused by kidney stones, the discovery that a troubled son or daughter is addicted to drugs — any one of these or like sufferings hammers home the bottom-line truth that we are easily breakable, small creatures. The upshot of authentic exploration of self is not the self-actualized (really self-centered) personality but the soul rendered lowly by the recognition of its handicaps and base propensities. In becoming lowly, we are invited to rise high. Prayer and praise amid blows and aches enable us to mount to the throne of God. When bathed somewhat in the sunlight of eternity, we see vividly that all flesh is grass, that the malefactor riding high will be abruptly unhorsed, his power and rank vanishing with him. This wisdom transfused with the eternal is not the fruit of analysis that builds metaphysics and theology. Concrete, existential understanding of the world of man through the eyes of God is won by the asking, seeking, knocking that is prayer in which the Christian comes to voluntarily offer sacrifice, i.e., to divest himself of self-interest, to surrender himself to the Father. It is only by looking up to God as his little children that we can look down on, i.e., properly assay, the pomp and glory of this world: its formidable figures flourish and fade as fast as the flower of the field.

> "For he has delivered me from every tribulation" (v. 9). For this reason I came to understand how good your name is. Suppose that, before suffering tribulations, I had recognized this goodness; perhaps then it would not have been necessary for me to suffer them. But tribulations served to admonish me, and the admonition moved me to praise you. For if I had not been admonished about my weakness, I might not have understood just where I was. So you delivered me from all tribulations. "And my eyes looked down upon my enemies" (v. 9); my eyes looked down upon those Ziphites. Indeed because my heart rose high, I passed over the flower of their lives, I attained you, Lord, and thence I looked down upon them, and I saw that all flesh is grass and all the glory of man like the flower of the field (Is 40.6). Along the same lines another psalm says, "I saw the evildoer towering and raised high as the cedars of Lebanon: I passed by, and then he was no longer there" (Ps 36[37].35-36). Why was he no longer there? Because you yourselves passed by. What do I mean in saying, "because you yourselves passed

by''? I mean this: because you have not idly heard the words, "Lift up your hearts''; because you have not remained on earth where you would have fallen into decay; because you have lifted up your souls to God and have risen above the cedars of Lebanon, and from that height you have fixed your eyes on him. And then he was no longer there, and you searched for him and could not find him. No longer does toil lie before you because you have entered into the sanctuary of God and have penetrated the meaning of the last things (Ps 72[73].16-17). So on this note the psalm concludes here: "And my eyes looked down on my enemies.'' Then do this very thing in your souls, brothers, lift up your hearts, sharply focus the gaze of your minds, learn to love God gratis, without thought of self, learn to despise the present world, learn to voluntarily offer a sacrifice of praise: so you will be able to rise above the flower of the field, so you will look down upon your enemies.[63]

Reflections

1. Jesus is the way that is everywhere, always going straight to you, Father. During his public career he called apostles and disciples in largely ordinary circumstances, and over the centuries he lets his glory be seen by lovers of your truth in uneventful routine. In his self-giving Jesus revealed your self-giving. Apostles and disciples and sundry others walking after him gradually came to understand him insofar as his self-giving prompted them to give themselves in return. Self-giving is the secret of living, the secret of praise, because it is the secret of your inner life. As at every moment you give yourself to me through Jesus in your and his Spirit, so at every moment I want to surrender myself to you as a whole-burnt offering. As through Jesus you say to me, "I am yours,'' so through Jesus I want to say to you, "I am yours.'' As I write this, let my scribbling say, "I am yours.'' As I stroll along a street, let my every step murmur, "I am yours.'' As I sit down for a quick bite, turn my eating and drinking into an act of self-giving, a sacrifice of praise in honor of your name. Were it not for your grace, I would fold up in despair. I am frequently thick-skulled, backtracking, frivolous, vacant-minded. Now and then the endeavor to live supernaturally seems to border on the farcical. I pray and meditate, I seek your Face in intimate colloquy, I am stirred by the bravery of your saints, I resolve to radically change my ways — then I sink back into self-indulgence, fritter away valuable time, drift into old ruts of mediocrity. Perhaps my actions will always fall shy of your luminous ideal, perhaps I will never live to the fullest your austere commands, but your grace, all perhapses brushed aside, will never stop urging me to give myself to you in the Spirit of Jesus. Trusting in your power, I will go on striving to become an ever-burning sacrifice of praise.

I must learn especially to give myself to you in tribulation. "Welcome to our little community of love and pain'': so went a note written by a coordinator of a lay religious group to a guest attending one of the community's religious services. The whole world of man is meant to be a community of love and pain. Unhappily so much does the pain incline us to whine that we miss the ingredient of love given, love to be returned to you, Father. Each visit to a hospital hones sensitivity to individual suffering. One Sunday afternoon I gave anointing of the sick and holy communion to Helen, an eighty-year-old woman preparing to undergo an operation for a broken right hip due to a fall. A pain-killer had so numbed her brain cells that she seemed partly disoriented. A strong, independent individual, perhaps a mite aggressive, she now found her world tumbling down about her. After recuperation in a rehabilitation center she had to face resuming life with a sister whose limbs are almost hopelessly gnarled by arthritis. For those two broken women every day henceforward is to be a day of infirmity and groping and remorseless decline. What can I do but adore your mysterious plan of love and pain? What can I do but absolutely trust that you will lead souls trapped in pain to offer anguish as an act of love, a sacrifice of praise celebrating your name? The pain you apportion to some calls forth love in others. A woman named Betty in the bed next to Helen seemed gently concerned for her and looked after her needs as best she could. Betty, by the way, was a special child of your love, who entered our holy faith about eight years prior to our encounter.

It bears repeating that my own tribulations have been comparatively minor. One morning during a recent winter when hurrying toward an appointment, I slipped on the ice but, fortunately sliding along on my left side, I sustained only bruised ribs. Betty, however, lay in her hospital bed because of a possible dislocated hip due to a like fall on the ice, and a university friend who fell on the ice fractured her fibula and spent weeks on crutches. Saddest of all, a young man of twenty-five, while rushing to climb on a train, slipped on the platform ice and, sliding under the wheels, lost both legs. Father, I thank you for covering me with your grace, won by prayers of friends. Garb all victims of tribulation in your consoling love, make their darkness and pain a source of light and love, their sense of helplessness a spring of fresh determination, their grimmest sorrows a fountain of tears of joy reflecting your bow in the clouds that bespeaks healing love.

While these tribulations find us, pursuing and overtaking us, often by surprise, another sort of tribulation, Augustine sagely notes, is one we find or should seek and find: a stinging perception that we are exiles who, however much we look for some measure of earthly security, can never settle down. Father, grant me this divine discontent that made your saints, ever inwardly joyful, long with unassuageable appetite for your lasting city. The Jewish people wandered in the desert for forty years; so must I go on hungering for the homeland where I will live forever as a member of your family. Today in West Germany, partly depopulated because of sedulously practiced contraception and abortion, millions of Turks live as guest workers, taxpayers without citizenship, isolated in part by their unfamiliarity with German, partially ostracized, misunderstood, and undervalued. How these resident aliens yearn for their homeland! Bless me with this feeling of living as a foreigner in a country not my own. Then will I understand that emptiness of heart due to nonbelonging, maltreatment by the in-group in any sector, snubs, minor persecution are permitted to implant deep within me this sense of estrangement. Day by day I am coming closer to my final hour on this earth; day by day then must I strip myself, shake myself free, of earthly baggage, so that, more and more alienated in this world, I may pant the more for another country in which I will rest Godlike with you, my God.

2. The brilliance and power of the words of Augustine well up from the abysses of your everlasting fire. At times I seem moved with a like desire to immolate myself as a whole-burnt offering. But more frequently night or at least twilight descends, and existence becomes drab, dreary, devoid of spiritual charm. Along with the apostles petitioning Jesus I cry out, "Lord, increase [my] faith" (Lk 17.5).[64] I have to believe that you are always there eager to receive my offering, I have to believe that the largely inconsequential segments and flying moments of my life are the stuff of sacrifice. Indeed especially when a slump of energy lowers my horizons, when a washed-out feeling blankets my plans in gloom, I can only turn to you in faith. I do believe that out of the scraps of my life, Father, you will rejoice in the petty holocaust I sacrifice to your praise.

The sacrifice of praise St. Polycarp offered you was a magnificent holocaust that culminated eight decades of self-giving. At eighty-six, when many are tottering and some doddering, he stood strong amid his pyre. According to one observer, the flames swelled and englobed his frame so that "his body was like bread that is baked, or gold and silver white-hot in a furnace, not like flesh that has been burnt."[65] An aroma like that of incense, miraculously sweet, signalized the beauty of his self-immolation. Polycarp lived the spiritual signification of his name; he was "many fruits," his spirit exhibiting practically all the fruits of your Spirit. Small-spirited as I am, I cannot be a Polycarp, I do not feel emboldened to embrace the stake. Nevertheless, Father, I ask you to let your flames englobe me so that, the least straw of my offering ignited by your love, my surrendered life may rise up to you as a pleasing sacrifice, little but great through your holy fire.

In giving me life through my dear parents many years ago, you first stamped your image upon me. Then laved in the waters of your Spirit, I took on a second image, one sharing in the perfect image that is your Son. It is an inner self partly tarnished by sin, sin I am abstractly aware of but concretely often insensitive to. Father, let your light bring before my eyes the tiniest sores and pockmarks of my soul, making me face up to my ugliness. Your light heals as it reveals. Let your devouring light caress me, entering my soul as a font of power, which cleanses me in the gentle Spirit of Jesus.

In your light a spiritual woman, a third-order laywoman now in her middle sixties, has come to read the major stages of her life as successive strippings. Many years ago her religious career was smashed by malignant forces within the Church itself. Part of her eyesight gone, she is crippled by arthritis and plagued by other infirmities. In recent years her household has been escaping economic ruin only by the skin of its teeth; her life along with that of her community is now a daily suffering. You are gradually despoiling her so that, like little Therese, she can go before you purified of self and empty of any fruit of her own. Father, send forth your light and your truth. Then will I see the need to strip myself of ties to world and flesh that blur your image within.

I must give myself to you as you give yourself to me: by love. It is love that draws me closer to you, it is lack of love that distances me from you. A wealth of insight there is in Augustine's words, "My affections are my feet." During your liturgy I may preach your word with eloquence, bidding others to be holy while perhaps harboring hatred in my heart. I may stand far off from you while speaking in the shadow of the tabernacle and the altar. So it was, Father, during the Last Supper that was the first Mass when John and Judas sat close to Jesus, both apparently intimate with him, both physically near but spiritually light years apart. For while the beloved disciple drank to the point of inner rapture from the heart of Jesus, the soul of Judas was a block of ice enchained by a traitorous resolve black as hell.

I imitate your love and, in particular I become holy as you are holy by forgiving enemies. A point already dealt with, true, but one so crucial that further mention will not be tedious. Forgiveness goes straight against the grain of nature. How can I forgive when bitter eyes throw daggers at me, a sneer curls on another's lips, overtures are cold-shouldered, a cheerful word invites a cutting reply or surly silence? Father, it is your love mediated through Jesus that alone can incite me to give to you by forgiving another made in your image. Take me step by step up the ladder of forgiveness; move me through Jesus to pray daily, without fail, for the inner healing of those who revile me. Show me how to bless rather than curse those who bad-mouth me; indeed tell me how to bless by word or smile at the very moment abuse is heaped upon me. But bear with me, as I tumble, then try to pull myself to my feet, in pursuit of your super-love: count my struggling as a testing that deepens my love of and likeness to you.

3. Not so long ago I ran across a picture of the Warwick B.C. baseball team on which I played many years back as a teenager. Halcyon days those; none of my teammates or friends were victimized by booze or drugs. A time of security too, a period sheltered from the shocks of existence, for we were young, and pain, distress, trauma, loneliness were by and large burdens taxing elders. Happy days those, but only superficially so because partially woven from the gossamer fancies of youth. In the succeeding years, Father, your mercy spared me from the major evils that beset body and spirit. Yet I do experience melancholy, vague apprehensions about the

future, dissatisfaction about the hurts I have inflicted on others in the past, disgust with my wallowing in mediocrity. Though a spiritually alothful sinner, I can sheet-anchor myself in your hope, and from that hope gain joy, and in that low-key delight truly praise your name. In 1982 a fifty-seven-year-old Philadelphia woman, a widowed mother of eleven children, entered a Philadelphia-area cloistered community of Poor Clares. This is one more sign that the Good News of Jesus brings transforming hope. It would be childish of me to hanker after a new career, but, whatever my past failings, however sluggish I now am, the ever-fresh impulses of your Spirit continue to call me to a new career of love. "Time brings roses," a German expression goes. Time that includes patience born of hope brings your roses aglow with the unchanging fires of your heart. If I wait, hold on, never give up, the roses will bloom in this cracked, unpromising soil even when locked in winter's icy grip.

No doubt roses will go on blooming within, but it would be running in blinders, Father, to make light of all the obstacles barring ascent to higher levels of praise. Through the saving grace of Jesus I dwell in a Godlike state, but much of its beauty and power are overlaid by the sheer down-drag of bodily existence. Yet, I promise, I will never stop praising you. I can praise you only "in my life," jejunely, half-heartedly, with mind yanked here and there by worldly concerns. I cannot praise you as Paul did, as Augustine did, as Catherine of Siena did, as Rose of Lima did. But I can praise you in my present half-muddled, half-irresolute state of heart. In your love you made me, Father; in your mercy you redeemed me; in your love and mercy, I trust, you will tenderly receive the sparse, at times tuneless bits of praise in this, my life.

Yet my life, deficient as it is, becomes more like yours through its very deficiency. On the human plane suffering hammers down and benumbs, making a patient lying seriously ill in a hospital feel helpless as a child. Stupefaction due to pain and medication slows down the stream of his thoughts, favorite meals and people and books and songs become insipid, perhaps repulsive, ravages of disease hollow out his cheeks and leave him a gaunt shell of himself. But through your power, Father, the blows of hammers beat the soul into a sweeter, stronger shape. Job suffered, and in his despoliation learned in the very marrow of his soul that all his blessings were pure gifts from you. The hammer fell on Paul, and in his anguish he learned anew that you were his sole strength. This is the frightful but inwardly delightful lesson you teach your saints throughout history: man grows more and more into superman through suffering. Archbishop Fulton Sheen was probably the finest preacher in the Church in the twentieth century, one whose like Catholics may not be graced with for another hundred years. A popular philosopher and theologian, a superb orator, he was most crucially marked not by the great books he had mastered, not by the personages he had hobnobbed with, but by the outer and inner sufferings he had been brought to endure. For all his energy, late on he mentioned that he had "never been a well man." A heart attack and open-heart surgery in his final years led him to identify more with Jesus of the passion. The inner pain he found the most longlasting and tormenting arose, he said in an interview, "from pettiness and jealousy within the Church." He went on, "We do such a disservice to our Lord and our people by being envious and jealous of others. This has been the hardest cross for me to bear."[66] The poisoned knives of fellow Catholics that stabbed his heart brought him a portion of the pain that convulsed Jesus when nails pierced his hands and feet. In his weakness he came to know, as never before, your strength. How depressing it is that your holy Church is soiled by unholy envy. Even on occasion in the strictest monasteries, historians relate, a power-hungry monk or nun goaded by envy spins a web of lies to besmirch and wreck a rival in authority. When bitterness bred of envy in another lashes out against me, let the tongue that whips and claws my spirit bring me to raise my hands to you; let me learn on my knees that in my weakness lies my strength. Put the names of Jesus and Mary on my lips to soften my speech, to daunt any inclination to growl or snarl in return. And let your strength relieving my inward hurt become strength for others as I spiritually stroke them, feeding them with the caring that every heart longs for.

Father, it is in Jesus crucified that envy and hatred of man for man are overcome. The yes of Jesus invited the hammer to destroy his earthly frame so to liberate us from our rebel self. By letting himself be devastated by the forces of hell, he opened the gates of heaven. With love and humility he fronted massive evil; in being conquered, he conquered; in dying, he won life; nailed in ignominy, he proclaimed the truth of your everlasting love. On the cross he showed himself as the king of love who wins empire over souls by love unto death. The crucified sovereign is also the perfect priest, offering you an inimitable sacrifice of praise. The Lord of Calvary stands out as the prophet of prophets, his saving death preaching the central meaning of your plan. The generosity and beauty of the death of Jesus, Father, are past all conception, past all praise. Were all men of all time to harmonize all their praise in one concerted outpouring, it would fall far short of the magnificence of his sacrifice. I cannot express the inexpressible; my praise cannot come near to matching the Jesus who is the highest sacrifice of praise. But I will not stop, I will not falter, I will go on praising you through him, I will cry out my thanksgiving in accents of love, squeaky and quavering though they sometimes be.

From the nether point and pinnacle that is the cross all that is of this earth looks tawdry. "He who exalts himself shall be humbled and he who humbles himself shall be exalted" (Mt 23.12). This golden truth is verifiable in our own century. Monsters of iniquity like Stalin and Hitler, in whose presence the hearts of confidants quaked, upon whose decree millions were executed, at whose command millions flung themselves into combat, have become symbols of almost universal infamy. But all the mighty ones of this world, along with the lesser lights who ambition worldly rank, will strut their brief hour on this world's stage, then will be pushed into the wings, with all that they have connived and battled for soon to fall to pieces. Raise me up with Jesus; sharpen the apex of my spirit so that through his crucified eyes I may perceive the meaning of the last things, and through that understanding see the earthly city as a doomed harlot (Rev 14.8). Inscribe on my heart the final words of Léon Bloy in The Woman Who Was Poor: "There is only one unhappiness... and that is — NOT TO BE ONE OF THE SAINTS."[67] Then will I come closer to enduring suffering, then will I quietly pray for the strength you will distill from the treacheries in your Church, then will I learn to rise above, by somehow pressing to my heart, my enemies, then will I share, however flimsily, in a prophet's reward by grasping even on this side a bit of the vision whose fruit is peace.

Praise

1. The peerless Aristotle described you with remarkable precision as self-thinking thought, the highest of beings whose bliss consists simply in contemplating the riches of his own intelligence. But you are more, Father, you are infinite existence, infinite understanding, infinite love, a trinity of persons in your one nature. Each of you not only thinks of but infinitely loves the other two. In a way that not even the minds of a trillion Aristotles rolled into one could prove, your self-giving to Son and Spirit makes you happy, and their self-giving to each other and to you fills tham with bliss. All your being, all your thinking, all your loving, all your rejoicing lie in your self-giving. I praise you for this incomprehensible self-giving, for your life of praise that is rooted in and identified with your self-giving. All is love, is it not, within the holy three? And does not this love have praise as its constant companion? All self-giving and therefore all praise: you are happy in praising the Son and Spirit and they are happy in praising you. How beautiful you are — you do nothing but praise you are all praise, as God you are, so to speak, self-praiser. I praise you for revealing yourself through Jesus, who came not to be served but to serve, to give his life as a ransom for the whole human race (Mt 20.28), who went about doing good (Acts 10.38), giving himself in your name for your glory, to your praise. His life of absolute surrender struck a spark in the hearts of Zaccheus, the apostles, the first disciples in the Greek cities, and billions since. Through Jesus you have set my heart aflame also. Fan that flame, whip it into a conflagration that images in some manner the fiery circle of self-giving unto praise in the hearts of the holy three. I praise you for drawing me into your eternal movement of praise. Let my life be an unbroken chant, my activity a never-stopping dance in rhythm with the celestial dance of the blessed everlastingly celebrating your name.

I praise you, Father, for ingredients of what is sometimes called the mid-life crisis: the fading of dreams, the braking of drive, the dashing of hopes, the feeling of being on the skids. At the end of a day your saints, battleworn though they may be, burst out in a song of victory. When my day winds down, my shoulders slumping, no vibrant hymn of triumph leaps from my lips, yet I will praise you, for, in never meeting my goals, I am experiencing inward tribulation that helps configure me to your crucified Son. Is this my particular cross, to admit without flinching that I am in so many ways a failure? Still I will praise you: this is the purgation marked out for me, a sense of futility over abortive efforts, promises without products, the one talent not buried but invested with scanty return. At wakes, as I pray over the body of a departed confrere or friend or someone to whom I have ministered, the thought steals over me: how many spiritual dreams have gone unrealized in this person. Yet, perhaps sooner than I imagine, I will join their company, equally unfulfilled, malformed in so many ways. Great God, Father of mercies, as a near-zero I will sing your glories. I am a saint manqué, a shadow of what I should be, a fourth-stringer, spiritually backward and underdeveloped, yet I will praise and praise you without end.

I praise you Father, for sowing in your saints an unquenchable thirst for endless union with you. So they lived in this world as if not living in it, so that they lived like displaced persons, transients, almost like gypsies (in a eulogistic sense), without fixed abode, ready to pull up stakes at a moment's notice. I praise you for your mercy: not a single one of my spiritual aspirations will you let go unanswered. As my praise pleads for more detachment, grant me, make me, a yearning for your heavenly country. I cannot ask for much ordinary pain, for I would buckle under extra sufferings, but I do seek the pain of exile that Augustine points up. Run me through with this holy longing for my true home, carve a crater in my soul, to be filled only by the downrush of your love. Let every word of praise sensitize me the more to the pathos of being a pilgrim, travel-stained and tired but bright-eyed with hope in looking toward the realm of your peace without cease. Wandering restless in search of everlasting rest, let me enjoy a "sabbath of the heart."[68] I praise you: this protracted tramp through the desert is the sacrament of your will, which knits a silver lining into every cloud of sadness.[69] Glory to you, most loving of fathers: you exile me only to excite longing for infinitely spacious tranquillity, for what Catherine of Siena called your sea of peace. Even here below the ache of alienation braces hope, and in the anguish of apartness I can rejoice in hope (Rom 12.12).

2. Just as I must cut below the surface to see the Christ-bearer beneath the livery of my brothers and sisters, so must I peer beneath the externals of my own life to descry your image within, however much I feel sordid and distant from your supernal life. Blessed one, I praise you for transplanting in me the eyes of your Spirit to believe in my dignity as your very

own son. Yes, that is what I am — the offspring of your supernatural love, formed out of the "genetic stuff" of your Spirit. Grounded on this faith in you, my Father, my works will praise you as I aim at acting as an inwardly superhuman being whose mission it is to help suffuse a sin-polluted planet with the aroma of your love. All praise to you for raising my drooping shoulders and sagging chest. I praise you for your saints, one and all souls of unflagging confidence, not smugly but humbly and invincibly certain that you would absolutely do what you longed to accomplish within them — the miracle of love seizing and transfiguring them into suns blazing in prayer and action. As I struggle hourly to open myself more to your grace that alone can pull me up out of the ditch, through your beauty shining in their beauty within, there surges new resolve to realize "the impossible dream," to reach "the unreachable star," to live wholly transformed in your image.

Precious Father, make me your child of forgiving love, so converted to littleness that I will, as toddlers do, almost immediately forget spats and slaps. No writhing, no standing on "principle," no attitudinizing about pseudo-rights: a simple cry of pain, perhaps a slap in return, and the scrap is over and done with, all feeling of hurt passing with the incident itself. Praise to you for the command of Jesus that we are to forgive not seven times but seventy times seven times (Mt 18.22), which he prescribed because we are your children whom you always forgive not seven times but seventy times seven times. Praise to you, Father in heaven, for deputing Jesus's putative father on earth to mirror your never-ending forgiveness. I praise you for schooling the human mind of Jesus in your forgiving spirit exercised in Joseph. How he forgave and forgave! At times customers, we may surmise, lied to and cheated him, abused and insulted him, but as your alter ego he forgave seventy times seven times.

Jesus told us, ". . . in heaven there will be more joy over one sinner who repents than over ninety-nine just people who have no need of repentance" (Lk 15.7). His last words on the cross bespoke not only triumph and serenity but also the profoundest of joy. Aware, while his life ebbed away, that his sacrifice would gather countless lost sheep into the fold, his heart sang with joy ineffable. In gasping, "Father, forgive them for they know not what they do" (Lk 23.34), Jesus rejoiced over the millionfold fruits of his forgiving love. Joy shone in his spirit as the Good Thief, a criminal who symbolized all the sin-sodden in mankind, said yes to his healing look. As I praise your mercy, make me merciful, and, as I stand in wonder at the joy in the crucified heart of Jesus, let me eat and drink of that joy. Praise to you, Father, for this delight locked within forgiveness. By giving myself, I can find the hidden treasure and buy the pearl of great price (Mt 13.44-46); by forgiving others I can experience the joy of storing in my heart the buried treasure and the precious pearl. Praise to you: it is your mercy I offer to others, it is your joy I feel in helping to bring them, along with myself, to contrite love.

3. The food of your Spirit that nourished the soul of Jesus was your will (Jn 4.34). Praise to you, Father: eating and drinking of the sacrament of your will, I can grow in love as did Jesus in doing your will. Glory to you for your justice that uses the no that suffering says to my spirit to help liquidate bills that the no of my refractory will has run up. With infinite care you have selected the blows that have fallen upon me to down my pride, muffle my wrath, and purge me of cowardice and meanness. Only your justice as the channel of your mercy can still the anguished why? why? why? rising from the lips of individuals imprisoned in pain. Praise to you for exploiting ordeals to compensate for sins, to curb passions, and to temper the spirit.

Most of all, Father, I praise you for Jesus crucified as priest, king, and prophet. His sacrifice canceled the debt of sin and transmuted thralldom into freedom of the sons of God. Praise to you for Jesus our victim: ground down into the dust, he was exalted as the very power of God (1 Cor 1.24). In being crushed, he reigned; he had to be last to become first. Praise to you for the crucifixion as witness to the truth. His death proclaims your mercy and evidences that the word of truth must be backed by the deed of truth. Praise to you for a Jesus whose death testifies that suffering welcomed with love conquers suffering and becomes a sacrifice of praise.

Still, hour by hour, Father, the key existential question presses down on me, at times haunts me: how can I translate the word of truth into the work of truth, how can I be yours wholeheartedly and "whole-actionally" as well as whole-mindedly? I praise you for gently nudging me on when pursuit of total union with you seems wishful thinking. Let my persistence in praising your power initiate fresh power to do your truth. As I praise you for vesturing Jesus as priest, king, and prophet, let your love persuade me to offer myself as a sacrifice of praise, fully submitted to his scepter of mercy, witnessing in action to the truth enfleshed in him.

I praise you, Father, for being eternally faithful and merciful. One single glance of your creative wisdom interlinks all the scattered events of past, present, and future, orienting them toward the denouement you have already written for the drama of man. Immersed in the flux and reflux of change, I can only grope toward a steady and whole picture of human destiny. How many times, kneeling before a casket, have I prayerfully sought to plumb the meaning of death — yet the impressions, though poignant, have not proved perduring. Glory to you for this chance to soar up on the pinions of your Spirit and view all history, especially my own brief tale, in your timeless vision. Praise to you, Father: even as I jot down these words, raise me up to the heights; make this moment and its every successor radiate with your everlasting now and sing with your peace and joy.

I praise you for the glory of your saints, which springs from their faith. What a vision of this world and its finale lit up their souls! All-generous one, grace me with more of this mysterious light, and I will remain poised, unwavering in the blasts of storms, in the sudden rufflings of waters, in the crosscurrents of the times, recognizing however dimly, that the majesty of your mercy will one day burst forth in unchallengeable triumph on the day of doom and pity. Glory to you for permitting your Church to reel from the shelling and pounding without and within during the twentieth century. Her truths have been derided, her salvation history reduced to a tissue of fabrications, her central claim of atonement attacked as bizarre improbability, her portrait of you as a Father scorned as the mere projection of men desperate for crumbs of solace. Praise to you for firm faith: I need not toss restlessly sometime during the night, upset by the modernist criticism that what the gullible call your revealed truth is nothing but a potpourri of irrationalities. Rather, it is the paltry scheme of naturalism that is implausible and pseudo-scientific. At this instant you are pouring your love into hearts, your light is blazing brighter in more minds; you are striving to work big and small miracles in our lives that will put down as nonsense charges that your plan of love is nonsense. Praise to you, Father, for tolerating sons of darkness within your Church who sow confusion in the name of charity, dissent in the name of unity. Lift my heart to your summit where, resting in your light, I will come to perceive that in the long vistas of the centuries error-mongers leave only shafts of darkness first dwarfed, then devoured, by your ever-burgeoning truth. The eye of my heart cleansed in the daylight of your eternity, I will see that even now judgment has come upon this world, even now the second coming of your Son is being made ready, even now you are executing the conquest of hosts of evil, even now you are glorifying your name in preparation for that day, your day, in which, after the heavens are torn asunder, you will make all things new for the rejoicing of those who whisper yes to your call to intimate love.

Notes

[1]EP 144 (145). 4; CC 40, 2090.
[2]EP 144 (145). 4; CC 40, 2090.
[3]EP 91 (92). 4; CC 39, 1281-82.
[4]EP 54 (55). 2; CC 39, 656.
[5]EP 144 (145). 4; CC 40, 2090.
[6]Mother Marie Thérèse, S.H.C.J., *Cornelia Connelly* (Westminster, Md.: Newman, 1963), pp. 49, 96-108, 305.
[7]Quoted in a collection of wise and warm sayings about friendship entitled *The Value of Friendship*, ed. Frederic Lawrence Knowles (Boston: Caldwell, 1904), p. 50.
[8]*Conf.* 13. 9. 10. In making an updated application of these words in the two sentences that follow, we are not suggesting that Augustine's equating of love and weight implies the modern notion of gravitation. As the context plainly indicates, he is invoking the ancient physical view of naturally light and naturally heavy elements.
[9]See *The Value of Friendship*, p. 29.
[10]Ruth Cranston, *The Miracle of Lourdes* (New York: McGraw-Hill, 1955), pp. 279-81.

[11]Michel de Saint-Pierre, *Bernadette and Lourdes*, tr. Edward Fitzgerald (Garden City, New York: Doubleday Image Books, 1955), pp. 208-09. The words, "charged with your grandeur," are adapted from the opening line of Gerard Manley Hopkins's sonnet, "God's Grandeur": "The world is charged with the grandeur of God."

[12]Franz Werfel, *The Song of Bernadette* (New York: Sun Dial, 1944), p. 459. Mgr. Vernon Johnson, *Suffering and Lourdes* (London: Catholic Truth Society, 1962), p. 12.

[13]Werfel, op. cit., p. 566. Several other accounts against which I have checked Werfel's moving portrayal of Bernadette's last moments make no mention of Abbé Peyramale's presence at her bedside. In case this scene is the product of Werfel's imagination, the familiar Italian comment may be germane: "Si non e vero, e ben trovato": "Even if it is not true, it makes a good story." In any event, whether or not Bernadette's childhood pastor uttered them, these words carry a ring of truth: Bernadette's death was a glorious birth into eternal life.

[14]S. 99. 6. 6; PL 38, 598.

[15]EP 148. 10; CC 40, 2172-73. It seems worth noting that in this sermon delivered in April, 395, Augustine does not appeal to the distinction, common in ancient physics, between the sublunary and superlunary spheres. Rather, as is clear in the commentary on Genesis begun in 401, he favors a division between a higher and more rarefied zone of air and a lower zone of air with its atmosphere marked by winds and rains; see *De Gen ad litt.* 2. 2. 5-3. 6; PL 34, 264-65. It is hard to pinpoint the author of this opinion that chance holds sway in the lower regions. According to P. Agaësse and A. Solignac in pt. 2 of n. 20, pp. 678-79, *La Genése au sens littéral*, tr. P. Agaësse and A. Solignac, *Oeuvres de saint Augustin*, 48 (Paris: Desclée de Brouwer, 1972), Augustine gleaned this view from the available doxographical literature, probably either from Cornelius Celsus' *Opiniones omnium philosophorum* or from a manual dependent on this first collection, the *Panarion* of Epiphanius.

[16]This objection was first formulated in its essentials by the Greek philosopher Epicurus (341-270 B.C.). As recounted by the Christian apologist Lactantius (c. 260-c. 340), *De ira Dei* 13; CSEL 27 (pt. 2, fasc. 1), 103-04, Epicurus's repudiation of divine providence rests on an exhaustive four-part division of the ways in which God can conceivably confront and blot out evil. (i) God wills to get rid of evil but cannot. (ii) He can but will not remove evil. (iii) He neither will not nor cannot remove evil. In implying that God is weak and/or envious, these first three alternatives incongruously construe God along unGodlike lines. (iv) God both wills to and can get rid of evil. This fourth possibility, the only one that harmonizes with the divine nature, seems nullified by insuperable difficulties. (a) In a world cared for by a God good and powerful enough to forestall all evil, how did, how could easily preventable evil arise? (b) Even granted that evil somehow unexplainably springs up in a universe controlled by a provident God, why does a God sufficiently good and powerful not exercise his will and power to immediately obliterate all evil? Within the constricted horizon of Epicurus's theology, which pictures gods as quasi-human in form and therefore finite, the objection against divine providence is indeed irresolvable. Hence, he concludes, the gods have to be aloof from and unconcerned about human weal and woe. As the selection in the body of this chapter evidences, Augustine repels this formidable attack by acutely perceiving that, precisely because he is God, i.e., unlimited in goodness and power, God can provide or make room for evil in the universe he creates and governs. Out of evil his infinite power miraculously harvests good planned by his infinite wisdom and flowing from his infinite goodness.

At present we cannot pinpoint the source or sources through which Augustine became acquainted with the gist of Epicurus's argument. Some scholars conjec-

ture that the third book of Cicero's *De natura deorum*, now lost, may have transmitted Epicurus's gravamen to Augustine. Whatever the value of such speculation,
it seems likely that fourth- and fifth-century Christian thinkers were commonly
aware of and engaged in informal as well as formal exchanges (independently
of explicit references to or reliance upon particular sources) concerning the kernel
of Epicurus's polemic against providence. In fine, the thorny issues Epicurus
raised probably constituted a stock but no mean part of the problem of God that
Christian theologians and apologists of Augustine's day had to grapple with.

[17]*Enchir.* 3. 10-11; PL 40, 2361.

[18]*De lib. arb.* 3. 9. 26; PL 32, 1283-84. The stony ground of faults may be turned
into a seedbed of immense spiritual fruit: this is one golden thread running
through the teaching of the saints   on trust and humility. See Paul de Jaegher,
S.J., *The Virtue of Trust* (New York: Kenedy, 1974), pp. 188-205. According to
Henri Marrou, *St. Augustine and His Influence through the Ages*, tr. Patrick
Hepburne-Scott (New York: Harper Torchbooks, 1975), p. 143, the broad understanding of *etiam peccata* goes back at least as far as the beginning of the twelfth
century.

[19]Quoted in Brand Blanshard, *Reason and Belief* (New Haven: Yale University Press,
1975), p. 562.

[20]*De corr. et grat.* 9. 23-24; PL 44, 929-31.

[21]*Conf.* 5. 8. 15; 8. 12. 30.

[22]For a sensitive, percipient treatment of good emergent from evil, along with other
strands of the problem of evil, see Thomas R. Heath, O.P., *In Face of Anguish*
(New York: Sheed and Ward, 1966), especially pp. 106-11.

[23]*Conf.* 1. 12. 19; 1. 18. 29; 10. 6. 10.

[24]St. Thomas Aquinas, *Summa theologiae* 3. 69. 2.

[25]Lewis Thomas, "How Should Humans Pay Their Way?", *New York Times*, August
24, 1981, p. A15. The fact that many scientists soberly and perhaps sorrowfully
realize the drastic limitations of science indicates that the portrait of the self-
assured scientist conquering all of nature is a myth invented by proponents, at
times propagandists, of an empiricistic reading of culture. Commenting on the
cognitive despair of Paul Ehrenfest, the theoretical physicist, Werner Heisenberg
remarked: "Out of this despair we must do something which leads a little bit
further, and that's all we can do. We certainly can't hope to solve the problems
once for all. That's just out of the question." T. S. Kuhn, J. L. Heilbron, P. Forman,
L. Allen, eds., *Sources for History of Quantum Physics* (Philadelphia: American
Philosophical Society, 1967), interview with J. Franck (February 27, 1963), pp.
20ff. See Enrico Cantore, S.J., *Scientific Man* (New York: ISH Publications, 1977),
p. 163.

[26]This fictive train of thought was originally prompted, I believe, by a short story
by Ray Bradbury set in a similar contracted time-frame — a story whose title I
have been unable to find.

[27]Albert Guérard, *France in the Classical Age* (New York: Harper Torchbooks, 1965),
p. 231.

[28]*Conf.* 3. 11. 19.

[29]S. 263. 1; PL 38, 1210.

[30]EP 44 (45). 3; CC 38, 495-96.

[31]EP 40 (41). 1; CC 38, 448. In remarking, "The pagans sit down and count the
years till Chistianity becomes extinct. . ." (this line occurs a little beyond the
midway point of this selection), Augustine is alluding to a claim made in an oracle
of pagan origin that Christianity would last 365 years, then would suddenly
collapse and shortly sink into oblivion. For details, some gruesome, and a critique
of the oracle see *De civ. Dei* 18. 53. 2 — 54.1; PL 41, 617-20. The most telling,
indeed unanswerable refutation of the oracle, Augustine says, is the fact that the
Catholic religion is still flourishing more than 365 years since its origin. According
to his calculation, the oracle's estimated duration of Christianity was the span
from 33 to 398. In 399, one year after its projected demise, leading officials

of the emperor tore down pagan temples and smashed their idols in Carthage. Between 411-13, close to or around fifteen years from the oracularly appointed death date, Augustine was preaching EP 40 (41), and close to thirty years after 398 he was exposing the falsity of the oracle in De civ. Dei. The anonymous author of the oracle was very probably a member either of the entourage of Julian the Apostate or that of Eugene, his successor. See the comments of G. Folliet in n. 59, pp. 774-75, in La cité de Dieu, tr. G. Combés, Oeuvres de saint Augustin, 36 (Paris: Desclée de Brouwer, 1960).

[32]EP 40 (41). 8; CC 38, 454-55.
[33]De civ. Dei 18. 51. 2; PL 41, 614.
[34]De civ. Dei 18. 51. 1-2; PL 41, 613-14.
[35]EP 109 (110). 20; CC 40, 1620.
[36]Conf. 3. 11. 19. The last eight words of this translation come from a prayer (whose lines are culled from various works and which is hence attributed to Augustine) in Harry Emerson Fosdick, The Meaning of Prayer New York: Association Press, 1962), p. 40.
[37]Conf. 9. 1. 1.
[38]Ep. 55. 6. 10; PL 33, 209.
[39]S. 163. 3. 3; PL 38, 890.
[40]EP 29 (30) (S. 2). 6; CC 38, 178.
[41]S. 116. 6; PL 38, 660.
[42]S. 91. 6. 7; PL 38, 570-71.
[43]Tract in Joh. 111.6; PL 35, 1929.
[44]EP 147. 19; CC 40, 2156.
[45]S. 329. 1; PL 38, 1455.
[46]De civ. Dei 12. 1. 2; PL 41, 349.
[47]Vincent P. Miceli, S.J., The Gods of Atheism (New Rochelle, N.Y.: Arlington House, 1975). p. 209.
[48]Quoted in Mary Lewis Coakley, Not Alone: For the Lord is Nigh (New York: Seabury, 1981), p. 37.
[49]C. litt. Petil. 1. 29. 31; PL 43, 259-60.
[50]Conf. 2. 6. 13-14.
[51]EP 92 (93). 3; CC 39, 1294.
[52]EP 137 (138). 2; CC 40, 1979.
[53]EP 49 (50). 21; CC 38, 590-91.
[54]EP 49 (50). 22; CC 38, 591-92.
[55]EP 137 (138). 2; CC 40, 1979.
[56]EP 115 (116). 8; CC 40, 656.
[57]EP 94 (95). 2; CC 39, 1331-32.
[58]EP 145 (146). 2; CC 40, 2105-06.
[59]EP 145 (146). 6; CC 40, 2109-10.
[60]EP 97 (98). 6; CC 39, 1374-75.
[61]EP 95 (96). 4; CC 39, 1345-46.
[62]EP 53 (54). 10; CC 39, 654.
[63]EP 53 (54). 11; CC 39, 654-55.
[64]S. 80. 6; PL 38, 497.
[65]"From a letter on the martyrdom of Saint Polycarp by the Church of Smyrna," quoted in The Liturgy of the Hours, 3 (New York: Catholic Book Publishing Co., 1975), p. 1396.
[66]Thomas J. Hartman, "The Last Days of Bishop Sheen," Catholic Digest (December, 1981), pp. 70-71.
[67]Léon Bloy, The Woman Who was Poor, tr. I. J. Collins (New York: Sheed and Ward, 1939), p. 356.
[68]EP 91 (92). 2; CC 39, 1280.
[69]EP 91 (92). 2; CC 39, 1280.

Chapter V

Jubilation

Jubilation, as already noted[1], is a species of praise, which may be spoken or unspoken. It is educed by the multifarious beauties of creation, the glories of divine grace, and the Church's ongoing triumph over its fiercest enemies.

This is praise affectively but not verbally possible, uttered when over-brimming joy prevents speaking or being silent in the conventional sense: "Our voice but not our affection is inadequate."[2] The voice may be mute but the heart will not stay still — inwardly it shouts the ineffable joy that is jubilation. From time to time, perhaps more frequently, this takes the form of "a voice of joy," i.e., a nonlinguistic sound unlisted in any known lexicon.[3] The heart in labor gives birth in outcry to the gladness that it has conceived but cannot put into words. Such jubilation is not uncommon among harvesters and vintagers who, overjoyed at the richness of the earth, launch into a familiar song or chantey and, while singing, slip in from time to time wordless cries of sheer joy that are the "vocabulary" of jubilation. So the soul, charmed by the presence of God and his superabundant gifts, revels in a joy that evades comprehension and defies ordinary articulation. Human language, helpless to transcribe what it feels, gives vent to word-less cries of joy. At other times, as was the case with the apostles imme-diately after Jesus ascended, souls in a sweetly confounding transport stand speechless before the latest epiphany of the all-holy, content to do nothing but jubilate within.

God and the outpourings of his love variously excite jubilation. Meditating on the magnitude and multitudinious diversity of a universe indescribably beautiful, the soul judges the whole panorama beyond analytical compass, and, in endeavoring to intimate its magnificence, speech lapses into stammering. But if words falter before creation, how can mere language be but powerless before its Creator? When words strain and crumble, the usual sacrifice of praise has to give way to the sacrifice of jubilation. The astounding fact that "All the ways of the Lord are mercy and truth" (Ps 24 [25].19) also fosters jubilation. No words suffice to tell how immeasurable is the grace unstoppingly and nuancively pouring from the bosom of the Father to heal and fortify uncountable pilgrims traveling to his city. The joy of the heart catching sight of the dimension of grace is bound to erupt in jubilation alone. Again, the vast picture of the indomitable Church built high on the rock that is Jesus triggers a sacrifice of jubilation. Hated, reviled, relentlessly besieged, the Church goes on conquering enemies as she bears fruit in every nation and culture under the sun. So the Church, delighting in rising triumphant over persecution, acclaims her savior-head in wordless accents of praise. We are at a loss for words as we behold infinite goodness, sheerly because he is good, bestowing being and life, unwearyingly gracing souls, and capitalizing on persecution to insure progress in the Church. In assembly or in solitude we can only burst forth in super-linguistic cheers, cries of gladness that by implication murmur within over and over: How good is the good God! Dearest beloved, you alone are my love!

Jubilation Spoken and Unspoken

Even when doing evil, Augustine remarks, man is seeking God.[4] The libertine trying to squeeze the last ounce of pleasure out of a lustful encounter is questing for the joy that comes from God alone. Any joy we experience participates in some way, perhaps perversely, in the joy of God. The greatest joy is reserved for us when we focus on God himself, the greatest of goods. As we have emphasized throughout, our knowledge of God cannot stop at the frontiers of the analytical. Surely we want to grasp as best we can his existence and attributes, but that is not enough. We must strive to know him in heart, by prayer, in communion and intimacy with his inner life. In close affective contact with him who is all-good we banquet on his being that is all joy and so realize some of his joy in a way that leaves us speechless. Some of the saints, we are told, leapt for joy as they lovingly dwelt on the truth that God is God, all goodness, all love. Their leaping symbolized the bounding of their hearts within: this wordless exultation within is jubilation. Lost for words, at times we also can only jubilate, shout for joy within, express the inexpressible by wordless cries within. The goodness of a God beyond comprehension is uttered in a joy beyond speech — the lyric and fire of jubilation.

> And what shall I do when I am crowned? See, the grace of God helped me when I wrestled with life's difficulties. Once the fight is over with, I will be crowned. I will no longer have to battle temptations of the devil or corruption of the flesh. In this life we are always struggling against this corruption. But what do we read in Scripture? "The last enemy to be destroyed is death" (1 Cor 15.26). Once death is destroyed, you will no longer fear any enemy. From that point on, "death is swallowed up in victory" (1 Cor 15.54). So then you will gain victory, then you will wear the crown. So I will be crowned after the fight, but what will I be doing after I am crowned? "God satisfies your desire

with good things'' (v. 5). Now you get wind of something good
and you pant after it, you get wind of some other good thing and
you sigh for that. Perhaps the reason why you sin is that you
are beguiled by your hot pursuit of the good you choose. In that
event you are blameworthy because you pay no heed to the good
counsel of God concerning what to reject and what to choose.
If you are deceived in the good you choose, this is perhaps due
to your failure to learn from God. Every time you sin, you are
seeking some sort of good, you are in search of some sort of re-
freshment within. These objects you are seeking are indeed goods
but in your case they will be evil if you turn your back on him
who made these goods. O my soul, seek your own good. For one
object is good to one thing, and another object to another thing,
and every creature has a certain proper good that makes for the
wholeness and perfection of its nature. Each thing differs in what
it needs to go from an unfinished state to full stature. Seek your
own good. ''No one is good but the one God'' (Mt 19.17). The
highest good is your good. What then does he not have who has
as his good the highest good? There are inferior goods which are
goods proper to various beings. Brothers, consider what is good
for cattle: to fill their stomachs, to be without want, to sleep, to
feel pleasure, to stay alive, to keep healthy, to reproduce. This
is good for them, and within a certain limit they have a measure
of proper good assigned and granted them by God, the Creator
of all things. Are you seeking a good such as this? Surely God
gives you this also, but don't seek this alone. You are a coheir
of Christ: why should you rejoice in being a companion of cattle?
Lift up your hope to the good of all goods. He himself will be
your good, he who has made you good after your kind and made
all things good after their kind. For God made all things very good.

So if we call that good which is God very good, creation as well,
we find, is called that: ''God made all things very good'' (Gen
1.31). What then are we to say about that good about which it
is said, ''No one is good but the one God''? Are we to say that
he is very good? We recall that we attribute this to all creatures,
where it is said, ''God made all things very good.'' What then
are we to say about God? Our voice but not our affection is inadequate. Let us call to mind our comment on a psalm we recently
dealt with: when we are unable to express ourselves, let us jubilate.
God is good. Who can say what sort of good he is? See, we cannot
say and we are not allowed to remain silent. So if we cannot say
and joy does not allow us to remain silent, let us neither speak
nor remain silent. What then are we to do as we neither speak
nor remain silent? Let us jubilate. ''Jubilate unto God, our
salvation, jubilate unto God, all the earth'' (Ps 94 [95].1). What

does "jubilate" mean? It means this: utter the unutterable cry
of your joys and burst forth your delights in his honor. And what
will that outburst be like on that day we feast to the fullest if even
now modest repasts delight our soul? What will our satisfaction
be like when our redemption from every bit of corruption will
be accomplished, as we are told in the psalm, "God satisfies your
desire with good things"?[5]

From time to time the soul, God-possessed and inundated with the
joy of the divine, breaks forth in sounds without ordinary signification,
in accents of joy that mark jubilation. In the contemporary world in which
sports constitute an alluring and exciting subculture, fans, some of whom
are distinguished scholars, burst forth in shouts of exultation not inscribed
in any lexicon when their favorite team wins a national championship.
These cries would seem to be faint secular analogues of sounds charac-
terizing religious jubilation. The joy of any secular achievement such as
winning a Nobel Prize, however grand and gripping, is surpassed by the
joy of the human spirit that is lit up by divine light and drinks from the
fountain of divine love. How can we express our delight in being seized
by and tasting the inexpressible life of God? We can only cry out our joy
in the language of jubilation untranslatable into any ordinary human
tongue. Even the merest musical neophyte, who fears that, if pushed to
sing an air on his own, he may make a fool of himself, can sing the song
of jubilation. It is a song that requires no special quality or style of voice,
no arduous rehearsing. It is the song of the new man whose union with
Jesus in the new covenant assures him that always and effortlessly he will
be spiritually on-key. Since the notes and melody of jubilation are sing-
able by all, are meant to be sung by all, jubilation is, for Augustine, an
additional sign that the Church of Jesus is the Church for all, the universal
Church, the Church that is Catholic.

> In a certain respect, my brothers, these foregoing words catch
> the whole spirit of this psalm. Fasten all your attention on what
> I have just said, on what I have presented to you. Do not let any
> other thought turn you away from this. This psalm is directed
> against the presumption of the Jews who were hoping that
> justification by the Law would win them resurrection. These were
> the Jews who crucified Christ, who was the first to rise again.
> The number who are to rise again include not only the Jews but
> all those who have believed in him, that is, all nations. From this
> point the psalm starts, "Jubilate in God." Who are told to rejoice?
> "All the earth" (v. 2). Thus not only Judea is to shout for joy.
> See, brothers, how this refers to the universal character of the
> Church, to the Church spread throughout the whole world.
> Mourn not only over the Jews who were envious because this
> grace was granted to the Gentiles but bewail even more the lot

of heretics. For if we are to mourn those who are not joined to the Church, how much more should we mourn those who, after belonging to the Church, split off from her? "Jubilate in God, all the earth." What does "jubilate' mean? It means this: burst forth in accents of joy if you cannot find words of gladness. Jubilation is not vested in words but in sounds expressing joy. The jubilating heart travails and gives birth in sound to its delight in the thing conceived, which cannot be uttered in words. "Jubilate in God, all the earth." Let no one jubilate in just one part of the earth, let all the earth jubilate, let the Catholic Church jubilate. The Catholic Church embraces the whole of the earth. Whoever is limited to just one part of the earth and has been cut off from the whole of the earth should want to wail rather than jubilate. "Jubilate in God, all the earth."[6]

"Sing to him the new song" (v. 3). Put off the old man and you will know the new song. The new man, the new covenant, and the new song imply one another. The new song does not belong to the old man. No one can learn it but the new man, renewed by grace from his old self, belonging now to the new covenant, which is the kingdom of heaven. And all our love sighs for this and sings the new song. Let your life, not your tongue, sing the new song. "Sing to him the new song. Sing well to him" (v. 3). Each one asks how he ought to sing to God. Sing to him but not off-key. He does not want his ears to be offended. Sing well, brother. Suppose that a good musician is in your audience and you are told, "Sing in a way that pleases him." You are afraid to sing because you lack training in the art of music and therefore you feel you may displease a skilled musician; for a skilled musician detects flaws that an unskilled listener misses. If this is the case, who can offer to sing well in the presence of God, who thoroughly appraises the singer, scrutinizes every part of the song, and listens with utmost acuity? When will you be able to achieve singing so polished that it will not offend in the least such perfect ears? See, he gives you, so to speak, the tune of your song. Do not go looking for the right words as if it were ever possible to find the right words with which to delight God. Sing "in jubilation" (v. 3). This is what singing well to God consists of: singing in jubilation. What does "singing in jubilation" mean? It means understanding that words cannot express what the heart sings. For singers during the harvest or at vintage time or in some other engrossing work, after they have begun to pour forth their delight in the words of their songs, find themselves overwhelmed by a joy that they cannot express in words, and so they stop using words and simply let themselves go in the spontaneous chant of

jubilation. Jubilee is a sound signifying that the heart is in labor
to give birth to what it cannot express in words. And who is the
most appropriate object of this jubilation other than the ineffable
God? God is ineffable in the sense that we cannot utter his nature.
And if you cannot utter him, and if you ought not to remain silent,
what is left to do but jubilate? The jubilation from your heart
can rejoice without words and you can voice the boundless expanse
of your joys without being cramped by the limits of syllables.
"Sing well to him in jubilation."[7]

The apostles experienced this jubilation, this rejoicing beyond human
grammar and syntax, when they saw Jesus ascending into heaven. At last
he was returning to the Father in his culminating glory. He had endured
the lowly human condition, had suffered execution reserved only for the
most depraved of criminals, had undergone the ultimate humiliation of
death on a cross. Then mysteriously and wonderfully he had rolled back
the stone and strode forth resplendent from the tomb. Now he was claiming
his throne as Lord of heaven and earth. The thrills and delights evoked
by the pomp and circumstance of earthly coronations hardly match the
rejoicing and unrestrained crescendo of triumph that filled the hearts of
men and angels as Jesus lofted himself into the skies. The apostles, sharing
in some way in some of the fruits of the glory of Jesus, were awestricken,
overwhelmed, seized by inner rapture, their hearts ascending, as it were,
with the glorified Jesus. As they observed the unutterable glorification of
Jesus, their souls leapt and bounded with transports of joy, they experienced
unutterable delight, they could only jubilate, cry out wordless, otherworldly
cries within. Happily the ascended Jesus is still there reigning in glory,
and in every century Christians can celebrate and thereby share in his glory.
He is still with us, still within us, still beckoning us to him with his eyes
of love, still arousing in hearts the extra-linguistic cries of exultation that
constitute jubilation.

"God ascended amid jubilation" (v. 6). It is our God, the Lord
Jesus Christ himself, who ascended amid jubilation. "The Lord
ascended with the peal of the trumpet" (v. 6). He ascended:
where did he go but where we know he did? There the Jews
did not follow him, not even with their eyes. When he was lifted
up on the cross, they mocked him (Mt 27.39), but, when he
was ascending into heaven, they did not see him. "God ascended
amid jubilation." Jubilation means the wonderment issuing in
a joy that words cannot express. How grand were the wonderment and the joy of the disciples when they saw going up into
heaven the Jesus whose death they had mourned (Acts 1.9)!
Words were simply inadequate to utter their joy, and only
jubilation could do justice to what no words could express. Those

on the scene heard the peal of the trumpet, the voice of angels.
For Scripture said, "Lift up your voices like a trumpet" (Is 58.11).
The angels proclaimed the ascension of the Lord. They saw the
disciples who watched the Lord ascending stayed rooted to the
spot, lost in wonder, astounded, uttering not a single word but
with hearts flush with jubilation. And now the trumpet pealed
in the clear voice of the angels: "Men of Galilee why are you
standing here looking up to heaven. This is Jesus" (Acts 1.11).
The angels spoke as if the disciples did not know that it was indeed
Jesus. Had they not shortly before seen him standing in front
of them? Had they not heard him speaking to them? Definitely;
not only had they seen his features but they had also touched his
members (Lk 24.39). So how could they really not know that this
was indeed Jesus? But their astonishment and the joy involved
in jubilation transported them outside themselves. That is why
the angels told them, "This is truly Jesus." It was as if they said,
"If you believe in him, it is the same Jesus whose crucifixion
made you falter in your steps, the same Jesus whose death and
burial made you think that all hope was lost. See, it is the same
Jesus." "He ascended before you, he will come back in the same
way, just as you saw him going into heaven" (Acts 1.11). His
body is taken away from your eyes but God does not distance
himself from your hearts. See him ascending, believe in him
although he is absent, hope in him who is to come back, but all
the while through his hidden mercy experience him as present.
For the very Jesus who ascended into heaven and vanished from
sight gave you his promise: "Behold, I am with you even to the
consummation of the world (Mt 28.20). Appropriately the Apostle
also made a like point in telling us, "The Lord is nigh: do not
worry about anything" (Phil 4.5-6). Christ is enthroned above
the heavens and the heavens are far distant from us, yet the very
Jesus enthroned there is nigh. "The Lord ascended amid the peal
of the trumpet." You are spiritually sons of Korah, and so if you
really understand yourselves and behold yourselves in the words
of the psalm, you should also rejoice because you see yourselves
present in this scene of jubilation.[8]

Jubilation Elicited by Creation, Grace, and the Victorious Church

In the mind undebauched by a false humanism the measureless
stretches of the universe always evoke cosmic piety, reverence, and awe
before the massive and interconnected ways of nature. As we have already

remarked, contrary to the expectations of some simplifying minds, the advance of modern science has sharpened awareness of the complexities of the material universe. Undoubtedly scientific formulas transcribe the workings of nature far beyond anything achieved by earlier eras. But new depths and levels, many nonplusing, disclosed by the advance of science apparently make it impossible to reduce all natural events to a few simple laws. The farthest regions of the remotest galaxies seem at present beyond the comprehension of man. But inner as well as outer space stimulates wonder. Who can explain "the vast deep" that is man?[9] Who can unravel all the layers of meaning that go into the making of a single human individual? Angelic life seems even more stupendous, even more resistant to adequate exposition. If the things of nature and created spirits escape full explanation and proper formulation, how can we come near to expressing the Author of nature? We are awestruck, rendered speechless, by the sublimity of the Creator of all things. Reverentially dumbfounded, mute, we can only proffer him a sacrifice of jubilation, a rejoicing beyond the cramping limitations of human speech. We go around his altar, around the universe, simply crying out in love and exultation.

"I have gone round and have offered in his tabernacle a sacrifice of jubilation" (v. 6). We offer a sacrifice of jubilation, we offer a sacrifice of gladness, a sacrifice of thankfulness, a sacrifice of thanksgiving, that no words can express. But where do we offer our sacrifice? We offer it in his own tabernacle, in holy Church. What is it that we sacrifice? We sacrifice a superabundant and inexpressible joy, a joy beyond words, one no voice can describe. This is the sacrifice of jubilation. Where do we seek it and where do we find it? We seek it and we find it by going round. "I have gone round," the psalmist says, "and I have offered in his tabernacle a sacrifice of jubilation." Let your mind go round the whole created universe. Everywhere creation will cry out to you, "God made me." Whatever you find delightful in a work of art you ascribe to the artist. And much more, if you go round the universe, does reflection on it elicit praise of its Maker. You view the heavens; they are the grand work of God. You view the earth; God made the numerous species of seeds, the various sorts of plants, the many kinds of animals. Go round the heavens again and go back to the earth, and leave nothing out. Everywhere all things cry out to you of their Maker. The very created species are voices, as it were, praising the Creator. But who can unriddle the whole created universe? Who can give it the praise it deserves? Who can worthily praise heaven and earth, the sea, and all the things in them? And these indeed make up only visible creation. Who can worthily praise the angels, thrones, dominations, principalities, and powers? Who can worthily praise the human soul, that power at work within us giving life to the body, moving the limbs, putting the senses to work, embracing so many things in the memory, distinguishing so many objects by the intellect? Who can worthily praise the soul? And if human language has so much trouble in doing justice to these creatures of God, how will it be able to do justice to the Creator? Words fail us, and we can have recourse to jubilation alone. "I have gone round and have offered in his tabernacle a sacrifice of jubilation."[10]

The wondrous world of nature is outshone by the super-wondrous world of grace. On the day of judgment all men, including the evil, will witness and recognize in some way the justice of God. Then, however they may rail at it, the haters of God also will plainly see the righteousness of God woven into all history. But even now he discloses his mercy and truth in souls, even now his loving kindness and fidelity overshadow and anoint faithful souls. So countlessly marvellous are the delicately interlinked works of grace that we cannot find words to utter our gladness and exultation. We can only exclaim in wordless cries, we can only jubilate over the glories of God that are the graces of men. Just as our jubilation shares in the unending super-ecstasy of divine joy, so our knowledge of God that grounds true joy streams down in part as the light of the divine Face. In his light we cry out in jubilation over his works of love. The zeal of some apparent devotees of God is spurious because it is no more than human. These counterfeit religionists do not walk in the light of the divine countenance; they do not know God in their hearts; they seek first and foremost their own glory. Any joy arising from self-glorification and inauthentic zeal cannot last, and at best it fitfully comes and goes, for it is the offspring of time and the lower self. Our praise is heavenly only when it is rooted in the loving knowledge of God and his ways. Humbling ourselves before his mercy and justice, we are exalted and, in being lifted up, we know and walk in the light of his Face, and our exaltation leads to the exultation transcending all human speech that is jubilation.

"Justice and judgment are the preparation of your throne" (v. 15). These words apply especially to the day of judgment. How then do they apply to the present? "Mercy and truth go before your face" (v. 15). I would be afraid of the preparation of your throne, your justice and your judgment to come, if your mercy and truth did not go before you. Why should I be afraid of your judgment at the end of time when your mercy going before you blots out my sins and when manifestation of your truth proves you faithful to your promise? "Mercy and truth go before your face." For "all the ways of the Lord are mercy and truth" (Ps 24 [25].10).

Won't all these things fill our souls with delight? Will our souls be able to grasp what is causing such delight? Or will words suffice for uttering our joy? Will our tongues be capable of expressing our joy? If then there are no words adequate, "Blessed are the people who know jubilation" (v. 16). O blessed people! Do you realize, do you understand just what jubilation is? You cannot be blessed in any true sense if you do not understand jubilation. What does "understanding jubilation" mean? It means this: you know the source of the joy that no words can express. For joy does not spring from yourself: "Let him who glories glory in the Lord" (1 Cor 1.31). So don't rejoice in your own pride but in the grace of God. Understand that his grace is so powerful that no tongue is adequate to express it, and you have come to understand jubilation.

Finally, if you have come to understand how jubilation stems from grace, listen now to the words of praise bestowed on that grace: "Blessed indeed are the people who know jubilation." What sort of jubilation is this? Realize it is due to nothing other than grace, that it flows from no one other than God, realize that in no way does it come from yourself. "Lord, they will walk in the light of your countenance" (v. 16). If that Tabor, which here means the coming light, does not walk in the light of your countenance, it will be a lamp blown out by the wind of pride. "Lord, they will walk in the light of your countenance and they shall rejoice in your name all day long" (v. 17). That Tabor and Hermon will rejoice in your name. If they so desire in your name, they will exult all day long. But if they rejoice in their own name, they will not rejoice all day long. For such a joy will not last, for it is a joy in themselves, one that brings with it a fall through pride. So in order to rejoice all day long "they will rejoice in your name, and they will be exalted in your justice" (v. 17). They are exalted not in their own justice but in yours, Lord, lest they show a zeal for God that is not according to knowledge. For the Apostle remarks certain individuals who show a zeal for God but not according to knowledge, men "who were ignorant of the justice of God and sought to establish their own justice." They did not rejoice in your light and "they did not submit themselves to the justice of God" (Rom 10.2-3). And why was this so? Because "they show a zeal for God but not according to knowledge" (Rom 10.2). But as for the people who know jubilation (for those Paul speaks of are not zealous according to knowledge: blessed are the people who are not ignorant of but know jubilation), for what other reason should they jubilate, for what other reason should they rejoice than in your name as they walk in the light of your countenance? And they shall deserve to be exalted but only in your justice. Let this people cast off their own justice and humble themselves. Then the justice of God will come and they will be exalted. "And in your justice they will be exalted."[11]

In addition, the people of God are exalted collectively, raised up in the Church through Jesus, the incarnate justice of God. In going round the world, we are struck not only by the beauty of creation but also by the Church that inevitably overcomes her enemies. The Church is always under siege, beleaguered by forces, direct and indirect, of the chief of the demons. Yet the Church is always coming forth triumphant. Powerless, she exhibits the power that wins victory. Flattened and trampled on, she rises anew, more energetic than before. Tortured and battered, she emerges more alluring and more stunning. Her secret of course is the divinity of her head, Jesus, through whom her weakness proves stronger than legions of carnal men and demons. It is Jesus who vanquishes the armies of evil, it is Jesus who unceasingly turns evil into good, it is Jesus whose wounds make his wounded Church ever more vigorous. Beholding the Church coming forth unfailingly victorious out of defeat, the soul is speechless with joy and can only cry out in exultation in the melody of jubilation.

> We may also read this verse in another sense, one that seems to me to be more in accord with the meaning of the psalm as a whole. Since the psalmist told us that he was lifted up on the rock that is Christ, and that his head, who is Christ, was lifted up above his enemies, he wants us to understand that he himself, who was lifted up on the rock, has likewise been lifted up above his enemies in the person of his head. Here he is referring to the glory of the Church, which triumphed over the persecution of her enemies. And since this victory has been won through the spread of the faith throughout the whole world, the psalmist tells us, ''I have gone round and offered in his tabernacle a sacrifice of jubilation'' (v. 6). In other words, I have reflected on the faith spread throughout the whole world, the faith that lifted up my head, Christ, above his persecutors, and in his very tabernacle, that is, in the Church spread throughout the whole world, I have praised the Lord with ineffable praise.[12]

As we celebrate in wordless wonder the mysterious conquests of the Church, our eyes are raised to go beyond or, rather, through Jesus to the interior of God himself. All the goodness that delights and jubilates us comes down from the Father of all goods. He is good, we know that, but he is good in a mode beyond our comprehension; he is infinitely good. So surpassingly is he good that his mode of goodness resists strict definition and appropriate expression in speech. In the presence of the all-good we can only voice our praise in glad shouts and cries of exhilaration irreducible to human language. It is the goodness of God that makes all his works deserving of jubilation: the vast, brooding cosmos, the marvels of grace, the triumphant march of the Church throughout history. In praising these works, we are implicitly praising his goodness. In jubilating over the beautiful outworking of his plans in nature, grace, and the victorious Church, we are jubilating over his goodness. Thus we sound near the close a note that we struck near the beginning. The universe draws its meaning from the momentous fact that God exists, its value from the thrilling fact that God is good; good not as men are good, imperfectly, flickeringly, undependably, gropingly, but unchangeably, everlastingly, infinitely good. How can finite hearts adequately praise a God of infinite goodness? Our bounded language cannot properly utter a boundless God. So we fall back upon or abandon ourselves to jubilation, a joy beyond words that is tendered as our sacrifice of praise to a God good beyond comprehension.

Reflections

1. A hospital, however finely staffed, well-run, and cheerily appointed, is not exactly a pretty place. In antiseptically clean and pleasant rooms hollow-eyed cancer victims shrink to a wisp of themselves, and in cardiac care units the lives of healthy-looking patients hang by a thread. As death in foreboding or fact casts its long shadow, relatives and friends of those mortally stricken dab their eyes or sob softly in sorrow. Every hospital imparts a lesson of the tragic frailty of the human condition. Yet it is a school of human life in another respect, teaching patients fortunate enough to be recuperating joy in and thanksgiving for the simplest things. Few culinary delights can rival the pleasure a patient feels when, after coming off intravenous feeding, he munches on scrambled eggs and toast for breakfast. How he smiles, perhaps giggles with glee when after six weeks in bed he manages to take his first faltering steps. How he blesses you, how he praises your name, Lord, for the gifts of food and legs. Father, three times a day I sit down before the banquet you have prepared for me, and all day long I am able to walk about. Again, I beg you, teach me to appreciate such blessings, to espy your finger in matter-of-fact eating and walking that are priceless. Every time I reach out for any good at all I am seeking you. When I eat an apple or orange, I am sharing in your goodness and in some way yearning to embrace you, my sovereign, my only fullest good. As I stroll on a mild summer day, my body soaking up the sunshine, it is your warmth that enfolds me. In the course of detailing his odyssey from the limp, senseless existence of a student-hippie to the moral freedom of the Catholic Church, Maclin Horton noted that one decisive turning point in his shift in values occurred in the summer of 1970 when he and a buddy were hitchhiking through central Florida. They were picked up by what he then castigated as a redneck, who was dedicated to middle-class American ideals Horton and his friend loathed. But when during the drive the Floridian recounted his long struggle to gain security for himself and his family, his concern for their needs and the weal of working-class citizens like himself, Horton's mind was lit up by the insight that exposed the sleazy fabric of his radical-liberal outlook. This man whose lifestyle he had sneered at was, even in his mediocrity, actually questing after values far superior to the claptrap-ideals of a bogus liberalism that had turned thousands of

college students into vagrants scarcely a cut above bums.[13] Teach me to
see your goodness radiating from working people faithful to their tasks.
Whatever their apparent lacks, these little ones are your people whose commitment imitates and points to your love keeping the whole universe
humming in harmony. Father, you are there, all around me, in commonplace goods, in the most ordinary people. Through nature and man you
"speak with a thousand tongues,"[14] you gaze upon me with a thousand
eyes. As I respond to your love in utterable things, I will learn to jubilate
over your unutterable goodness.

It is in the family that a child grows in knowledge of prayer, and it
is in the worldwide family that is your Church that I can slowly absorb
more about jubilation. Father, you bind and blend hundreds of millions
into one supernatural organism, one spiritual person, through your Spirit
continuously poured out on us. Your Spirit never stops nurturing us, never
stops drawing new members into the body of Christ. For many years a
nonCatholic physician who was married to a Catholic and had reared his
children as Catholics had been attracted to the Church. Yet for various
reasons he held back, always hesitating, always reluctant to take the final
step. One afternoon as he lay in a hospital bed after some repair work on
a broken shoulder, he was greeted by a priest-friend, who blurted out,
"Dick, old pal, you know I don't think there is anyone in the whole world
who is more a Catholic by desire than you." The doctor nodded. "Then
why don't you go the whole way? Why not just become a Catholic?" Again
the physician gave silent assent. "O.K., then I'll send you a Baltimore
Catechism and in a few weeks we'll have you on the road to baptism."
A brief scene but pregnant with lasting import for that doctor and his family.
Father, this signaled another conquest for your people, whose prayers go
up endlessly for the full coming of the kingdom. Under the prompting of
your Spirit that priest spoke with abrupt holy boldness, and through the
urging of your Spirit the physician said yes to your call. But you employed
the praise unto jubilation born of the prayers and works of your tiny ones
all over the world to ready the doctor's heart for the tenderly compelling
movement of your Spirit. Father, so often am I the captive of appearance,
the dupe of incidentals, eyes sealed to the inner reaches of your Church.
Plunge me into the mystery of her vitality one with your own divine life,
and under the urging of the Spirit of Jesus I will cry out in awe over your
goodness with ineffable shouts of joy.

The song of the new man in your Church, Father, is a song of joyful
praise that rises to the pitch of jubilation. No one is tone-deaf, no one need
sing out of tune, all can sing pleasingly, for all can love with the love of
the heart of your Son. How is this love expressed? For years the obvious
but elusive answer slipped through my fingers, partly because I leaned to
the view that this core love was embodied in near-heroic achievements,
in extraordinary acts of ardor and self-abnegation. Yet again and again Jesus
plainly spells out the answer. "If you love me, keep my commandments"

(Jn 14.15). "If you keep my commandments, you will abide in my love just as I keep my Father's commandments and abide in his love" (Jn 15.11). Disbelievers, dissidents, mavericks inside your Church cosseted by the media are the destroyers of the dream that is divine, their racket threatening with dissonance the song of freedom. But unhighlighted by opinion-molders are your little people of love who sacrificingly keep your commandments, say their rosary and attend Mass, deny themselves for their children, and rise daily to do their jobs, whatever the outer or inner weather. Stumble and fall and drift away at times from righteousness they sometimes do, but their never-slackening will is to heed your word of love. These secret pillars uphold me as I strive to sing the song of jubilation in love by observing your commandments. I am never alone, for I am borne up by your family that encircles the globe. I am never alone, for the Spirit of Jesus in your bosom sweetly drives me to trudge along the way of your commandments, exulting inwardly with a microscopic fraction of the jubilation that transported Jesus as he gazed upon your Face and kissed you in his Spirit. Because your and his commandments are mine, his love is mine, his joy is mine, his praise is mine, his jubilation is mine.

2. Who can conceive the wordless praise with which the soul of Jesus rang as he went back to you? Some of his jubilation Jesus shared with his apostles and disciples, lifting their hearts to skyey realms of mystical prayer. The enraptured Jesus communicated to them some of his transport so that in spirit their souls ascended with him to you, Father. Many of your choicest sons and daughters have been favored with ecstasies and divine seizures enabling them to savor in part what the apostles felt at Jesus's unique leave-taking. Legging behind in the race for eternity, my heart will never leap with the elation of these elect, my soul will never be wounded by flaming darts piercing with the pain of your love. Only let me know the abiding presence of Jesus and in his company rejoice in his quiet glory. Jesus is nigh, so, so near, within me, at the very center of my being, the fires of his heart enwrapping my own right at this moment. Yet for all practical purposes, for most of the day I hardly accord him a passing nod. Father, several near-incredible tales are told of the prodigies you worked through Padre Pio. On one occasion while physically present in his monastery, he appeared in a bedroom hundreds of miles away to lay healing hands on a farmer suffering from a double embolism in the lungs. During World War II an American squadron-leader saw a brown-robed figure in midair waving his bombing plane away from the vicinity of Foggia, where Pio's San Giovanni Rotondo monastery was located.[15] These miracles of bilocation proclaim your glory in your Son. More astonishing is the omni-location of Jesus in the lives of the just. He is always there, pressing his hand on my soul to heal it of spiritual disease, steering me to oases of fresh strength and consolation, whispering his love in my ear, squeezing my hand, and clasping me in the hugs only a divine lover can give. Yet in my aloofness I am like a lover who frigidly shrugs off signs of affection in a spouse's

tireless ardor. No matter, Father, ready me for a fresh inflow of fire from the Spirit of Jesus to consume all the trash within. Let me know as the apostles knew, as all your saints knew, the "hidden mercy" of Jesus. Then I will think his thoughts, desire with the glow of his heart, mount with him to your bosom, praise your name with his lips, jubilate with his heart in a way that ear has not heard.

3. A great scientist with the soul of a poet would kneel down before the universe to kiss it, salute its order and majesty, pay homage to its mystery, and, without suggesting nature-worship, do some unsophisticated honor to its grandeur. But wait — should this seem to border on the idolatrous, let me add this: genuine cosmic piety flowers from a religious root, and the spellbound thinker kneeling on the earth has to recognize you, Father, as its mighty Maker. In honoring your universe, he implicitly honors you and worships your holy name. Scientific analysis and poetic wonder help release adoration. In all of us lies at least the germ of scientist and poet, and in some dim way all of us can realize that yours is a universe of beauty and can cry out our delight. And so we kneel down to hug your universe in love, to praise you, grand, magnificent, all-beautiful one. Infinitesimal-looking in size but gigantic in spiritual stature and lofty in dignity is man. An unkempt member of the street people huddled over a steam vent near a big-city building is more splendid in his body and spirit than all the stars of our Milky Way. And who can fully understand the human soul with its layer upon layer of spiritual power? Father, outstripping men are the angels, the depth and scope of whose intelligence staggers us. Father, if your creation leaves me speechless, how can I rightly homage your grandeur and your goodness? Trying to praise you, I am forced to break out in cries of jubilation. You are God! You are God! You are God! Holy, holy, holy! Going on, I can only shout for joy in sounds translatable in no human tongue, utterances linguistically unutterable. Kneeling on your earth, arms outstretched, eyes raised, heart pulsing with exultation, I can only wordlessly praise you, I can only jubilate.

Father, your works of nature are surpassed only by your works of grace. Each of your saints is a colossus, a super-giant of prayer and love, formed by the recreating flow of your own divine life. Through Jesus your life and power course into and remake the most prosaic and unenchanting of lives. A Lucie Christine outwardly busy about her household chores is inwardly transformed and dwells in the vestibule of heaven, breathing sighs of love in answer to your nuptial caresses. Too your marvels of grace are at work in all redeemed souls, and it is only my fuzzy faith-perception that leaves these concealed. To an associate upon whom he had vented his spleen Evelyn Waugh, the distinguished English Catholic novelist, apologized, then remarked: "My nastiness shows me to be a poor Christian. But think of how vicious I would be if I were not a Christian in some sense." It is not idle to muse over the might-have-beens in the lives of men who could have gone unredeemed. So many sucked up into the world-system are enslaved by greed and pursuit of power. Without the delicate advances of your love I might be peddling drugs or bribing my way upward in some corrupt economic or political network. I say this not in a self-righteous spirit but with gratitude and love, with compassion for those chained in darkness. Let me see the glory of your grace not only in what might have been but also in what actually is, in the gold beneath the clay surface of fellow Christians. How much goodness, how much Godness, inspires them! These are, in spite of their sins, truly your people, little ones who raise their children in the faith, support their churches and schools with unfailing generosity, never vacillate for a minute in their fealty to the mystical body of Jesus, never flinch in the face of hostility, overt and covert, directed against your holy Catholic Church. These are your people born anew and burgeoning in you through your mercy and truth, walking in the light of your countenance. Once more, Father, send forth your light and truth. Then I will learn to jubilate as I see hundreds of plain, unassuming folk of every description pouring in and out of any one of your parish churches every Sunday. These are the treasures of your love: penetrating that truth, I can begin to shout with inexpressible joy over the awesome reality that is the Catholic Church.

A thing of beauty and joy forever, this holy Catholic Church, still flourishing after nineteen centuries, still attracting souls of every race and nation, of every age and station, deeper into your heart, Father. But it is a Church that has been vilified and assaulted over and over again. Your Son, the purest and most virtuous of men, was baited, insulted, slandered, and scorned even by apparently religious men of his day. As he prophesied, his followers have been equally abused. Attacked and beleaguered, the Church of Jesus seems at times to waver, wobble, reel, and stumble under blows of venomous foes. But from every assault she emerges erect and serene, for you have built her on the rock that is Christ. Impregnable, unshatterable, invincible, the Church below shares in some of the exaltation of the Church above. Without vainglory I too am exalted; I too can exult in her triumph out of darkness all over the world; with Augustine and his flock I too can go round the world and offer you the sacrifice of jubilation. I am a Catholic! Mine is the glorious privilege of belonging to an indestructible Church resting upon your eternal power. Grant me the joy of your saints so that I can cry out in ineffable gladness over the day-by-day miracle that is your Church. Fill my heart with the spirit of jubilation that alone does credit to your Church: then will I sing, perhaps with a tiny bit of the charm of the tongues of angels, the sacrifice of jubilation due your Church.

Praise

1. When your home becomes our home, we will see and love and praise you beyond human concepts, singing your glory in your own super-

language beyond human language. All our seeing, loving, alleluia-ing will fuse in the joy that is the root of jubilation. Heaven is all jubilation because it is all praise of you, Father, and your Son and Spirit. I praise you for preparing through Jesus numberless mansions of jubilation. On this side I cannot jubilate daily any more than I can attend a formal banquet daily. Teach me then to grow in the self-abnegating love of Jesus so as to be the more ready to praise you and, in praising you, to be more open to special events that evoke jubilation. I praise you for the festive mood your Spirit breathes into your people along with the balance your Church wisely recommends in the realm of prayer. I cannot continually cheer, I cannot continually chant psalms, I cannot continually cry out words of praise, I cannot continually jubilate. Yet the nagging thought persists: am I lackadaisacal about grasping opportunities for jubilation? If at present I am free of all major diseases, shouldn't I now and then interiorly vault in the air and click my heels, jubilating because you keep me healthy? I praise you for incorporating me into the mystical body of your Son. What a gift this is! Yet how often have I inwardly jubilated in the privilege of being a Catholic? Too self-centered, not wholly cleaving to the one thing necessary, I frequently miss Jesus passing by; I miss your presence, reacting like an iceberg to the joy bubbling up all around and within me.

I praise you, Father, for your Church that is truly Catholic, whose worldwide extent perhaps images your omnipresence. Praise to you for her authentic pluralism, diversity of cultures, many devotional styles, and variety of festivals. Each country boasts its favorite saints and cherished feasts, and not a month goes by that does not carry some special celebration somewhere around the world, which triggers outbursts of joy leading to jubilation. Glory to you for your Church: her feasts are my feasts, her jubilation my jubilation. It might be presumptuous to ask for daily jubilation — the narrow frame of my soul cannot abide such supernatural stretching, yet, because your generosity always outruns my needs, I pray for some filaments of this jubilation springing up from Catholic hearts throughout the year. In these throbs of joy, be they as short as wingbeats of a fly, I will be hearkening to the word your Spirit speaks in the psalm, "Jubilate in God, all the earth": for to be a Catholic is to jubilate over all the earth.

Your Church sings with a unique jubilation. Cheers and chanteys along with other vehicles of jubilation are, if not monotonous, only slightly structured, containing only elementary melodies that gain in power by sheer repetition. The jubilation of your Church is multi-thematic and polymelodious, rich and indefinitely varied in its accents and chords and cadences. Yet the diverse voices and musical lines harmonize in a strange beauty. It is your love that makes us sing the new song and sparks its upward flight into jubilation; it is the search for your hidden Face that makes us break forth in jubilation of every sort. Let me understand that each Catholic singing the new song is aiming at jubilation over your beauty. Let me see the face of each Catholic soul reflecting your sweet Face, and, loving you in them and them in you, I will be the more ready to jubilate in you through them. Father, I praise you for the jubilation in heaven, in which I can now participate by loving your Face in the faces of my brothers and sisters: in them I will jubilate in you all over the world.

2. Jesus jubilated, his apostles jubilated, all heaven sang and rang with super-joy as he was enthroned at your right hand in glory. To jubilate with the glorified Jesus let me live by the words of Augustine: "Why do we who are laboring on earth not find our rest with him in heaven even now through the faith, hope, and love that makes us one with him? While reigning above, he is also with us and we, while here below, are also with him. He is one with us here below by his divinity and power and love. With him reigning above we cannot be one by divinity, but we can be one with him by love in him."[16] Jesus died, rose, and ascended long ago, but by faith, hope, and love I can be quickened by his life and by a touch of his glory cry out in jubilation. I praise you, Father, for true faith that makes the unseen and remote as inwardly seen and near as the paper now in front of me. I believe, yes, I believe so strongly that at times I feel as if confirmed in belief. I cannot put any faith in the cloudy, ambiguous faith-events conjured by the non-faith of modernist theology. Rather, I believe that Jesus really died, rose in his physical body, factually ascended into heaven. I praise you for the hope channeled through your Church. To use a pregnant saying ascribed to Augustine, "We are an Easter people, and alleluia is our song."[17] We are, I dare add, an Ascension people, and our alleluia vaults to jubilation. I see by faith, but my hope limps and lags behind, sometimes shuffling along like a nonagenarian. Renew my confidence that Jesus is with me now, ascended to your side but still "descended" as head of the body, his Church, into which he pours his Spirit without stop or stint. I praise you for the pure charity of the Jesus of the ascension, the focus of my jubilation: he is king of kings, Lord of lords! It is by his love, your love, that I live at this very instant. Without Jesus, my lover, I cannot go on, I cannot take a single step farther. If he had not ascended into heaven, I could not rejoice in him by my side on earth. Precious Father, I praise you for hearing my requests before I tender them, and, as I praise you, I beg you again: lift me up by love to the ascended Jesus so that, companioning with him every moment, I can, though on earth, dwell with you in heaven.

Some intellectuals of our day, including self-styled cultural Catholics (i.e., nothing but nominal Catholics), dismiss claims of the truly super-natural as pious twaddle, at best idealized formulations of infantile fantasies spawned from a fevered religious temper. Nice, pretty, perhaps elevating, we are told, but at bottom proclamation of a divine calling for man is rubbish because it is impossible. Father, I praise you for being a God of the impossible, a Lord of miracles. Along with my fellows, I am a man of earth, and my existence is a grubby thing, a life at times dismal, a life with all sorts of loose ends. Like most Christians, I do not "have it all"; mine is far from a model existence. Only in Jesus revealed through your

Spirit are resolved enigmatic questions that vex my mind and haunt my spirit: why am I here? what must I do to be healed? how can I become happy? I praise you: happiness is a possibility only through the impossibility of the divinity, power, and love of your ascended Son. I can become fully human only by being dowered with superhuman power and love.

I praise you once again for the mother of Jesus. Apparently she was not among the onlookers who witnessed his final exaltation, but certainly she knew of it — perhaps he paid her one last, secret visit the evening before his departure. How did she respond to her Son's ascension? With immense motherly peace: now all possible suffering lay behind him. With immense joy and jubilation: he was king of glory! I praise you, Father, for the faith of Mary; as her Son left human sight, she joined herself more closely to him by faith. I praise you for her serene confidence that Jesus would pour himself out anew in light and courage through his Spirit; and for her trust that in a few short years she also would be reunited with him in an ecstatic physical encounter, a melting of two persons into one love that best reflects the threefold union of persons in your divine nature. At the ascension Mary sang anew her *Magnificat*: "Father, all-loving one, sweet doer of the impossible, you do marvels for me through my Son — holy is your name!" Father, let me appropriate Mary's *Magnificat* to sing my praise, to experience some of the jubilation that thrilled her heart to the fullest as Jesus went up with the blare of trumpets. Put her desires in my heart, her *Magnificat* on my lips, and I will jubilate in Jesus as the apostles did, as Mary superbly did.

3. Though not a sharp-eyed naturalist or a trained natural scientist, I praise you for the marvels of a world so accommodating that we can call it our natural home. Bring me to pause and praise the sunshine and the rain, the squirrel hunting for provisions, the bird chirping, the azalea and the dogwood trees, the faithful German shepherd. As I hail the wonders of a world created by your love, let me look behind its processes to see your Face, catch the beating of your heart, drink in the glory of your eyes. Ineffable one, I want to offer you ineffable praise. Father of joy, I want to lift up to you praise transfused with joy, jubilation echoing the unutterable felicity that is yourself. I praise you, true God, God beyond time, God without limits: let the wordless delight you favor me with arise as my sacrifice of jubilation to your glory.

Edgar Allan Poe was not indulging in hyperbole when he hailed "the glory that was Greece and the grandeur that was Rome." The fruits of these outstanding civilizations are worked into and infixed in the tissues of our science, technology, law, and language. But the underside of these bright monuments of the human spirit was dark, hideous, here and there grisly. Slaves in the lead mines of third-century Sardinia were brutalized. After having his left eye cut out, each slave was partially lamed, branded on the forehead, chained so as to be permanently bent over, and flogged; then he was forced to work twenty hours a day. Usually no slave lasted more than two years, those literally worked to death being replaced by a fresh batch of wretches.[18] Yet on occasion even Christians sank to depths of comparable wickedness. The sack of Rome in 1527 spewed unbelievable abominations on the populace. Monks were executed, nuns repeatedly raped before being killed, churches defiled and desecrated, religious places and secular residences stripped of vessels and ornaments. Rape, rapine, looting, pillage, and killing went on practically unabated for five hellish months.[19] Sex-pleasure, money, and power can transmogrify the human heart into an abyss of corruption, whose crimes are more unspeakable than the most revolting depredations of the most ruthless of wild beasts.

I praise you for purifying and consecrating the human heart in your truth and love, changing what is potentially a hireling of Satan into a son of God. Father, I praise you for your canonized saints, heroes and heroines who fight with love and humility, the weapons of your Spirit. I praise you too for the millions of ordinary saints, colorless-looking men and women who zealously serve and honor you in your Church. In the early nineteen-eighties a Visitation nun died about the age of ninety. Born and raised in a well-to-do Mexican family, she entered a Visitation convent in her homeland, but the outbreak of anti-clericalism then raging under dictatorial "liberators" drove her community to a new foundation in Philadelphia in 1926. The superior of her monastery summed up her life, "She was a faithful religious." What a brief powerful tribute! She was faithful: a virginal bride of Jesus, exact in observance, child of the faithful Abraham, daughter of Mary, our mother of faith. Bending her will to the good of her monastery, she meshed her personal desires with those of her sisters, all for the building of her community as a hidden shrine of love. I praise you for a lay caretaker of this monastery who dropped dead suddenly in his home in the presence of his wife shortly after the Mexican nun's death. According to the superior, hardly a room or section of the monastery does not bear some imprint of his handiwork: a repaired doorknob, a new window pane, new pipes in the cellar, an extra electrical outlet in the kitchen, fresh plaster on one part of the chapel. A devoted Catholic this man, who departed as he lived, without fanfare. I praise you for the marvels you worked in him, strengths that enabled him to live peaceably with his wife as he spent himself in the rearing of five children in the faith. I have remarked this before, but it cannot be said too often: in such little ones who live and die leaving scarcely a world-significant trace behind you form hearts pulsating with the love of Jesus. Ungifted as I am, I do not frequently discern your secret wonders in ordinary souls. Still I praise you in anticipation of the day of full vision when I will rejoice in your super-glory shining in little ones. Then will I shout your joy without end, then will I jubilate with your everlasting jubilation.

At present your little ones in the West are generally not undergoing overt persecution. But there is hardly a segment of Catholics whose past history does not carry the scars of hatred. I praise you, Father, for your

Church that has been many times rocked and apparently reduced to rubble by the huge cannons of enemies — and yet she stands, her fortifications firm. She lives, she goes on mystically renewing herself. To the consternation of his murderers Jesus lives. To the bafflement and dismay of her persecutors the Church lives — more precisely, it is Jesus who lives in his Church. What a spectacle: besieged, hammered down, left for dead, the Church rises afresh, breathing by the deathless life that ceaselessly wells up from your Spirit. I will go round the world and, seeing her erect and undyingly energetic, I will offer you a sacrifice of jubilation for this Church one with Jesus. Outwardly begrimed, smelly, disfigured, uncomely because of the human element that spurns your grace, she is inwardly glorious, ever more resplendent, increasingly bursting with life, waxing stronger and stronger as the blows of enemies beat upon her yet leave her intact. I praise you for this Church so human, so weak, so divine, so powerful with the life of Jesus that flows from you. My faith and love insufficient, I can only praise you, praying that my tepid praise do duty in your merciful eyes for the divinely wild and passionate jubilation that the sight of your Church excites in the hearts of your saints.

As I draw near to the end of these lame praises, I turn once more to Mary immaculate and to Jesus. In the words of Samuel Coleridge, "All knowledge begins and ends with wonder, but the first wonder is the child of ignorance, while the second wonder is the parent of adoration."[20] All the love of Mary begins and ends in the wonder your grace begot in her soul, a first wonder that is the child of wisdom, a second wonder that is the parent of adoration and jubilation. Mary is the mother of wonder, the mother of adoration, the mother of praise, the mother of jubilation. Prostrate yet uplifted before you, Father, and your Son and Spirit, she ceaselessly sings her song of love, her *Magnificat*, offering herself as a sacrifice of love and jubilation. Even while burying herself in your glory, Mary my mother, purest of the pure, smiles at me, coaxes me to lose myself under her mantle, and enfolds me in her arms, bidding me prostrate myself with her and lovingly praise the holy three. Then her hands on my shoulders, she leads me to Jesus, and so, in imitation of John, I can lean my head on his Sacred Heart to drink in and be intoxicated by the mysteries of your love and joy. What words will Jesus speak to me? He murmurs the magnificent line that sums up you, Father, and the meaning of human history: "God is love" (1 Jn 4.16). And with these words comes his command: "Believe, hope in, love with that Love." Without you, without love, Father, the world is a melange of farce and tragedy, a nightmare that provokes mocking laughter. Barbarity, savagery, cruelty, cunning, lying, cheating, double-crossing, lust, depravity, greed — sins without cease darken and pollute not only men of the world but Christians of every rank, most shamefully some in the highest places. It is the charity of Jesus that saves this sin-cursed world, that strikes off the shackles, that turns dusk into dawn again and again. It is love that makes sense of my own life, one with so much false ambition, pettiness, meanness, impatience, anger, self-seeking, coldness toward you, indifference toward my brothers and sisters; a life in part a shambles, in part a trash heap, apparently beyond renovation, beyond reshaping. Then your love in the heart of Jesus enters in, making all things possible. I can put the shabby and shoddy behind me, I can sweep out all that is disorderly and disgusting, I can become new — not only once but over and over again. While making me more conscious of my inner sicknesses, you make me more acutely aware of your goodness. You are sweet with all love, joy, peace, and kindness. So looking into your eyes, I dare to say, "Abba, my dearest Father," and stand boldly yet comfortably in your presence by resting my head on the heart of Jesus.

The final word is confidence in your love, and my never-ending words must be those with which your Spirit brings to an end the inspired words of Scripture: "Come, Lord Jesus!" (Rev 22.20). Come, Word of the Father, heal me, embrace me, hold me in the love of your Father and my Father. Come, make me the all that is love, the all that is the Father. Come, fill me with dauntless trust. Come, set me on fire with love. Come, Jesus, make me a Jesus, make me all love, pure fire, that will burn forever as a holocaust, a sacrifice of jubilation before the everlastingly Burning Bush that is Father, Son, and Holy Spirit.

Notes

[1]See Chapter I, p. 38, n. 33.
[2]EP 102 (103). 8; CC 40, 1458.
[3]EP 65 (66).2; CC 39, 839.
[4]Conf. 2. 6. 13-14.
[5]EP 102 (103). 8; CC 40, 1457-58.
[6]EP 65 (66). 2; CC 39, 839.
[7]EP 32 (33) (En 2. S. 1). 8; CC 38, 253-54.
[8]EP 46 (47). 7; CC 38, 532-33.
[9]Conf. 4. 14. 22.
[10]EP 26 (27) (En. 2). 12; CC 38, 161.
[11]EP 88 (89) (S. 1). 15-17; CC 39, 1229-30.
[12]EP 26 (27) (En. 2). 13; CC 38, 161-62.
[13]Maclin Horton, "Bringing It All Back Home," in Reassessments (a supplement to the National Catholic Register), May 16, 1982, p. 3.
[14]Karl Adam, Christ Our Brother, tr. Dom Justin McCann, O.S.B. (New York: Macmillan, 1931), p. 6.
[15]John McCaffery, Tales of Padre Pio (Kansas City: Andrews and McMeel, 1978), pp. 2-3, 31-32. At the time of each apparition neither the Padua-area farmer nor the American pilot had ever seen Padre Pio in person or in a photograph. After inquiries each traveled to the monastery and recognized his miraculous visitant. Significantly in each encounter it was Padre Pio who first commented on the circumstances of the particular apparition. Additional bilocationary incidents are related on pp. 5, 24-31, 33-36, 49, 75-76, 135.
[16]Serm. Mai 98; MA 342-43.
[17]Over the last decade or so I have occasionally encountered this rich line in spiritual writers or homilists, always accredited to Augustine but never referenced in his

corpus. A combing of relevant texts for an exact citation has so far drawn a blank. If this attribution is veridical, this spiritual gem compactly reproduces his insights on alleluia as the new song that the people of God are to sing on their lips outside the lenten season but to sing in their hearts in all seasons amid the ruck and moil of life in this world as they march forward on the dusty road of time toward the eternal city on high where alleluia is unceasingly chanted. See S. 255. 1. 1 and 5. 5; PL 38, 1186, 1188. S. 256. 1-3; PL 38, 1190-93. EP 104 (105). 1; CC 40, 1535. EP 106 (107) 1; CC 40, 1570. *Serm. Mai* 92; MA 332-33.

[18]Malachi Martin, *The Decline and Fall of the Roman Church* (New York: Putnam, 1981), p. 261. Though engagingly styled, this work, it should be noted, paints a superficial and distorted picture of the papacy in support of its one-dimensional theory of Church and state, according to which the Church since Constantine has been essentially and tragically politicized.

[19]E. R. Chamberlin, *The Bad Popes* (New York: New American Library, 1969), pp. 271-74.

[20]Quoted in J. Arthur Thomson, "The Wonder of Life," in Frances Mason, ed., *The Great Design* (New York: Macmillan, 1935), pp. 308-09.

Index

Abraham, faith of, 239; God of, 12; poor in spirit, 27; spirit of sacrifice, 32
Adam, K., 242 n. 14
Agaësse, P., 218 n. 15
Angela of Foligno, St., 179
Angels, 14, 69, 86, 92, 110, 114, 115, 118, 121, 186, 190, 227
Angels, fallen, 184, 190
Allen, L., 219 n. 25
Aristotle, 64, 179, 213
Augustine, St., affections are feet, 210; chance and design, 148-51;
Christ, Jesus: beautiful in every phase of existence, 167-70; bridegroom, Church his bride, 78-80; chorus of, 76; cries for help in Church, 80-81; death of, greatest sacrifice of praise, 206; divine physician, 14; lowly, 77-78; mediator, 13-14; one with Church in prayer, 77-78; speaks in the psalms, 77;
Christian, incarnate praise, 115, 118-19;
Christians are Christ himself, 181;
Church: an Easter people, 238, 142-43 n. 17; enemies within, 172-73; flourishes amid persecution, 174-76, grows through suffering, 170-72; one with Jesus in ascension, 238;
Confessions, 107, 193; dignity of individual in Christ, 177-79; each Catholic speaks in all tongues, 181; each Christian life a song of praise, 121-22; cross, trap for Satan, 167; encyclical on, xvi n. 5; evening, time of sadness, 135-36
evil: good derived from, 110 ff.; man's infinite capacity for, 148;
faith, prior to understanding, xiv;
God: beauty of, 68-71; attributes paired, 6-7; idea of, 3-4; love of, for each one, 178-79; merciful, 136, 190-91; nature of, 5-6;
good, derived from evil, basic law, 166 ff.; work of divine love and power, 151-53, 158, 218-19 n. 16; glory, defined, 38 n. 33; healing of eye of heart, relatively supreme, 40; heart, restless, 60; humble, rocklike, 190; humility, way to repentence, 153-56; Job, 137-38;
jubilation: of apostles, 221, 226-27; defined, 38 n. 33; forms of, 221-22; in regard to Church, 222, 231; in regard to creation, 228-29; in regard to God, 221-24, 225; in regard to grace, 229-30;
likeness to God: by inner cleansing, 45-47; through love, 47-48;
love of God by God, 60-61; love sinner, hate sin, 190; love as weight, 144-45, 217 n. 8; Massa candida, 131 n. 5; morning, time of gladness, 135, 136; new Christians baked by fire of Holy Spirit, 133 n. 51; new song brings serenity, 44-45; on pagan oracle, 171-72, 219-20 n. 31; physical theory of heavens, 218 n. 15;
praise: as confession, 28; distinguished from prayer and thanksgiving, 22; of divine attributes, 7; of God by God, 59-60; greater when sins forgiven are greater, 28-29; lifts to heaven, 88; as living well, 115-20; meaning of, 1-2; of mercy, 178-79; proper work of man, 1; relatively supreme, 39-40; song of new man, 42-45; in tribulation, 135-36;
prayer: as begging, 25-26; as conversation with God, xiv; expands heart, xiv; of petition, 23-25;
psalter his joy, 88, 111;

245